TRUMP
REVEALED

An American Journey of
Ambition, Ego, Money, and Power

Michael Kranish
and Marc Fisher
The Washington Post

SCRIBNER

New York   London   Toronto   Sydney   New Delhi

Scribner
An Imprint of Simon & Schuster, Inc.
1230 Avenue of the Americas
New York, NY 10020

First Scribner hardcover edition August 2016

SCRIBNER and design are registered trademarks of The Gale Group, Inc.,
used under license by Simon & Schuster, Inc., the publisher of this work.

For information about special discounts for bulk purchases,
please contact Simon & Schuster Special Sales at
1-866-506-1949 or business@simonandschuster.com.

The Simon & Schuster Speakers Bureau can bring authors to your live event.
For more information or to book an event, contact the Simon & Schuster Speakers
Bureau at 1-866-248-3049 or visit our website at www.simonspeakers.com.

Interior design by Jaime Putorti

Manufactured in the United States of America

10 9 8 7 6 5 4 3 2 1

Library of Congress Cataloging-in-Publication Data
Names: Kranish, Michael, author. | Fisher, Marc, author.
Title: Trump revealed : an American journey of ambition, ego, money, and power /
Michael Kranish and Marc Fisher.
Description: First Scribner hardcover edition. | New York : Scribner, 2016.
Identifiers: LCCN 2016032645 (print) | LCCN 2016033114 (ebook) | ISBN
9781501155772 | ISBN 9781501155789 (ebook) | ISBN 9781501155789
Subjects: LCSH: Trump, Donald, 1946– | Trump, Donald, 1946—Political and
social views. | Presidential candidates—United States—Biography. | Presidents—
United States—Election—2016. | United States—Politics and government—2009– |
Republican Party (U.S. : 1854–)
Classification: LCC E901.1.T78 K73 2016 (print) | LCC E901.1.T78 (ebook) | DDC
973.932092 [B]—dc23
LC record available at https://lccn.loc.gov/2016032645

ISBN 978-1-5011-5577-2
ISBN 978-1-5011-5578-9 (ebook)

ABOUT THIS BOOK

Every four years, reporters at the *Washington Post* explore the lives and careers of the presidential nominees. The idea is to learn as much as possible about how the candidates think, decide, and act; to examine their past in order to glean how they might behave in the future. In late March 2016, with both parties' nomination contests still unresolved, the *Post*'s editors decided they had to get started on the extensive research and reporting necessary to produce comprehensive biographical studies of each candidate in the general election. *Post* editors assembled large teams of reporters to look into the work and backgrounds of the likely nominees, Donald Trump and Hillary Clinton. Both teams had the same charge, but Trump presented a unique challenge: he would be the first major party nominee for president in more than half a century—the first since Dwight Eisenhower—to rise to that status without having held elective office.

The *Post* assigned more than twenty reporters, two fact-checkers, and three editors to examine Trump's life. In about three months, they were to produce this book and more than thirty articles for the *Post*, with the goal of chronicling and understanding everything from Trump's family background through his childhood, career, and political evolution. We sent reporters to his ancestral homes in Germany and Scotland, to his childhood neighborhood in Queens and his boarding school in upstate New York, to his college campuses in the Bronx and Philadelphia, and to his business ventures in Atlantic City, Panama, Russia, and Azerbaijan. We visited and spoke with Trump's relatives, classmates, friends, competitors, business partners, executives and employees, boosters, and critics.

This book is the work of an extraordinarily dedicated and talented group of reporters and editors: Jenna Johnson and Frances Sellers traveled far and wide to explore the Trump family's roots. Michael Miller and Paul Schwartzman reached back to Trump's childhood to find playmates, classmates, teachers, and neighbors. Robert O'Harrow and Shawn Boburg explored Trump's complicated finances and real estate transactions in Atlantic City and New York, and Bob Woodward provided key interviews and guidance as we learned how Trump built his businesses. Drew Harwell traced the roots of the Trump Organization in Manhattan and Will Hobson delved into the evolution of Trump's decades-long love-hate relationship with the news media as well as his ventures in the world of professional sports. Mary Jordan and Karen Heller chronicled Trump's relationships with women, including his wives, girlfriends, and female executives. Amy Goldstein and Jerry Markon examined the ups and downs of Trump's casinos and other ventures during a particularly difficult stretch of his career, and Rosalind S. Helderman and Tom Hamburger traced how Trump reshaped his empire into a brand based on his name and popular image. Robert Samuels explored Trump's politics through the years and Kevin Sullivan traveled around the globe to examine the international ventures. Dan Balz went deep inside the 2016 campaign to understand how and why Trump emerged from the big pack of Republican candidates. Nearly all of these reporters also worked on other aspects of this book, which also benefited greatly from work by *Post* reporters Dan Zak, Ben Terris, Michael Birnbaum, Ian Shapira, Steve Hendrix, David A. Fahrenthold, Karen Tumulty, Robert Costa, Philip Rucker, and Janell Ross; researcher Alice Crites; and financial columnist Allan Sloan. Researchers Julie Tate and Lucy Shackelford painstakingly fact-checked the book, and photo editor Bronwen Latimer organized the book's picture section. Editors Scott Wilson, Steven Ginsberg, and Peter Wallsten played a critical role in shaping the reporting and reading every draft as the process unfolded. The *Post*'s executive editor, Martin Baron, and managing editor, Cameron Barr, were adamant from the start that this biography be as comprehensive and penetrating as possible, and they made an extraordinary commitment of resources to back that goal.

Trump made himself available for more than twenty hours of interviews with many of the reporters who worked on this book. He also made his lawyer and some members of his campaign staff available. He turned down our requests to speak to his siblings or to lift the restrictions he'd imposed on his many current and former executives who signed nondisclosure agreements when they worked for Trump. He also declined to give us access to his income tax returns, something that every other presidential nominee in modern history has made available to the public. Throughout the process, Trump said he hoped and expected that this book would be accurate and fair, and we assured him that that was indeed our chief goal. At many points along the way, he also told us that if he didn't like the book, he wouldn't hesitate to denounce it or to take action against it. On the same day that he first agreed to be interviewed for this book, he told the *New York Post* that the project was "ridiculous."

Donald Trump has lived by the credo that all attention, fawning or critical or somewhere in between, accrues to his benefit, that his personal image defines his brand, that he *is* his brand. We began this reporting on the theory that Trump, like anyone else, is far more than his reputation or brand. We conclude this work on that same note, having discovered that the man who would be president is far more complex than his simple language might indicate, that his motivations and values are informed by his parents, his upbringing, his victories and his defeats, and his lifelong quest for love and acceptance. What follows is the man we have come to know.

CONTENTS

TRUMP
REVEALED

"Presidential"

He was the front-runner now, and for his next act, he would become presidential. His son and his daughter and his wife had told him he had to do this, had to show his more thoughtful, calmer side. And he had told them, "I can be very presidential." He had laughed and said, "I can be more presidential than any president that this country has ever had, except for Abraham Lincoln, because . . . you can't out-top Abraham Lincoln." And now here he was, in the nation's capital, in the belly of the beast, showing them all that he could do this. He would meet with a US senator—a senator who was supporting *him*, the kid from Queens, the bad boy of New York real estate—at the offices of one of the capital's top law firms. He would talk foreign policy with a roomful of Washington wonks. He would read a speech from a tele-prompter, the tool he'd long made fun of, the crutch that political los-ers used. He would name some of the insiders who would advise him in the White House, even though he would, of course, remain his own chief adviser, because he knew this stuff better than anyone else. On one crystalline spring day in 2016, the leader in the race for the Repub-lican nomination for president of the United States would field what-ever sharp questions the editorial board of the *Washington Post* might throw at him. He'd address the tough crowd at AIPAC, the American Israel Public Affairs Committee, one of the most influential lobbies in the most important city in the world, a group whose members were increasingly calling his campaign frightening, even demagogic. And just because he was in Washington—where he was, by the way, building what would be one of his company's signature hotels—he'd lead the jackals of the media through the construction site, showing off the thick granite and the top-shelf marble. He would beam and jut his jaw as he announced that his hotel was coming in way ahead of schedule and under budget, "and we have almost three hundred rooms, super-luxury," and "we are going to employ substantially more than five hundred people, at least five hundred people."

It would be an important day in the grand campaign to Make America Great Again. He would show just how multifaceted he was, now the populist man of the moment, egging on huge crowds in ever-bigger arenas, complimenting them for bursting out of silent-majority status and becoming "a very, very aggressive, very, very noisy, loud majority," and then, the next day, he would be the elegant, serious, principled—yes, *presidential*—front-runner. This is the real deal, he was saying, and there would be no denying the will of the people. Donald Trump—scion of a self-made man who built modest homes for the middle class, brash kid who crossed the bridge and took Manhattan, braggadocian developer who plated everything with gold, the man who made Atlantic City great again (until it collapsed again), the entertainer who was a self-described "ratings machine"—stood now in the biggest room in the nation's capital, delivering an address, every word of which would be examined as if he were already the president. Trump—the fringe candidate who turned the Republican Party upside down, the billionaire who persuaded millions of Americans that he best understood their frustrations and aspirations—this political novice, this proud outsider, had outsmarted the experts and the consultants and the insiders, the whole cabal of the powerful and the self-righteous who had driven this city into an embarrassing paralysis. In weeks, the sideshow had become the main event. Now he was the star of just the kind of day that there would be hundreds of once he became *President* Trump, days devoted to "making this a country again," taking it back, making it great, bringing back the jobs, keeping out the Mexicans and the Muslims, "winning, winning, winning." "Bam!" he'd say at his raucous rallies. Bam!—and the evil terrorists of ISIS would be wiped out. Bam!—and the same companies that had exported American jobs would bring them back. Bam!—and Mexico would pay for the wall to keep illegal immigrants from crossing into the United States. Bam!—a great country, again.

HE'D BEEN IN THE spotlight nearly all of his adult life. He was still in his thirties when he became a single-name celebrity, like Madonna or Beyoncé, like a rock star or a president, his name, in ALL CAPS, gold plated, on buildings and airplanes and shirts and wine bottles (even though he says he's never had a drink in his life). He was the rare billionaire who shunned privacy, who invited cameras to focus on the ego wall in his office. He flaunted his wealth, spent ostentatiously, worked the media to keep himself on the gossip pages and the business pages and the sports pages and the front pages. He would, his detractors said, attend the opening of an envelope.

He was, almost from the start, his own brand. He got there in good part by making a close study of everything said about him. He began his days with a sheaf of press clippings, his daily mentions. Even now, running for the most powerful position on the planet, a job that relies almost entirely on the power to persuade those around you, a job heavy on running a team and winning loyalty, even now Donald J. Trump said he made most of his decisions by himself, consulting no one: "I understand life," he said. "And I understand how life works. I'm the Lone Ranger."

He knew how to be famous, he knew how to win numbers, get ratings, make people take notice. More than three decades before he decided he wanted to be president, he showed up on Gallup's list of the ten men Americans most admired, running behind only the pope and some presidents. He'd made a lifelong study of how to create buzz. He had a hierarchy of attention in his mind. Glitz was one level up from flash, he said. Good PR was better than bad PR, but both were good. He was a curious, perhaps unique, blend of savvy showman and petulant, thin-skinned street brawler. He promoted himself with abandon, generating both fawning and ridicule. He was as likely to sue his critics as he was to tout his achievements. He was a proud, boastful winner who had also failed at more businesses than many moguls start in a lifetime. He took pride in demanding respect. He was rarely seen without jacket and tie. Even people who had worked closely with him for decades addressed him as "Mr. Trump."

Yet his language could shock people and he consistently laced his perceived enemies—and especially women—with slashing, coarse insults. His language sometimes seemed a string of slogans and simple, declarative sentences delivering simplistic ideas. This led some people to conclude that he was boorish, unthinking. He kind of liked that; it was the sort of thing he expected from the elitists who had sneered at him all his life. He boasted about a great deal, but he mostly kept quiet about what was going on deep inside. That came out only rarely, such as when he talked about the movies he loved. When he was asked about *Citizen Kane*, the Orson Welles classic about an idealistic newspaper owner who acquires great wealth and loses his soul, Trump said, "*Citizen Kane* was really about accumulation, and at the end of the accumulation, you see what happens, and it's not necessarily all positive. Not positive . . . In real life, I believe that wealth does in fact isolate you from other people. It's a protective mechanism. You have your guard up, much more so than you would if you didn't have wealth."

He fancied himself a man of the people, more interested in the praise of cabdrivers and construction workers than in accolades from the rich and the powerful. The people knew him and admired him, he said, and so he had always thought maybe the ultimate move might be to the White House. "Because I've had great success," he said. "I've been very successful for a long period of time. I've always maybe had it in the back of my mind . . . always toward making the country better, or, as we say, making the country great again, right? . . . A very good slogan, which I came up with."

ONE YEAR EARLIER, TO the day, this was all a dream, a fantasy. Trump was doing what he'd done just about every election cycle for decades, toying with the reporters, making the rounds of the radio talk shows and TV newscasts, hinting, teasing, smirking at the incompetent politicians, tantalizing audiences with the idea that he might bring his talent to bear on the woes of the world. On that March day in 2015, exactly one year before he would make his first "presidential" rounds in Washington, DC, the first wave of Republican wannabes had started to declare their intentions, and Trump was mentioned eighty-six times in the press. The *Chicago Sun-Times* asked him to weigh in on a local controversy about the possible landmarking of a skyscraper; Trump hated the idea of hemming in his fellow developers—if they, like Trump, wanted to make changes in historic buildings, they should be allowed to. In Palm Beach, Trump was lining up with homeowners to oppose an airport runway extension that would result in noisy jets roaring above his Mar-a-Lago estate. In Scotland, Trump reversed course and announced he was going ahead with a hotel and golf course development. At home in New York, an entertainment company staging a music, dance, and fashion show at Radio City Music Hall put out word that the performances would include a "celebrity video cameo" by Donald Trump.

But in March 2015, Trump's usual array of business controversies and promotional forays was starting to be crowded out by a gathering storm of political murmurs and putdowns. On MSNBC that day, host Chris Matthews offered "a little comic relief" in the form of a discussion about Trump's presidential hopes. "Let's not treat Donald Trump like a serious candidate," replied *Chicago Tribune* columnist Clarence Page. "He's a marketing genius, and that's what he's doing." Over on CNN, analyst Jeffrey Toobin rejected the topic: "Donald Trump is engaging in one of his fictional presidential campaigns." A *Washington Post* rundown of the Republican field lumped Trump in "a growing swarm of longshot contenders" with Carly Fiorina, Senator Lindsey Graham, Ohio governor John Kasich, and former New York governor George Pataki. *BuzzFeed*'s McKay Coppins, speaking on MSNBC, dismissed Trump's talk of running as "this pageant of pretend presidential ambitions" and stated, "I still would bet my entire year's salary that he will not actually be on a ballot in Iowa." And on the online gambling sites, oddsmakers were betting on the inevitability of Jeb Bush and the absurdity of Trump. Bush on that day in 2015 was riding on 4–1 odds; Trump was at the bottom of the heap, at 150–1.

But away from the country's media centers of New York and Washington, the first murmurs of a different tune were coming through. In the *New Hampshire Union Leader*, publisher Joe McQuaid wrote that other candidates and the news media "underestimate Donald Trump at their peril. People are so tired of glib talk and polished images and position papers that they may find to their liking a guy who goes against the grain and gets dissed by the talking head know-it-alls." Trump himself appeared on Megyn Kelly's Fox News program, and when she asked "whether you're just a tease," he replied, "I see everything through. Everything in my life, I've seen through. . . . I love what I'm doing, but I love the country more. And I can straighten it out."

Nine months later, in the last days of 2015, Trump was nobody's idea of a tease. In a packed arena on a cold, rainy night in Grand Rapids, Michigan, he stood before a massive American flag, beaming as his supporters—many wearing his red MAKE AMERICA GREAT AGAIN baseball caps, "Made in U.S.A." and available on the shop.donaldjtrump.com website for $25—chanted his name. The first primary was still a few weeks off, and already Trump's opponents were falling away. Trump opened the rally by noting that Lindsey Graham had dropped out that day: "He was nasty to me. Everybody that goes against me, X, X," and he drew X's in the air, X-ing out the losers as the crowd inside the Delta-Plex Arena roared. "That should happen with our country," Trump said. "Everybody goes against us, down the tubes." Another roar.

Already, dozens of rallies into his campaign, his routine was set. There was no script, but rather a small menu of stories that he deployed between riffs about the day's events and narrations of the removal of protesters from the room. (The crowds never minded hearing stories they'd heard before, such as the one about how Ford was building a big plant in Mexico, and President Trump would make them bring those jobs back. "Has anyone heard that story?" Trump asked.

"Yes!" the people shouted.

"Do you want to hear it again?"

"Yes! Yes!" they cried.)

On this day, Trump had some new zingers, some new cuts of red meat for a crowd that relished his every shot against the powerful and the pompous. Today, the first target was news reporters. Trump noted that Russia's leader, Vladimir Putin, had been quoted saying that Trump was brilliant. Trump smirked at American media accounts suggesting it maybe wasn't a great thing for a presidential candidate to be praised by the autocratic leader of one of the country's most difficult rivals. "Oh, isn't it *terrible* that Putin said nice things?" Trump mocked. "That's not terrible, that's good. . . . Wouldn't it be nice if we could get along with people?" Reporters were forever twisting his words, making it sound as if Trump supported Putin, he said. "By the way, I hate some of these 'reporters.' But I'd never kill them. I hate them." The cheers reached a new pinnacle, and Trump, his voice rising with the crowd's lusty shouts, added, "Some of them are such lying, disgusting people, it's true, it's true. But I would never kill them."

He would insist on his right, his obligation, to tell it straight. His language, the belittling little "bye-bye" wave he gave when security guards ushered out protesters who shouted "You're a bigot!"—Trump would never apologize for that. He explained to the crowd, "I went to an Ivy League school. I'm very highly educated. . . . I don't have to be plainspoken. I have, like, this incredible vocabulary. But, honestly, how can I describe our leaders better than the word *stupid*? . . . I used to say 'grossly incompetent,' but *stupid*'s stronger, isn't it?"

The crowd agreed, with gusto. "Trump, Trump, Trump," they shouted. "USA, USA, USA," they chanted. The candidate joined in. Then he ordered the newspeople to "turn the cameras" around and show the crowd, pan the room because "there's so much love in the room." He kept at it, pestering them over and over to turn their cameras, and finally some of them did, and the crowd roared its approval, and another protester shouted something, and Trump directed the guards to "Get him out," adding, with a mischievous smile, "Don't hurt him! Be very nice!"

He turned back to the audience: "Look, is there more fun than a Trump rally?"

It was a happy crowd, even if they had queued up in the rain for hours, wrapped around the arena; even if a few dozen protesters, standing in silent witness, waved placards saying NO TO HATE, NO TO TRUMP and HEIL TRUMP, AMERICAN FASCIST. Most people were glad finally to hear Trump for themselves, not because they loved the guy, or even thought he'd make a fine president, but because they were glad someone was finally saying what he was saying. Kevin Steinke was fifty-three and had been finding lately that he sometimes had to make decisions about paying for health care or paying the mortgage. He came to the rally and brought his two teenaged sons with him so they could hear for themselves, understand that other people were also struggling and that maybe there was a way to get things back to how they used to be. Trump's language, Steinke said, was a little strong, but "he's hitting the nerve. People are getting frustrated by the fact that we don't seem like we're getting anywhere as a nation. A lot of us feel like we're going backwards." Steinke, a college graduate, and his wife, a music teacher, weren't doing as well as they once had, and though he was neither a left-winger nor a right-winger, and though he'd never been to a political rally before, he liked the idea of Trump as a CEO for the country, some-one who wouldn't divide "us against them," but would change the atmo-sphere so that people could "say what you think and not feel like you're Islamophobe or homophobe or add a word on the front for *-phobe*." Trump was scary enough that he was "causing some of the establish-ment people to panic, and I kind of like that," Steinke said. "Donald just says it in plain English, a little too plain. For me, it's refreshing."

Steinke was under no illusion that Trump was "squeaky-clean—nobody is." And he thought some of the things Trump said were "a little too far on the edge, and he can't always walk them back like he wants." But Steinke liked hearing Trump talk tough about dealing with foreign leaders, because America didn't need to win everything, but did need to be "a little more forceful on that stage, to say we need to be the leaders. We're not going to be, 'We're sorry that we're Ameri-cans.' That's really what it feels like: parenting gone wrong, with no consequences across the globe." Trump, Steinke said, "knows how to trade off: you scratch my back, I'll scratch yours. So I think as much as his rhetoric is hot air out-front, when he gets behind closed doors, he wants to make a deal."

On this day, Trump came up with a new line about Hillary Clin-ton and what a loser she was, having gotten "schlonged" by Barack Obama in the 2008 primaries. Trump needled Clinton over her use of the restroom midway through the last Democratic candidates' debate, calling it "disgusting, I don't want to talk about it." He explained that he'd once gotten along well with her, back "in my previous job," where "a guy gives you five million bucks and . . . you know, you sort of feel obligated." Now, though, he was not taking big donations, he was funding his own campaign, "and it's very hard for me to say no, 'cause all my life I take. I take money, I love money, I take money. Now I'm telling these people I don't want your money. Because I know what happens."

And the people cheered, louder now, because he was saying what they'd been saying, he was admitting what the glad-handing, platitude-mouthing politicians would never admit. He just said it: "The truth is, the American Dream is dead." The people cheered, not because they were pessimists or cynics, but because they were hurting and they'd been betrayed and finally someone acknowledged that. He finished with a promise, a big one, one they chose to believe: that the American Dream was dead but not gone. "I'm going to make it bigger and better and stronger than ever before. Ever before. Bigger, and better, and stronger."

AND NOW IT WAS three months later, in March 2016, a fine spring day in Washington, and Trump had victory after victory under his belt, well on his way to the presidential nomination, all but two of his opponents gone. The party bosses were holding secret meetings to talk about how they might turn the summer convention against Trump, and the same pundits who had dismissed him a year earlier were saying that his nomination appeared all but inevitable. He was still holding several rallies a week, and going on TV and radio all day, mixing the usual promises of revival and greatness with new bursts of political incorrectness. When women get abortions, "there has to be some form of punishment," he said one day, and then he backtracked a few hours later. He was confident enough of victory now that he said that if the party denied him the nomination, "I think you'd have riots." He was sure enough that he decided it was time to start showing the pivot that he'd long said he would make after the rough-and-tumble of the primary campaign was over. He'd prove, easily and quickly, he said, that "I can be very presidential."

And so Trump went with a more conservative navy-blue tie, more muted than the flashy reds he favored at rallies. At the *Washington Post*'s editorial board, his voice was calmer, gentler, too. His rhetoric was toned down—he went out of his way to praise one of the paper's political reporters (though Trump also noted, "I've been treated very, very badly by the *Washington Post*") and even offered kudos to the federal agency that controls the DC building, next door to the IRS, that Trump was converting into a hotel. Trump had readily agreed to do the hour-long interview entirely on the record—a break from the editorial board's usual custom of keeping its conversations with candidates private to maximize frank discussion as the board decided whom to endorse. In Trump's case, no one on the board was kidding himself or herself about any chance that the *Post*, with its tradition-ally Democratic editorial page, would seriously consider backing a candidate whom its editorials had been blasting in unusually strong language, calling him a threat to American democracy. So the only value of the interview would be to see if the editors and columnists could press Trump on his more extreme statements and test whether he really knew his stuff.

The board members had discussed in advance a strategy designed to home in on Trump's command of tough foreign policy issues, and to push him on why he chose to be so inflammatory. Now it was show-time. Trump walked in and extended his hand—doughy, with surpris-ingly rough skin—to each editor. This was perfectly ordinary for most visitors, but something new for Trump, who spent much of his life avoiding handshaking because, as he put it, "Guys come in, they have a bad cold, you shake their hands, you have a cold." (Becoming a can-didate required a change, he said, because people expect a handshake: "You know, it's very rude if somebody comes and wants to shake and you won't do it, so you do it, you shake it. I wash my hands as much as possible . . . and that's not an insult to anybody, it's a fact: you get germs on your hands and you catch colds.") At the *Post*, Trump's tone remained even and his sentences grew longer and more complex than they'd been in debates or TV appearances. But he would not be pushed. Six times, his questioners tried to get him to talk about whether police treat blacks more harshly than whites.

"You know, I feel very strongly about law enforcement," Trump replied. "Law enforcement, it's got to play a big role."

Asked again if he believed there were racial disparities in law enforcement, Trump replied, "I've read where there are and I've read where there aren't. I mean, I've read both. And, you know, I have no opinion on that."

The conversation turned to Trump's frequent incendiary comments at his rallies, urging security officers to remove protesters, commands such as "Knock the crap out of him." Don't such remarks condone violence?

"No, because what I am referring to is, we've had some very bad people come in. We had one guy . . . he had the voice . . . and I said, 'Boy, I'd like to smash him.' You know, I said that. I'd like to punch him. This guy was unbelievably loud. He had a voice like Pavarotti. I said if I was his manager, I would have made a lot of money for him, because he had the best voice. I mean, the guy was unbelievable, how loud he was."

The news coming out of the meeting was about Trump saying that maybe the United States didn't need to put so much money into NATO, the core of the European-American security alliance since the Cold War—the kind of statement that might win nods or applause at a rally, but sparked shock and ridicule in the corridors of think tanks and policy shops in Washington. Was Trump just winging it? Was he toying with the self-serious policy wonks? Or did he really have an informed, thought-out position?

"NATO was set up when we were a richer country," Trump said. "We're not a rich country. We're borrowing, we're borrowing all of this money."

But you do know, editorial writer Charles Lane said, that South Korea and Japan pay half of the administrative cost of keeping the American military in those countries, right?

"Fifty percent?" Trump asked.

"Yeah," Lane confirmed.

"Why isn't it one hundred percent?"

Trump never sounded angry in the meeting. His face didn't turn red the way it did in heated moments at debates. The editors who wanted more than anything else to figure out how much of Trump's campaign manner was shtick and how much was real venom emerged thinking that they had seen the genuine Trump—a man certain of his views, hugely confident in his abilities, not terribly well informed, quick to take offense, and authentically perplexed by suspicions that he had motives other than making America great again.

A few weeks later, Trump would hire a new chief strategist, a seasoned Washington lobbyist named Paul Manafort, who would quickly assure the Republican National Committee that Trump was only play-ing a role on the campaign trail. "The part that he's been playing is now evolving into the part that you've been expecting," Manafort said. But Trump himself wasn't buying that line, and neither were members of the *Post*'s editorial board. Strangely enough, the least presidential moments of the visit persuaded some of the *Post*'s editors that Trump wasn't putting on an act for them. Fred Hiatt, the paper's editorial-page editor, had to ask, How could a man running for president justify going on a nationally televised debate and talking about the size of his penis? "You are smart and you went to a good school," the editor said. "Yet you are up there and talking about your hands and the size of your private parts."

"No," Trump said, Marco Rubio had brought up the issue of Trump's hands. "He started it."

"You chose to raise it," said columnist Ruth Marcus.

"No, I chose to respond." Trump stuck out his jaw. "I had no choice."

"You chose to raise it during a debate," Marcus persisted. "Can you explain why you had no choice?"

"I don't want people to go around thinking that I have a problem."

He started it. Like a schoolyard taunt. And Trump had reacted. He *had no choice.* He'd never been one to stand down in a battle, not as a kid in military school, and certainly not on the national stage. So, yes, he was a fighter, and a winner, he'd tell anyone who asked. But he was also loyal, respectful, chivalrous.

On the way out of the meeting, Trump stopped to shake hands with one of the editors, Karen Attiah, who had asked him a question about his divisive rhetoric and its impact on a country that is getting browner and blacker. "I really hope I answered your question," Trump said. Then he smiled, looked directly at Attiah, and added, "Beautiful." He wasn't talking about her question.

Attiah didn't respond. Astonished that a candidate for president would remark on her looks, she wasn't angry, "just stunned," she said. "He'd been charming, charismatic, not cagey or reluctant. I thought about what he said, and I remembered, this is the guy at the beauty pageants, who parades his wife and daughter around, who said if she wasn't his daughter, he might be dating her. And I concluded, well, we got the full Trump experience."

A few blocks away, at the sports arena where the Washington Wizards and Capitals play, thousands of Jewish activists gathered for Trump's long-awaited speech to AIPAC on his approach to the Israeli-Palestinian stalemate. Dozens of rabbis and others had announced plans to boycott the event, both because Trump had pledged to be "neutral" in talks between Israel and the Palestinians, and because Trump's call to ban Muslims from entering the United States struck many Jews as a frightening echo of the policies that their own parents and grandparents had faced in Europe. Even though Trump's daughter Ivanka had married an Orthodox Jew and converted to Judaism, the candidate had alienated many Jews with comments at a Republican Jewish Coalition meeting where he said he might not win the support of many in the room because he did not want their money. Trump said he was best-positioned to get a Middle East peace deal because he's a negotiator, "like you folks."

So Trump had some repair work to do. He took no chances. Though he'd said that teleprompters should be banned on the campaign trail, he now used one, his eyes darting from one screen to the other. This time, he was squarely on Israel's side. He railed against the Palestinians' demonization of Jews. He reminded the crowd that he'd lent his personal jet to New York mayor Rudy Giuliani when he visited Israel weeks after the 9/11 attacks and that he'd been grand marshal of the Israel Parade in New York in 2004, at the height of violence in the Gaza Strip. He made sure everyone noted that Ivanka would soon give birth to a "beautiful Jewish baby."

But before Trump's speech won repeated standing ovations, at the start of his remarks, six rows from the stage, one rabbi wearing a Jewish prayer shawl stood up and shouted in solitary protest, "This man is wicked. He inspires racists and bigots. He encourages violence. Do not listen to him." Rabbi Shmuel Herzfeld, who leads an Orthodox congregation in Washington, did not rise out of any passion of the moment. He had wrestled with this decision for days. He consulted with his own mentor rabbi, with his lawyer, with his wife and seven children. He told his kids that he felt obliged to say something, "to say 'we know who you are, we see through you.' " His children asked him not to stage his protest because he might get hurt, but Herzfeld concluded that he had no choice. He knew he would lose members of his synagogue (and he did). He knew he would be accused of taking an inappropriately political stance (and he was). But he had concluded that Trump posed "an existential threat to our country. I've never seen this type of political figure in my life. He's shameless in inspiring violence. He used vile language about people from other countries. He's opened a space for ugliness to come out of the shadows."

Herzfeld was immediately ushered out of the arena and Trump continued speaking without incident. But the next day, AIPAC's president, choking back tears, apologized for the Trump speech, saying that it had violated the group's rules against personal attacks. Trump had been unusually restrained in his language, but he had called President Obama "maybe the worst thing to happen to Israel," and he'd slipped an unscripted "Yeah!" into the part of his address in which he noted that Obama was in his final year in the White House. He could appear in presidential settings, but he was still Trump being Trump.

Indeed, the only appearance that day where Trump looked and sounded like the plain-speaking billionaire of the people that he'd been on the campaign trail—by turns playful, angry, passionate, persuasive—was a wholly different kind of event, a sales pitch at the ornate old post office building on Pennsylvania Avenue that he was rapidly transforming into the Trump International Hotel. An hour before Trump was to appear, the queue for media credentials to cover the event stretched around the block. A couple of hundred reporters showed up, and only maybe a handful of them had any interest in the renovation of a nineteenth-century federal office building into a luxury hotel five blocks from the White House. The bait was the chance to toss questions at Trump.

The ringing of hammers on steel and the whir of power tools sounded until just before Trump was due to appear. Then the men in hard hats and orange vests melted away, leaving only placid piano music, a striking departure from the aggressive, pulse-pumping playlists Trump deployed to amp crowds at his rallies. Trump's motorcade arrived, two gleaming black SUVs preceded by four DC police squad cars and several motorcycle cops. Trump—followed by more than a dozen aides in dark suits, a rotund man in chef's whites, two construction workers, and lots of hotel executives—stepped into the atrium over a pathway of plywood and settled in front of two American flags. The hotel, he promised, would be "incredible, with beautiful marble from different parts of the world . . . I think it's a great thing for the country, it's a great thing for Washington."

For forty minutes, reporters peppered Trump with questions, none of which had to do with the post office project. They wanted to talk, instead, about delegate counts, Middle East policy, NATO, violence at Trump rallies. Trump took all comers, then asked if anyone might like to see that great, great ballroom. A throbbing clot of reporters and camera people, a mass bristling with boom mics and cameras held aloft, squeezed through a doorway, surrounding Trump like amoebas. Trump seemed not to notice. He stopped, peered up the building's Romanesque Revival exterior, and pointed: "That window is from 1880. Hard to believe, right? It's special glass. It has a kind of patina." Building materials weren't what this crowd had come to study, but this was what he knew. This was where he lived. The rest of this—the throngs, the people chanting his name, the politics of the nation gone topsy-turvy—was all new and exciting, and unsettling, too. He was the front-runner now, and for his next act, some people told him he should be presidential, and yet he knew he would be what he'd always been.

1

Gold Rush: The New Land

On a June day in 2008 by the northwest coast of Scotland, a cluster of townsfolk in the Outer Hebrides gazed skyward at an approaching airplane. The islands on which they lived were shaped like a medieval club, narrow at the southern end, thick at the north, splayed amid choppy gray-blue waters. Much of the lightly populated land appeared from afar to be an endless greensward, fields reaching to ragged cliffs and rocky beaches, beyond which lay a string of islets. The islanders waited as the Boeing 727 banked toward them.

The jet was an unusual visitor, nothing like the propeller-powered puddle jumpers or rattling Royal Mail craft that frequented the island. Having traversed the Atlantic Ocean on its voyage from Boston, the craft cut through the winds, bounced its wheels on the tarmac, and taxied toward the small terminal in Stornoway, population eight thousand, the main city on the Isle of Lewis. The plane had been retrofitted to the exacting specifications of its owner, Donald J. Trump, of Manhattan. It had a master bedroom, spacious seating for twenty-four passengers, a dining area for five guests with accompanying china and crystal serving, and, for good measure, two gold-plated sinks. A single word in capital letters, TRUMP, streaked across the fuselage. As the plane's engines shut down, Trump's underlings unloaded cases of his books, which would be given like totems to the islanders. One case was labeled TRUMP: HOW TO GET RICH and another NEVER GIVE UP.

Trump, dressed in a dark suit, white shirt, and blue tie that hung well below his belt, his thatch of blondish hair flapping in the breeze, greeted the islanders. Then he and his fellow travelers headed to a black Porsche Cayenne and two BMW X5s. The entourage drove along winding roads for seven miles, past green hills rolling down to a bay, through neighborhoods of waterfront homes and small industrial buildings, until they arrived at a gray house known as 5 Tong, named for the village in which it was located. Trump exited his car and peeked inside. The dwelling was so modest that Trump remained inside for only ninety-seven seconds. Photos were taken, and the story line seemed neatly complete: Trump visits the birthplace of his mother, Mary Anne MacLeod.

"I feel very comfortable here," Trump told the gathered reporters. "When your mother comes from a certain location, you tend to like that location. I do feel Scottish, but don't ask me to define that. There was something very strong from my mother." In case anyone had failed to notice, Trump added, "I have a lot of money."

Trump had been here only once before, when he was three or four years old, and this stay seemed as brief as possible, barely three hours. There was talk of Trump's turning a local castle into a luxury hotel. Then it was off to another part of Scotland, where Trump hoped this rare reminder of his heritage might help persuade politicians to let him build a massive golf resort and housing development on environmentally sensitive land near Aberdeen.

Trump's mother's story was a classic one of desire for a new life in a strange land, freighted with a seemingly unrealistic dream of unimaginable riches. The wealth, in the case of Trump's family, would one day come. But that result could hardly have been envisioned if one could step back in time to a scene captured in a grainy photograph taken near the very spot that Trump visited so briefly on that June day.

THE BLACK-AND-WHITE PHOTO WAS taken in 1930 at 5 Tong. A woman is slightly hunched over, wearing a full-length dress, her hair tied back, a strap around her shoulder. The strap is attached to a bundle on her back that is about ten times the size of her head. She is, according to the caption written by the Tong historical society,

Trump, dressed in a dark suit, white shirt, and blue tie that hung well below his belt, his thatch of blondish hair flapping in the breeze, greeted the islanders. Then he and his fellow travelers headed to a black Porsche Cayenne and two BMW X5s. The entourage drove along winding roads for seven miles, past green hills rolling down to a bay, through neighborhoods of waterfront homes and small industrial buildings, until they arrived at a gray house known as 5 Tong, named for the village in which it was located. Trump exited his car and peeked inside. The dwelling was so modest that Trump remained inside for only ninety-seven seconds. Photos were taken, and the story line seemed neatly complete: Trump visits the birthplace of his mother, Mary Anne MacLeod.

"I feel very comfortable here," Trump told the gathered reporters. "When your mother comes from a certain location, you tend to like that location. I do feel Scottish, but don't ask me to define that. There was something very strong from my mother." In case anyone had failed to notice, Trump added, "I have a lot of money."

Trump had been here only once before, when he was three or four years old, and this stay seemed as brief as possible, barely three hours. There was talk of Trump's turning a local castle into a luxury hotel. Then it was off to another part of Scotland, where Trump hoped this rare reminder of his heritage might help persuade politicians to let him build a massive golf resort and housing development on environmentally sensitive land near Aberdeen.

Trump's mother's story was a classic one of desire for a new life in a strange land, freighted with a seemingly unrealistic dream of unimaginable riches. The wealth, in the case of Trump's family, would one day come. But that result could hardly have been envisioned if one could step back in time to a scene captured in a grainy photograph taken near the very spot that Trump visited so briefly on that June day.

THE BLACK-AND-WHITE PHOTO WAS taken in 1930 at 5 Tong. A woman is slightly hunched over, wearing a full-length dress, her hair tied back, a strap around her shoulder. The strap is attached to a bundle on her back that is about ten times the size of her head. She is, according to the caption written by the Tong historical society,

1

Gold Rush: The New Land

On a June day in 2008 by the northwest coast of Scotland, a cluster of townsfolk in the Outer Hebrides gazed skyward at an approaching airplane. The islands on which they lived were shaped like a medieval club, narrow at the southern end, thick at the north, splayed amid choppy gray-blue waters. Much of the lightly populated land appeared from afar to be an endless greensward, fields reaching to ragged cliffs and rocky beaches, beyond which lay a string of islets. The islanders waited as the Boeing 727 banked toward them.

The jet was an unusual visitor, nothing like the propeller-powered puddle jumpers or rattling Royal Mail craft that frequented the island. Having traversed the Atlantic Ocean on its voyage from Boston, the craft cut through the winds, bounced its wheels on the tarmac, and taxied toward the small terminal in Stornoway, population eight thousand, the main city on the Isle of Lewis. The plane had been retrofitted to the exacting specifications of its owner, Donald J. Trump, of Manhattan. It had a master bedroom, spacious seating for twenty-four passengers, a dining area for five guests with accompanying china and crystal serving, and, for good measure, two gold-plated sinks. A single word in capital letters, TRUMP, streaked across the fuselage. As the plane's engines shut down, Trump's underlings unloaded cases of his books, which would be given like totems to the islanders. One case was labeled TRUMP: HOW TO GET RICH and another NEVER GIVE UP.

a Trump ancestor, possibly Donald's grandmother, "carrying a creel of seaweed on her back." In the background is a young lady, perhaps Trump's mother, Mary MacLeod, then eighteen years old, and already planning to leave her increasingly destitute island and find her way to America.

Mary grew up in this remote place speaking the local Gaelic dialect. Tong had been home to Mary's parents, grandparents, and great-grandparents, as well as countless cousins. The land around the home was known as a croft, a small farm typically worked by the mother, enabling the father to spend much of his time fishing. It was a spare existence, with many properties "indescribably filthy, with doors so low it is necessary to crawl in and out," according to a local history. Families struggled to cobble together incomes through a combination of farming in the acidic soil and raising animals, fishing in the nearby bay and rivers, and collecting peat to be sold or used as fuel and seaweed to be used as fertilizer on the difficult land. It was all too common for men to sink with their sailing ships, a fate that in 1868 befell Mary's thirty-four-year-old grandfather, Donald Smith, who had the same first name Mary gave decades later to her son, Donald Trump.

Mary was born in 1912 during the height of a boom in herring, the fatty fish that had become a delicacy throughout Europe. Many young residents worked the trade, gutting the fish or traveling with the fleets. Mary was a child during World War I, when the island's fishing industry collapsed. Ten percent of the male population died. A wave of emigration took place as families searched for economic opportunity elsewhere. One Tong man was said to have done so well that when he returned for a visit, he arrived in a big American car with white tires and gave local children a ride.

Then, in 1918, one of the greatest businessmen of the era, Lord Leverhulme, known for his family's Lever soap empire, paid 143,000 pounds to purchase the Isle of Lewis, on which Tong was located. He moved into the sprawling Lews Castle and announced a series of grand schemes, including the marketing of local fish at hundreds of retail shops across the United Kingdom. Most of all, he urged residents to trust him.

Amid this brief period of hope came another tragedy. On New

Year's Day 1919, a yacht carrying British soldiers went off course, hit rocks, and killed 174 men from Lewis, again diminishing the island's male population. Soon, it became apparent that Leverhulme's grand promises would not pan out, and the islanders rebelled. A group of Tong men invaded a farm owned by Leverhulme and staked claim to the land. By 1921, Leverhulme had halted development on Lewis and focused just on neighboring Harris, best known for the wool fabric called Harris Tweed. His business dealings elsewhere were struggling, especially in a global recession, and in 1923, Leverhulme's dream of a Lewis utopia went bust. Leverhulme died two years later, and as Mary entered her teenaged years, hundreds of people fled the island.

The MacLeods took pride in the island's sturdy stock; their family crest featured a bull's head and the motto HOLD FAST. But that became nearly impossible with the onset of the Great Depression in the fall of 1929; opportunities for a young woman to be anything other than a farmer or child-bearing collector of seaweed were scarce. So on February 17, 1930, after Black Tuesday and all the other blackness brought on by the Depression, Mary Anne MacLeod boarded the SS *Transylvania*, a three-funneled ship built four years earlier. The vessel spread 552 feet from stem to stern, 70 feet across the beam, and carried 1,432 passengers. Mary, an attractive young woman with fair skin and blue eyes, appears to have been on her own, filing on board between the McIntoshes and McGraths and McBrides. She called herself a "domestic," a catchall for "maid" or whatever other labor she might find once she reached New York. She told immigration officials at Ellis Island that she planned to stay in Queens with her older sister, Catherine, who had married and just given birth to a baby boy. Mary declared that she planned to be a permanent resident, hoping to gain citizenship in her adopted land.

THE UNITED STATES HAD welcomed immigrants for much of its history, importing laborers and encouraging settlement in the West. But a combination of economic downturns, nativism, and the rise of the eugenics movement had recently made it increasingly difficult for certain groups of people to become US citizens. Crackdowns began in the early 1920s. The Ku Klux Klan sought to all but take over the 1924 Democratic National Convention in New York City, urging severe limits on immigrants and bashing Catholics, prompting brawls in the aisles of sweltering Madison Square Garden. More than twenty thousand Klansmen rallied nearby, celebrating when the convention narrowly failed to pass a platform plank condemning the group. The ensuing Klanbake, as the days of rage became known, so disrupted the convention that it took 103 ballots to select nominee John W. Davis, who lost the general election to Republican Calvin Coolidge. Nonetheless, the KKK continued to wield political power, and an anti-immigrant mood gripped the country as the economy weakened. The Democrats' 1928 nominee, Al Smith, was pilloried by the KKK because he was Catholic, and he lost to Republican Herbert Hoover. By 1929, Congress passed legislation cutting the immigration quotas for many countries, including European nations such as Germany. Soon, hundreds of thousands of Mexicans would be expelled. Those from China, Japan, Africa, and Arabia were given little chance of gaining US citizenship. At the same time, Congress nearly doubled the quota for immigrants from much of the British Isles. Mary, coming from the preferred stock of British whites, would be welcomed at a time when the United States was closing its doors to many others.

As Mary made her way across the Atlantic, the *Transylvania* battled a horrific storm. Finally, as the vessel reached New York Harbor, a driving rain stirred the swells, and bolts of lightning knocked out power, including the torch in the Statue of Liberty, which nonetheless welcomed the world's tired and poor. The lead story on the front page of the *New York Times* on the day of Mary's arrival seemed reassuring: "Worst of Depression Over, Says Hoover, with Cooperation Lessening Distress." Hoover pinned his hopes on a construction boom, which he insisted had accelerated "beyond our hopes." His hopes would prove far too optimistic. Hoover was soon replaced in the White House by New York's governor, Democrat Franklin Delano Roosevelt, and it would take years of government intervention for America to dig itself out of the Depression. But one of those who shared Hoover's hopes for a construction boom was a young man named Fred Trump. He was the son of a German immigrant and was on his way to making a fortune by building modest homes in the same area of New York City where Mary MacLeod now was headed.

THE TRUMP SIDE OF the family's American saga begins with Donald's grandfather, Friedrich. He was raised in a wine-producing village in southwest Germany called Kallstadt, which looked appealingly verdant and prosperous to the casual eye, but which held little future for the ambitious teenager who would later be Donald Trump's paternal grandfather.

The steep-roofed two-story house on Freinsheim Street where Friedrich grew up was just a few minutes' walk from the bell tower of the Protestant church in Kallstadt's center. With two or three bedrooms to accommodate a family of eight, it was far from the grandest vintner's house. But if the Trumps weren't the richest winemakers in late-nineteenth-century Kallstadt, they secured a decent income. They owned land on which to grow grapes, and their house had several outbuildings for livestock and a great arched cellar adjoining the ground-floor rooms where the annual harvest would be fermented.

Kallstadt lies in the Pfalz, or Palatinate, a lush, undulating region of the Rhine Valley to which millions of German-American families such as the Trumps trace their roots and where the Nazis later created a *Weinstrasse*, or wine route, to market produce after they had driven out the local Jewish merchants. Sheltered by the Haardt Mountains to the west, the gentle topography created a Mediterranean-like climate, a so-called German Tuscany, where almonds, figs, and sweet chestnuts thrived. Grapes had been cultivated for at least two thousand years since the Romans built a villa on a hill above the village. Orderly rows of Riesling crisscrossed fields and filled tiny plots between village houses.

Years of unrest prompted many to flee, establishing a history of emigration, and cementing the interdependence of the families who stayed. Outgoing and proud of their shared past, the people of Kallstadt came to be known as *Brulljesmacher*, or "braggarts." It is uncertain when the Trumps first came to the Palatinate or when they settled on the spelling of the family name. Family genealogists and historians have found various spellings, including Dromb, Drumb, Drumpf, Trum, Tromb, Tromp, Trumpf, and Trumpff. More recent headstones in Kallstadt spell the family name Trump, though in the local Palatinate dialect, the final *p* is pronounced with emphasis, almost like *Tromp-h.*

Friedrich, Donald Trump's grandfather-to-be, was born on March 14, 1869. He was a frail child, unfit for backbreaking labor in the vineyards. He was eight years old when his father, Johannes, died of a lung disease. His mother, Katherina, was left to run a household of children ranging in age from one to fifteen, as well as the winery. Debts began to mount. Katherina sent Friedrich, her younger son, off when he was fourteen for a two-year apprenticeship with a barber in nearby Frankenthal.

Friedrich, however, saw no future in the Palatinate village and decided to join the stream of Germans looking for a better life in the United States. Friedrich traveled 350 miles north to Bremen, a port teeming with emigrants, and boarded the SS *Eider*. The two-funneled German ocean liner was bound for New York City, where Friedrich would find his older sister, Katherine, who had already married a fellow emigrant from Kallstadt. Friedrich arrived in New York on October 19, 1885. Immigration records list his occupation as "farmer" and his name as "Friedrich Trumpf," although he would soon be known by Trump. He was sixteen years old.

But Friedrich's departure ran afoul of German law. A three-year stint of military service was mandatory, and to emigrate, boys of conscription age had to get permission. The young barber didn't do so, resulting in a questionable status that would undermine any future prospect of return: Friedrich Trump was an illegal emigrant. Luckily, US officials didn't care about the circumstances under which he left Germany. US immigration law at the time granted Germans preferred status; they were viewed as having the proper white European ethnic stock and an industrious nature. Friedrich was one of about a million Germans who immigrated to the United States in 1885, more than had ever before come in one year.

The SS *Eider* delivered him to Castle Garden, the main entry point for immigrants before the federal government opened Ellis Island in 1892. Friedrich had left a rural European town of fewer than a thousand residents for the chaos of New York City, which then had a population of more than 1.2 million, about one-third foreign-born. Friedrich moved in with his older sister and her husband, Fred Schuster, joining a community of fellow Palatinates on Manhattan's Lower East Side. He started out as a barber, but that proved unsatisfying.

Friedrich, like many before him, was lured by tales of gold strikes and other riches to be found in the West. By 1891, the ambitious young man—a government document described him as five feet nine, with a high forehead, hazel eyes, straight nose, prominent chin, dark complexion, and a thin face—headed to Seattle. The booming city of fifty thousand was crisscrossed by streetcar lines and visited by vast fleets of ships. Friedrich saw an opportunity to offer food and lodging. He set up shop among the dance halls in a seedy area of town and changed the name of an establishment known as the Poodle Dog to the more salubrious-sounding Dairy Restaurant, operating among the pimps and gamblers who haunted the district.

Trump, granted US citizenship in Seattle in 1892, began investing in land. He headed to the mining community of Monte Cristo, nestled in the nearby Cascade Range. A New York syndicate backed by John D. Rockefeller had allowed a railroad to be built, bringing ore down from the mountains. Just as Friedrich eschewed toiling in Kallstadt's vineyards, he did not join the grueling and often unrewarding work of digging for gold and silver. Instead, he built a hotel and put placer claims on land in questionable deals that allowed him to claim mineral rights. He won the 1896 election for Monte Cristo justice of the peace by a vote of 32–5.

After returning briefly to Seattle, Friedrich joined the Klondike gold rush in the Yukon, where he and a partner opened an establishment called the Arctic, later renamed the White Horse. A vivid portrait of the Arctic, which offered food and lodging, appeared in a local newspaper, suggesting that the hotel catered to the more questionable mores of the miners. "For single men," wrote the *Yukon Sun* in 1900, "the Arctic has excellent accommodations as well as the best restaurant in Bennett, but I would not advise respectable women to go there to sleep as they are liable to hear that which would be repugnant to their feelings and uttered, too, by the depraved of their own sex."

Friedrich sold his shares in the business just as authorities began cracking down on drinking, gambling, and prostitution. While he now seemed firmly planted in the United States, he hadn't entirely forgotten Kallstadt or his German roots. And he didn't yet have a wife. That gap in his life was filled on one of his visits to Kallstadt, during which he saw his mother and attended family weddings. On that trip home in 1901, Friedrich met twenty-year-old Elizabeth Christ, who'd grown up across the street from the Trump family house. The following year, Friedrich returned to marry her and bring her back to New York, where their first child, another Elizabeth, was born in 1904.

Despite the close-knit community of fellow Kallstadters on the Lower East Side, Elizabeth Christ Trump never felt at home in New York, and in 1904, Friedrich renewed his passport to travel to Germany, listing his profession as "hotelkeeper" and saying he would return to the United States within a year. This time, though, he brought his savings to Germany with him—some eighty thousand marks, the equivalent of several hundred thousand dollars in 2016 currency. Kallstadt officials, happy to welcome the wealthy young American back into their village, testified to his good character and ability to support his family members. But regional and national officials asked why Trump hadn't come back sooner to perform his military service. To them, he looked like a draft dodger, and they pressured him to leave. In early 1905, he received notification that he had to depart by May 1. On April 29, Trump pleaded that his baby daughter was too sick to travel. He won a three-month reprieve. On June 6, Trump made another attempt to stay, this time writing a personal letter to Bavaria's prince regent, Luitpold of the House of Wittelsbach, describing in increasingly desperate and obsequious terms how he and Elizabeth were paralyzed by horror at the prospect of returning to America.

"My dear wife and I . . . are faithful, loyal subjects, true Palatinates, good Bavarians who are bound with unlimited love and devotion to the magnificent princely house of the illustrious Wittelsbachs," he wrote. He would readily give up his right to live in the United States, Trump continued, if he could only secure permanent residence in the land of his birth. No luck: on June 28, Trump resigned himself to returning immediately to New York with the now-pregnant Elizabeth and their young daughter. The Trumps arrived in New York in the middle of the summer and settled into an apartment in a largely German neighborhood in the South Bronx, where on October 11, their first son, Frederick Christ Trump, who would become Donald Trump's father, was born.

On December 20, Friedrich Trump made one last attempt to win the right to return to his homeland. Once again, his plea was rejected. By May of 1907, the case was closed. Friedrich and Elizabeth Trump would remain in America and raise their three children as US citizens.

RESPONSIBLE FOR RAISING A young family in this new land, Friedrich Trump made his way to Wall Street—not as a broker or financier, but in his old profession of barber. He clipped the hair of countless residents of lower Manhattan in a block that would later be well-known to his grandson. The address was 60 Wall Street. Friedrich could have hardly imagined that, a century later, the family name would grace a seventy-two-story tower nearby at 40 Wall Street, known as the Trump Building. Friedrich eventually became a hotel manager and moved to Jamaica Avenue in Queens in the middle of a building boom—a move that would help shape the family's future and fortune.

Then, in 1914, World War I broke out, and suddenly Trump and hundreds of thousands of others with German ancestry became targets of their own government. A German-American newspaper, the *Fatherland*, ran a 1915 cover story titled "Are Hyphenated Citizens Good Americans?"—a question that many unhyphenated citizens were asking at the time. A government-sanctioned volunteer group called the American Protective League, with 250,000 members, spied on German Americans amid growing fear that the immigrant families were working for their fatherland and against their newer homeland.

Soon, use of German was discouraged, and many Germanic names were Americanized. The tone was set from the top. On June 14, 1917, two months after the United States entered World War I, President Woodrow Wilson declared, "The military masters of Germany [have] filled our unsuspecting communities with vicious spies and conspirators and sought to corrupt the opinion of our people." It was known as the Flag Day speech, a moment German Americans would long remember. Anti-German views would only intensify in later years, as World War II renewed the animus, and Donald's father, Fred Trump, would for much of his life be defensive about his roots, sometimes insisting his family was Swedish, a claim that his son would repeat. There was never serious discussion about expelling Germans, however, and in the end the Trumps mixed into the melting pot that was America.

SHORTLY AFTER THE UNITED States entered World War I, Friedrich Trump, then forty-nine, walked down Jamaica Avenue with his twelve-year-old son, Fred. The elder Trump casually mentioned that he felt sick. He went home, took to bed, and soon died, a victim of a worldwide flu epidemic. Friedrich had left the family with a considerable estate, and his widow, Elizabeth, made herself the head of the family real estate business, which she called E. Trump & Son. Her eldest son, Fred, had a passion for the building trades and soon took on a leading role in the company his mother led. Given enormous responsibility at a young age, he grasped it, determined to become a leading builder in booming postwar New York City. Fred constructed his first home at seventeen, then another and another, using the profits from one to finance the next.

As Fred surveyed New York City of the 1920s, he saw a landscape of opportunity. The boroughs of Brooklyn and Queens still held large swaths of undeveloped land, and streetcars and subways were being extended deeper into the outer boroughs, opening new areas to developers. The population of Queens, where Trump did most of his early building, more than doubled from 469,000 in 1920 to 1.1 million in 1930, remaining 99 percent white throughout the decade.

Even with that separation, racial and ethnic tensions were bubbling over. After the Klanbake of the 1924 Democratic convention, the Klan kept up its nativist drumbeat. The tensions climaxed anew on May 30, 1927, at a Memorial Day parade that wound through Fred Trump's Queens neighborhood. The police had been concerned for weeks that the KKK would try to take over the event, and they had said Klan members could only join the march if they agreed to abandon their white robes and hoods. Trump, a twenty-one-year-old Protestant and now the head of the family business, joined the tens of thousands of New Yorkers who attended the parade. The KKK did not heed the police mandate. Dressed in their robes and hoods, carrying giant American flags, they passed out handbills in Trump's neighborhood alleging that Catholic members of the police force were harassing "native-born Protestant Americans." The KKK appealed to "fair-minded citizens of Queens County to take your stand in defense of the fundamental principles of your country." This typical Klan tactic tried to pit Catholics against Protestants, while stirring up anti-immigrant feelings.

Having sown the seeds for a clash, more than a thousand Klansmen assembled at the intersection of Jamaica Avenue and Eighty-Fifth Street, where the Memorial Day parade was slated to begin. The commander of a small police contingent was outraged that the Klan had defied his order against wearing the robes and hoods. A policeman rushed toward a hooded Klan member with his nightstick, about to hit the marcher on the head, a moment vividly captured in a photograph published in the *Brooklyn Daily Eagle*. "Women fought women and spectators fought the policemen and the Klansmen, as their desire dictated," the *New York Times* reported the next day. "Combatants were knocked down, Klan banners were shredded." Fred Trump wound up in the thick of the melee, and he was arrested.

The charge against Trump was "refusing to disperse from a parade when ordered to do so." But a Queens newspaper, the *Daily Star*, reported that the charge was promptly dismissed. News accounts did not say whether Trump was for or against the Klan, or whether he was at the parade merely to see the spectacle, but the implication of the *Star* story was that he was unjustly charged. Whatever happened, the parade and arrests underscored that the Klan remained prominent and influential, as demonstrated by the imposition of immigration quotas two years later.

Trump, meanwhile, methodically built his empire, buying vacant land mostly in Queens. Even as the Depression devastated New York City, he looked for opportunities. When housing sales fell off, he invested in what became one of the city's thriving grocery stores. In March 1931, with the Depression still at its height, Trump announced that he was nearing completion of an upscale project in the Jamaica Estates section of Queens. Trump said he expected to build $500,000 worth of dwellings in just a few months. "The homes are of English Tudor and Georgia Colonial styles," reported the *Times*, which was otherwise filled with gloomy news that day.

Trump found opportunity in gloom. When a mortgage firm called Lehrenkrauss & Co. was broken up amid charges of fraud, Trump and a partner scooped up a subsidiary that held title to many distressed properties. Trump used that information to buy houses facing foreclosure, expanding his real estate holdings with properties bought on the cheap from people who had little choice other than to sell.

At a time of financial ruin, with unemployment rising to 25 percent, and the streets lined with the destitute, Trump emerged as one of the city's most successful young businessmen. As the economy recovered, Trump snatched up more property, building more Tudor-style homes in Queens. In 1935, Trump began to focus on Brooklyn, and he sold seventy-eight homes in twenty days, each for about $3,800. Soon, his home sales reached into the thousands.

One day, Trump, dressed in a fine suit and sporting his trademark mustache, attended a local party. He saw a pair of sisters, and the younger one caught his eye. Her name was Mary Anne MacLeod. In the several years since she had first arrived in the United States, she had gone back and forth to her little village on the Outer Hebrides island of Lewis, unsure what her future held. She was about to go on another return voyage when her sister Catherine took her to the party in Queens. Mary MacLeod, twenty-three, and Fred Trump, thirty, spent the evening together, and something clicked between the maid and the mogul. When Trump returned that night to the home he shared with his mother, he made an announcement. He had met the woman he planned to marry.

THE WEDDING WAS HELD on January 11, 1936, at a Presbyterian church on Madison Avenue in Manhattan, and a reception followed at the Carlyle Hotel, an elegant thirty-five-story art deco confection that had opened six years earlier. Then it was off on a brief honeymoon and quickly back to work. Fred, now described in the newspapers as president of the Trump Holding Corp., of Jamaica, soon announced that he was building thirty-two homes in Flatbush in an "exclusive development." As World War II approached, Trump boasted that the threat of combat had helped business. "In the event of war, I believe that the profit will be quicker and larger," Trump said, trying to gin up sales. The remark might have seemed impolitic, but it proved correct, at least for his company. He showed a flair for salesmanship and showmanship, hoisting fifty-foot-long banners that were seen by "millions of bathers" at city beaches. He promoted his homes from a sixty-five-foot yacht that broadcast music and advertisements while filling the air with "thousands of huge toy balloon fish," which resulted in "a series of near riots" as people tried to catch the souvenirs. Those who caught the balloons found coupons giving them a discount on a house purchase. The Trump Boat Show, as the marketing extravaganza was called, ensured that the family name was known throughout the metropolis.

Mary Trump focused on her new role as wife and mother to a family that would eventually include five children. On June 14, 1946, the fourth member of that brood was born. Fred and Mary named him Donald John Trump, and he would ensure that the family name would endure long after the immigrant stories of his ancestors had passed from memory.

2

Stink Bombs, Switchblades, and a Three-Piece Suit

In 1958, when they were twelve years old and hungry for adventure, two boys from the quiet, low-slung edges of Queens liked to board an E train bound for Manhattan, the island of soaring, exotic promise they knew as "the City." Donald Trump and Peter Brant never asked their parents for permission for their Saturday-afternoon expeditions. The answer would have been an emphatic no. Manhattan was too far, too risky, an unsettling cacophony of comic-book superheroes and millionaires, con men, movie stars, gangsters, and worse.

For the boys, that blend of glamour and danger was only part of the allure. Times Square hadn't yet become the nation's most prominent back alley, the open market of sex, drugs, and sleaze that it descended into in the late 1960s. But in 1958, it was already a neighborhood in steep decline, its sidewalks dotted with streetwalkers, its shops cluttered with novelties. Donald and Peter were fascinated by Times Square shops where they could buy stink bombs and hand buzzers and fake vomit—perfect accessories for pranking their pals back at school. Exiting the train a few blocks away, at Fifty-Third Street and Fifth Avenue, the boys climbed the station stairs to a thrilling swirl of honking horns and police sirens, hot dog vendors, and a dizzying blur of humanity. Manhattan, the boys knew, would be their testing ground, a new frontier for them to conquer. A lanky blond boy on the cusp of adolescence, Donald Trump came from a neighborhood where the tallest buildings were only a few stories. On the city's border with suburban Long Island, Jamaica Estates was populated mainly by middle- and upper-income Jews and Catholics. The streets were defined by neat front lawns, massive oak trees, and handsome homes, among the largest of which was built by Fred C. Trump.

After a long slog through the Depression and World War II, much of New York was booming, with the world's most vibrant ports, factories, and financial center. More than a quarter of the country's top five hundred corporations, a roster that included IBM, RCA, and US Steel, had their headquarters in a city that was now recognized as a world capital. The prosperity extended beyond Manhattan. As veterans returned to neighborhoods in Queens and Brooklyn, Fred Trump saw a burgeoning market for modestly priced, easy-to-build homes that some New Yorkers called "Trump's dumps on stumps." In Bath Beach, a neighborhood just off Gravesend Bay in Brooklyn, Fred Trump planned his most ambitious project to date, a complex of thirty-two six-story apartment buildings—a total of 1,344 units—renting for as little as $60 a month.

When Donald was born, less than a year after World War II ended, Fred and Mary Trump and their four children lived in a two-story Tudor revival on Wareham Place, a couple of blocks from Grand Central Parkway, a major commuter thoroughfare. But when a fifth child, Robert, was on the way, Fred bought two adjoining lots across the backyard and built a twenty-three-room manse on Midland Parkway. It looked like a faux Southern plantation. Seventeen brick steps led up a sloping hill to the front door, which was framed by a colonial-style portico, a stained-glass crest, and six imposing white columns. The house was the talk of the neighborhood of lawyers, doctors, and business executives, if not for its size than for Fred Trump's apparent wealth, as suggested by the navy-blue Cadillac limousine in the driveway, with a license plate boasting his initials, FCT.

The Trumps had other things hardly anyone else possessed, including a chauffeur, a cook, an intercom system, a color television, and a sprawling electric train set that was the envy of the neighborhood. Later, while his pals were riding Schwinn bikes, Donald would cruise on a ten-speed Italian racer. But wealth was not all that set the Trumps apart. When Fred Trump asked if he could put a television antenna on a nearby house, thinking its higher elevation would improve his signal, the neighbor, Chava Ben-Amos, agreed. But when Fred told her she could not use the antenna for her own television, Ben-Amos told him the deal was off.

Fred Trump's children apparently inherited their father's chilly attitude toward the neighbors. When a neighbor's ball accidentally bounced into the Trumps' spacious backyard, young Donald growled, "I'm going to tell my dad; I'm going to call the police." Another neighbor, Dennis Burnham, grew up a few doors away from the Trumps. When he was a toddler, his mother placed him in a backyard play-pen. Once, after going inside for a few minutes, she returned to find that little Donald—five or six at the time—had wandered over and was throwing rocks at her son, Burnham said. Donald's fearlessness impressed his sometime babysitter Frank Briggs. As afternoon turned to dusk one day, Briggs led Donald into a sewer that was under construction in Forest Hills. They remained belowground for two hours. "All of a sudden, it was pitch-black and you couldn't see the entrance or anything," Briggs recalled. "And the thing that amazed me was that Donny wasn't scared. He just kept walking."

WHEN DONALD WAS READY for kindergarten, the Trumps sent him to the private Kew-Forest School, where they had enrolled his older brother, Fred Jr., a fun-loving boy who dreamed of becoming a pilot. Donald's two older sisters, Maryanne, who had her father's drive, and Elizabeth, sunny like her mother, also went to Kew-Forest. In high school, Maryanne, who would grow up to be a lawyer and a federal judge, emerged as the family's academic star. She joined Kew-Forest's debating team and student council and wrote poetry, including a maudlin riff entitled "Alone," which was published in the school yearbook: "On the familiar school grounds, where groups of boys and girls stop to chat, laugh and then move on to see their other friends, she stands disregarded by all. She, alone and friendless, cannot even hope to join their happy crowd as they walk toward the corner candy store."

Donald spent the most time with Robert, his little brother, a quiet, sensitive youngster and easy prey for an aggressive older sibling. As an adult, Donald liked to tell the story of when he appropriated Robert's building blocks for his own and glued them together because he was so pleased with what he had made. "And that was the end of Robert's blocks," Donald recalled.

At Kew-Forest, Donald encountered a dress code—ties and jackets for boys, skirts for girls—and a strict set of rules, including the requirement that students rise at their desks when a teacher entered the classroom. From the start, Donald and his friends resisted their teachers' commands, disrupting class with wisecracks and unruly behavior. "We threw spitballs and we played racing chairs with our desks, crashing them into other desks," recalled Paul Onish. Donald spent enough time in detention that his friends nicknamed the punishment DTs—short for "Donny Trumps."

Their classmates did not always appreciate their antics. In second grade, after Trump yanked her pigtails, Sharon Mazzarella raised her metal lunch box in the air and brought it down with a clunk on Donald's head. No matter the consequences, Donald's behavior did not change. "He was headstrong and determined," said Ann Trees, a Kew-Forest teacher who monitored students in the cafeteria. "He would sit with his arms folded, with this look on his face—I use the word *surly*—almost daring you to say one thing or another that wouldn't settle with him." Steven Nachtigall, who lived a couple of blocks away from the Trumps in Jamaica Estates, said his own impression of Donald was cemented when he saw him jump off his bike one afternoon and pummel another boy. "It's kind of like a little video snippet that remains in my brain because I think it was so unusual and terrifying at that age," Nachtigall would say six decades later.

By his own account, Trump's primary focus in elementary school was "creating mischief because, for some reason, I liked to stir things up and I liked to test people. . . . It wasn't malicious so much as it was aggressive." As a second-grader, as Trump has described it, he punched his music teacher, giving him a "black eye" because "I didn't think he knew anything about music, and I almost got expelled. I'm not proud of that, but it's clear evidence that even early on I had a tendency to stand up and make my opinions known in a very forceful way." Peter

Brant, his best friend at Kew-Forest, is among several of Donald's pals who recall neither the incident nor Trump's ever mentioning it. When Trump was asked again about the incident decades later, he said, "When I say 'punch,' when you're that age, nobody punches very hard. But I was very rambunctious in school."

The teacher, Charles Walker, who died in 2015, never told anyone in his family about a student's striking him. Yet Walker's contempt for Donald was clear. "He was a pain," Walker once said. "There are certain kids that need attention all the time. He was one of those." Just before his death, as he lay in bed in a hospice, Walker heard reports that Trump was considering a run for the presidency. "When that kid was ten," Walker told family members, "even then he was a little shit."

TRUMP'S GRADES SUFFERED AND his behavior got him in hot water, but he found success in the gymnasium and on the ball field, where his athletic prowess was unmistakable. In dodgeball, Donald was known for jumping straight up in the air and pulling his knees up to avoid being struck. "The Trumpet was always the last man standing," remembered Chrisman Scherf, a classmate, invoking his old nickname for Donald. Donald and his buddies played punchball and basketball, football and soccer. But his favorite sport was baseball, which inspired him to write an almost Zen-like ditty that was published in the school yearbook:

> *I like to see a baseball hit and the fielder catch it in his mitt. . . .*
> *When the score is 5–5, I feel like I could cry. And when they*
> *get another run, I feel like I could die. Then the catcher makes*
> *an error, not a bit like Yogi Berra. The game is over and we say*
> *tomorrow is another day. —Donald Trump*

In the mid-1950s, New York City was America's undisputed baseball mecca, with the Yankees in the Bronx, the Dodgers in Brooklyn, and the Giants in upper Manhattan. On a fall afternoon in 1956, when he was ten, Donald lined up with fellow Kew-Forest students outside the school to wave at President Eisenhower as he passed by in a

Chrysler Imperial limousine taking him to throw out the ceremonial first pitch at the Yankee-Dodger World Series. Donald's favorite players were Yogi Berra of the Yanks and Roy Campanella of the Dodgers, both catchers whose championship heroics Donald followed by sneaking a transistor radio into class, the wire of an earplug concealed beneath his shirtsleeve.

By sixth grade, Donald's ability as a right-handed hitter was fearsome enough that opponents shifted toward left field to defend against him. "If he had hit the ball to right, he could've had a home run because there was no one there," said Nicholas Kass, who was a couple of years older. "But he always wanted to hit the ball through people. He wanted to overpower them." When he played catcher, his favorite position, Trump's uniform was the dirtiest on the field. He shrugged off foul balls that clanged against his mask and used his big frame to block errant pitches. "He was fearless," Peter Brant recalled. "If he stole a base, he came in all guns a-blazing." He did not like to fail, as his neighbor Jeff Bier discovered when Donald borrowed Bier's favorite bat and made an out. Frustrated, Donald smashed the bat on the cement and cracked the timber. He was too lost in his fury to apologize.

In those years, young ballplayers wanted the new, webbed fielders' mitts that Rawlings was beginning to make. Peter convinced his father to buy him one for $30, as long as the youngster earned $15 doing chores around the house. But Donald could not persuade Fred Trump that the more modern glove was worth the price. Fred bought his son a cheaper model.

For all his wealth, Fred did not want to spoil his children, encouraging them to earn money by collecting empty White Rock soda bottles and turning them in for the nickel deposit, and by delivering newspapers (when it rained, he'd drive them on their routes in his Cadillac). A workaholic, Fred would take Donald with him to construction sites and to his headquarters, a converted dentist's office near Coney Island, where the boy would absorb his father's attention to detail and obsession with cutting costs. At Kew-Forest, where Fred served on the board of trustees, he complained that the school was wasting funds by adding bathrooms for the new gymnasium. The school already had enough toilets, he groused. On his own projects, Fred would pick unused nails off the floor and return them to his carpenters. He saved money on floor cleanser by ordering lab analyses of store-bought products, buying the ingredients, and having them mixed to produce his own.

A fastidious, formal man who wore a jacket and tie even at home, Fred could be dour and socially awkward. His wife, Mary, relished attention, thrusting herself to the center of parties and social gatherings. She also loved pomp, sitting for hours to watch the coronation of Queen Elizabeth. A homemaker, Mary devoted herself to charitable work and volunteering at Jamaica Hospital, where Donald was born. Mary had various medical problems, including a hemorrhage after Robert's birth that required an emergency hysterectomy. From his mother, Donald inherited a wariness about catching germs that led to years as an adult when he avoided shaking hands.

Fred and Mary Trump ran a disciplined household, forbidding their children to call each other by nicknames, wear lipstick, or go to bed past their curfew. The Trumps questioned their children each night about their homework and demanded that they perform their chores. Just as he did at school, Donald rebelled against the rules, arguing with his father. Nonetheless, Fred always told his son that he was a "king" and that he needed to become a "killer" in anything he did.

Hungry for a sense of autonomy, Donald and his friend Peter created a routine that they kept secret from their parents. On Saturday mornings, after playing soccer at school, they put on their pressed chinos and dress shirts and walked to the Union Turnpike subway station, where they boarded the train for Manhattan. The city was far more exciting and enticing than the quiet, orderly streets that defined deep Queens, a feeling that would not dissipate as they approached adulthood. Wandering the city, the boys fancied themselves urban Davy Crocketts, exploring Central Park's bucolic expanse, watching black men play pickup basketball on outdoor courts along the East River, observing panhandlers in Times Square, eating hot dogs bought from street vendors, and hopping on stools at a diner to drink egg creams. At their favorite novelty shops in Times Square, the boys were drawn to the selection of switchblades. On Broadway, *West Side Story* was a smash hit, and Donald and Peter, imagining themselves gang members on the city's mean streets, bought knives to fit the part. Back in Queens, the boys played a game they called Land, in which they flung their knives at the ground and then stepped on the spot where the blade had pierced the dirt. At first, the knives they used were six inches long, but they graduated to eleven-inch blades as they became more daring. (Trump denied ever being "a knife person. . . . I never had a switchblade in my life. That's crazy.")

Near the end of seventh grade, Fred discovered Donald's cache of knives. Fred called Peter's father, who found his own son's collection. The parents were infuriated to learn about the youngsters' trips to the city. As an adult, Peter Brant would see those adventures as an early sign of independence and ambition, a drive that would propel both men to fame and vast wealth. (Brant became a paper-industry magnate, publisher, and movie producer.) But Fred Trump, alarmed by how his son was evolving, decided Donald needed a radical change.

In the months before eighth grade was to begin, Donald seemed to vanish. Peter heard from a friend that his buddy would be attending another school. When Peter telephoned him, Donald, his voice thick with dejection, said that his father was sending him to New York Military Academy, a strict boarding school seventy-five miles north of Queens. Peter was stunned. His best friend was being sent away, and for reasons that seemed, at least to a thirteen-year-old, almost inexplicable.

DONALD ARRIVED AT NEW York Military Academy in September of 1959, a stocky teenager bewildered by his new surroundings. An hour north of Manhattan, the school was located in tiny Cornwall-on-Hudson, on a campus with a culture so strict and unforgiving that one desperate cadet was rumored to have jumped into the Hudson River to swim to freedom. Instead of the delicious steaks and hamburgers served by the Trump family cook back home, Donald had to sit in a mess hall alongside fellow cadets and fill his plate from vats of meat loaf, macaroni and cheese, and something the students called "mystery mountain," a concoction of leftovers that were deep-fried and shaped into balls. Instead of his own room in a vast mansion, he slept in a barracks, awakened each morning before dawn by a recording of a bugle playing "Reveille." Instead of having his own bathroom, he had to stand beneath an oversize showerhead and bathe with other boys. Instead of adhering to his father's commands, Donald had a new master, a gruff, barrel-chested combat veteran named Theodore Dobias.

Dobias, or Doby as he was known, had served in World War II and had seen Mussolini's dead body hanging by a rope. As the freshman-football coach and tactical-training instructor, Doby smacked students with an open hand if they ignored his instructions. Two afternoons a week, he would set up a boxing ring and order cadets with poor grades and those who had disciplinary problems to fight each other, whether they wanted to or not. "He could be a fucking prick," Trump once recalled. "He absolutely would rough you up. You had to learn to survive." To glare at Doby, or suggest the slightest sarcasm, Trump said, caused the drill sergeant to come "after me like you wouldn't believe."

Whether his students were the sons of plumbers or millionaires, Dobias did not care. They would follow his orders, no questions or whining tolerated. Donald was no exception. "At the beginning, he didn't like the idea of being told what to do, like make your bed, shine your shoes, brush your teeth, clean the sink, do your homework, all that stuff that a kid has to do when you're a cadet at an academy of four hundred kids," Dobias said. "We really didn't care whether he came from Rockefeller Center or whatever. He was just another name, another cadet, just like everybody else."

Founded in 1889 by a Civil War veteran in what had been a summer resort hotel, the academy modeled its strict code of conduct and turreted academic building after West Point, located five miles south along the Hudson. About 450 students were enrolled, all of them white except for a couple of dozen Latin Americans. The school did not admit blacks until Donald's senior year. Women would not arrive for another decade. The military academy was a place where, as the school's slogan put it, the boys were "set apart for excellence"; the idea was to inject discipline and direction into boys who arrived on campus unformed and untamed. That involved breaking them down to build them up. Every student received a blue booklet titled "General Order No. 6," which laid out the punishments for a variety of infractions. A dirty uniform, unpolished shoes, uncut hair, an unmade bed, "not walking properly," "holding hands with a young lady," and nudity in the barracks all resulted in demerits. Hitchhiking, stealing, drinking, gambling, and possession of pornography could result in immediate dismissal. Every day, the cadets had to line up and face rigorous inspection. An officer wiped a white glove along the top of the lockers to check for dirt. A misspelling or missed punctuation on a term paper was enough to lower a grade.

The academy offered few distractions. Entertainment was limited to theater staged by an all-male cast and old movies in the chapel on Friday and Saturday nights. If a film included starlets, the cadets would erupt in howls and whistles, prompting commanders to order a punishing round of drill marches on the quadrangle. Only high-ranking student officers were allowed off campus in groups on Sunday afternoons, although cadets could leave for a meal with their parents. Fred Trump often came up to see his son. Once, when Fred arrived in a limousine driven by his chauffeur, Donald was too embarrassed to meet him. From then on, Fred drove his own Cadillac to check up on Donald.

The academy celebrated masculine excellence with a message carved above the school's main entrance: COURAGEOUS AND GALLANT MEN HAVE PASSED THROUGH THESE PORTALS. When they weren't studying or playing a sport, cadets were required to learn to clean an M1 rifle and fire a mortar. Physical brutality and verbal abuse were tolerated, even encouraged. Hazing was a part of freshman life, with upperclassmen pummeling new cadets with broom handles or forcing them to stand fully dressed in their uniforms atop radiators or in steam-filled showers until they passed out. Michael Scadron, a close Trump friend at the academy, said his own hazing culminated with upperclassmen requiring him to kiss the school's mascot—a donkey—"on the ass."

DONALD'S COMPETITIVE DRIVE TOOK over as he learned to master the academy. He won medals for neatness and order. He loved competing to win contests for cleanest room, shiniest shoes, and best-made bed. For the first time, he took pride in his grades; he grew angry when a study partner scored higher on a chemistry test, even questioning whether he had cheated. Donald also learned to manage Dobias, projecting strength—especially in sports—without appearing to undermine the sergeant. "I figured out what it would take to get Dobias on my side," Trump said. "I finessed him. It helped that I was a good athlete, since he was the baseball coach and I was the captain of the team. But I also learned how to play *him.*"

To fellow cadets, Donald could be friendly, aloof, and cocky, once telling Jeff Orteneau, "I'm going to be famous one day." When meeting classmates for the first time, he liked to ask, "What does your father do?" Most of Donald's friends knew that his family was wealthy because he would talk about his father's business. Donald told David Smith, his senior-year roommate, that Fred Trump's wealth doubled every time he completed a project. "He was self-confident and very soft-spoken, believe it or not, as if he knew he was just passing time until he went on to something greater," said classmate Michael Pitkow. Despite his affluence, Donald's tastes were often plebeian. In the waning months of the Eisenhower administration, in a culture defined by conformity, Donald used the record player in his dorm room mostly to listen to Elvis Presley and Johnny Mathis albums. Sometimes, Donald would screw an ultraviolet lightbulb into the overhead socket and announce to his roommate that it was time to tan. "We're going to the beach," he'd say.

As a senior, Donald drew notice for bringing women to campus and showing them around. "They were beautiful, gorgeous women, dressed out of Saks Fifth Avenue," said classmate George White. Trump was never shy about judging a girl's appearance, pronouncing one of White's visitors a "dog." Ernie Kirk went on double dates with Donald and two girls who lived in town. Because the boys weren't allowed off grounds, the girls came to campus, where they watched a ball game and had burgers and Cokes in the canteen. Donald was cordial and talkative with his date, a brunette. A few months later, Trump was identified as "Ladies' Man" in his senior yearbook, posing for a photo alongside an academy secretary.

On occasion, Donald demonstrated that he was still capable of the aggression that had defined him at Kew-Forest, and he seemed to enjoy wielding authority. As a junior supply sergeant in Company E, Trump commanded that a cadet be struck on the backside with a broomstick for breaking formation. On another day, when he was on inspection duty, Trump came upon fellow student Ted Levine's unmade bed. Trump ripped the sheets off and threw them on the floor. Levine, a foot shorter than Trump, threw a combat boot at Donald, then hit him with a broomstick. Infuriated, Trump grabbed Levine and tried to push him out a second-floor window, Levine recalled. Two other cadets intervened to prevent Levine from falling. Trump and Levine clashed again when they became roommates. Disgusted by Levine's messiness, Trump often shouted at him to clean up. Trump, his roommate would later say, would try to "break" anyone who did not bend to his will.

AS AT KEW-FOREST, TRUMP could rely on his athletic ability to win respect from his teachers and classmates. In his second year at NYMA, Trump played on the freshman football and baseball teams, the latter coached by Dobias. By his sophomore year, as he shed baby fat and continued to grow, Trump had made the varsity in both sports. He particularly excelled at baseball, playing first base and developing a reputation for stretching his long body to scoop up balls that the team's shortstop, Gerald Paige, threw in the dirt. Donald could also swing the bat, inspiring a caption beneath an action photo in the yearbook that read, "Trump swings . . . then HITS." A headline in the local paper— "Trump Wins Game for NYMA"—may have been the first to celebrate his exploits. "It felt good seeing my name in print," Trump said years later. "How many people are in print? Nobody's in print. It was the first time I was ever in the newspaper. I thought it was amazing." Dobias taught his players the line famously attributed to legendary Green Bay Packers head coach Vince Lombardi: "I taught them that winning wasn't everything, it was the only thing," Dobias said. "Donald picked right up on this. He would tell his teammates, 'We're out here for a purpose. To win.' He always had to be number one, in everything. He was a conniver even then. A real pain in the ass. He would do anything to win . . . [Trump] just wanted to be first, in everything, and he wanted people to know he was first."

On the football team, Trump played tight end for two years. He wasn't the fastest player, but he was a "big, strong kid" who was "hard to bring down," said Paige, a running back. As a junior, however, Trump quit the team. He didn't like the head coach, and the feeling was apparently mutual. "The coach was nasty to him," Levine said. Trump "got personally abused by authority and was not appreciated." Trump's teammates, who valued his play on the field, were angry that he left the team. John Cino, the head coach, had his own theory: Trump quit, he said, because his father wanted him to concentrate on academics.

Off the field, Trump rose steadily from private to corporal to, in his junior year, supply sergeant, an important if dull position that required him to procure supplies for his company, including deactivated M1 rifles. New cadets were required to meticulously clean their weapons. Trump went further, demanding that the boys memorize their rifle numbers. "Being a new guy, it was overwhelming," said Jack Serafin, who was a freshman when Trump was a supply sergeant. "But you could always go to Donald and he would figure out how to get things done."

IN JUNE OF 1963, as Donald was completing his junior year, the National Guard escorted two black students into the University of Alabama, pushing their way past Governor George Wallace as he made his stand in the schoolhouse door. Three months later, New York Military Academy accepted its first two African American cadets. On his first day at the academy, after arriving from Harlem, Vincent Cunningham was tying his shoes when a corporal called him a "nigger." Cunningham knocked the corporal down and wound up in a commandant's office. The abuse continued all year. "You had to have thick skin and know how to carry yourself," Cunningham said. "If you overreacted to everything and were in disagreement to everything, they'd make your life miserable." David Prince Thomas, another black student, got into a fight on his first day after a white student called him a "jungle bunny." At night, fellow cadets would call up toward Thomas's room, saying the Ku Klux Klan was coming to get him. "It was almost socially accepted," Peter Ticktin, a classmate of Donald's, said of the abuse. But when Ticktin and Trump heard a student call a black cadet "nigger," they were both disgusted, Ticktin recalled.

On November 22, 1963, a Friday, Donald was sitting in class when an alarm bell rang. The cadets were called to the chapel, where an administrator announced that President Kennedy had been assassinated. At home, Donald had grown up absorbing his father's enthusiasm for Republicans such as Barry Goldwater. Donald had gone to school wearing an I LIKE IKE button for Eisenhower. Yet because of his business interests, his father also had many allies in New York's Democratic establishment. Kennedy's death was a seismic moment, and many of the cadets assembled that afternoon broke out into tears at the news. It was an unsettling time: along with racial and political crises, US involvement in Vietnam was escalating.

At NYMA, Trump was focused on more personal tumult as senior year unfolded. Scadron, his friend, left the academy after a younger cadet accused him of beating him with a stick. At the same time, Trump was promoted to captain of A Company, a prestigious position. Ticktin served as Trump's platoon sergeant, helping him "set the pace for all the parades" and managing their forty-five-man platoon. As a captain, Trump was "even-keeled," Ticktin said, inspiring respect without screaming at his cadets. Often, he left his officers to manage the younger cadets. "You just didn't want to disappoint him," Ticktin said. "I came back from a trip to New York once, and I was five minutes late, and he just looked at me. He never yelled at anyone. He would just look at you, the eyebrows kind of raised. The kind of look that said you can't disappoint him."

A month into the school year, one of Trump's sergeants shoved a new cadet named Lee Ains against the wall after the freshman didn't stand to attention fast enough. Ains complained. With administrators still reeling from other hazing incidents, a colonel relieved Trump of duty in the barracks and reassigned him to the academic building as a battalion training officer. "They felt he wasn't paying attention to his other officers as closely as he should have," said Ains, who left the school at the end of the year. By Trump's account, his transfer was a promotion and had nothing to do with hazing under his command. "I did a good job, and that's why I got elevated," he said. "You don't get elevated if you partake in hazing." After his transfer, Trump was put in charge of a special drill team for New York City's Columbus Day parade. In white gloves and dressed in full uniform, Trump led the procession south along Fifth Avenue toward St. Patrick's Cathedral, where he shook hands with Francis Cardinal Spellman. Turning to Major Anthony "Ace" Castellano, one of NYMA's commanders, Trump said, "You know what, Ace? I'd really like to own some of this real estate someday."

When Trump graduated from NYMA in May of 1964, striding across the quadrangle in full uniform in front of his family, his ambition was to follow his father into real estate. Despite his military preparation, Trump apparently had little desire to go to war. He registered for the draft—he was listed at six feet two, 180 pounds, with birthmarks on both heels—but his decision to go straight to college earned him the first of four educational draft deferments on July 28, 1964. For a time, he flirted with signing up for film school at the University of Southern California—reflecting his lifelong love of movies—but he enrolled instead at Fordham University because he wanted to be closer to home.

In the summer between high school and college, Donald worked for Fred, traveling to Cincinnati, where his father had purchased a rundown, twelve-hundred-unit apartment complex called Swifton Village for $5.7 million. Fred would leave his son in Cincinnati for a week at a time to take care of menial tasks. "He'd get in there and work with us," remembered Roy Knight, a Swifton Village maintenance man. "He wasn't skilled, but he'd do yard work and clean up—whatever needed to be done."

STARTING IN FALL OF 1964, Trump commuted from Jamaica Estates to Fordham's leafy Bronx campus in his red Austin-Healey. After being away at school for five years, Donald could spend more time with his father, joining him that November for the opening ceremony for the elegant, daring Verrazano-Narrows Bridge, then the world's longest suspension bridge, connecting Brooklyn and Staten Island. Amid the pageantry, Donald noticed that city officials barely acknowledged the bridge's eighty-five-year-old designer, Othmar Ammann. Although the day had been sunny and cloudless, Trump would remember pouring rain years later when he recalled Ammann's standing off to the side, alone. "Nobody even mentioned his name," Trump said. "I realized then and there that if you let people treat you how they want, you'll be made a fool. I realized then and there something I would never forget: I don't want to be made anybody's sucker."

At Fordham, Trump's wealth was evident to classmates, most of them public school graduates from working- and middle-class families across the New York area. At a time when college students were beginning to experiment with drugs and dressing more casually, Trump showed up for school in a three-piece suit and carrying a briefcase. In classes, Trump often raised his hand to participate. Yet what caught the attention of Robert Klein, an accounting major who sat next to him in philosophy class, were Donald's doodles. He drew pictures of buildings—skyscrapers. Klein discovered that Trump was not like his classmates in other ways, too. One afternoon, Donald invited Klein to a Mets game. Donald drove his convertible with his friend to Shea Stadium, where an attendant parked the car for Donald. He and Klein sat in the stadium's front row, near the team's owner, Joan Payson.

Trump joined Fordham's squash team, cramming with teammates into his coach's station wagon for rides to practice. Squash was not Donald's game, but he was an eager learner and was aggressive on the court, preferring to smash the ball past opponents than to outlast them in a volley. "Way to go, Trumpie!" his teammates shouted after Donald won a decisive match. "He had a certain aura," said Rich Marrin, a teammate. "He didn't have tantrums, and he was never late. If anything, he was more of a gentleman than we were, more refined, as if brought up in a stricter family, with more emphasis on manners. We weren't that rowdy, but we didn't always know the right forks." Trump made the first-string team, which traveled across the Northeast and mid-Atlantic. He sometimes drove teammates in his sports car, requiring them to chip in for gas and tolls even though the coach gave Trump travel money. Sometimes, at practice, a teammate would look over to see Trump, taking a break, reading the *Wall Street Journal* or the *New York Times*. On road trips to Yale and Georgetown, he snuck out at night with teammates to bars, even though he did not drink. After a crushing loss to the Naval Academy in Annapolis, Trump tried to boost his team's spirits. As they were driving back to New York, he told a teammate to pull over at a Montgomery Ward department store, where Donald bought golf clubs, tees, and dozens of balls, which they took to a bluff overlooking Chesapeake Bay. Trump grabbed a club and hit a few balls into the water, inspiring his teammates to join in. After all the balls were gone, Trump and his teammates got back into the car, leaving the golf clubs on the side of the road.

Yet, for all the fun he seemed to have with his team, Trump also exuded restlessness at Fordham, as if the school's reputation and its culture did not meet his standards. Brian Fitzgibbon, who lived near Donald in Queens, sometimes commuted to school with him in Donald's car and did not think Trump "had a keen sense of belonging at Fordham. His family wealth and the fact that he was not Catholic may have made him feel different from others." Trump, he said, sometimes complained "that there were too many Italian and Irish students at Fordham," an assertion that struck Fitzgibbon as "elitist." Fitzgibbon suspected that Trump's attitude reflected his belief that he had really always belonged at an Ivy League school. After his sophomore year, Trump got his wish, transferring to the University of Pennsylvania. He left Fordham behind without saying good-bye to his buddies on the squash team.

TRUMP ARRIVED AT THE University of Pennsylvania's Wharton School in the fall of 1966 as a man in a hurry. In the school's tiny real estate department, Trump's bragging stood out from the start. The kid with the big blond mop of hair told classmates that he was going to be the next Bill Zeckendorf, the Manhattan developer who once owned the Chrysler Building and amassed land for the United Nations headquarters (and who was also the son of a major builder). Trump promised he'd be even bigger and better than Zeckendorf.

Trump's two years at the sole Ivy League school with an undergraduate business school would be the only time he ever lived outside New York, but even then, he returned home frequently on weekends to work with his father. Trump saw Wharton from the beginning as a place to pick up a patina of prestige. "Perhaps the most important thing I learned at Wharton was not to be overly impressed by academic credentials," Trump said. "It didn't take me long to realize that there was nothing particularly awesome or exceptional about my classmates, and that I could compete just fine. The other important thing I got from Wharton was a Wharton degree. In my opinion, that degree doesn't prove much, but a lot of people I do business with take it very seriously."

Yet Trump himself would come to take Wharton very seriously. Wharton became a name to be dropped, another "best" to burnish the Trump brand. For a time, Trump bragged of being a top student among his 333 Wharton classmates, even claiming to have been first in the class. But Trump is not included on the honor roll printed in the *Daily Pennsylvanian*, the student newspaper, and classmates don't recall Trump as an exceptional student. "Trump was not what you would call an 'intellectual,'" said Louis Calomaris, his classmate. "He wasn't a dumb guy. He had a specific interest. I don't think he ever studied for an exam. Trump was interested in trading and leveraged deals. . . . He did what it took to get through the program." Trump lived off campus in a modest apartment and left town most weekends. He wasn't prominent in extracurricular activities. Many classmates don't remember him at all.

At the height of the anti–Vietnam War protests on college campuses, in the first, volatile years of the Nixon administration, Penn students staged sit-ins, demonstrating against university contracts with the US military to research biological weapons and potent herbicides. Trump, like many other Wharton students, steered clear of the campus unrest; his focus was on getting his career going. Soon after he arrived at Penn, Trump had his second US military physical, but he remained exempt from the draft because he was still a student. Trump would be declared 1-A—eligible for service—after he completed college, in 1968. But another armed forces physical that fall ended with his being classified 1-Y, medically disqualified except in case of national emergency. Military records do not detail the reason for that finding; Trump said it was because he had bone spurs in both heels. In 1969, young men who shared Trump's birthday—June 14—drew number 356 out of 366 in the draft lottery, almost certainly sparing them from mandatory military service. But Trump didn't need the luck of the lottery because his medical disqualification remained in effect through 1972, when it was changed to 4-F, meaning not qualified for service. (During his presidential campaign, a Trump spokesman said that Trump was "not a fan of the Vietnam War, yet another disaster for our country, [but] had his draft number been selected, he would have gladly served.")

Far from joining the hundreds of thousands of young American men who were in the jungles of Southeast Asia, Trump was already spending nearly as much time working for his father in New York as he was in class in Philadelphia. "He sniveled every Monday about having to go home on the weekends to New York and work for his dad," said classmate Terry Farrell. "He was a rich whiner." Trump may have felt like a prince of Queens, but he was by no means the wealthiest student in his class or even in his major. The real estate department, with about six undergraduate majors in each class, was stocked with scions of some of the country's titans of property development, including Gerald W. Blakeley III, whose father ran Boston's venerable Cabot, Cabot & Forbes; and Robert Mackle, whose father and uncles were prominent in postwar Florida real estate.

Trump was eager to get going in his field, and he spent many hours looking to buy apartments near the West Philadelphia campus to rent them to students. Trump recalled being focused on acquiring property, but his name does not come up in searches of real estate transactions during that period. Some classmates said he was equally interested in being seen with beautiful women. "Every time I saw him, he had a pretty girl on his arm," said classmate Bill Specht.

Candice Bergen, the actress and model, had left Penn before Trump arrived on campus, but she recalled a blind date with him: "He was wearing a three-piece burgundy suit, and burgundy boots, and [drove] a burgundy limousine. He was very coordinated. . . . It was a very short evening." Trump's recollection is different: "She was dating guys from Paris, France, who were thirty-five years old, the whole thing. I did make the move. And I must say she had the good sense to say, 'Absolutely not.'"

In the years after Trump graduated, Wharton became synonymous with financial success. Many of its graduates grew rich, and Penn's endowment soared. Alumni gave generously, their names emblazoned all over campus. But although Wharton's place in Trump's biography expanded, his contributions to the school did only rarely. In the 1980s, a Penn development officer said Trump had given the school more than $10,000, but declined to elaborate. "I don't know why he has not supported the school more," Wharton's associate director for development, Nancy Magargal, said then. One of the only places his name appears on campus is the Class of 1968 Seminar Room plaque in Van Pelt Library, donated at his class's thirty-fifth reunion. Classmates and former university officials believe the contribution was in the $5,000 range. Despite Trump's professed love of Penn and boasts of his financial success, university fund-raisers tired of asking for large donations. One sizable gift came in 1994, when he gave enough to be listed as a "founder" of the Penn Club's new location in midtown Manhattan. The minimum gift for that category was $150,000. Two autumns later, Donald Trump Jr. arrived at the leafy campus. In all, three of the four older Trump children—including Ivanka (transferring after two years at Georgetown) and Tiffany—would attend Penn, making the school almost an inheritance, a family emblem.

In May 1968, William S. Paley, founder of CBS and an alumnus, delivered Wharton's commencement address. Standing with Fred Trump, Donald posed for a photograph in his black gown, a gold sash bordering his collar. Father and son beamed, their hands posed similarly by their sides. Donald's commuting days were over. Wharton had been a footnote, a pit stop on the way to the career he had announced to classmates as soon as he arrived on campus. Walking down Spruce Street during graduation festivities, his classmate recalls Trump yelling, "Hey, Louis, wait up!" Calomaris turned to his new girlfriend and future wife and said, "Linda, you're about to meet the next Bill Zeckendorf of Manhattan."

3

Father and Son

For years, Donald Trump had spent summers with his father, touring developments, learning the basics, but now Fred asked his college graduate son to join him full-time in Brooklyn, where Trump Management had a modest office on Avenue Z, near the timeworn Coney Island boardwalk. There, the capstone of Fred Trump's career now dominated the skyline: Trump Village.

For close to a century, Coney Island had been a thriving urban resort; hundreds of thousands of New Yorkers crowded the beaches and queued up for the amusements. But over the years, the area had declined, and city officials were anxious for redevelopment. They condemned a forty-acre parcel, authorized demolition of existing buildings, and gave Fred Trump permission to build near the site of the famous Parachute Jump, the 250-foot-high "Eiffel Tower of Brooklyn," which once let riders plunge, safely, to the ground. The elder Trump seized the opportunity in the early 1960s and, for the first time, put the family name on a development.

As Donald drove his Cadillac from Queens to Coney Island to join his father, he could see his father's greatest accomplishment. Trump Village was no bucolic refuge, as its name implied. It was a gargantuan series of seven twenty-three-story high-rises dwarfing the Parachute Jump and all that stood around it, built in a utilitarian style—thirty-eight hundred apartments near the beachfront, the largest rental complex in Brooklyn at the time. The apartments, nobody's idea of grand or elegant, were nonetheless a proud step up for the striving middle-class families, many of them Jewish immigrants or their children, who left the city's badly aging, cramped row houses to enjoy the ocean breezes and live a few blocks from Nathan's hot dog stand and Mrs. Stahl's Knishes on the boardwalk.

Fred had insisted Trump Village be built as cheaply as possible, with the least expensive brick and few architectural niceties. He carried the frugality to his nearby office, shag carpeted, strewn with metal furniture, and decorated with cigar-store wooden Indians. This would now be Donald's office as well. Just a few years out of Wharton, around the time he turned twenty-five in 1971, Donald became president of Trump Management, while Fred took on the role of chairman. Donald's ascendancy was both an extraordinary gift and a great responsibility. He now oversaw fourteen thousand apartments throughout the outer boroughs, including those at Trump Village. It could be rough work. Tenants came and went by the hundreds. Some missed payments. The city pressured the Trumps to accept lower-income families, who sometimes fled when bills were due, leaving the apartments wrecked. Donald later told tales of standing to the side of the door after he knocked, fearing someone might greet him with a gun. This cost was all part of running large apartment complexes in such neighborhoods, familiar to Fred but a culture shock for his son.

Fred, in his midtwenties at the start of the Depression, worried about his financial condition and shouldered as little personal risk as possible. He said he was successful because he squeezed nine days out of a seven-day week and made sure every penny was spent wisely. He liked to say that he could turn a lemon into a grapefruit. These were the lessons he hoped to convey to Donald: work hard, be humble and thankful, and stick to the winning formula of building middle-class housing in Queens, Staten Island, and Brooklyn.

"There is no secret" to success, Fred explained years later in accepting the Horatio Alger Award, given to people who overcame adversity. "There are just two things. One, you must like what you do. You must pick out the right business or profession. You must learn all about it . . . so you become enthusiastic about it. Nine out of ten people don't like what they do. And in not liking what they do, they lose enthusiasm, they go from job to job, and ultimately become a nothing." Such was the challenge Donald faced as his father's son: he was given everything at the start—and thus never able to qualify for the Horatio Alger Award—and he wanted to avoid failing in his father's eyes and becoming a nothing.

Fred made his millions with care and frugality, but also with more than a little help from government housing programs. As Fred became more successful, he increasingly faced questions about how he ran his business. The first big fight had come in 1954, when Donald was eight years old, and Fred was called to testify before Congress. A congressional committee was investigating whether Fred had misused a government-insured loan on a Brooklyn apartment project called Beach Haven. He had borrowed $3.5 million more than he needed, according to a Senate report. Trump angrily responded that the allegations had done "untold damage to my standing and reputation." He testified that he built apartments for less than the loan amount because of reduced costs, not because he was trying to make an illicit profit. No charges were brought against him.

Then, in 1966, Fred faced allegations that he netted a "windfall" of $1.8 million in building Trump Village through a state program. New York investigators said that Trump's project costs had been inflated, and that he had blocked the appointment of a government official who might have opposed his plans. Trump, as he had in the Senate hearing, dismissed the complaints as nonsense, saying the profits were "peanuts, compared to a sixty-million-dollar job." Again, no charges were brought.

Fred Trump could proudly point to tens of thousands of working-class residents of Brooklyn, Queens, and Staten Island who lived in houses that he built or apartment complexes that he managed. Countless New Yorkers, including many immigrant families, got their start in the city in the housing on which Trump had made his fortune. Many apartment complexes were in gritty neighborhoods, often divided by race. The federal government, which helped finance many Trump projects, bore some of the blame for this balkanization; the Federal Housing Administration had all but sanctioned segregation, advising against what were euphemistically called "inharmonious" projects.

One Trump tenant disturbed by the de facto segregation was the

Oklahoman Woodrow Wilson Guthrie—or Woody, as the folksinger was known. He had moved to New York City in 1940, the same year he wrote one of the nation's most revered ballads, "This Land Is Your Land." Ten years later, he had moved to Beach Haven, the Trump complex a few blocks from the Coney Island beachfront. Guthrie later wrote a number of verses that suggested Fred Trump was responsible for steering blacks away from the property: "I suppose / Old Man Trump knows / Just how much / Racial Hate / He stirred up / In the bloodpot of human hearts / When he drawed / That color line / Here at his / Eighteen hundred family project."

For years after Guthrie left Beach Haven, Fred's company faced allegations of discrimination. Every now and then complaints would be filed with local agencies, and the Trump company would agree to rent to someone who had allegedly been denied admission, and the matter was settled. But by the time Donald joined the business, investigators were again monitoring the company for racial discrimination. Local activists suspected that rental agents steered black applicants away from buildings that were mostly occupied by whites. That had been a common practice in many parts of the country for years, but it had been outlawed by the Fair Housing Act of 1968. The legislation was passed during the Johnson administration at a time when many whites were relocating to the suburbs, and minorities often moved into the city properties that whites had vacated. Concern about the issue peaked following race riots that broke out across the country after the 1968 assassination of the Reverend Martin Luther King Jr. In 1971, after a major New York City landlord settled a case alleging discrimination, undercover testers stepped up their focus on Donald and Fred Trump. They quickly found evidence of what they believed to be racial discrimination.

On March 18, 1972, Alfred Hoyt, a black man, heard about a vacancy at a Trump apartment complex on Westminster Road in Brooklyn. When he sought to rent the place, he was told by the superintendent that no two-bedroom apartments were available. The following day, his wife, Sheila Hoyt, who is white, was offered an application to rent a two-bedroom apartment at the same complex. Unbeknownst to the superintendent, Sheila Hoyt was a tester for the New York City Human Rights Commission, a city agency that investigated housing discrimination. Two days later, she returned to sign the lease. What the superintendent didn't know was that she had brought along her husband and a housing commissioner, who had been waiting outside and now entered the apartment. The commissioner demanded to know why Alfred Hoyt had been denied an apartment offered to Sheila Hoyt. Hoyt said the superintendent told her he was "just doing what my boss told me to do. I am not allowed to rent to [black] families." The commissioner placed a placard at the building that said no business could be transacted there, per order of the Human Rights Commission. Then the superintendent brought the Hoyts and the commissioner to the Trump office on Avenue Z. Sheila Hoyt couldn't recall if she met Donald, but said that after the group met at the Trump office, Alfred Hoyt was allowed to rent the apartment for himself and his wife.

The initial refusal to rent to Alfred Hoyt helped set off a chain of events that would lead to one of the most controversial and defining moments in Donald Trump's early years. More testers secretly made the rounds of Trump buildings. In a July 1972 test at Shore Haven Apartments in Brooklyn, a superintendent told a black woman, Henrietta Davis, that nothing was available. A white woman, Muriel Salzman, a tester for the Urban League, followed Davis into the office, and the same superintendent told Salzman that she could "immediately rent either one of two available apartments."

The tests revealed a pattern. White testers were encouraged to rent at certain Trump buildings, while the black testers were discouraged, denied, or steered to apartment complexes that had more racial minorities. After local activists realized the scope of their findings, they alerted the Justice Department's civil rights division, which was looking for housing cases to pursue.

THE TRUMP FILE LANDED on the desk of an idealistic young Justice Department lawyer named Elyse Goldweber. It was a fateful moment, and she seized it. One of Goldweber's clearest childhood memories had been taking a ferry in southern Virginia to visit her grandparents. Two signs greeted her as she came on board: WHITE and COLORED. As the ferry reached Newport News, Virginia, Goldweber's parents vowed the family would not patronize stores that practiced segregation. Growing up on Long Island, she watched reports of blacks being chased by police dogs and pushed back by spray from high-powered water hoses; she decided she wanted to work for the government as a civil rights lawyer.

For years, the Justice Department had sought Ivy League law school graduates to represent the US government. Goldweber graduated from Brooklyn Law School and figured she had little chance to fulfill her dream. But just as she graduated, the Justice Department said it wanted to expand its pool of job candidates, and a number of lawyers had left the housing division to join the presidential campaign of Democrat George McGovern. Goldweber won a plum spot from the start.

When the allegations against the Trump company arrived at the Justice Department office in Washington, the file came to Goldweber, whose bosses had given her jurisdiction over New York cases. She went to New York and talked to housing activists and Trump company workers, learning that in a sampling of ten Trump buildings, only 1 to 3.5 percent of the occupants were minorities, far below the rate of the local population. This was as strong a case as she had seen. She recommended that the Justice Department file suit against Fred and Donald Trump and their company.

Two former Trump employees, a husband and wife, said they were told "by Fred Trump and other agents" that the company only wanted to rent to "Jews and Executives" and "discouraged rental to blacks." The couple said "a racial code was in effect, blacks being referred to as 'No. 9.'" Other rental agents employed by the Trumps told the FBI that only 1 percent of tenants at the Trump-run Ocean Terrace Apartments were black, and that Lincoln Shore Apartments had no black tenants. Both were on Ocean Parkway in Brooklyn. Minorities, however, were steered to Patio Gardens, a different complex on Flatbush Avenue in Brooklyn, where the tenant population was 40 percent black. One black woman was turned away at a heavily white complex but was told she should "try to obtain an apartment at Patio Gardens."

Phyllis Spiro, a white woman, went undercover in 1973 at Beach Haven, the same property that Woody Guthrie had lived in and written about two decades earlier. She told investigators that a building superintendent acknowledged to her "that he followed a racially discriminatory rental policy at the direction of his superiors, and that there were only very few 'colored' tenants" at the complex. More than four decades later, Spiro remembered the case vividly and said she and her fellow housing activists found "a constant pattern and practice of discrimination" at Trump buildings.

Goldweber's bosses had heard enough. Citing the experiences of the Hoyts, Spiro, and many others, the Justice Department announced the filing of one of the most significant racial bias cases of the era: *United States of America v. Fred C. Trump, Donald Trump and Trump Management, Inc.* On the morning of October 15, 1973, a Justice Department official reached Donald Trump on the phone. This courtesy call was to let the twenty-seven-year-old developer know the federal government was suing him and his father. Within minutes, the Justice Department issued a news release that said the Trumps had violated the law "by refusing to rent and negotiate rentals with blacks, requiring different rental terms and conditions because of race, and misrepresenting that apartments were not available." The news media promptly picked up the story. Trump later said the first time he heard the news was when he turned on the radio in his Cadillac, not from the Justice Department official's phone call. The following morning, Trump was on the front pages, including a *New York Times* story headlined "Major Landlord Accused of Antiblack Bias in City." Trump was livid, saying the charges were "absolutely ridiculous. We never have discriminated."

THE TIMING WAS TERRIBLE, coming just as Donald was growing increasingly anxious to pull away from his father's shadow. He had lost patience with his father's strategy of catering to lower- and middle-income residents of Brooklyn and Queens, and what was required to manage them. When he found tenants throwing trash out of the windows, he began a program "to teach people about using the incinerators." Company employees warned him that he was "liable to get shot" if he tried to collect rent at the wrong time. He thought his father's buildings lacked style, with their "common brick facades." All for a profit margin that he called "so low."

Though a creature of his father's business and a beneficiary of it, Donald yearned for something more. Fred, now sixty-eight, was settled in his routine of going to lunch, every Monday, Wednesday, and Friday, at Gargiulo's, an Italian restaurant a couple of blocks from Trump Village, a neighborhood fixture since 1907. Fred was often accompanied by his administrative assistant, a woman named Ann, and his order was always the same: tortellini Bolognese with white cream sauce.

It was a calamitous time for New York City. The metropolis lost 10 percent of its population in the 1970s, as crime escalated, whites fled, and the city teetered on the edge of bankruptcy. Graffiti-filled subways rattled along, badly in need of repair. A popular television show, *All in the Family*, featured the bigoted Archie Bunker character, who lived in Queens, near Trump's childhood home. Coney Island had fallen into further decay, a shadow of its merry heyday. Donald, meanwhile, could look across at Manhattan and see a skyline in transition; when the twin 110-story towers of the World Trade Center were dedicated in April 1973, President Nixon hailed the moment as the inauguration of an era of revitalized international commerce. As the Vietnam War wound down, the protest music that had filtered out of folk clubs was being replaced by the pulse of disco.

Donald preferred everything about Manhattan—the fancy restaurants, the slinky fashion models, the skyscrapers, the money to be made and spent. He disparaged his experience in the grittier parts of the city. His father's outer-borough empire, Trump wrote, "was not a world I found very attractive. I'd just graduated from Wharton and suddenly here I was in a scene that was violent at worst and unpleasant at best." This "unpleasant" world was the reality faced by millions of people, but it was far away from everything Trump knew—his luxurious surroundings in Jamaica Estates, the order of a military academy, the elite education at Wharton. He wanted something better. His father had found one path to riches; Donald saw a different one to even greater wealth. "The real reason I wanted out of my father's business— more important than the fact that it was physically rough and financially tough—was that I had loftier dreams and visions," Trump wrote. "And there was no way to implement them building housing in the outer boroughs."

In 1971, Trump moved into a Manhattan apartment on the seventeenth floor of a building on East Seventy-Fifth Street, which he furnished with velvet couches and crystal with help from an interior designer. He hired an Irish woman to be his maid. He parked his Cadillac convertible in a garage next door and each day drove the sizable distance to work at the Trump Management office on Avenue Z. The Upper East Side apartment had a certain appeal for a young man, in part because it was rent-controlled; city law prohibited the landlord from increasing the rent substantially each year. (In 1975, Trump handed the apartment over to his brother Robert. About that time, Donald spoke out against rent-control laws: "Everybody in New York gets their increases but the landlords, and we are going to put an end to that practice.")

After living in Manhattan for two years, Trump moved closer to his goal of building his own real estate business. Then the government filed suit against him and his father. Just as he was envisioning a new, Manhattan-centric Trump brand, the first thing most people heard about him was the accusation that he discriminated against black people. The prudent thing to do might have been to settle. The Justice Department wasn't seeking a financial penalty or jail time; the government basically wanted a settlement in which the Trumps would promise not to discriminate. At that transitional moment, with authority passing from father to son, Donald needed guidance. One day shortly after the suit was filed, Trump and his father visited a top New York law firm, where attorneys advised them to give in to the government. Donald was torn. That evening, as he pondered the decision, Donald walked into a Manhattan discotheque. There he met the man who would help shape his life's course as his father began to recede from the picture. This new acquaintance was adept at working the private and public corridors of power. He knew mayors and judges and senators. He moved at a whole other level than Donald Trump. The man's name was Roy Cohn.

4

Roy Cohn and the Art of the Counterattack

The nondescript stucco building at 416 East Fifty-Fifth Street bore little hint of what lay inside. No name was on the doorway or awning, just MEMBERS ONLY on a brass plaque. Known as Le Club, this discotheque was where Gotham's glitterati gathered on a small dance floor, around a billiard table, and at a second-floor dining room. Club membership was limited to twelve hundred, including "13 princes, 13 counts, four barons, three princesses, two dukes."

Trump wanted in. In 1973, Le Club was a gathering spot for "some of the most successful men and the most beautiful women in the world," Trump wrote, "the sort of place where you were likely to see a wealthy seventy-five-year-old guy walk in with three blondes from Sweden." But this young newcomer hardly qualified for such an exclusive venue. The club rejected him. Trump cajoled and pleaded with management. Acceptance was granted on one condition: he had to promise not to go after married women who came to the club "because I was young and good-looking." He boasted that he went there almost every night and "met a lot of beautiful, young, single women," but said he never got "very seriously" involved with them in these early years and, in any event, couldn't take them back to his apartment because his place wasn't glitzy enough.

It wasn't just about the women or the music. To Trump, the wish to belong was part of his quest for connections. He wanted to befriend those who held sway in New York City, the power brokers who moved easily between the dealmakers and the politicians. On the evening after a lawyer advised Donald and his father to settle the racial-bias case, Donald went to Le Club, where he spotted a balding man with a memorable face: high forehead, piercing blue eyes, heavy eyelids, a fighter's nose with a crooked streak running down it. He looked like Hollywood's vision of a tough, a sharp contrast to tall, dashing Trump. Yet Trump was drawn to Roy Cohn—or, at least, to the power he represented, a power Trump could use at this difficult moment.

ROY COHN WAS BORN into power. His father, Albert C. Cohn, was a member of New York's Democratic machine who became a justice on the state Supreme Court. Roy went to the elite Fieldston and Horace Mann prep schools in the Bronx and on to Columbia, graduating from its law school at age twenty. Through his family's political connections, Cohn landed a job with the US Attorney's Office in Manhattan. Just months later, Cohn received an assignment that transformed his career. He was asked to write a memo about Alger Hiss, a State Department official suspected of spying for the Soviet Union. After FBI agents told Cohn about alleged "Kremlin cells" in federal agencies, he became convinced communists had infiltrated the government. Cohn rose quickly in the US Attorney's Office and later boasted that he took advantage of his family's ties to New York's five main crime families. (Years later, Cohn said he arranged for an ally to get the job of US attorney with the help of Frank "the Prime Minister" Costello, boss of the Luciano family, later renamed the Genovese. "In those days, nobody became US Attorney in New York without the O.K. from the mob," Cohn wrote.)

In 1951, Cohn worked on the prosecution of Julius and Ethel Rosenberg, who were convicted of espionage and passing atomic-bomb secrets to the Soviet Union. The couple were later executed, and Cohn claimed he had privately convinced the judge to send Ethel—not just Julius—to the electric chair. After that sensational case he worked in 1952 for the federal Internal Security Division, a new Justice Department office focused on rooting out communists. He soon learned that Senator Joseph McCarthy was launching an inquiry into whether communists had infiltrated the government, and the Wisconsin Republican hired Cohn as chief counsel to the Senate's Permanent Subcommittee on Investigations.

McCarthy made headlines by claiming he had a list of 205 State Department employees who were members of the Communist Party. Newspapers were filled with headlines about McCarthy's "Red scare" and his claim that the government was filled with "loyalty risks." With Cohn's help, McCarthy launched a series of hearings about the supposed communist threat in the United States. He called scores of professors, Hollywood writers, government employees, and others to answer for their alleged ties to the Communist Party.

McCarthy ramped up the allegations, claiming the nation's armed forces had been infiltrated by spies and subversives. Cohn's friend G. David Schine, who worked for McCarthy as an unpaid consultant, had been drafted into the army and faced the possibility of being sent to serve overseas. Cohn allegedly said he would "wreck the army" if Schine wasn't allowed to stay stateside. That prompted the army to accuse McCarthy and Cohn of trying to get Schine special treatment. Facing heavy criticism, McCarthy launched a counterattack. He suggested that a junior attorney at the law firm that employed Joseph Welch, the army's counsel at the hearings, once belonged to a communist front group. Welch famously turned the tables on the senator, saying, "Have you no sense of decency, sir, at long last?" The Senate censured McCarthy and Cohn resigned. *McCarthyism* became shorthand for political witch hunts; the senator's influence dissipated and he died in 1957. Cohn, however, insisted he had "never worked for a better man or a better cause." He not only survived, he returned to New York to become one of the city's most influential men.

Working from a Manhattan town house, Cohn represented clients ranging from the Catholic archdiocese to discotheque owners, real estate moguls, and mobsters. He boasted of avoiding federal taxes, which got him in trouble with the government. In the two decades following the McCarthy hearings, he was indicted on charges ranging from obstruction of justice to bribery to extortion, but he always seemed to get off. To fight his legal battles, Cohn honed a set of hard-boiled tactics and a rhetorical style that would serve him far beyond the courtroom. By the early 1970s, Cohn was looking for a client with wealth and connections, one he could mold to his liking.

ON THE MORNING OF October 15, 1973, the day the Justice Department announced it was suing the Trumps for racial bias, an op-ed appeared in the *New York Times* written by Roy Cohn. The column was in the form of a letter to Spiro Agnew, the former vice president of the United States. Agnew had resigned days earlier after pleading no contest to federal income tax evasion. Cohn, who had famously avoided federal income taxes for years, was outraged.

"Dear Mr. Agnew," he wrote. "How could a man who made courage a household word lose his? How could one of this decade's shrewdest leaders make a dumb mistake such as you did in quitting and accepting a criminal conviction? If you had stood your ground as you promised the public you would, I give you my opinion that your chances for legal and political survival were excellent. That opinion might mean something, because I went through three separate criminal proceedings very similar to those with which you were threatened. . . . I was offered 'deals' and 'plea bargains.' I turned them down and fought. When it was over, I had obtained three unanimous jury acquittals."

Trump, up against a discrimination charge, was being urged to settle, but hated the idea. Cohn, appalled that the vice president would cave in to the allegations against him and resign from the second most powerful office in the land, represented the argument against settling. Then Trump wandered into Le Club. And there was Cohn, the man who never settled. Trump sat down and explained the dilemma he faced.

"I don't like lawyers," Trump told Cohn. "I think all they do is delay deals. . . . Every answer they give you is no, and they are always looking to settle instead of fight."

Cohn agreed.

Trump continued, "I'd rather fight than fold, because as soon as you fold once, you get the reputation of being a folder."

"Is this just an academic conversation?"

Trump was thrilled that Cohn was listening to a "nobody" like him. Now he courted Cohn: "No, it is not academic at all." Trump explained how the government had just filed suit, "saying we discriminated against blacks in some of our housing developments." Trump said he didn't discriminate, and he didn't want the government forcing him to rent to welfare recipients. "What do you think I should do?"

"My view is tell them to go to hell and fight the thing in court and let them prove that you discriminated. . . . I don't think you have any obligation to rent to tenants who would be undesirable, white or black, and the government doesn't have a right to tell you how to run your business." Cohn assured Trump, "You'll win hands down."

Trump liked what he heard—not just about the case, but the whole "go to hell" philosophy. From that moment, he adopted the Cohn playbook: when attacked, counterattack with overwhelming force. One of the most influential relationships in Trump's life was now under way. As their relationship grew, he admired Cohn's brilliance, but worried that he could at times be unprepared and a "disaster."

When Cohn boasted that he had spent much of his life under indictment, Trump asked whether Cohn had really done what was alleged. "What the hell do you think?" Cohn responded with a smile. Trump said he "never really knew" what that meant, but he liked Cohn's toughness and loyalty.

Cohn worked hard to polish his reputation as gritty, cooperating with an *Esquire* profile titled "Don't Mess with Roy Cohn," which described him as a man who enjoyed getting indicted and fought every case as if it were a war. "Prospective clients who want to kill their husband, torture a business partner, break the government's legs, hire Roy Cohn," Ken Auletta wrote. "He is a legal executioner—the toughest, meanest, loyalest, vilest, and one of the most brilliant lawyers in America. He is not a very nice man." Trump served as a supporting witness in the piece. "When people know that Roy is involved, they'd rather not get involved in the lawsuits and everything else that's involved," Trump said. Cohn "was never two-faced. You could count on him to go to bat for you," which was exactly what Trump wanted Cohn to do in the racial-bias case.

Cohn unveiled his strategy two months after the Justice Department filed suit. On December 12, 1973, Trump walked before a phalanx of cameras at the New York Hilton to announce Cohn's audacious plan. Cohn filed a counterclaim against the government, saying the Justice Department had made false and misleading statements. He sought $100 million for the Trumps. Donald told reporters that the government was unfairly trying to force his company to lease apartments to people on welfare. If that happened, Trump said, "There would be a massive fleeing from the city of not only our tenants, but communities as a whole."

Trump rejected any suggestion that his view was based on race. "I have never, nor has anyone in our organization ever, to the best of my knowledge, discriminated or shown bias in renting our apartments," he swore in an affidavit. Cohn filed his own affidavit lamenting what he called an "abuse" of government powers. "The Civil Rights Division did not file a lawsuit," Cohn said. "It slapped together a piece of paper for use as a press release, and only secondarily as a court document. It contains not one fact concerning the discriminatory practices against blacks by the Trump organization."

Making his case for a $100 million payout to the Trumps, Cohn said, "No matter what the outcome of this case, I suppose the damage is never going to be completely undone because you are never going to catch up with these initial headlines."

FIVE WEEKS LATER, DONALD and Fred Trump, accompanied by Cohn, took their seats at a table at the US courthouse in Brooklyn for the Eastern District of New York. Goldweber, the idealistic twenty-six-year-old Justice Department lawyer, made a dramatic appearance, drenched from a downpour because she had been unable to find a cab. She felt nervous as she settled in and prepared to face the famously cutthroat Cohn.

At issue was whether the judge should let the Trumps' countersuit continue or, as the government wanted, to toss it out. Cohn spoke first, ridiculing the government for requesting racial breakdowns of the residents in Trump buildings. There are "a number of blacks who live in there, that we know visibly," Cohn told the court. "I have taken a ride and looked at some of them and blacks walk in and out and I assume they are not there for any improper purpose and they live in the place.

But they want us to go, apparently, and canvass all fourteen thousand of these units and find out how many blacks live there and how many nonblacks live there, and I suppose how many Puerto Ricans live there or non–Puerto Ricans."

Goldweber urged the judge to let the government's discrimination case go forward: "The defendants have refused to rent apartments to persons on account of their race and color. They have made discriminatory statements with respect to the rental of these dwellings. . . . They have represented that their dwellings were unavailable for rental, when, in fact, such dwellings were available."

Judge Edward R. Neaher sided with Goldweber, dismissing Cohn and the Trumps' $100 million counterclaim and ordering that the case go forward. Goldweber promptly requested depositions from the Trumps and said she had no patience for delay tactics. That prompted Cohn to write to Goldweber: "Dear Elyse, I never knew you were such a hot-tempered white female! . . . We will see you with Mr. Trump and the other witnesses next week."

Trump said in his deposition that he was "unfamiliar" with the Fair Housing Act that banned discrimination. He also initially said that he didn't count a wife's income when calculating whether a couple qualified financially to rent a Trump apartment, saying he relied only on income from "the male in the family," although he subsequently revised that statement.

The Trumps went on the counterattack. Cohn sought to undermine the government's assertion that Trump employees used coded language to refer to minorities. The government had offered evidence that a Trump employee was instructed to mark rental applications from blacks with the letter *C* for "colored," and that "he did this every time a black person applied for an apartment." The employee didn't want to be identified in the case. He said he feared that the Trumps would have him "knocked off."

Cohn visited the employee and came away with a different story. Cohn drafted a new affidavit for the employee, in which he denied saying he was told to discriminate. Now the employee claimed that a Justice Department lawyer who had replaced Goldweber, Donna Goldstein, told him to "lie" or risk being "thrown into jail." The employee described himself as a "Spanish-speaking Puerto Rican hired directly by Mr. Donald Trump."

Cohn then tried an unlikely gambit. Cohn, who was Jewish, said in an affidavit that Goldstein, also Jewish, was conducting a "Gestapo-like interrogation." A Cohn colleague wrote to the Justice Department that its agents were "descending upon the Trump offices with five storm-troopers." Cohn asked the judge to hold Goldstein in contempt. But Cohn's comparison of Justice Department lawyers and FBI agents to Nazis backfired. "I find no evidence in the record that anything of the nature of Gestapo tactics was permitted by the FBI in doing the tasks assigned to them," Judge Neaher told Cohn. Cohn asked the judge to find Goldstein in contempt for allegedly trying to get witnesses to change their stories. Neaher again dismissed the effort.

Finally, in late spring 1975, Cohn sought a settlement, notwith-standing Trump's claims that he hated to settle or Cohn's claim that he could win by telling the government to "go to hell." Nearly two years of fighting was about to end, and the settlement was much like what the Trumps could initially have gotten. But Trump had one more ploy. He viewed the signing of a consent order as a new chance to negotiate, and he started haggling.

As part of the settlement, the Justice Department wanted the Trumps to place ads in local newspapers assuring prospective renters that Trump housing was open to people of all races. "This advertising, while it's, you know—I imagine it's necessary from the government's standpoint, is a very expensive thing for us," Trump said. "It is really onerous. Each sentence we put in is going to cost us a lot of money over the period we are supposed to do it." When government officials persisted, Trump said, "Will you pay for it?" The government said the Trumps had to pay for the advertising.

On June 10, 1975, the Trumps signed a consent order prohibiting them from "discriminating against any person in the terms, conditions, or privileges of sale or rental of a dwelling." The Trumps were ordered to "thoroughly acquaint themselves personally on a detailed basis" with the Fair Housing Act. The agreement also required the Trumps to buy the ads assuring minorities of their equal access to housing.

Decades later, Trump tried to put the best possible spin on the case, insisting, "That wasn't a case against us. There were many, many landlords that were sued under that case." This case was, in fact, filed against Trump, his father, and their company; other companies had been sued in separate cases. In any case, Trump stressed it was settled "with no admission of anything" and he "ended up making a better settlement by fighting."

The Justice Department claimed victory, calling the decree "one of the most far-reaching ever negotiated." Newspaper headlines echoed the view. "Minorities Win Housing Suit," said the *New York Amsterdam News*, which told readers that "qualified Blacks and Puerto Ricans now have the opportunity to rent apartments owned by Trump Management." As it turned out, the battle was hardly over.

FIFTEEN MONTHS LATER, IN September 1976, Fred visited Maryland, where local authorities had for years complained that he had failed to properly maintain a housing complex he owned in Prince George's County, just outside Washington, DC. Donald had worked there a number of times, often collecting rent, and had told his father, "Pop, this is a rough piece of property here." When Fred arrived, local officials stunned him with an arrest warrant for a series of housing code violations at the 504-unit development called Gregory Estates, arrayed in forty three-story buildings. The violations included broken windows, rotted rain gutters, and the absence of fire-prevention equipment. Bond was set for $1,000. "N.Y. Owner of P.G. Units Seized in Code Violations," the *Washington Post* reported. Fred was livid, but he arranged for the bond and eventually paid a $3,640 fine. Donald was later quoted in the *Post* saying it was "terrible" the company had been hit with housing code violations, but forty years later he said that he "never knew" his father had been arrested.

FRED RETURNED TO New York and more trouble from the feds. The authorities suspected that the Trumps were reneging on their agreement to provide housing to anyone regardless of race. The Justice Department eventually accused the Trumps of failing to comply with the settlement and continuing to make apartments "unavailable to black persons on account of race." For three years after the Trumps signed off on the settlement, Cohn battled on their behalf against the Justice Department.

In time, Cohn would be a constant presence by Donald's side, serving not only as lawyer, but also as informal adviser, publicist, and intermediary with the city's powerful. Donald, meanwhile, tried to put the racial-bias case behind him, and he began to cultivate the image he craved. As Trump ventured into Manhattan real estate, he cooperated with a *New York Times* profile, which began with a paragraph of a publicist's dreams:

"He is tall, lean and blond, with dazzling white teeth, and he looks ever so much like Robert Redford. He rides around town in a chauffeured silver Cadillac with his initials, DJT, on the plates. He dates slinky fashion models, belongs to elegant clubs and, at only 30 years of age, estimates that he is worth more than $200 million."

With those words, the definition of the man who would be known as The Donald was etched. The piece made a passing reference to the discrimination allegations, which Trump denied, and emphasized his genius at real estate (although one anonymous "money man" called him "overrated" and "obnoxious").

How Trump estimated his worth at $200 million was unclear. He was involved in real estate deals that might pay off handsomely, and this may have been the first time he projected the intangible value of his name. The company his father founded might have been worth $200 million, or Donald may have valued his ownership in various properties that highly. But he reported income in 1976 of a relatively modest $24,594, in addition to some payments from family trusts and other assets. All told, he owed $10,832 in taxes, according to a report later issued by the New Jersey Division of Gaming Enforcement. But the nuances of net worth didn't matter, at least at the time. All that Donald J. Trump had worked for—the jet-setting, club-going, model-dating image of a savvy, tough dealmaker—all of that was now set. Trump was finally on his own, and on his way.

5

Crossing the Bridge

New York City was desperate for cash and in danger of insolvency. In the early seventies, the city lost 250,000 jobs, gutting its tax base even as the cost of city services soared. President Gerald Ford's press secretary Ron Nessen compared the city's dependence on federal aid to "a wayward daughter hooked on heroin." It was a miserable time to be a developer. In 1971, the year Donald Trump first moved to Manhattan, hotel occupancy plunged to 62 percent, its lowest point since World War II. By 1975, cutbacks forced the city and state to freeze new construction of subsidized housing, the core of the Trump family business. At his father's Avenue Z office, Donald was itching to break away from building basic housing for middle-class, outer-borough families. When Fred Trump did branch out beyond Brooklyn, it was to buy cheap plots from desperate sellers in California, Nevada, Ohio, and Virginia. Donald wanted something bigger. He had long urged his father to tap the tens of millions of dollars in equity Fred had accumulated in more than eighty apartment buildings, to use that value to invest in Manhattan, where the action was. Donald had taken to walking the urban grid, sizing up buildings, daydreaming about what he could do with each lot.

Fred Trump was wary of Manhattan's expense and the difficulty of building there, but Donald couldn't turn away from the place that had captivated him since childhood. As New York City crumbled, he saw the opportunity that would change his life. Penn Central, the once-iconic railroad giant, was going under. By 1970, in what was then the largest bankruptcy case in US history, the railroad had chewed through a $300 million emergency bailout from fifty-three banks. Now, its creditors were eager to chop up Penn Central and sell its most lucrative parts, including some of Manhattan's last big open tracts—vast train yards in midtown and on the Upper West Side. The railroad's bankruptcy trustee fielded interest from Arab sheikhs, bank financiers, and hotel land scouts. But some pieces were more attractive than others. Penn Central owned four once-renowned midtown hotels that had long ago slid into decay. Multiple offers were made for some of the properties, but the decrepit, rat-infested Commodore on East Forty-Second Street, directly next to Grand Central Terminal, didn't receive a single bid.

Three of Penn Central's holdings had captivated Trump's imagination: a strip of the Hudson riverfront, from Fifty-Ninth to Seventy-Second Streets; an unused rail yard at Thirty-Fourth Street; and the Commodore, the crummiest hotel, which Trump believed was an overlooked jewel. In the summer of 1974, Trump began making overtures for the properties, telling the *New York Times* that he planned to buy them for more than $100 million. Although the *Times* called him a "major New York builder," he didn't yet have the financing to buy such properties. Still, he started wooing the man in charge of selling Penn Central's assets. Trump even sent him a television set as a Christmas present, delivered by chauffeur. The official turned the gift down. Trump had more luck wielding his father's reputation. Donald coordinated a meeting with the railroad man and New York mayor Abe Beame, a longtime friend of his father's. Beame wrapped his arms around the two Trumps and declared, "Whatever Donald and Fred want, they have my complete backing."

Trump was a construction neophyte, but he was already adept at turning around his opposition. David Berger, a lawyer who represented the railroad's shareholders, initially opposed selling Trump the Commodore, but at a crucial moment in the negotiations, Berger flipped to support a deal with Trump. A few years later, federal prosecutors investigated whether Berger's sudden change of heart was connected to Trump's decision to help Berger out and join his unrelated, $100 million suit by New York landlords against nine major oil companies for fixing

the price of heating oil. The federal probe ended without any indictments. Both Trump and Berger denied there was any quid pro quo.

In March 1975, a bankruptcy judge questioned whether Penn Central's trustees had given other developers who wanted the railroad's
land the same opportunity they gave Trump. But the court nevertheless
approved a deal giving Trump an option to develop the Thirty-Fourth
Street property, where he discussed building a city-funded convention center and twenty thousand apartments, in one swoop creating an
empire that would rival his father's. The apartment element of the plan
soon collapsed, but Trump moved ahead on the convention center by
using a prized political connection. In 1974, he hired Louise Sunshine,
then chief fund-raiser for Hugh Carey's gubernatorial campaign, to help
him persuade city leaders to build their convention center on the rail
yards where Trump now held the option. Donald and his father were big
supporters of Carey, having donated $135,000 ($390,000 in 2016 dollars)
to his campaign, more than anyone else except the candidate's brother.

Donald first got to know Sunshine when, after Carey was elected
governor, Trump thought she could get him a license plate customized
with his initials—then a rare privilege. He was right. Every morning,
Donald would ride from Manhattan to Brooklyn, now in a chauffeur-
driven Cadillac limo with DJT plates—his version of his father's blue
Cadillac, with its FCT plates. Sunshine became one of the young
builder's most effective advocates. "Everybody thought Donald was
this brash, hard-charging young kid," Sunshine said. "I was the one
who took Donald everyplace . . . no matter who it was, because they
didn't really know Donald. I was Donald's credibility factor."

Trump was not shy about using Sunshine's political connections.
He had a notion to buy the World Trade Center, which was owned
by the Port Authority of New York. He asked to meet with its executive director, Peter Goldmark, and over lunch in the Port Authority's executive café on the Trade Center's forty-third floor, Goldmark
pressed Trump for specifics on what a deal would look like. Trump
stuck to generalities. As a new player in town, Trump was an unlikely
candidate to take over the iconic towers, and several other developers
had already expressed interest in the buildings. But Trump's chances
truly soured when he started flexing his connections. "He threatened,
'You wouldn't last in your job very long if Governor Carey decided

you weren't doing the right thing on this,'" Goldmark recalled. "'You should know I have a lot of weight in Albany.'" Trump dropped Sunshine's name. "As soon as he threatened, I made clear I didn't want to talk anymore," Goldmark said. "He'd expected me to quake and shake." Trump denied Goldmark's account, saying, "I really don't talk that way."

In 1978, the city decided to build its convention center at the Thirty-Fourth Street site, whereupon Trump argued that his option on the property entitled him to a commission of more than $4 million. But he offered to waive the fee if the city named the facility the Fred C. Trump Convention Center. The city was considering the idea when, a month later, an official revisited Trump's contract with Penn Central and saw that his option actually entitled him to barely a tenth of the commission he was claiming. The city ultimately paid Trump an $833,000 fee when it bought the land for the Jacob K. Javits Convention Center. Trump did not deny that account but said, "If someone came to me properly, I would have given up my commission without asking that they put my father's name on the building. But they didn't."

WINNING THE RIGHT TO rebuild the Commodore Hotel gave Trump a corner of Grand Central, a blighted neighborhood even he believed was a disaster. Crime was rampant in midtown, and fewer and fewer straphangers coursed through the subway lines under Grand Central. The Chrysler Building, the neighborhood's art deco landmark across the street from the Commodore, fell into foreclosure. Texaco, its core tenant, followed some of America's top companies in fleeing to the suburbs. The nineteen-hundred-room hotel, one of New York's largest, was an eyesore, its business gutted by the postwar shift from luxury trains to airports and interstates. When it opened in 1919, the hotel—named after "Commodore" Cornelius Vanderbilt, the robber baron who became one of America's first tycoon celebrities—boasted a palatial lobby, then the largest room in New York City, adorned in the style of an Italian courtyard and featuring an indoor waterfall. In the lounge, workers posted updated stock prices on the walls; another room boasted its own orchestra.

Modernizing the Commodore was going to be a massive undertaking. The hotel had no garage. Its basements, hemmed in by two subway lines, couldn't be expanded. The rooms were too cramped to convert to apartments, and they lacked modern gas and electric lines. The rooms remained empty half the time, and the few dingy storefronts included a questionable massage parlor called Relaxation Plus. ("Nobody ever got into what the *Plus* meant," Trump joked.) A real estate expert estimated that the building was worth "the true land value minus the cost of demolition"—in other words, nothing. Losing $1.5 million a year, the hotel was scheduled to be shut down in the summer of 1976, right around when the city would host the Democratic National Convention at Madison Square Garden.

Fred Trump was dubious about his son's plan. The father had never understood the draw of Manhattan, which commanded some of the world's highest land prices and biggest development headaches. "Buying the Commodore at a time when even the Chrysler Building is in receivership," he said, "is like fighting for a seat on the *Titanic*." But Donald was determined. "I'm basically an optimist," he said, "and frankly, I saw the city's trouble as a great opportunity for me. Because I grew up in Queens, I believed, perhaps to an irrational degree, that Manhattan was always going to be the best place to live—the center of the world." Despite his doubts, Fred came through, pledging his own equity toward his son's success—an early sign that although the father himself had no interest in taking on Manhattan, he would stand by his son, helping him at key moments in the formative years of Donald's career. Fred would also personally back construction loans from Manufacturers Hanover Trust, guaranteeing that the bankers would be paid even if Donald's venture collapsed.

For Donald's plan to succeed, Penn Central had to sell him the hotel, New York City's bureaucracy had to approve his approach and give him a tax break, a management company needed to join him to run the hotel, and the banks had to front him the money to pay for the whole thing. Donald wooed Hyatt, the hotel chain owned by the deep-pocketed Pritzker family, to manage the remade Commodore. Since opening its first hotel near the airport in Los Angeles, the company had exploded in popularity, but lagged behind its rivals in one key way: it had no hotel in New York. Trump launched a charm offensive. Before lunch with Ben Lambert, a real estate investor friendly with the Pritzkers, Trump gave the potential partner a ride in his limousine (which was actually leased by his father's company). In the backseat, he had propped up sketches of his renovation plans. Trump suggested that the hotel would benefit from dramatically reduced real estate taxes—an alluring notion, but a deal he had not yet secured.

Trump played the city, the sellers, and the hotel chain off one another, using one to leverage a deal with the other. He assured Penn Central's negotiators that he had a solid deal with Hyatt when he had no such thing, and the railroad gave him a nonbinding, exclusive opportunity to buy the $10 million property. Trump didn't have the $250,000 he needed to secure that option, let alone financing to cover the estimated $70 million project; his father had even fronted him the money to hire an architect. But in May 1975, Trump called a press conference anyway. Joined by Hyatt cofounder Jay Pritzker, Trump presented elaborate renderings of the Commodore's revival: fourteen hundred rooms, seventy thousand square feet of retail space, a daz-zling Hyatt-style atrium, and walls of mirrored glass surrounding the aging hotel's steel bones. Trump announced that he had a signed con-tract with Penn Central to buy the hotel. It was signed, but only by him; he had yet to pay the $250,000. Then came a feat of misdirection he would later boast about. When a city official asked for proof of Penn Central's commitment, Trump sent what looked like an agreement with the sellers. Trump then used the city's resulting approval to push his deal with Hyatt to closure.

Now Trump needed money. With no collateral to back his debt, he struggled to persuade banks to front him a construction loan. After one rejection, Trump wanted to quit, telling his real estate broker, "Let's just take this deal and shove it." But Trump, who grew up watch-ing his father build an empire based on subsidized development, was saved by New York's first-ever tax break for a commercial property. The Urban Development Corporation—a nearly bankrupt agency launched in 1968 to build integrated housing—had the power to make properties tax-exempt. It could buy the hotel for $1, then lease it back to Trump and Hyatt for ninety-nine years—an arrangement that would save Trump's project an estimated $400 million over the next forty years. Sunshine helped Trump land a meeting with the UDC's chairman, Richard Ravitch, who had grown up in the construction business. Ravitch's father, Saul, was the founder of HRH Construction, which Fred Trump had hired to build Trump Village. Now Ravitch saw that the younger Trump had a different way of doing business. Donald came to see Ravitch and told him he had bought the Commodore to convert it into a Grand Hyatt. "I want you to give me a tax exemption," Trump said.

A Hyatt would be great for the city, Ravitch replied, but the project didn't qualify for a tax break because it would likely be successful on its own. Trump stood up and repeated his request: "I want an exemption." When Ravitch again declined to support the idea, Trump said, "I'm going to have you fired," and walked out of the office, Ravitch said. (Trump denied Ravitch's account and called him a "highly overrated person.") Rival hoteliers agreed with Ravitch and opposed what they saw as a sweetheart deal for Trump. The Hotel Association of New York City said its members paid more than $50 million a year in real estate taxes and asked why a brash young developer who had never built a hotel and would invest none of his own money deserved a helping hand.

On the day before New York's influential land-use authority, the Board of Estimate, was to vote on the tax exemption, three Manhattan lawmakers called a press conference outside the hotel to demand the city push for a better deal. When the politicians had finished, Trump, who had shown up to refute their argument, told reporters that if the city did not approve the assistance, he would walk and the Commodore would rot. To dramatize how decrepit the Commodore would be without him, Trump had directed his workers to replace the clean boards covering up hotel windows with dirty scrap wood.

In fact, other investors were interested in the hotel and had offered to renovate it, pay more in taxes, and share more of the profits with the city than Trump would. But the alternative offer was ignored because of Trump's contract with Penn Central—even though that deal was not yet signed and sealed.

Ultimately, Trump's purchase option, energy, political connections, and profit-sharing promises turned the desperate city to his side. A few weeks after the last tourists were booted out of the Commodore, the Board of Estimate agreed to waive all real estate taxes as long as Trump's project was run as a "first-class" hotel. Trump took a victory lap in the

Times, boasting about his "financial creativeness" in cobbling together tax credits, and making clear the distinction between his father's success and his own Manhattan ambitions: "My father knew Brooklyn very well, and he knew Queens very well. But now, that psychology is ended." Trump had asserted to the *Times* that he was worth "more than $200 million," even though a year earlier, Penn Central negotiators had estimated the Trump family holdings at about $25 million, all of it under Fred's control. In December 1976, a month after that article appeared, Fred Trump opened eight trusts for his children and grandchildren and transferred in $1 million each. Over the next five years, Donald would reap about $440,000 in income from that trust alone.

Despite winning the Commodore battle, Trump maintained a grudge against those who had opposed him. Five years after Ravitch and Trump's contentious meeting, the counsel of the Metropolitan Transportation Authority, where Ravitch had become chairman, told him Trump's bulldog attorney, Roy Cohn, was calling. Cohn informed Ravitch that Trump wanted the MTA to spend taxpayer funds to connect the Commodore to the Forty-Second Street subway station. Ravitch was opposed. The next morning, Mayor Ed Koch called and asked him, "What did you do to Donald Trump? He wants me to fire you." Ravitch pointed out what the mayor already knew: Ravitch had been appointed by the governor. He stayed on the job.

IN 1977, AS TRUMP scrambled for loans, New York City plunged further into decay. Its financial crisis grew more severe. A serial killer known as Son of Sam terrorized the city. During a July heat wave, a historic blackout shrouded the city in darkness, touching off devastating fires, storefront lootings, and arrests. But the real threat to Trump was far more subtle. Mayor Beame, a longtime friend of Fred Trump's and powerful supporter of Donald's project, lost his reelection campaign to Koch, a vocal opponent of political cronyism and largesse. Trump's tax abatement was suddenly at risk. But he was saved again when he found a key ally in Stanley Friedman, Beame's outgoing deputy mayor. With his goatee and a Te-Amo Toro cigar forever stuck between his teeth, Friedman was a Hollywood caricature of a big-city dealmaker.

His DNA was pure New York. He grew up in the Bronx, son of a cab-driver named Moe, before attending public school, City College, and Brooklyn Law School. In Trump, Friedman saw another guy from the outer boroughs trying to establish himself in Manhattan, where they'd run into each other at social hot spots such as Le Club and Maxwell's Plum.

In the closing weeks of Beame's term in 1977, Friedman worked feverishly during marathon meetings to seal the deal on the Com-modore. By the time Beame left office, Trump's taxpayer-supported hold on the hotel had been made virtually bulletproof—and Fried-man had found new work, at Roy Cohn's law firm. "Grand Central was turning into Times Square—a dead neighborhood," Friedman said. "Regardless of whose money he was going to use—the city's, his own, the Hyatt's—he was going to take a shit building and put up a first-class operation. It was the first major thing done in the city in years."

TRUMP DIDN'T CROSS THE bridge solely to build a business. He wanted the Manhattan life, too. He now lived in a three-bedroom spread at the Phoenix apartments on East Sixty-Fifth Street, a mile uptown from the Commodore. When Mike Scadron, his friend from New York Military Academy, visited, he was struck by the apartment's sparse furnishings—mirrored wall, shag rug, glass coffee table, a ren-dering of the Commodore. Trump's attention was on making it in the big city. He told Scadron he was going to surpass his father's success by conquering Manhattan, where Fred Trump had never laid a brick. Another time, at the Avenue Z office, Scadron watched father and son go at it, "talking past each other. They could have been in separate rooms. Donald had something to prove." But back at Donald's apart-ment, one other item was on prominent display: a photo of Trump's new girlfriend.

The story of how Trump and Ivana Zelníčková Winklmayr met has two versions. Trump recalled that the two first saw each other at the summer Olympic Games in Montreal in 1976. Ivana, according to the official story, had been a member of the 1972 Czech Olympic ski team in Sapporo, Japan. Both Trumps said so at one point. Later,

Trump wrote that Ivana was an alternate on that Olympic team. But when *Spy* magazine interviewed the Czech Olympic committee secretary, he said there was no such person in their records.

The more popular story about how the couple met has Trump introducing himself to Ivana in the queue outside Maxwell's Plum, Warner LeRoy's over-the-top East Side singles bar stuffed with Tiffany lamps and topped with a stained-glass ceiling. In New York for a fashion show promoting the upcoming Olympics, Ivana was standing with her friends waiting to get into the bar when Trump tapped her on the shoulder, told her he knew the owner, and said he could get them inside. They got in. Trump paid for the night's festivities, whisked the ladies to their hotel, and further charmed Ivana the next day with three dozen roses.

Ivana, raised in Czechoslovakia under Communist rule, was an only child, a model who emigrated to Canada before coming to the States. Once she and Trump started dating, her life story became as infused with Trump superlatives and hype as any of his properties. Ivana was "one of the top models in Canada," Trump wrote. She had modeled at Montreal department stores and posed for furriers. She had also been married, briefly, to Alfred Winklmayr, an Austrian skier. But this marriage disappeared from the official narrative, going unmentioned in her 1995 memoir, *The Best Is Yet to Come: Coping with Divorce and Enjoying Life Again*. Winklmayr had helped Ivana move to the West, and the marriage broke up promptly thereafter.

At age thirty, Trump was ready to settle down. His parents' marriage was his model. "For a man to be successful, he needs support at home, just like my father had from my mother, not someone who's always griping and bitching," Trump said. Ivana, an immigrant like his mother, appeared to fit the mold. "I found the combination of beauty and brains almost unbelievable," he said. "Like a lot of men, I had been taught by Hollywood that one woman couldn't have both." Ivana saw Trump as "just a nice all-American kid, tall and smart, lots of energy: very bright and very good-looking." She defined Trump by what he had yet to achieve. He "wasn't famous" and he "wasn't fabulously wealthy."

On New Year's Eve of 1976, Trump proposed to Ivana, later presenting her with a three-carat Tiffany diamond ring. But before there could be a wedding, less than a year after they met, there was the prenup—

ultimately, as many as four or five contracts. The negotiations between Trump and Ivana—Roy Cohn urged Donald to begin married life with codified financial arrangements—followed a pattern that came to define Trumpism: boasts of wealth and influence, a highly public airing of grievances, and dramatic battles staged in gossip columns and court-rooms. The marriage would start—and later explode—to the accompa-niment of lawyers. Cohn negotiated the prenup, which was signed two weeks before the wedding. Ivana was represented by a lawyer Cohn had recommended. At a negotiating session at Cohn's house, Cohn wore only a bathrobe. Ivana was ready to sign off on a deal, but balked when she learned that Cohn's proposal called on her to return any gifts from Donald in the event of a divorce. In response to her fury, Cohn added language allowing her to keep her clothing and any gifts. With Trump's consent, Cohn also added a "rainy day" fund worth $100,000; Ivana could begin tapping that fund one month after the wedding.

Even as Cohn helped Donald and Ivana arrange their marriage, he was leading them through the hedonistic, drug-fueled disco scene of the late seventies. Although he cherished his reputation as a tee-totaler, Donald loved to be in the late-night mix of boldface names and beautiful women. In April 1977, Trump and Ivana went to the opening night of Studio 54, the midtown club that would become the iconic home court of the disco movement. The owners, Steve Rubell and Ian Schrager, relied on Cohn for legal advice, and he in turn served as an informal gatekeeper, ushering the rich and the famous past the queue of desperate night people trying to get in to party with the likes of Andy Warhol, Liza Minnelli, Truman Capote, Margaux Hemingway, and David Bowie. Cohn also used his pull to win admission for groups of young gay men; although Cohn always maintained that he was straight, his friends knew better. (Despite his sexuality, Cohn remained strongly antigay on policy matters; asked to represent a teacher fired for being homosexual, Cohn refused, telling a group of gay activists that "homosexual teachers are a grave threat to our children; they have no business polluting the schools of America.")

Trump became a regular at the club and later recounted seeing "things happening there that to this day I have never seen again. I would watch supermodels getting screwed, well-known supermodels getting screwed on a bench in the middle of the room. There were seven of them and each one was getting screwed by a different guy. This was in the middle of the room. Stuff that couldn't happen today because of problems of death."

On the Saturday before Easter, Donald and Ivana were married by the Reverend Norman Vincent Peale—author of the 1952 motivational bestseller *The Power of Positive Thinking*, a pillar of America's self-help culture, and pastor at New York's Marble Collegiate Church, which Donald's parents occasionally attended. Peale was the only person other than his father whom Donald called a mentor (he resisted using that term for Cohn, insisting that the lawyer was "just a lawyer, a very good lawyer"). Peale "would give the best sermons of anyone; he was an amazing public speaker," Trump said. "He thought I was his greatest student of all time." Trump's parents first took him to hear Peale's sermons as early as the 1950s, when the minister was at the apex of his fame, with a newspaper column and radio show that reached millions. "I know that with God's help, I can sell vacuum cleaners," Peale once said, a perspective that appealed to entrepreneurs, including Fred Trump and his son. As Donald Trump found success, Peale predicted Donald would become "the greatest builder of our time." Trump, in turn, credited Peale with teaching him to win by thinking only of the best outcomes: "The mind can overcome any obstacle. I never think of the negative."

Donald and Ivana's wedding reception was held at the 21 Club, a former speakeasy famed for its celebrity clientele. About two hundred people attended, including Mayor Beame, Cohn, and a bevy of politicians and Trump lawyers. Only one member of Ivana's family, her father, Miloš, was on hand.

On December 31, 1977, a year after their engagement, Ivana gave birth to Donald John Trump Jr., the first of their three children. Ivanka arrived in 1981 and Eric in 1984. The new family moved into an eight-room apartment at 800 Fifth Avenue, decorated with modern sectionals and little of the excess that would eventually become a hallmark of the Trump style. They soon offered reporters a tantalizing photo op featuring the stunning skier-model and the boyish real estate dynamo. "He'd walk into a crowded room and everyone would look at him," said

Stanley Friedman. "The whole world revolved around Donald. He was always the guy who would talk to you but was looking over his shoulder for the next person. Always working . . . He was always looking for the next deal, he was always looking for the next something."

That next something usually involved more work than being a father. As his own father had done, Donald saw his children mainly at the office, where they were always welcome. "I was always there for my children when they needed me," he said. "Now, that doesn't necessarily mean pushing the baby carriage down Fifth Avenue for two hours." Trump "didn't know what to do with the kids when they were little," Ivana said. "He would love them, he would kiss them and hold them, but then he would give it to me because he had no idea what to do." The children would come to look back on their early years with a strong confidence in their father's love and a certain wistfulness about his priorities. "It wasn't a 'Hey, Son, let's go play catch in the backyard' kind of father-son relationship," Donald Jr. recalled. "It was 'Hey, you're back from school, come down to the office.' So I would sit in his office, play with trucks on the floor in his office, go trick-or-treating in his office. So there was a lot of time spent with him, and it was on his terms. . . . He never hid from us, he never shied away, but it was on his terms. You know, that tends to be the way he does things."

TRUMP QUICKLY ADDED IVANA to his executive staff, putting her to work as a vice president overseeing interior design at the Commodore, and later at Trump Tower, the Plaza Hotel, and one of Donald's Atlantic City casinos. "It was unheard of for a businessman in those circles to give his wife, his *new* wife, someone who wasn't somebody who had been around for a while, such great responsibilities," said Nikki Haskell, a friend of both Trumps. "Many rich men don't allow their wives to come to their office. Many women don't know what their husbands do."

"Donald and Ivana were cut from the same cloth," said Louise Sunshine. "They were just exactly the same kind of people—very, very determined, laser-focused, very sharp . . . very synergistic and very much alike, too much alike. It was hard to tell them apart. They could have come from the same sperm."

At the Commodore site, Ivana often clashed with foremen. But when the work hit snags, Donald tended to fault his project manager and assistants—not his wife. The Commodore was a difficult gut job; a massive, twenty-six-story rehab more complicated than anything his father had attempted. As demolition crews got to work in May 1978, they found conditions fouler than they had expected. Homeless men had moved into a warm, lice-ridden boiler room. The steel frame Trump had wanted to build upon was rusty and compromised. In the basements, workers released cats to chase out a horde of jumbo-size rats; the cats died, and the rats survived. Costs soon ballooned. Twenty-six stories of exterior stonework were to be curtained in mirrored glass. Whole floors were to be gutted. Suppliers and contractors were anxious to get paid. When Barbara Res, an assistant project manager at HRH Construction, which Trump hired to run the job, arrived on-site, her boss handed her the contract and instructed her to make sure every second of work was tracked and paid for: "Read this and learn it. . . . These people will kill you. Keep records of everything."

Leading his first project, Trump was "very brash and extremely self-confident," Res said, even as many of his decisions struck experienced construction workers as amateurish. Architects and contractors were afraid to challenge him, creating what Res called a "deadly combination: . . . an aggressive and powerful person in charge who is also inexperienced." With his lenders watching, Trump scoured the work for savings. He believed he could recoup some dollars by salvaging the old Commodore's pipes and steel. The impulse was copied directly from his father, a legendary penny-pincher who once boasted that he had saved $13,000 in one day by convincing a contractor to shave the price of painting thirteen thousand apartments by a dollar each. Donald's attempt at thrift backfired. Union workers spent many hours spray-painting color codes on every metal object—red for trash, green for keep—slowing construction to a crawl.

For his architect, Trump had recruited Der Scutt, a pipe-smoking rising star of New York modernist design. After their first meeting, on a Friday night at Maxwell's Plum, Trump invited Scutt back to his apartment. Like Trump, Scutt had his own blend of ego-driven eccentricities—he had changed his first name from Donald to the German word for "the." He was ruffled by Trump's "extremely aggressive" sales technique and tendency toward exaggeration. Still, he was energized by Trump's unceasing demands. "He thinks nothing of calling me at seven a.m. on a Sunday and saying, 'I've got an idea. See you in the office in forty minutes,'" Scutt said. "And I always go."

The modernized Grand Hyatt opened on September 25, 1980, six years after Trump had first targeted the Commodore. Designed initially to serve middle-class travelers, the fourteen-hundred-room hotel had taken on considerable luxury, with brass fixtures and room rates that started at $115 a night (about $330 in 2016 dollars). To toast its opening, the Grand Hyatt hosted a star-studded party in the ballroom, attended by the governor, mayor, former mayor, Cohn, and others from New York's real estate elite. The Grand Hyatt would prove the exemplar of Trump's development style: generous tax breaks, leveraging rival interests against each other, and a hefty dose of financial chutzpah and sleight of hand. Trump claimed that the hotel helped jump-start the Grand Central neighborhood and usher in a new age of glamour for Manhattan. Trump said the project changed his life: "If I hadn't finally convinced the city to choose my West Thirty-Fourth Street site for its convention center and then gone on to develop the Grand Hyatt, I'd probably be back in Brooklyn today, collecting rents."

The doom Trump had predicted for the neighborhood never came to pass. By the time crews first started working on the Commodore, a dozen other office, apartment, and hotel projects were already rising in surrounding blocks—without the government assistance Trump said was essential to get anything going in the dreary area. Now, as hotel visitors rolled in, he tightened his grip on one of the few concessions he'd made to land his tax break. In 1987, Trump told his accountants to change their reporting methods, limiting the amount that the Grand Hyatt's profit-sharing deal would deliver to the city government. When the city's auditor general, Karen Burstein, reviewed hotel records, she found that "aberrant" accounting practices had shortchanged the city by millions of dollars in taxes. Asked years later about the changes, Trump said he did not remember the investigation.

In the years that followed, Trump would spar often with Hyatt's ruling family, including a messy lawsuit-countersuit that ended with the Pritzkers agreeing in 1995 to pay $25 million for renovations. Battling against heavy debts as his empire expanded, Trump ended up selling his half of the Hyatt to the family in 1996, ending his involvement in the project that launched his career. Trump kept about $25 million of the $142 million sale price, but most of the money would go toward paying off part of the billions his businesses then owed, including hundreds of millions that Trump had personally guaranteed.

IN THOSE DAYS, TRUMP and Sunshine would tool around Manhattan in the back of Trump's limousine, looking for potential projects. One day, they passed the Fifth Avenue flagship of Bonwit Teller, an upscale women's department store that had fallen on hard times. "Oh, I love that site, let's find out who owns it, let's tear the building down," Trump said. This, Trump decided, would be the spot for his signature project, Trump Tower, a glittering statement on New York's most majestic boulevard. Sunshine led Donald to a major stockholder of Genesco, the conglomerate that owned Bonwit Teller's lease. In November 1978, when Trump learned the company was open to selling, he secured, for no money, an option allowing him to buy out the lease for $25 million—a free shot at one of the most pivotal blocks in midtown Manhattan. When rival developers learned of the deal and offered better prices, Trump fought back, threatening a trip to court if the trustee didn't honor his word.

Trump now controlled the lease to the building at what he called "the best location anywhere in the world"—but he needed two other pieces: the land below, owned by insurance giant Equitable, and the air rights above, which were controlled by Tiffany & Co., the iconic jeweler, whose landmark building was next door, where Audrey Hepburn window-shopped in *Breakfast at Tiffany's*, and where Trump had bought Ivana her diamond engagement ring. With the Grand Hyatt built and open, Trump didn't have to fight for loans anymore. Chase Manhattan fronted him funds covering the rights above and below Bonwit Teller, plus more than $100 million for construction. Trump persuaded Equitable, one of his lenders for the Grand Hyatt, to sell him the land in exchange for a 50 percent stake in the project.

Der Scutt again signed on as architect and sketched a striking saw-tooth-edged building, resembling a staircase on its side. Trump Tower's upper condos would have two city views, a rationale for Trump to charge higher prices. *Times* architecture critic Ada Louise Huxtable praised the black-glass tower as a "dramatically handsome structure" with "28 shimmering sides." City zoning laws would have blocked a tower of such height on such a small site, but Trump cleverly used Tiffany's air rights and more lenient rules for mixed-use office-retail-residential projects to expand skyward. The tower also took advantage of a zoning provision that allowed greater height if the builder provided public spaces such as atriums. City planners had grown leery of new skyscrapers, especially in a time of growing public backlash against more shadowy canyons in Manhattan. But Scutt's plan and Trump's dealmaking won out. City officials did trim his design from sixty-three to fifty-eight stories, but Trump got the last word, simply renumbering the fifty-eight-story tower's floors so they extended up to sixty-eight.

FIRST, BONWIT TELLER'S ELEGANT storefront had to go. But some New Yorkers loved the art deco building, especially a soaring bronze grillwork above the entrance and a pair of fifteen-foot-tall bas-relief sculptures, or friezes, of nearly naked goddesses dancing over Fifth Avenue. ("A poor advertisement, one might think, for a shop devoted to women's apparel," a *New Yorker* architecture columnist wrote in 1930.)

Robert Miller, owner of an art gallery across the street, and Penelope Hunter-Stiebel, a curator at the Metropolitan Museum of Art, believed they could persuade Trump to preserve the pieces by donating them to the museum in exchange for a generous appraisal—estimated at more than $200,000—that he could use as a tax write-off. Hunter-Stiebel had experience appealing to landowners' sense of history: the Met had acquired from Rockefeller Center a 1930s-era elevator cab that represented the art moderne style. Perhaps Trump would cooperate, too. He seemed enthusiastic. "This is going to be a great deal!" Trump said when they met at his office.

But on June 5, 1980, Miller called Hunter-Stiebel from his gallery and told her he could see construction workers on scaffolding out-side Bonwit Teller. They were blasting the sculptures to smithereens. Hunter-Stiebel, nine months pregnant, raced out of the Met, jumped into a taxi, and, when her driver got stuck in traffic, ran the last ten blocks to Bonwit Teller. Meanwhile, at the site, Miller offered the con-struction foreman cash to spare the sculptures. The foreman refused, telling him, "Young Donald said there's a stupid woman uptown at a museum who wants them and we have to destroy them." Hunter-Stiebel arrived and gasped "in incredulous horror," she recalled. "They were jackhammering through the neck of one of the figures. It was unbelievable."

"Developer Scraps Bonwit Sculptures," read the front-page head-line on the next morning's *Times*. The article quoted "John Baron," a "vice-president of the Trump organization," explaining that the com-pany had decided on demolition after three independent appraisers concluded that the sculptures were "without artistic merit," were worth less than $9,000, and would have cost $32,000 to move. John Barron— usually spelled with two *r*'s—was a pseudonym that Trump often used when he did not want to identify himself to a reporter. Two days later, Trump, using his real name, addressed the incident, saying that remov-ing the sculptures could have cost more than $500,000. "My biggest concern was the safety of people on the street below," he insisted. "If one of those stones had slipped, people could have been killed."

The incident became Trump's first public-relations fiasco. "Mr. Trump may assume that esthetic vandalism soon vanishes from civic memory," the *Times* wrote in an editorial. "But what he has destroyed with the sculptures is the public image he was build-ing with his new Fifth Avenue skyscraper." Kent Barwick, chairman of New York's Landmarks Preservation Commission, said the demoli-tion established Trump "as a bad guy. Afterwards, rightly or wrongly, there was a question of trust." Trump later expressed "regret" for the demolition and argued that he had to move quickly on the demolition to avoid long delays caused by historic preservationists. In *Trump: The Art of the Deal*, though, he said he was delighted by the negative cover-age because it generated free publicity and helped him sell apartments. In the eighties, Trump said that the sculptures "were nothing" and "junk." A decade later, visitors to Trump's fifty-three-room penthouse would remark on a particularly notable piece of relief artwork in his two-story dining room: a carved ivory frieze.

BONWIT TELLER WAS SO tightly wedged into Fifth Avenue's streetscape that crews could not use traditional demolition tools such as wrecking balls or dynamite. Instead, the historic building had to be dismantled piece by piece. To handle the grueling job, Trump turned to Kaszycki & Sons Contractors, which had submitted a rock-bottom bid.

The work was done by hundreds of undocumented Polish immigrants known as the "Polish brigade." The men toiled through spring and summer of 1980 with sledgehammers and blowtorches, but without hard hats, working twelve- to eighteen-hour days, seven days a week, often sleeping on Bonwit Teller's floors. They were paid less than $5 an hour, sometimes in vodka. Many went unpaid and were threatened with deportation if they complained. In 1983, the year Trump Tower opened, members of the Housewreckers Local 95 union filed suit claiming that Trump had illegally permitted undocumented immigrants to work on the tower. John Szabo, an immigration lawyer representing the workers, said a Mr. Barron—that name again—had called him from the Trump organization and threatened a lawsuit if the workers didn't drop their demand for back payments. In 1990, after years of delays, Trump testified that he did not know the workers were undocumented. He blamed Kaszycki & Sons.

The judge ruled against Trump and the contractor, saying that one of Trump's top aides at the site, Thomas Macari, "was involved in every aspect of the demolition job." Trump appealed and won a partial reversal, but the court ruled that Trump "should have known" about the Polish workers. The case was settled and sealed in 1999. Years later, Trump would call illegal immigration "a wrecking ball aimed at U.S. taxpayers."

WITH BONWIT TELLER DEMOLISHED, the complicated construction of Trump Tower began in earnest. A few days after the Grand Hyatt's opening party, Donald and Ivana had invited Res up to their gleaming Fifth Avenue apartment. The living room offered breathtaking vistas of Central Park, and the furniture, curtains, and carpets were harmonized in the same stylish white. When Ivana offered Res an orange juice, she declined, worried she'd leave a stain. At the Grand Hyatt, Res—five feet four with shoulder-length brown hair, often seen in a hard hat, flannel shirt, corduroy pants, and work boots—had held her own as one of the few women at the construction site, where workers openly urinated on columns and covered walls in crude nude sketches of her and Ivana. But although Res knew she'd won the Trumps' respect, she didn't expect Donald's next request.

"I want you to build Trump Tower for me," he said. The high-rise would feature the glitziest shops, top-of-the-line offices, and the most luxurious condos. Trump didn't have the time to be as involved as he had been at the Grand Hyatt. He needed someone to be his eyes and ears, a "Donna Trump," as he called her, in charge of construction for "the most important project in the world." Res would become the tower's chief engineer, in charge of all construction, when she was only thirty-one. She was one of a very few women in an executive role in real estate development at the time, and Donald appointed her over the objection of his father, who told his son that that kind of work wasn't for women.

The tower's first five floors were to be filled with a high-end shopping arcade. Stacked on top would be eleven floors of offices, thirty-eight floors of luxury condos, and several mechanical floors to keep the whole thing running. Trump wanted his tower, unlike most steel-boned skyscrapers, to be built largely with reinforced concrete, allowing for more flexible floor plans. Construction, Res said, was designed as a "fast-track" job, with crews starting work before the full drawings were complete. Crews worked six days a week, pouring a new concrete floor every two days. One concrete foreman, Eddie Bispo, said the construction schedule was so demanding that he would get to work at 6:00 a.m. and sometimes not leave until 11:30 p.m.

The decision to hurry the job forced Trump to intersect with New York's powerful "concrete club," a cartel of Mafia-controlled unions and contractors who colluded to drive up prices, block out rivals, and punish resistant developers with costly strikes. Many other New York developers at the time felt compelled to enter the same thorny arrangement. The concrete for Trump Tower came from S&A Concrete, then owned by the heads of two New York crime families: "Fat" Tony Salerno, of the Genovese family, and Paul "Big Paul" Castellano, of the Gambinos (Castellano was assassinated in 1985 outside Sparks Steak House on Manhattan's East Side in a Mafia hit organized by the mobster John Gotti). Roy Cohn had represented Salerno and other mob figures and been friendly with another boss, John Cody, who ran the Teamsters union that controlled cement truckers. Documents cited by the House Subcommittee on Criminal Justice in 1989 called Cody "the most significant labor racketeer preying on the construction industry in New York."

In 1982, when union strikes froze developments across the city, construction at Trump Tower didn't miss a beat. When the tower opened the next year, three large duplexes on the sixty-fourth and sixty-fifth floors, just below Trump's penthouse, were sold to Cody's girlfriend, Verina Hixon, whose apartments benefited from costly upgrades, including the tower's only indoor swimming pool. Trump Tower's structural engineers did the work, including designing a special frame to accommodate the pool. For six months after she moved in, Hixon had thirty to fifty workmen in her units every day, installing cedar and lacquer closets, large mirrors, and a sauna at a total cost of $150,000. When Trump resisted one of Hixon's requests, she called Cody, and construction deliveries to the building stopped until work at her apartment resumed.

Hixon stood out among Trump Tower's ultrawealthy condo clientele. In a 1986 deposition, conducted after she failed to make payments on a $3 million loan, Hixon said she had never been employed, owned one checking account with $2 in it, and had no savings accounts, stocks, or property besides her lushly appointed Trump Tower condo. She said her ex-husband, a wealthy Texas businessman, sent her $2,000 a month in child support, covered her $7,800 monthly condo maintenance fees, and paid for the prep-school tuition of their sixteen-year-old son. Hixon said her apartment was mostly unfurnished, with only a couple of chairs and "beat-up tables" to go along with the indoor pool. She had other furniture in storage, but could not remember where it was: "In America somewhere, Brooklyn, who knows where these things go?" She said she never ate at home, but rather at fine restaurants, including La Côte Basque, La Grenouille, and 21. How did she pay for it all? "I have rich friends," she said. "They love to invite me." After Cody was convicted on racketeering charges in 1982 and sent to prison, Trump took Hixon to court. After she missed $300,000 in condo maintenance payments, Hixon went bankrupt and lenders seized her Trump Tower apartments.

Subpoenaed by federal investigators in 1980, Trump denied giving away apartments to keep his project on track. Cody, meanwhile, said he "knew Trump quite well," adding that "Donald liked to deal with me through Roy Cohn." After Cody died in 2001, Trump called him "one psychopathic crazy bastard" and "real scum."

EVEN AS THE TOWER was going up, Trump pushed ahead with plans for a massive condo complex on the southern edge of Central Park. In 1981, he bought two grand old buildings—the Barbizon Plaza Hotel, and a fifteen-story apartment building next door at 100 Central Park South—for $13 million. Trump bought them to demolish them, but he ran into hard resistance from tenants eager to keep their rent-controlled units. Trump decried his opponents as "millionaires in mink coats, driving Rolls-Royces." Some of the residents were seniors on fixed incomes; others were indeed well-to-do stars.

Trump, tenants said, tried to force them out by annoying them. He proposed to move homeless people into at least ten vacant apartments; the city declined the generous offer. Maintenance workers ignored leaky faucets and broken appliances and covered up windows of empty apartments with ratty tinfoil. A tenants' group accused Trump of harassment, but he denied all. "Let me tell you something about the rich," he said. "They have a very low threshold for pain."

After a five-year standoff, Trump dropped his demolition plans and said he would renovate 100 Central Park South into twenty-six luxury apartments. The existing tenants could stay. The Barbizon Plaza Hotel was closed so its 950 rooms could be converted into four hundred luxury apartments. In early 1983, before Trump went ahead with the conversion, he asked Stephen N. Ifshin, a niche commercial broker, if he could find a buyer for both the Barbizon Hotel and the apartment house next to it. Ifshin was sure he could.

I want $100 million for the two buildings packaged together, Trump said.

It's a lot of money, Ifshin said, astounded by such a huge ask. Such a price was unheard of in Manhattan's real estate scene at the time, even as an unofficial high number to be floated to favored buyers, called a "whisper number." But brokering such a sale could earn Ifshin several million dollars in commissions, and he put out the word that the buildings could be had. Sherman Cohen, a tough negotiator in the Manhattan properties market, expressed interest and Ifshin set up a meeting in Trump's office. Before taking a seat at Trump's conference table, Cohen lit up a cigarette. But when he reached for the ashtray in the middle of the table, it would not budge.

Donald, Cohen said, do you have this thing screwed down?

This conference table comes from my hotel, the Barbizon, Trump said, and we screwed down all the ashtrays because people were stealing them as souvenirs. Trump's self-satisfied grin suggested he was just protecting his investment. They got down to business, and Trump announced that the buildings were for sale, for $100 million, firm. When I give out a price, that's the price, he said. Cohen replied that he didn't have $100 million to offer, but he could see his way to $90 million.

They were close, so close, Ifshin thought. Now a serious negotiation could begin. But Trump merely thanked Cohen and repeated the price, $100 million, nothing less. Cohen said no more. Trump said no more. It was a stare-down, an impasse. The meeting ended in less than half an hour. Cohen left, but Ifshin stayed behind, flabbergasted. Why? he asked Trump. Why turn such an offer down? You were close.

It wasn't what I was asking, Trump said. I never sell for less than I'm asking.

Presposterous, Ifshin thought. There's always a negotiation. And then it dawned on Ifshin that he had been used. Donald, he said, this was your way of getting an informal appraisal, to see if someone would bite, and for how much. Trump denied it, but Ifshin pushed back: This was just a ruse to see what the buildings might be worth in the marketplace, and now Trump knew, at least $90 million. You owe me a commission for getting you an informal appraisal from my buyer, Ifshin said. You owe me $10,000.

Trump looked at him like he was insane, but said he'd pay him back with a favor in the future. That never happened. Ifshin never dealt with Trump again and Trump didn't sell the buildings. "He wasn't upfront," Ifshin said. "He sort of hid his intentions. And that's the part that bothered me—very clever but not straight." Trump, Ifshin concluded, was someone who was unreliable, didn't care about long-term relationships, and burned through people.

Trump kept the buildings. The Barbizon was later renamed Trump Parc East, offering wood-burning fireplaces; the apartment building became Trump Parc. Three decades later, Trump's son Eric lived on the thirteenth floor.

FRED TRUMP'S FIRST SON, Freddy, was supposed to follow his father into the family business. Carrying his father's first and middle names (Frederick Christ), Freddy was the first focus of the father's sky-high expectations. (Freddy was the second child, behind Maryanne, a year older.) Freddy attended an Episcopal school on Long Island, then enrolled at Lehigh University, where his passion was aviation. But after graduating in 1960, he returned to the Avenue Z office and joined his father. Fred was a stern taskmaster, and mild-mannered Freddy struggled to live up to his father's demands. When Freddy installed new windows in an old building during a renovation, his father rebuked him for being wasteful. Freddy complained to his fraternity brothers that his father didn't appreciate him.

Donald looked up to his older brother. In the early sixties, Freddy would take Donald, then in high school, on summer fishing trips in his Century speedboat. In his dorm at New York Military Academy, Donald kept a photograph of his brother standing next to a plane. Early on, growing up in his older brother's shadow, Donald competed for his father's affection. But as he watched his brother fall short of Fred's approval, Donald came to believe that his brother lacked the toughness to survive in his competitive family. "Freddy just wasn't a killer," Donald said, echoing the term his father liked to use for a successful son.

After a proposed Trump development set for Coney Island's Steeplechase Park fell apart, Freddy left the business and went to work as a pilot with Trans World Airlines. At age twenty-three, he married a stewardess, and the couple had two children, Fred and Mary. Freddy seemed far happier than he had been under his father; Donald, however, couldn't help but pick on Freddy's run-of-the-mill ambitions, asking him, "What's the difference between what you do and driving a bus?" Freddy's smoking and drinking, which worsened in his midtwenties, would lead Donald to avoid cigarettes and alcohol for the rest of his life. Freddy divorced and quit flying. By the late seventies, he had moved back in with his parents and was supervising a maintenance crew at one of his father's Brooklyn apartment complexes. In 1977, Donald asked Freddy to be best man at his wedding to Ivana, saying he believed it would be "a good thing for him."

On September 26, 1981, Freddy, eight years Donald's senior, died of a heart attack following years of alcoholism. He was forty-three. Freddy was buried in Queens at a family plot in a Lutheran cemetery. Donald called his death "the saddest part in what I've been through." He said he learned from his brother's failure "to keep my guard up one hundred percent." "Man is the most vicious of all animals, and life is a series of battles ending in victory or defeat," Trump said two months after his brother's death. "You just can't let people make a sucker out of you."

TRUMP TOWER WAS A HIT. Its 266 condos, which went on sale in late 1982 and started at $500,000 for a one-bedroom apartment, sold for a combined $277 million, enough to pay off the entire building even before the first tenant moved in. Interested buyers would meet with Sunshine and Trump, who would sometimes join them for a tour. Sales brochures touted a hidden Fifty-Sixth Street entryway advertised as "totally inaccessible to the public." Trump explained his strategy for winning over apartment buyers: "You sell them a fantasy." Many units were sold as corporate apartments or pieds-à-terre for wealthy foreigners. But to Trump's promotional delight, several celebrities bought in, including Steven Spielberg, Michael Jackson, and Johnny Carson, who would accuse two building workers of stealing his vicuña-wool coat.

After Trump fired the men, Carson found the coat in his closet. Trump spread a rumor, printed in the New York papers, that Britain's royal family—Charles, Prince of Wales, and his wife, Princess Diana—were interested in spending $5 million to buy a twenty-one-room condominium, an entire floor of Trump Tower. They never showed. Trump didn't confess to creating that rumor, which the *Times* attributed to "one real estate official," but he did say that the rumor "certainly didn't hurt us."

To boost the tower's image, Trump sought world-renowned upscale brands for his shopping atrium. The first forty-eight retail tenants included Mondi (clothes), Botticellino (fashion), Charles Jourdan (shoes), Buccellati (Italian jeweler), Ludwig Beck (German department store), Harry Winston (jewelry), and Asprey (London jeweler), some of whom paid rents as high as $1 million a year. Within the first few years, some initial tenants bailed out after struggling to turn a profit from the tower's many middle-American tourists.

As Trump Tower reached for the sky, so, too, did the Trump mythos. In 1982, Trump made *Forbes*'s inaugural list of America's four hundred wealthiest people; the magazine estimated his worth at $100 million. But although Trump's deals were starting to expand his wealth, his income remained more modest. New Jersey investigators sizing him up for a casino license said that in 1982, Trump made $100,000 working for his father, got a $1 million commission from the Grand Hyatt, and had $6,000 in savings and a $35 million line of credit from Chase, arranged with his father's help.

The tower, which some Manhattan traditionalists disdained as a gaudy display of nouveau riche excess, won accolades from *Times* architectural critic Paul Goldberger, who admitted that he'd assumed the building "would be silly, pretentious and not a little vulgar." Instead, he found the atrium to be "warm, luxurious and even exhilarating . . . the most pleasant interior public space to be completed in New York in some years." In the tower's early days, homeless people moved onto the atrium's marble bench to listen to the music; Trump dispatched security guards and instructed landscapers to cover the bench with potted plants. It was "kind of comical," Res remembered. "All this glass and marble in the ultimate tower of opulence, a brilliant musician playing show tunes on this $50,000 piano, and the city's poorest citizens sitting with their paper bags just passing the day."

Trump Tower permanently ingrained Trump, his name, and his celebrity into the firmament of Manhattan, just as he had dreamed about as a young boy looking over the bridge from Queens. He moved into a honey-colored office on the twenty-sixth floor, where he would work for decades to come, his custom-made mahogany desk stacked with magazines featuring himself, his walls jammed with awards and tributes; all framed by a dramatic view of the Plaza and Central Park. Ivana moved into the office next door, at least for a time (in the design phase, Trump asked the architect to plan for a second apartment just for Donald, in case the marriage fell apart). In March 1984, the Trumps—Donald, Ivana, and their three children—moved into the three-story penthouse. The fifty-three-room gilded triplex boasted a twenty-nine-foot-high living room, maid's quarters, ceiling murals of Renaissance cherubs, crystal chandeliers, a remote-controlled Romanesque fountain, blue onyx mined from "deepest, darkest Africa," and its own elevator. The couple had his-and-her bathrooms: Donald's was dark brown marble; Ivana's, translucent pink onyx. Trump reserved an apartment below his penthouse, with an imported marble mantelpiece, for his parents. They mostly stayed in Queens.

The Grand Hyatt had made Trump famous in New York. Trump Tower made him famous everywhere. *GQ* sized up his hands ("small and neatly groomed"), his stature ("trim but well-nourished"), and his instincts ("I know what people want"). *Lifestyles of the Rich and Famous*, Robin Leach's breathless TV juggernaut, said Trump's Greenwich, Connecticut, mansion was a $10 million estate—three times what he had actually paid. "I believe in spending maybe more money than other people would think almost rational," Trump told the camera.

Banks were finally willing to lend him enough to meet Trump's appetite. In 1985, he bought a 118-room Palm Beach mansion called Mar-a-Lago with an $8.5 million loan. "Every lender was a starfucker," said Jon Bernstein, a former partner at Dreyer & Traub, Trump's principal law firm in the eighties. "They all wanted to be attached to Donald Trump in any way they could."

• • •

THAT SAME YEAR, TRUMP returned to one of the first pieces of Manhattan real estate he had fallen in love with—the Penn Central railroad's large block of land on the Upper West Side. He bought the property from another developer for $115 million and declared his intention to build the world's tallest building, a 150-story tower overlooking the Hudson River, accompanied by six 76-story towers, eight thousand apartments, a shopping mall, eighty-five hundred parking spaces, forty acres of parks, and a headquarters for the National Broadcasting Company, which Trump hoped to lure from Rockefeller Center. "Television City" was, his own press release said, "the master builder's grandest plan yet."

The neighbors were having none of it. They promised a hell of a fight. The *Times* called the proposal Trump's "bid for immortality." Opponents lined up to block Trump's path, creating a not-for-profit called Westpride, which hosted a fund-raiser that drew celebrities such as TV host Bill Moyers, feminist Betty Friedan, and Robert Caro, Lyndon Johnson's biographer. One year into the battle, Trump switched architects and shrank his plan. He and Koch got into a verbal war, with the developer calling the mayor a "moron" and a "disaster" for New York. "If Donald Trump is squealing like a stuck pig, I must have done something right," Koch declared, before adding, "piggy, piggy, piggy."

Under financial pressure, Trump eventually surrendered his ambition to construct the world's tallest building. He embraced the opponents' alternative plan, with less than half the density Trump had proposed. Trump praised the new plan at a meeting with Roberta Gratz, a prominent opponent, saying, "This is brilliant! My architects have been wasting my time for years." Stunned to hear such a concession, Gratz replied, "Donald, someday I want to hear you say that in public." Trump shifted in his seat and did not respond.

ON MAY 28, 1986, Trump wrote Koch a letter: "Dear Ed, For many years I have watched with amazement as New York City repeatedly failed on its promises to complete and open the Wollman Skating Rink." For years, Trump had gazed out his office window at the shuttered rink in Central Park, appalled by the city's inability to fix the public facility. Now he was ready to do what the city couldn't—and show up the mayor while he was at it. Building the rink, he promised Koch, "which essentially involves the pouring of a concrete slab, should take no more than four months' time."

Trump offered to pay for the construction and run the rink himself.

Koch wrote back the same day, saying he'd be "delighted" if Trump managed the repair work, but rejecting his offer to then manage the rink. And the mayor discouraged Trump from seeking to rename the rink after himself: "Remember, the Bible says that those who give charity anonymously or, if not anonymously, then without requiring the use of their names, are twice blessed."

Trump quickly turned the Wollman project into a free-media gold mine. He held half a dozen press conferences as the work unfolded, irritating city officials. Parks Commissioner Henry Stern arrived at the first news conference to find a sign that said OWNER: TRUMP ICE INC. He ordered his staff to remove the sign. Instead of naming the rink for Trump, Stern offered to plant a tree in his honor. Parks workers chose a ten-foot-tall Japanese pine, which they dubbed the Trump Tree. The developer happened to arrive at the rink as workers prepared to plant the tree. Infuriated, he shouted, "Tell Ed Koch and Henry Stern they can shove the tree up their asses." Thirty years later, when Trump was running for president, the mature tree, now forty feet high, stood tall outside the rink.

Free from the bureaucratic regulations that had stymied the city's efforts to rebuild the rink, Trump got it fixed two months ahead of schedule and under budget, winning the PR battle against the mayor— and the hearts of many New Yorkers.

TRUMP PARLAYED THAT GOODWILL into a new wave of celebrity, portraying himself as a can-do dealmaker with a showy billionaire's tastes and a populist's penchant for plain talk. Media magnate Si Newhouse noticed that sales of his *GQ* magazine spiked when Trump appeared on the cover, so he approached Trump with an idea: write a book for my publishing house, Random House. Ghostwritten by Tony Schwartz, *Trump: The Art of the Deal* packaged Trump's celebration of ego, excellence, and expansive business ambitions into an

easy-to-read book of prescriptions. His business bible reviewed the joy
of tax abatements, the power of a sensational story, and the importance of playing to customers' fantasies. The book tore into critics (the
Koch administration was "both pervasively corrupt and totally incompetent") and boosted his cachet ("Deals are my art form. I like making
deals, preferably big deals"). In an echo of the Reverend Norman Vincent Peale's "positive-thinking," Trump offered an eleven-step formula
for success. In step one ("Think Big"), Trump said "many highly successful entrepreneurs" exhibited a level of focus he called "controlled
neurosis."

Reviewers trashed the book as shallow, pompous, and self-
promotional. A *Washington Post* critic said, "The man's lack of taste is as
vast as his lack of shame." But in the first few weeks after its release, the
book rocketed to the top of bestseller lists. It sold more than a million
hardcover copies, in part thanks to a Trump publicity blitz that looked
like a presidential campaign: taking out full-page newspaper ads calling
for a tougher US foreign policy; giving a speech in New Hampshire at
the cusp of the primary season; handing out I ♥ DONALD TRUMP bumper
stickers. But that campaign was not about running for office, just about
selling books—and himself. "It was all about being high-visibility,"
said Peter Osnos, who edited the book for Random House. "Trump
had this urge to be a really big name, so he cultivated celebrity. But his
lifestyle was surprisingly unglamorous. He's quite disciplined in some
ways. Doesn't smoke, doesn't drink, lives above the store. He was not a
big New York socialite, never was. He basically enjoyed going upstairs
and watching the tube. What he was interested in was celebrity and his
businesses—construction, real estate, gambling, wrestling, boxing."

AS TRUMP'S EMPIRE SPREAD, some of the people closest
to him noticed a change. He grew more distant, sometimes petulant,
sometimes explosive. In the Grand Hyatt days, the Trump organization, as much as it talked big, thrived with a small office and tight
crew: Sunshine; Trump's attorney and adviser Harvey Freeman; a
close group of leasing agents, lawyers, and secretaries. Trump's vanity
instilled a strong tribalism in his team: his workers, he often said, were
the best. Though he would later become known for the catchphrase

"You're fired," Trump usually felt uneasy getting rid of an employee. If it had to be done, he would rather delegate the task to an underling. "We always felt that if you were close enough to Donald that he would have to be the one to let you go, you had a job for life," Res said.

In the early eighties, Res walked the sidewalks with Trump to meetings, making small talk about buildings or deals. By the end of the decade, when Trump went to lunch with other executives, he would surround himself with three security guards. The office had always been competitive, but the door to Trump's inner lair had stayed open, even when he was making calls under the fake name John Barron. But after the first big successes, the mood around Trump began to change. He surrounded himself, Res said, with sycophants who applauded his moves rather than questioning his logic. "He was not the same Donald that you would sit and chew the fat with so much," she said. "He doesn't want to be argued with anymore. He's too big a star." He began drinking his diet sodas through a straw, and only when they came from Norma Foerderer, his executive assistant, because he was too afraid of others' germs. Executives began calling Norma "the barometer." If Donald was in his office in a particularly combative mood, she would stop visitors, saying, "Don't go in there."

Trump's demands seemed to shift into overdrive. One morning around two, while passing Trump Parc in his limo, Trump saw a soda can lying on the sidewalk near the entrance. He called Blanche Sprague, who oversaw project development for Trump, and told her, "Call me when it's gone." She got a superintendent to fix the problem, then called Trump to report back. "Then I got to sleep until six, when Donald called about something else," she said. As his businesses grew and became more complicated, Trump's temper flared. After being told a project was running behind schedule, he kicked a chair across a conference room. "He always has to have his way," said Scutt, the architect.

Some of his closest executives began to leave: Trump's chief New York counsel, his top sales executive, his chief financial adviser; even Res, the engineer who had lifted his name into the sky, the woman he'd once anointed "Donna Trump." But that was all behind the scenes. In public, Trump had become what he'd always wanted to be: a star. *Playgirl* magazine called him one of the sexiest men in America, and in March 1990, he adorned the cover of *Playboy*, brushing against a cover girl eyeing him adoringly. Trump's wife didn't push back against the cover photo, at least not in public, but some women in Trump's offices were dismayed. "I think that was the beginning of the end of him being a serious businessman," Res said. "And he moved into being a cartoon." Undaunted, Trump relished the publicity. "The show is Trump," he said, "and it is sold-out performances everywhere."

6

"Best Sex I've Ever Had"

The show began back at the start of Trump's career, when he built not only buildings but an image as the consummate dealmaker. In 1978, a young investigative reporter decided to explore the facts behind the image. Wayne Barrett hadn't told anyone where he was going, so when the phone rang in the conference room of an obscure government agency where he was poring through documents, he ignored it. Barrett had a lot of work to do. Boxes and folders containing thousands of pages of records covered the table in front of him. Somewhere in these stacks, he suspected, were documents that would explain how a brash young developer from Queens had gotten the inside track on a series of big real estate deals in Manhattan. A few weeks earlier, veteran *Village Voice* journalist Jack Newfield had walked over to the thirty-three-year-old newbie reporter with an assignment: Trump was getting fawning press coverage portraying him as a self-made success and an urban visionary. Newfield, who had spent years covering the Brooklyn Democratic machine, saw not a precocious businessman, but a child of privilege playing off his father's political connections in a city wracked by corruption.

Barrett knew that a little-known government agency called the Urban Development Corporation had played a pivotal role in Trump's deal to buy the derelict Commodore Hotel and turn it into the gleaming Grand Hyatt. Barrett asked to see all records connected to that deal. When Barrett got to the agency's nondescript office in midtown Manhattan, an employee led him to this conference room, and an intimidating ocean of paper. Now the phone rang again. This time, an agency staffer ducked her head in and told Barrett the call was for him. As far as Barrett knew, the only people aware that he was in that room were the employees at the office. Puzzled, he picked up the phone. A stranger with a distinct Queens accent greeted him: "Wayne! This is Donald. I hear you're doing a story on me."

"Like we were old buddies," Barrett recalled. "We had never spoken." Barrett, one of the first reporters to take a deep look at Trump's deals, was about to become one of the first to experience a media strategy, then in its infancy, that would become familiar to reporters around New York, then across the country. As Barrett dug into Trump's business over the next few months, Trump handled him with carrot and stick—attempts to ingratiate himself with the reporter, followed almost immediately by thinly veiled threats.

First, the carrot. Barrett lived in Brownsville, then one of the poorest areas of Brooklyn. "I could get you an apartment," Trump told Barrett. "That must be an awfully tough neighborhood." Barrett replied that he chose to live in Brownsville and worked as a community organizer. "So we do the same thing!" Trump replied. "We're both rebuilding neighborhoods. . . . We're going to have to really get to know each other." Then, the stick. "I've broken one writer," Trump told Barrett another time. "You and I've been friends and all, but if your story damages my reputation, I want you to know I'll sue."

While other developers might refuse interviews or issue carefully worded statements through publicists, Trump was almost never unavailable to talk for a few minutes or a few hours. One of Barrett's first interviews with Trump, in his Fifth Avenue apartment, lasted three hours, ending only because Ivana Trump interrupted with a request to go to the opera. Even as it became clear that Barrett's story would not be favorable, Trump's demeanor altered only slightly. At their last interview, Trump read a prepared statement: "I really value my reputation and I don't hesitate to sue. I've sued twice for libel. Roy Cohn's been my attorney both times. I've won once and the other case is pending. It's cost me one hundred thousand dollars, but it's worth it." Right after the stick, another carrot. Trump flashed a smile:

"But everything'll be all right. We're going to get together after the story."

They did not get together after the story. Barrett's article—published in two parts in 1979—was the first to reveal the prominent role that Fred Trump's political connections and campaign contributions, along with legally questionable favors granted by government and bankruptcy-court officials, played in Donald's meteoric rise. Trump's response to the story was, compared to the media wars that would develop in the years to come, tame. He stopped taking Barrett's calls, criticized him to other reporters.

Barrett wasn't entirely surprised by Trump's carrot-and-stick strategy. Trump's adviser was, after all, Roy Cohn, a man who, while combative with reporters, always saw the value of publicity, regardless of its tone. Cohn would often greet Barrett when the two bumped into each other, usually at the 21 Club, with a running tally of the damage the reporter had inflicted. "You've written thirty-four stories about me and you've never written a good word," Cohn said one day. "You have no idea how much money you've made for me."

IN HIS BOOK *Trump: The Art of the Deal*, Trump plainly spelled out his media philosophy, the product of three men who influenced him and New York's unique media environment in the 1970s and 1980s—his father, Fred; developer William Zeckendorf; and Donald's lawyer, Roy Cohn. Trump wrote:

> *One thing I've learned about the press is that they're always hungry for a good story, and the more sensational the better. . . . The point is that if you are a little different, or a little outrageous, or if you do things that are bold or controversial, the press is going to write about you. I've always done things a little differently, I don't mind controversy, and my deals tend to be somewhat ambitious. . . .*
>
> *Sometimes they write positively and sometimes they write negatively. But from a pure business point of view, the benefits of being written about have far outweighed the drawbacks. It's really quite simple. If I take a full-page ad in the* New York

Times *to publicize a project, it might cost $40,000, and in any case, people tend to be skeptical about advertising. But if the* New York Times *writes even a moderately positive one-column story about one of my deals, it doesn't cost me anything, and it's worth a lot more than $40,000.*

The funny thing is that even a critical story, which may be hurtful personally, can be very valuable to your business. . . . The final key to the way I promote is bravado. I play to people's fantasies. People may not always think big themselves, but they can still get very excited by those who do. That's why a little hyperbole never hurts. People want to believe that something is the biggest and the greatest and the most spectacular.

I call it truthful hyperbole. It's an innocent form of exaggeration—and a very effective form of promotion.

Fred Trump knew the value of good publicity. As a young developer, he routinely sent out press releases promoting his latest projects, sometimes referring to himself as "Brooklyn's Largest Builder." Donald's touch for the dramatic probably drew more inspiration, however, from another developer. Zeckendorf employed a press agent to keep his name in the papers, ideally in stories emphasizing his lavish lifestyle, or announcing outlandish building plans that never came to fruition, such as an airport atop buildings in Manhattan. As Donald started getting press in the late seventies, some reporters referred to him as a young Zeckendorf. Trump was flattered, even if Zeckendorf's company did end up in bankruptcy.

On November 1, 1976, readers of the *Times* were introduced to a flashy young developer who was moving ahead on three big projects (though none had actually been built). Headlined "Donald Trump, Real Estate Promoter, Builds Image as He Buys Buildings," the story was one of the first to draw the Trump/Zeckendorf parallel. Written by Judy Klemesrud, a society reporter, the story described a day in the life of "New York's No. 1 real estate promoter of the middle 1970s." Dozens of reporters after Klemesrud would learn the core challenge of covering Trump. As Barrett, one of his biographers, put it, "He was born with bullshit capabilities beyond what you and I could possibly imagine." The *Times* profile gave Trump an early taste of how easy it was to use the media to burnish his reputation. Klemesrud reported that he had graduated first in his class at Wharton, which was untrue. The *Times* profile also noted that Trump called himself "publicity shy." But it was Trump's gift for self-promotion that appalled many of New York's most prominent developers. Manhattan's real estate barons—families such as the Rudins, Tishmans, Fishers, and Roses—saw little benefit to having their names in the papers. Trump struck them as a showboat. "He was an outsider in that group," said Paul Goldberger, the *Times*' architecture critic, "and never really became central to it. I think they were annoyed by him presenting himself as the most important, biggest builder in New York."

TRUMP'S MOST IMPORTANT MENTOR in media as well as legal matters was Cohn, himself a lifelong student of the tabloid trade. As a thirteen-year-old, Cohn wrote a gossip column for the *Bronx Home News*, and while still a teen, he learned big-city newspapering from Leonard Lyons, a *New York Post* columnist. In his twenties, Cohn, by then a lawyer, helped enlist legendary gossip columnist Walter Winchell to promote Senator Joseph McCarthy's campaign against communist sympathizers. By the time Trump and Cohn crossed paths, Cohn's media connections included publishers such as Si Newhouse and another man, an Australian whose expansion into the New York media market changed the city's media culture just as a young real estate mogul was looking to generate free publicity.

Gossip reporting has a storied tradition in New York, but in the early seventies, the art seemed nearly lost. The *New York Daily Mirror* had closed in 1963, and with that tabloid's coarse voice silenced, the *Daily News* and the *Post* felt less drawn to salacious material. Then Rupert Murdoch came to town. In 1976, the Australian press baron bought the *Post*, then a liberal paper with an intellectual bent. Murdoch imported staffers from his other publications to lend the *Post* a different sensibility. The paper was soon blaring eye-grabbing headlines such as "Boy Gulps Gas, Explodes," "500-Pound Sex Monster Goes Free," and "Granny Executed in Her Pink Pajamas." Inside the paper, Murdoch created a full-page gossip sheet—Page Six—with a focus on celebrities' romantic dalliances, nighttime wanderings, and personal indiscretions. "People sell the paper," said the *Post*'s new editor, Roger Wood, and especially people from New York City. Gone were the days when gossip columnists fed mainly on Hollywood starlets three thousand miles away. Now, Page Six feasted on Manhattan media moguls, power brokers, and even real estate developers.

One of Page Six's first, most dependable sources was Cohn, who was friendly with both Murdoch and Wood. Claudia Cohen, an early Page Six reporter, started writing about the parties Roy threw, listing the names of judges who attended. This would have infuriated many lawyers. Not Cohn. "He loved it and started inviting me to cover every single party he had," Cohen said. "He loved seeing his name on the page so much that he would also become a source for great stories. And nobody knew where more bodies were buried in New York City than Roy Cohn." And Cohn had a young friend with a powerful desire to get his name in the papers.

The journalism establishment sneered at the remade *Post*. The *Columbia Journalism Review* called the paper "a force for evil." But Murdoch's paper was flying off the newsstands, and competitors took notice. Across town at the *News*, Liz Smith, a gossip columnist who had previously focused on Hollywood, turned toward New York's elite. One day, Smith recalled, she was in a car, headed up Park Avenue with her friend Parker Ladd, when Ladd mentioned a new power couple in town, a young building tycoon and his blond, Eastern European wife. It was the first time Smith heard two names that would one day become inextricably linked with hers. As the car neared a statue of Commodore Cornelius Vanderbilt, Ladd asked Smith, "Have you ever met Ivana and Donald Trump?"

FOR DECADES, TRUMP'S DAILY morning routine included a review of everything written or said about him in the previous twenty-four hours. The clippings were usually culled by Norma Foerderer—for two decades Trump's ever-present chief assistant—who also handed her boss a spiral notebook containing media requests, most of which he would handle himself. As his celebrity grew, the daily pile of Trump-related news coverage swelled; still, he diligently tried to review everything written or said about him. He often handed the positive pieces to other visiting journalists as examples of how to do it right. No matter how famous he became, no publication was too small for a kind word about Trump to go unnoticed. Trump handed a reporter from *Fortune* magazine a copy of *New York Construction News* in which Trump was named "owner and developer of the year."

Trump kept the negative stories, too. When *Wall Street Journal* reporter Neil Barsky arrived for an interview, Trump's desk was covered with a series of articles Barsky had written about the developer's financial struggles. Trump flipped on a tape recorder, motioned to the articles, and told Barsky he had three sworn affidavits from people saying that the reporter was spreading rumors about Trump's having a cash-flow problem. Trump informed Barsky that he'd already retained a prominent libel lawyer in anticipation of Barsky's next piece. Then the interview began.

While other business magnates hid behind publicists and spokespeople who put reporters off for as long as possible, Trump usually returned calls personally, within hours if not minutes. For some publications, Trump's constant availability and interest in coverage crossed into annoyance. One year, when *Fortune* assembled its annual list of wealthy businesspeople, it assigned an intern to deal with the barrage of calls from Trump, who disagreed with the magazine's assessment of his net worth.

Trump inherited from his father a connection to one of New York's most influential publicists, Howard Rubenstein, who served as spokesman for many other prominent real estate barons. Rubenstein quickly found that the younger Trump didn't need his help. Once Trump established himself as someone who mattered in media circles, virtually everything he and Ivana did was deemed newsworthy. When *Daily News* gossip columnists George Rush and Joanna Molloy ran an item about Trump cutting the ski-lift line in Aspen, they had two sources to verify the incident, including a ski resort employee. The day the item ran, Rush says he heard from an angry Trump: "It didn't happen. This story is total bullshit. Who told you this? Whoever it was made it up. You tell him I said he's a motherfucking liar. Tell him to call me. Whoever it is doesn't have the balls because he knows I'll beat the fucking shit out of him."

One summer, Jim Brady, an early Page Six editor, heard that Donald and Ivana had been granted a temporary summer membership at a club in East Hampton, where they were renting a home. The Trumps wanted to become permanent members, but Brady learned that the club's board would never approve them. Brady put that news on Page Six and got a quick call from Trump. "He was cursing me with every four-letter word," Brady said. "'You SOB. You bleeping this. You bleeping that. I'm going to sue you. I'm going to sue the *Post*. I'm going to sue Murdoch. I'm going to sue everyone.'"

A moment later, the phone rang again. It was Cohn. Expecting another tirade, Brady told Cohn if he was going to sue, he should call the newspaper's lawyer. "Jim, Jim, Jim," Cohn said. "There's going to be no lawsuit. It's very good for Donald to let off steam. That's just Donald. And we encourage that kind of thing, but no one's going to sue anybody. I'm just telling you that there will be no lawsuit." There was no lawsuit.

Trump quickly figured out that some tabloid reporters would publish an item just on his say-so; he took advantage of that to float notions that might help his business. Among the tall tales he fed the tabs, according to former Trump Organization executive Barbara Res, was one that the White House was considering moving the president's New York suite to the Trump-owned Plaza Hotel. "Donald had a way of getting to print whatever he would say, even if it weren't necessarily the whole and honest truth," Res said. "He had tremendous self-confidence, which is important. He managed to say what he would say, and people would write it and then it would be the truth. That was the thing with him that they call the big lie. You say something enough times, it becomes the truth. And he is the master of that."

Trump had a knack for laundering quotes or rumors under the cloak of anonymity. If he didn't want his name connected to something, he'd persuade reporters to attribute statements to "a friend of Trump's" or "a high-ranking official in the Trump organization." Years later, reporters unfamiliar with Trump would express confusion when, during an initial interview, he would say something was "off the record, but you can use it." "He knew how to play the game," George Rush said. "A lot of things would come from 'a friend of Donald's,' and so he would talk in the third person about what Donald was thinking."

Some reporters criticized the tabloids' willingness to be used. Mark

Singer, a reporter at the *New Yorker* who profiled Trump in 1997, said Trump used the tabloids as "his mythmaking apparatus." But reporters at the tabloids said their readers—and especially blue-collar New Yorkers—loved any item about Trump. "When we would talk particularly to immigrants, recent immigrants who were the readers of the *Daily News*, they would always want to know about Donald Trump," Rush said. "He embodied the American Dream to them. Excessive, conspicuous consumption is not a bad thing in New York to a lot of people. It's kind of comic what he was doing. I've always felt like Donald was in on the jokes. He knows he's over the top, but that's where he likes to live."

Trump's fan base was particularly strong outside Manhattan. "New Yorkers are very attuned to accents, and he had an outer-borough accent," said Ed Kosner, the former editor of *New York*, *Esquire*, and the *Daily News*. "Even though he went to Penn and all the rest of it, he sounded like a guy who grew up in Queens, which is what he did, and I think people recognize that in him. They didn't think he was a snooty guy. They thought he was a regular guy who's made a lot of money."

As impressed as Trump's fans were, many reporters concluded that the payoff for all the media attention was greater for the celebrity than for his admirers. "He was literally addicted to publicity and recognition," said former *New York* magazine writer John Taylor. "He would get this, like, dopamine surge in his brain. I would walk with him into some building or room, and Trump would kind of hang back and watch the room, and wait until the room had filled, and he could have that moment of recognition, when you'd see waves of people turn and realize it was him. . . . He lived for those moments."

Sometimes it seemed as if recognition was the only thing that mattered. In 1988, when Jeffrey Breslow, one of the country's leading inventors of board games, visited Trump Tower to pitch Trump on a Monopoly-like game that would be named after him, the inventor was prepared to get down on the floor and pit his strategic wiles against the guy whose picture would be on the box of Trump: The Game. But Trump had no interest in playing or even hearing the details of the game. He took a quick glance at the mock-up of the box's cover and said, "I like it—what's next?" What came next was a lightning-fast negotiation, a promotional blitz, and the sale of about a million units.

Trump happily made appearances to sell the game, but wanted no role in determining its content.

Trump's focus on getting his name onto products, buildings, and news stories left some of his top executives, as well as reporters, wondering if there was more to the man than his public persona. He would grant an in-person interview, in the hospital room, on the day his daughter Tiffany was born. For many years, he would call columnists and ask for their assessment of his latest romantic conquest, preferably with a numerical rating on a 1-to-10 scale. "Everywhere Donald Trump turns, he sees Donald Trump," Singer said. "He doesn't see the other guy much. It becomes really hard to distinguish [how much] of the promotion and publicity . . . is good for business and how much of it is to fill that hollowness inside of him."

IN THE FALL OF 1984, Roy Cohn fell ill. A year later, he entered the National Institutes of Health hospital in Bethesda, Maryland, maintaining that he had liver cancer. But he was suffering from the effects of HIV infection. As Cohn struggled to stay alive, Trump pulled back from his friend for a time. Trump had always known that Cohn was gay. Cohn was "invariably with some very good-looking young man," Trump wrote in his first book. "But Roy never talked about it. He just didn't like the image. He felt that to the average person, being gay was almost synonymous with being a wimp." If someone brought up gay rights, Trump noted, "Roy was always the first one to speak out against them."

Now Cohn, fighting his final battle, was miffed by Trump's apparent betrayal: "I can't believe he's doing this to me. Donald pisses ice water." As Cohn's health deteriorated, his unethical behavior as a lawyer caught up to him. The Appellate Division of the New York State Supreme Court accused him of "dishonesty, fraud, deceit and misrepresentation." A host of luminaries rose to defend Cohn's good character, including Trump, who pivoted again, returning to his friend's side and inviting him to visit Mar-a-Lago.

In 1986, Cohn was disbarred. "For an attorney practicing for nearly 40 years in this state, such misconduct is inexcusable," the court said. Cohn died five weeks later. He was fifty-nine. His friends held a memorial service for him. Trump attended, standing silently in the back.

"MY AREA IS CONTROVERSY," Cohn once said. "My tough front is my biggest asset. I don't write polite letters." Throughout his first decades in business, Trump littered New York with his own aggressive correspondence. Sometimes handwritten, sometimes typed, usually on the distinct gold-embossed Trump-organization letterhead, the letters landed on the desks of competitors and detractors. When Trump wanted media attention, he'd send a copy of a letter to selected reporters or columnists. When *New York* magazine's architecture critic Carter Wiseman panned a Trump building, Wiseman got a letter calling him a loser and a poor dresser who wore corduroy suits. *Times* architecture critic Goldberger found his dress habits critiqued on Page Six after Goldberger wrote negatively about Trump's Television City plans. Sometimes Trump eschewed the company letterhead and just annotated a copy of the offending piece of journalism and sent it to the author. When *Times* columnist Gail Collins called Trump a "financially embattled thousandaire," he sent her column back with her face circled. Next to it, Trump had written, "The Face of a Dog!"

Sometimes letters weren't enough—for example, when the offending party was dead. In 1990, *Forbes* magazine published an article downgrading Trump's wealth from $1.7 billion to $500 million. The magazine's owner, Malcolm Forbes, had died a few months earlier of a heart attack at the age of seventy, but Trump believed the deceased publisher was to blame for the article. About to publish his second book, *Trump: Surviving at the Top*, Trump called his coauthor, Charles Leerhsen, with a request to add a few pages about Forbes. In a television interview a few weeks later, Trump said his book would be "very interesting with regard to Forbes. It's nothing I wanted to tell, but after [Forbes] did that number on me, I figured I might as well." In the book, published later that year, Trump criticized Forbes for having kept his homosexuality secret. In New York's elite social circles, Forbes's sexual orientation was well known, but publicly he was closeted; he'd been married for thirty-nine years and had four sons before divorcing. Trump wrote that it was a "double standard" that Forbes "lived openly as a homosexual—which he had every right to do—but expected the media and his famous friends to cover for him." The story about Trump's diminished wealth, he wrote, was payback after Trump refused to let Forbes bring two underaged young men into the bar at the Trump-owned Plaza Hotel.

WHILE SOME JOURNALISTS FOUND themselves in the midst of a Trump media feud by accident, or merely by doing their jobs, one fledgling publication actively courted the tycoon's fury: *Spy* magazine, an acid, brilliantly funny monthly that delighted in popping the inflated egos of the Reagan years. *Spy*'s founders, Kurt Andersen and Graydon Carter, had coincidentally both written profiles of Trump—Andersen for *Time* magazine, Carter for *GQ*. Andersen and Carter started *Spy* in 1986 with the mission to be "smart, fun, funny, fearless." The monthly quickly developed a reputation for an acerbic tone and creative insults. In *Spy*, CBS president Laurence Tisch was a "dwarf billionaire," and Vice President Dan Quayle a "dumb blond rich white kid plunked down in water far over his head." No public figure drew as consistent, heated attacks, though, as Trump. Andersen and Carter targeted Trump because he epitomized what their magazine was created to mock: the "ostentation, brashness, and vulgarity of New York in the '80s."

In *Spy*'s debut issue, Trump was included on a list of the Ten Most Embarrassing New Yorkers. The next year, the first *Spy* 100 list of "the most annoying, alarming, and appalling people, places and things" ranked Trump number three. In 1989, *Spy* explained that Trump had become so appalling that he had advanced to "another plane altogether." That year's *Spy* 100 ranked people by how much they were like Trump, or according to their "Trumpscore." *Spy* staffers coined epithets to refer to Trump, a lengthy list that included "well-fed condo hustler," "shuttle-owning dilettante-megalomaniac," and "joyless punk millionaire." One insult bothered Trump more than any other, though, outliving the magazine that created it: "short-fingered vulgarian." Soon after *Trump: The Art of the Deal* was published in 1987, Trump sent a copy to *Spy*'s office. On the book's cover, Trump had circled his own fingers in gold marker, an apparent rebuke of the suggestion that his digits were short. *Spy* staffers thought perhaps Trump had a better sense of humor about himself than they had given him credit for—until they opened the book. There, Trump had tucked a handwritten note that could have been penned by Cohn: "If you hit me, I will hit you back 100 times harder."

The more *Spy* hit him, the more Trump struck back. He told *Playboy* that *Spy* was "a piece of garbage." He repeatedly threatened to sue the magazine. He told the *News'* Liz Smith that *Spy* would close in a year; *Spy* embraced the prediction and added a monthly feature: a countdown to its own extinction. "He made it like a volleying sport," former *Spy* editor Susan Morrison said. "It was so fun to poke at him. It was like bearbaiting because he would respond and write us letters and call us losers. He was the gift that kept on giving." The magazine didn't just poke Trump with inventive epithets. *Spy* fact-checked the financial claims Trump made in *Trump: The Art of the Deal*, and in 1990 included him in its prank experiment, "America's Cheapest Zillionaire." The magazine created a company—the National Refund Clearinghouse—and, starting at $1.11, mailed checks of decreasing amounts to dozens of well-known wealthy people. When *Spy* got down to its smallest refund checks—for thirteen cents—only two people deposited them: Adnan Khashoggi, a Saudi Arabian arms dealer and billionaire, and Trump. (Years later, the *New Yorker's* Singer, who became a Trump target after Singer wrote a critical profile, mailed Trump a check for $37.82, also as a joke. Trump deposited it.)

Trump's prediction of *Spy's* demise eventually proved right; the magazine briefly folded in 1994, then closed for good in 1998. *Spy's* insults left a lasting sting, though. For years Carter, who became editor of *Vanity Fair*, periodically received photos of Trump torn from magazines and newspapers, sent by Trump, who circled images of his hands in gold. As recently as April 2015, Trump sent a picture with a note affixed: "See, not so short!" Carter sent it back, with his own note: "Actually, quite short."

IN LATE 1989, SOMEONE sent a photograph of a blond model named Marla Maples to the newsroom of the *New York Post*, along with a note saying the woman was dating a prominent married businessman. Maples was of little intrinsic interest to the tabloids; she was a homecoming queen from Dalton, Georgia, America's carpet capital, who had done some modeling for a ceramic-tile adhesive maker and Delta Airlines before she arrived in Manhattan and rented a $400-a-month studio apartment in Chelsea, determined to make it in the big city. But Page Six published her picture, along with a short, cryptic story, because the rumor was that the model was having an affair with a "business tycoon"—Donald Trump was cheating on Ivana.

In the newsroom of the *Post*, word spread that the story was off-limits. Murdoch had sold the paper to Peter Kalikow, a real estate developer who was friendly with Trump. A *Post* staffer had once walked into Kalikow's office to hear Trump on the phone berating the publisher for what he perceived as negative coverage. When word got to Kalikow that some of his reporters were pursuing rumors of Trump's infidelity, he told Lou Colasuonno, the paper's managing editor, "We cannot break this story." Why not? the editor asked. "Please," Kalikow said. "I'm going to have so much grief at home." He explained that his wife was close to Ivana, and his paper simply couldn't be the one that made public the rumored trouble in the marriage.

In her East Thirty-Eighth Street home office, Liz Smith was hearing the same rumors. Smith had been writing regularly about the Trumps for more than a decade. She'd been socializing with the couple, too, traveling with them on their private jet, attending their family anniversaries, weddings, and birthdays. When the Trumps refurbished Mar-a-Lago, Smith spent a weekend at the estate with a group of Ivana's girlfriends, including ABC-TV's Barbara Walters. Smith made no secret of her friendship, and when Donald's name appeared in her columns, it was often preceded by two words: "my pal." This may have bothered journalism ethicists, but Smith explained that she was a gossip columnist, not an "authentic journalist." Anyway, Smith liked Trump. When they bumped into each other at parties, he would pull Smith in for a hug, turn her toward the next person, and say, "She's the greatest! Isn't she the greatest?"—an act Smith always found embarrassing and a bit endearing, given Trump's germ phobia.

In 1990, Smith called Donald and told him a "strong story" was going around about him cheating on Ivana. She tried to sell him on giving her the exclusive, offering to print it in a way that wouldn't be "too inflammatory." Donald didn't deny the rumors, but he wasn't ready to go public. A few weeks later, Smith sent Trump a letter: "Give me this story or you are going to be in someplace a lot worse than the Liz Smith column." Trump never replied.

In early February, as Smith sat at her desk cranking out a column, she got a call from Ivana. Donald was in Japan to watch a Mike Tyson fight and talk to Japanese investors about buying the Plaza Hotel. Ivana invited Smith over, and when she arrived, Ivana was in tears. She told Smith the whole story. Even before Ivana discovered his affair, Donald had told her he'd lost sexual interest in her, and even a battery of plastic surgery she'd gotten recently hadn't made a difference. Now, like her husband, Ivana didn't want to go public about the affair. She feared that when Donald inevitably left her, he'd take away friends like Smith and Barbara Walters. Smith tried to allay Ivana's fears and urged her to call a prominent publicist, John Scanlon. The three of them developed a plan. On Friday, February 9, 1990, Smith had her Sunday column hand-delivered from her apartment to her editor at the *News*. She attached a note, half joking, "After Donald gets off the plane [from Japan] Sunday night, I'm afraid he's going to kill her—or me."

"Exclusive! Love on the Rocks," the headline blared across the bottom of the front page on Sunday, next to a smiling picture of Smith. The story inside had few details, but was accompanied by a biography of Donald and a story chronicling his twelve-year marriage to Ivana— a full two-page spread on the couple. "The marriage of Ivana and Donald Trump seems to be on the rocks, and inside sources say lawyers are already at work trying to divide the complex Trump holdings," Smith wrote.

It's unclear whom the story infuriated more: the *Post* staffers who had wanted to break it, or Donald. With the story finally out, Kalikow no longer stood in the way. An old-fashioned tabloid war broke out. It would be several months before Smith's editors let her write about a different topic. As the paper assigned an army of reporters to the story, an editor explained to Smith, "If this isn't a tabloid story, then there are no tabloids." The next day, the *Post*'s front screamed, "Split." A story inside offered Donald's version: he already had left Ivana. A source described only as "one intimate" of Trump's provided this quote from

Donald: "I like Ivana, but we've grown apart. Her level of arrogance has grown steadily worse in recent years." The *Post* reported that what angered Trump most was not that his private marital issues were now public, but rather one phrase in Smith's story: "The megadeveloper became positively apoplectic over a newspaper item yesterday suggesting that Ivana was his business partner."

February 1990 was a newsy month. Nelson Mandela was freed from prison. Drexel Burnham Lambert, a major Wall Street investment banking firm, went bankrupt. President George H. W. Bush welcomed the new president of Czechoslovakia, the former dissident playwright Václav Havel, to the White House, as the collapse of the Soviet empire accelerated. But for weeks, one story dominated the front pages of the city's tabloids: Donald vs. Ivana. After putting Mandela on the February 12 cover, the *Daily News* plastered Trump items on its front for twelve straight days. The *Post* ran page-one Trump items for eight days in a row. The obsession in the nation's media capital spread to serious national publications. No morsel of news was too small. When the AP reported that Trump and Marla Maples had attended the same church, the *Post*'s front page blared "They Met in Church." When Trump flew to Mar-a-Lago for Ivana's birthday, it led the *Daily News*; the *Post* returned fire the same day with "Trumps Share Fla. Palace, but in . . . SEPARATE BEDS." The *News* ran a reader poll gauging support for Donald or Ivana and put cardboard cutouts of both in its lobby and let readers pose for pictures next to their favorite Trump. The *Post* compared vital statistics for Marla and Ivana—age, height, weight, dress size—under the headline "Tale of the Tape in the Battle of the Belles." The next day's *Daily News* included a chart breaking down which members of New York social circles sided with Donald or with Ivana. Donald had Cher, Elton John, Frank Sinatra, and "everyone in Atlantic City," while Ivana's supporters included Calvin Klein, Oprah Winfrey, Princess Diana, and "all of N.Y. City's florists." (Barbara Walters was part of a smaller group of "fencesitters," along with George and Barbara Bush.)

The sensational headlines reached their apex with the *Post*'s February 16 front-page "Best Sex I've Ever Had," a statement supposedly uttered by Maples in reference to Donald. The headline would become a tabloid classic. Bill Hoffmann, a *Post* reporter known for his stories on celebrities, wrote the article after interviewing two of Maples's friends from her acting class. The women said they saw Trump pick up Maples after class, and that Marla had gushed to them about their love affair and their sex life. He pressed them for details, but the women knew little more. No matter: Hoffmann had the nugget he needed—a quote from an unidentified friend in which Marla said that Trump provided the "best sex I've ever had."

The *Post*'s managing editor, Colasuonno, read the quote on his computer and knew he had the next day's front page. Editors discussed whether the story was actually true: Did Marla really say what the *Post* was about to trumpet on page one? Colasuonno wasn't worried. "Guys, this headline is libel-proof," he said. "Donald will never complain about this one." A photo editor found the perfect photo: Trump grinning like the Cheshire cat. Under the front-page headline, the *Post* wrote, "We always knew that Donald Trump was a tiger in the corporate boardroom, but now we know he's a wildcat in the bedroom, too." (A couple of years later, when Colasuonno became editor of the *Post*, he'd get occasional calls from Trump, including an invitation one day to lunch at the Plaza. There, according to Colasuonno, Trump told the editor he would fly him down to Atlantic City for a weekend and "get a couple of chicks," or Colasuonno could go to a Yankee game and sit in owner George Steinbrenner's box. Trump wanted Colasuonno to write an article saying that Trump was solvent. "Look, there are a lot of rumors out there that I'm broke—it's all bullshit," Trump said. He wanted Colasuonno to write the story, but the editor instead offered to have his best business reporter look into Trump's finances. Trump never followed up. There was no more talk about going to Atlantic City and Yankee Stadium.) The day after "Best Sex" appeared, the *News* responded with a Smith report that Donald was "delighted" with the headline, which prompted a follow-up in the *Post*: "Trump: Fire Liz Smith."

The frantic coverage continued for months, giving *Spy* the opportunity to add to its collection of Trump epithets: "wife-dumping Atlantic City strongman" and "debtor-adulterer." Donald and Ivana did ultimately divorce, and during Trump's stint as a single man in his forties, one of his stranger media-massaging habits came to light. Since the beginning of his business career, Trump had occasionally called reporters using the name John Miller or, more often, John Barron. (Trump's fascination with that name persisted for years; when he was seeing Marla while still married to Ivana, he sometimes used the code name "the Baron" when he left messages for her. And when Trump and his third wife, Melania, had a son, they named him Barron.)

In 1991, a young reporter at *People* magazine named Sue Carswell called Trump's office to request an interview. Carswell had recently been given the Trump/Marla/Ivana beat and was calling about a recent *Post* story claiming that Trump had dumped Marla for Italian model Carla Bruni. Five minutes later, Carswell got a call from Trump's publicist, who introduced himself as John Miller. Miller confirmed the *Post* story. Yes, Trump had dumped Marla, and he had a bevy of beautiful women to pick from for his next love interest. "Important, beautiful women call him all the time," Miller said. He listed some names, including Madonna. "He mentioned basically every hot woman in Hollywood," Carswell said. Something struck the reporter as odd about Trump's publicist. He sounded a lot like, well, Trump. Conveniently, Carswell had been recording the interview. She played it for some colleagues, who agreed that it sounded like Donald. Then she called Marla and played the tape. Maples burst into tears and confirmed the voice was Trump's.

Carswell was far from the only reporter Trump called under an assumed name. *Daily News* columnist Linda Stasi said he once left her a voice mail as an "anonymous tipster" who wanted it known that Trump had been spotted going out with models. Quotations from "John Barron" appeared in *New York* magazine, the *Washington Post*, and the *Times*, where a "John Baron," described as a "vice-president of the Trump organization," showed up in a front-page article in 1980. Barron was variously quoted as a "Trump spokesman," "Trump executive," or "Trump representative." Although Trump at times denied making calls as John Barron, he admitted in a 1990 deposition that "I believe on occasion I used that name." Some reporters found the calls from Miller or Barron merely playful, if a bit weird. Others thought the calls were disturbing or even creepy, as Barron seemed to take pleasure in describing how prominent women were drawn to Trump sexually. "Actresses," Miller said in the call to Carswell, "just call to see if they can go out with him and things." Madonna "wanted to go out with him." And Trump's alter ego boasted that in addition to living with Maples, Trump had "three other girlfriends."

As the tabloid battles raged, Trump maintained that all publicity was good for business, but some of his close advisers had severe doubts. Longtime Trump employee Barbara Res worried that tabloid coverage of Donald's personal life would hurt the organization's bottom line. The day the "Best Sex I've Ever Had" story ran, Trump held up the *Post* with pride to show Res. "We all thought, the people in serious positions in the company, thought that was terrible," she said. "I mean, he's got a six-year-old at home. He's got a twelve-year-old that can read the papers. I mean, it was just—we thought that was terrible. He thought it was the greatest thing." (Donald Jr. later fought for his father's pride, getting into a tussle at the Hill School, a boarding school in Pennsylvania, after a fellow student confronted him with a racy newspaper picture of Donald's mistress. Donald Jr. went a year without speaking to his father around that time. "You're in an environment where every day you're seeing something on the front page of the paper, you're getting one side of the story, and it became a feeding frenzy," he recalled.)

Still, some reporters thought Trump's decision to fan the flames of coverage rather than trying to stamp out the fire demonstrated a counterintuitive, media-savvy genius. "He understood that if you're completely shameless and have the knack to turn things to your advantage, there's no such thing as bad publicity," said Taylor, the former *New York* magazine writer. "That situation with Marla and Ivana was a perfect example; he was able to spin it like he was this irresistible macho guy who was being chased by these blond beauties all over town." The day the "Best Sex" story ran, Taylor interviewed Trump in his office. His marriage was in shambles, yet he had personally called Taylor back within hours. Taylor arrived, walked past the gallery of magazine covers featuring Donald Trump, and found his subject sitting behind his desk, relaxed as ever. Trump didn't seem particularly troubled. All he could talk about was how much press attention his and Ivana's impending break was getting: "I've never seen anything like it in my life. I don't think there has been anything like this. One day it was eight pages in the tabloids. Even the *Times* is doing it. . . . One of the papers has twelve reporters on it."

Taylor noted that the recent divorce of director Steven Spielberg and actress Amy Irving was also generating a lot of press attention, but Trump dismissively waved away the comparison, calling it "a one-day wonder." Trump called the "Best Sex" story "cheap," but added that he had just heard the paper was impossible to find on newsstands citywide. Later, Taylor mentioned that he had just gotten back from London. Trump wanted to know how his breakup was playing across the ocean: "Was it big over there, too? I heard it's a monster over there."

Taylor's story, titled "Trump: The Soap," quoted "one Trump executive" about how the sensational tabloid coverage resulted in booming casinos and a booked-up Plaza Hotel. A few weeks later, a similar quote appeared in a *Wall Street Journal* story about Trump's decision to invest in Atlantic City. This time, the words came not from an anonymous source, but from Trump. His Trump Taj Mahal casino was about to open, and since his breakup and the crush of coverage, the casino's staff had seen a spike in media requests to cover the opening. Trump was pleased: "A divorce is never a pleasant thing, but from a business standpoint, it's had a very positive effect."

The business was always at the center of life; Trump had absorbed that from his father. Success was defined—and created—in good measure by reputation and image; he learned that from Roy Cohn. Now Trump added his own ingredient: as he pivoted from real estate developer to a far more expansive sense of Trump the brand, he began to use his celebrity not merely to promote his buildings but to erect a network of ventures in gambling, sports, beauty pageants, television—an ever-morphing array of ways to send the message that *Trump* meant ambition, wealth, and a distinctly personal expression of success. Some of his initiatives would flop and some would make piles of money, but at the core of all of them would be his identity, his carefully honed image as artisan of the deal, his insistence that he—and not a staff or a corporation, but he himself—was the rainmaker. Everything else served that idea—his relations with women, bankers, the media, the broader public. People were always asking him who the real Donald Trump was—was the bombastic, boastful billionaire he played in the media merely a character designed to enhance his business? They didn't get it, he insisted. He was exactly what he presented to the public: a man of business, in it for himself, in it to win. He would speak in "truthful hyperbole." He would crush opponents. He would demean "losers." He would choose to spend time in the office rather than with his wives or children. He would do what it took. And he would gamble, reaching now beyond Manhattan to a sorry seaside city in New Jersey that he believed he could remake in his own image.

7

All In

In the summer of 1978, thirty-two-year-old Donald Trump boarded a seaplane to Atlantic City, anxious to learn about the millions of dollars in profits reaped by Resorts International, the owner of the first casino on the East Coast. So much cash was coming in so fast that Resorts stored it in bags stashed in hotel rooms before it could be counted. Yet as Trump strolled the boardwalk and viewed the dilapidated buildings, he saw a city in need of a savior.

For generations, Atlantic City had conjured an image of seaside beauty and romance. City dwellers flocked to its shores, at first seeking a health retreat. The cool ocean breezes earned it the nickname "the lungs of Philadelphia." In 1921, the city played host to the first Miss America contest, one of many events that made Atlantic City an East Coast entertainment magnet. Hotels lined the beachfront boardwalk, and the city's accessibility by train made day trips a possibility for families—known as shoobies—who packed their picnic lunches in shoeboxes.

The city's fortunes waned as tastes and fashions changed. During World War II, the army and air force took over the city's hotels, and in 1944 a hurricane destroyed much of the famous seven-mile-long boardwalk. The number of visitors fell over the next two decades as white flight and urban blight drove up crime and depleted the city of jobs, and interstate highways drew people to new suburban developments. Atlantic City's population dropped from sixty-six thousand in 1930 to around forty thousand in 1980. The resort remained in the public imagination as a place of wedding-cake hotels, saltwater-taffy stands, and beauty pageants, but the financial reality was harsh. Atlantic City seemed to be dying, and nothing city officials attempted was helping. In desperation, New Jersey legalized gambling in 1977 and enshrined in the law the dream of "the restoration of Atlantic City as the Playground of the World and the major hospitality center of the Eastern United States." A year later, as Resorts International's casino-hotel provided evidence the dream was becoming reality, Trump arrived on his scouting mission.

Trump had hoped his home state of New York would legalize gambling. He had suggested putting a casino in his midtown Manhattan property, the Grand Hyatt. This visit to New Jersey sent a not-so-subtle message: if New York wouldn't let him build a casino in Manhattan, Trump would shift his focus across the Hudson River. Property in Atlantic City was cheaper than in Manhattan, and partners were willing to bear much of the risk on Trump's behalf. The legalization effort in New York faltered, and Trump decided to invest in New Jersey. On his visit to Atlantic City, Trump stopped at an ice cream shop and met with a real estate broker to discuss acquiring land for a casino. Trump had no experience with gaming or casino management, but local officials didn't mind; they were interested in his reputed wealth. Anyone was welcome to apply for a casino license, so long as the applicant followed a strict set of regulations and had no ties to organized crime. The first year after legalization, thirty-six corporations filed proposals for gaming halls. As Trump pondered his plans over the next two years, half a dozen casinos began operation. Trump toured one of the new hotels, the Tropicana, insisting that the casino's gaming chief show him every floor of the building.

As Trump focused on key parcels along the Boardwalk, he portrayed himself to Atlantic City officials as a young mogul. Indeed, he had received millions in commissions on deals in New York, including a fee for brokering the acquisition of land for Trump Tower. He drove a Mercedes-Benz SL two-door coupe and used a Cadillac limousine leased by his real estate company. At thirty-four years old in early 1981, however, he still tapped his father for cash. He had recently borrowed $7.5 million from Fred Trump to help pay off debt he had accumulated partly while advancing plans for Atlantic City.

Trump had to be licensed to run a casino, and that required a financial review and background check. When gaming regulators examined Trump's finances, they concluded that his organization would carry a lot of debt. Trump told regulators that he would raise $175 million to launch his business in Atlantic City by leveraging his existing real estate holdings. Under his plan, one loan for $100 million was to be secured by his 50 percent stake in the Grand Hyatt. The remaining amount was to be secured by a lien on a casino hotel in Atlantic City— a building that did not even exist. Trump was asking state gaming officials to have faith in him, not necessarily in the money that he had on hand.

Under state law, Trump was obligated to disclose whether he had "ever been cited or charged with or formally accused of any violation of a statute, regulation or code of any state, county, municipal, federal or national government other than a criminal, disorderly persons or motor vehicle violation." Trump initially neglected to tell the Casino Control Commission about the Justice Department's civil rights lawsuit that he had faced for racial bias several years earlier. Eventually, as his background check unfolded, Trump disclosed the case in conversations with gaming regulators.

THE BACKGROUND CHECK ALSO found that Trump had been in contact with people associated with organized crime. This was supposed to be a red flag. When Governor Brendan Byrne signed New Jersey's gambling law, he declared, "I've said it before and I will repeat it again to organized crime: Keep your filthy hands off Atlantic City. Keep the hell out of our state." There was good reason for concern. A review by the State Commission of Investigation found that as early as 1974, not long after gambling had been proposed, there was an "incipient pattern of organized crime infiltration of certain legitimate enterprises," including cigarette-vending firms and local Atlantic City taverns. The mob wanted a piece of the action.

In June 1980, as Trump intensified his search for property, he focused on a piece of land along the boardwalk that had been acquired weeks earlier by two men with questionable connections. One was an associate of the Scarfo crime family in Philadelphia, a violent organi-zation that had a tight grip on the twenty-thousand-member union that represented hotel and casino workers in Atlantic City. The Scarfo associate, Kenny Shapiro, was a former scrap-metal dealer in Philadel-phia who became a real estate developer on the Jersey Shore. Shapiro served as a financier for Scarfo in South Jersey and Philadelphia. He worked closely with Daniel Sullivan, a former truck driver and Team-ster who owned a trash-hauling business and would later be named in a court case as an FBI informant.

The parcel's location was perfect, next to the city's landmark Con-vention Hall. Trump and his organization came calling almost imme-diately. In July, Trump agreed to pay tens of millions in leasing fees for the property over the next fifteen years. The windfall for Sullivan, Shapiro, and their small firm was extraordinary. In addition, Trump told investigators that he was so impressed with Sullivan's negotiating skills that he recommended him for a job at the Grand Hyatt in New York. Trump hired Sullivan as a negotiator to smooth out "labor prob-lems" with the union representing hotel and restaurant employees at the Grand Hyatt. Trump arranged for Sullivan to meet with Trump's personal banker at Chase Manhattan Bank, an introduction that led to a multimillion-dollar loan for Sullivan. Casino regulators became concerned and began to examine the connections.

Trump said years later he had not known Sullivan or Shapiro well. He considered them "tough guys" and once heard a rumor that Sullivan had been the one who had killed onetime Teamster union chief Jimmy Hoffa, who famously went missing in 1975 and was never seen again. "Because I heard that rumor, I kept my guard up," Trump remembered. "I said, 'Hey, I don't want to be friends with this guy.'" But Trump told the Casino Control Commission in 1982, "I don't think there's anything wrong with these people. Many of them have been in Atlantic City for many, many years, and I think they are well thought of."

Trump, however, was aware of mob involvement in Atlantic City. In confidential conversations with FBI agents, who contacted him in April 1981 about the Mafia's role, Trump said he "had read in the press media and had heard from various acquaintances that organized crime elements were known to operate in Atlantic City." An FBI summary said Trump had told agents "he wanted to build a casino in Atlantic City, but he did not want to tarnish his family's name." After questions surfaced publicly about Sullivan and Shapiro's involvement in Trump's proposal, the commission delayed final approval of his casino license. The commission told him to disentangle himself from the Scarfo association by canceling the lease on the property and buying the land outright instead.

Even then, the sale provided a hefty windfall for Sullivan and Shapiro. Trump paid them $8 million—nearly three times what the pair had paid for the land just three years before.

ON MARCH 14, 1982, the Casino Control Commission took up Trump's application for a casino license. Trump wanted to build the city's largest casino-hotel, thirty-nine stories with 614 rooms. Atlantic City officials all but bowed before him. It didn't matter that he had no experience running a casino, had not assembled financing, and had been investigated for dealings with organized crime figures. To the officials, Trump's presence showed the city was on its way back. "People were excited that someone was coming who was not just another operator out of Nevada," said then-commissioner Carl Zeitz. The license was approved in less than two hours.

Now, as Trump moved ahead with his plans, he stoked his image with flair, wearing a black suit, white shirt, and blue or red tie under a black overcoat with a velvet collar. New York City reporters and gossip columnists regularly followed him. His timing seemed grand. Some analysts predicted Atlantic City might overtake Las Vegas as the country's premier gambling mecca by the end of the decade. Yet Trump needed a partner who could help him finance and run the casino. To entice someone to join him, he performed an illusion.

In June 1982, Trump hosted board members from Harrah's, a subsidiary of Holiday Corp., the company that also owned Holiday Inn, at the site of his proposed casino—the land Trump had leased and later bought from Sullivan and Shapiro. The Trump Organization had done little work at the construction site. To impress the Harrah's officials, Trump told a crew to dig up dirt and push the piles around the two-acre lot. Trump instructed the workers to make it look like "the most active construction site in the history of the world." On the tour, a Harrah's official asked why one of the workers was quickly filling a hole he had just dug. Trump was relieved when the questioner was not more skeptical. Trump would recall with glee his little deception: "The [Harrah's] board walked away from the site absolutely convinced that it was the perfect choice."

Three weeks later, Harrah's agreed to invest $50 million up front, arrange for construction financing, and manage the casino-hotel after it was completed. For his part, Trump assumed virtually no risk. In exchange for half the profits, he supplied the casino license and the land, and he agreed to build the property for an additional construction fee. When the casino-hotel was under construction in 1983, Trump's father, Fred, paid a visit to Atlantic City. As a field engineer on the project gave him a tour of the site, Fred looked out over the steel framework taking shape along the boardwalk and marveled with pride, "I told Donald to stay out of Manhattan and now look at him."

Trump now had a stake in his first casino, Harrah's at Trump Plaza, which opened in spring 1984. It towered above the boardwalk, the tallest building in Atlantic City, with sleek lines and neon lights that contrasted with the monolithic dome of the Convention Hall next door. But the debut was marred by malfunctioning slot machines and fire alarms, and the money didn't come rolling in as expected. The first year's results brought in half of projected profits. Trump blamed part of the problem on the name and began a campaign to eliminate the reference to Harrah's. He reasoned that gamblers confused the casino with the other Harrah's Atlantic City property. Trump insisted the property should be called Trump Plaza, saying he "created the value that exists in my name" and accusing Harrah's of running the property poorly. "I gave them a Lamborghini, and they didn't know how to turn on the key," Trump said. A Harrah's executive responded that Trump's "unsupportable falsehoods" had undermined their partnership. After lawsuits and countersuits, Harrah's sold its 50 percent stake, giving Trump full ownership of what was now unambiguously the Trump Plaza Hotel & Casino.

• • •

TRUMP HAD A VICTORY, but he wasn't satisfied with one casino. In February 1985, a remarkable opportunity to acquire another presented itself. The Hilton Corp. was putting the finishing touches on a $270 million casino-hotel across town in the marina district. The company, run by chairman Barron Hilton, had already hired more than one thousand workers. But with opening day just three months away, the Casino Control Commission surprised Hilton by denying the company an operating license because of Hilton's ties with a reputed mob lawyer. (The commission did not make an issue of Trump's reliance on his lawyer, Roy Cohn, who had represented New York's Mafia families.)

Trump seized on Hilton's misfortune, offering to buy the place since he had already been qualified for a license. That spring, he agreed to pay $320 million, beating out Las Vegas casino mogul Steve Wynn. It was an extraordinary gamble. Trump had never set foot inside the casino, ignoring his father's admonition to carefully inspect even small properties before making an investment. As a young man, Trump had watched his father check everything from the sink to the boiler. "If I'd told my father" that he hadn't gone inside the Hilton property, Trump later confessed, "he'd have said I'd lost my mind." Trump acknowledged that he would have to take financial responsibility amid doubts that the market could support the casino, but he was convinced the property would "earn a ton of money."

Trump now had his second casino, comparable in size to his first, a sixty-thousand-square-foot hotel with 615 rooms and a three-thousand-space parking garage. It would become known as Trump Castle Hotel & Casino. It sat on the west side of the barrier island, away from the boardwalk and next to a marina, featuring bright lights arrayed as crowns, inspiring its advertising slogan as the "crown jewel of Atlantic City." Now Trump just needed somebody to help run it. He consulted friends, colleagues, experts. His choice shocked nearly everyone: he picked his wife, Ivana. She, like Donald, had no experience running a casino. But she did have a sense of style, albeit an expensive sense, and she did have Donald's trust, at least at the start. He called her "a natural manager." Some of Trump's friends later wondered whether he put her there so he could have affairs with women in Manhattan, or to get her away from his construction projects in New

York. In any case, she had an important role, serving as vice president and chief operating officer of Trump Castle, where she was now finally treated as the boss, not just the boss's wife. She would often infuriate other Trump executives, who viewed her as boosting the Castle at the expense of the Plaza casino. The intracorporate competition, other Trump officials believed, was a sign of difficulties to come.

TRUMP EVENTUALLY REALIZED THAT he needed executives with a strong background in running casinos. He scouted the competition and picked Stephen Hyde, a devout Mormon with a large family. The Church of Latter-day Saints opposed gambling, but the casino industry employed many Mormons in key positions, in part because executives believed the faithful wouldn't be tempted to bet. Hyde was soft-spoken, unflappable, and widely considered one of the nation's savviest gaming executives, having most recently worked for Trump's competitor Steve Wynn. Trump, who once wrote, "I can be a screamer," would occasionally humiliate Hyde by cursing him out in front of other executives. Yet Trump recognized Hyde's capabilities and entrusted him with a business potentially worth billions of dollars. Hyde was, Trump wrote, "a very sharp guy and highly competitive, but most of all, he had a sense of how to manage to the bottom line." Trump throughout his career would rely on small circles of advisers, and Hyde became one of Trump's most trusted associates at the time. That meant some other senior executives felt shut out, unable to convey their concerns to Trump without going through the tight inner circle. Hyde was at the top of that chain of command.

Hyde's colleagues marveled at his ability to anticipate Trump's moods and protect midlevel staff from outbursts. Trump sometimes dropped in on his casinos without warning, polling low-level employees about the performance of managers and commenting on the appearance of the facilities. He once fired a director at the Castle after he found four cigarette butts in a stairwell used exclusively by casino employees. At the Plaza casino, Hyde often followed Trump, smoothing over abrasive or awkward interactions with workers or customers. Hyde became adept at gently steering the boss to see things his way. The two would talk on the phone for hours, sometimes late at night, about personal matters. One former colleague said Hyde "may have been the only person Donald truly trusted . . . as close a friend as Trump ever had." He was one executive Trump could not afford to lose.

AS HE BUILT HIS empire, Trump became increasingly aggressive fighting his competitors. Starting in mid-1986, he went on a stock-buying spree using borrowed money. He spent $70 million to snap up shares of Holiday Inn—the parent of Harrah's, his bitter rival and former partner. Next, he spent about $62 million to buy 10 percent of Bally Manufacturing Corp., which also owned a competing casino in Atlantic City. Trump insisted he was merely pursuing investment opportunities. The competitors saw the stock purchases as precursors to a hostile takeover and they took drastic action, taking on additional debt to make themselves less desirable takeover targets. Trump backed off, but made big profits. He sold his Holiday Inn stock for more than $12 million in gains. Bally agreed to buy back Trump's stock at a premium in a private transaction. The companies were left reeling.

These deals did not sit well with the Casino Control Commission, in part because Bally's efforts to fend off Trump had sent it into a financial tailspin. Commission members accused Trump of "greenmail," the practice of threatening a takeover to extract premium prices for stock. At an April 1987 hearing, Trump was asked if he had intended to damage the company. "Not at all," he said. "The practice is a totally legal practice."

Outraged, the commission's chairman, Walter N. Read, accused the Trump Organization of using its casino licenses "as a weapon to weaken or undercut the financial integrity of its competitors." Read warned that he would vote to revoke the license of any casino operator who did the same in the future. But in the end, the commission gave Trump a pass, renewing his license. The Federal Trade Commission, however, said Trump was not in compliance with regulations designed to prevent anticompetitive mergers or acquisitions. In 1988, the US Justice Department alleged that Trump had not provided timely notice to authorities when he bought the stock in Holiday Corp. and Bally, as required by federal antitrust laws. Trump did not admit violating the law but agreed to settle the complaint by paying a $750,000 penalty.

TRUMP WAS ALLOWED TO own three casinos in Atlantic City, and he had only two, so he began scouting properties. His strategy would prove risky. One company, for example, could market two casinos to different types of gamblers, working-class in one and high rollers from around the world in another. But a third casino might cannibalize customers and earnings of the other two, sending all three into a tailspin. Still, Trump had made up his mind. He wanted more. A troubled casino project being built by Resorts International caught his eye. The Resorts property became available unexpectedly, just as the Hilton casino had. Resorts' founder, James Crosby, had died during surgery the year before, and the firm's profits waned. Over the previous three years, Resorts had poured as much as $500 million into Crosby's grand vision for a new casino: the one-thousand-room Taj Mahal. It was only half completed, with construction funding running low, when Trump made his move. Some would have considered the Taj a money pit. Two of Trump's closest advisers argued against investing in it. Trump, now forty, saw it as a potential money machine. He made deals to buy shares of Resorts stock from Crosby's heirs, seeking to take control of the company. With three casinos, he expected to dominate gambling on the East Coast.

Trump seemed poised for triumph. A year earlier, *Forbes* had estimated that he was the fiftieth wealthiest American, worth $700 million. He kept buying "trophy" properties that fed the image that he had money to burn. He spent $29 million on one of the world's largest yachts, formerly owned by Saudi arms dealer Adnan Khashoggi, and another $8 million to refurbish it. He called it the *Trump Princess* and planned to offset the expense by leasing it to the Castle for $400,000 a month—a major financial drain on the property. The 282-foot-long vessel came with a helipad, a swimming pool, a disco, a movie-screening room, and two hundred telephones and could accommodate a crew of fifty-two. Trump gold-plated the sinks and even the screws. He didn't care much about sailing. The *Princess* was to be a docked spectacle to enhance the Trump brand, a place where high-roller gamblers could cavort. After the yacht was unveiled to an admiring public, Trump headed from the *Princess* to the Castle with an entourage in tow. A bystander shouted, "Be our next president, Donald."

It seemed that Trump couldn't spend fast enough. In 1988, he had paid $365 million to buy airplanes and routes from Eastern Airlines, which he turned into a Northeastern shuttle service. And he shelled out $407 million for the Plaza Hotel, the iconic château-style building across from Manhattan's Central Park. In both cases, he borrowed most of the money, and analysts said he overpaid. The purchases loaded him up with debt at the same time he was ramping up his gambling empire by the boardwalk, and both moves would come to haunt him.

To Atlantic City boosters at the time, however, Trump appeared to be the savior he had promised to be, and they applauded his verve. Here was the ultimate showman, reputedly one of the nation's richest men, almost single-handedly reviving the resort town. "He came in, in 1988, and said, 'I've done this, I've done that, I've done the other thing, everything I've ever touched has been successful,'" said Steve Perskie, a state legislator who drafted the bill that legalized gambling and later became chairman of the Casino Control Commission. "Everybody said, 'Great, terrific, you're Donald Trump, you're too big to fail.'" There was, however, a potential downside. If Trump failed, he might bring down much of Atlantic City with him. Trump had bet on the city, but it had also bet on him. And there was reason to be nervous.

Trump's plan to take over Resorts and complete the Taj was audacious. The projected completion costs of the Taj had ballooned to more than $800 million and were rising. To profit from his investment, Trump had to finish the Taj and do it as financing was becoming difficult to arrange. At the same time, the gambling market was becoming more complex. Revenue in Atlantic City had risen to record levels, but casino profits had dropped because of mismanagement and fierce competition. In 1986, the city's casinos recorded $2.5 billion in gambling revenue but only $74 million in profit. One man in particular began to express concerns—a man little known outside the casino world, but whose judgments were closely watched within the industry.

• • •

MARVIN ROFFMAN SAW PROBLEMS looming. He had long been fascinated by the casino business, which led him to be a gaming-securities analyst for the Philadelphia-based Janney Montgomery Scott. He specialized in the Atlantic City scene, and he spoke out about both the promises and risks of the business, providing strong opinions and data to reporters, casino operators, and investors, including Trump and his executives. Roffman was like the theater critic in a city with a handful of playhouses; his words mattered. So when he said in June 1987 that the opening of the Taj Mahal would put pressure on profits, Atlantic City operators paid attention. When he predicted that tougher years lay ahead, casino owners listened.

Trump was undaunted. In July 1987, he completed the $79 million purchase of 72 percent of Resorts' voting shares, became chairman, and installed his brother Robert and another associate on the board. Donald promptly began looking for side deals that could bring him quick riches. He didn't act merely as an investor or a manager; he pushed for a lucrative "comprehensive services agreement" that would require Resorts to pay him to arrange for financing and manage the Taj's construction. The agreement was estimated to be worth $108 million over five years. Resorts would eventually bend to Trump's request.

Trump's power seemed to be hitting new highs. He had just finished working on his first book, *Trump: The Art of the Deal*, with journalist Tony Schwartz, which was already creating buzz. Trump's Atlantic City casinos were ordered to boost sales by buying eight thousand copies, which they would first try to sell to guests and then give away. The book portrayed Trump as a brilliant dealmaker who got the better of his partners, not to mention his enemies.

Then, just days before *Trump: The Art of the Deal* was to be published, the economy tanked. On October 19, 1987, which became known as Black Monday, the Dow Jones Industrial Average plunged by almost 23 percent. The crisis presented an intriguing opportunity for Trump. The crash accelerated a decline in the price of Resorts stock. While Trump had bought a majority of voting shares, known as Class B, he now offered to buy all of the common shares, known as Class A. This brash, unexpected move would allow Trump to take the company private and, he reasoned, more easily raise money to finish the Taj. In a news release, Trump offered gambling regulators a tough choice: they could support his new direction, or he would walk away and the Taj project would languish. He warned, "Only with the financial backing of the Trump Organization will it be possible to build the Taj Mahal."

Trump would need to go deeply in debt to build the Taj. In a city of gamblers, Trump would be one of the biggest.

IN FEBRUARY 1988, TRUMP appeared at a licensing hearing before the state Casino Control Commission. A major issue was whether, in the wake of the market crash, Trump could still get financing. Trump replied that after he took control of the Taj casino, bankers would respond well to his request for a loan. Trump even suggested that the bankers would line up to give him money. There was one thing he would not do, he assured the commission. He would not seek risky, high-interest junk bonds, which had propelled a takeover craze. Junk bonds, Trump testified, "are ridiculous. The funny thing with junk bonds is that junk bonds [are] what really made the companies junk." Trump said banks were willing to give him loans at prime rate—then 9 percent or less—far below what other developers could hope for: "I mean, the banks call me all the time. 'Can we loan you money? Can we do this? Can we do that?'"

The commission and its lawyers expressed skepticism. How could Trump get such a good deal when others had to pay so much more to borrow? "It's easier to finance if Donald Trump owns it," he explained. "With me, they know there's a certainty they would get their interest." Trump said he held another appeal for bankers: "I get it done, and everybody is happy and it turns out successfully."

Michael Vukcevich, the state deputy attorney general, asked Trump, "Is there anything that can go wrong, that you're aware of?"

"Can go wrong? Yes. We can have a depression," Trump replied. "The world could collapse. We could have World War Three. I mean, a lot of things can go wrong. I don't think they will."

Commissioners pressed Trump about his plans to raise spending on the Taj to $1 billion, with added luxury suites, gourmet restaurants, and opulent fixtures, something the commission referred to as "extras." "Don't people have to live within their means?" asked commissioner E. Kenneth Burdge.

Trump said the added costs were insignificant yet necessary to impress customers. "We are probably talking about a difference of fifty million dollars or so," he said. "I mean, the worst thing to happen with the Taj Mahal is for the building to open and for people to have been disappointed with it. Because word of mouth on something like this, it's like a Broadway show." Trump later assured the commission, "My basic attitude has always been that I want to do what is good for Atlantic City."

This was welcome news for a legion of small-business owners, many of whom considered Trump one of the city's great benefactors. The Taj would only add more luster to the city's greatest boom in decades, building a solid foundation for the local contractors, suppliers, and others whose work was integral to casino operations. Marty Rosenberg, who co-owned Atlantic Plate Glass Co., a family-owned company, had great confidence in Trump, who had paid him money he was due from the stalled Resorts construction. Trump's organization gave the firm as much work as it could handle, including installation of the reflective exterior glass that helped give the Taj its glitz. It was a lucrative time, and laborers worked around the clock. The dollars flowed, and the goal was to open on time. "It was an explosion, absolutely an explosion," Rosenberg said. "It meant financial stability. It was a boom time."

AS TRUMP TRIED TO persuade regulators that he had the money to complete the Taj, trouble arose with one of his existing properties, the Castle casino, the one he had put under Ivana's control. "Isn't this the best property in town?" Trump asked a top aide. "What's wrong? Why isn't this place working?"

One reason was the construction of a fourteen-story addition to the hotel, a tower that was well under way by early 1988 and already straining the Castle's bottom line. Ivana had insisted on the $40 million addition with ninety-seven luxury suites to attract high rollers, and Trump had agreed, against the advice of his other executives. Now the Castle was in the red and would end up with a net loss that year for the first time. Ivana's clashes with other Trump executives had escalated. One former Trump aide said Ivana resented having to report to Hyde, as well as the close relationship between Hyde and Trump. Trump's executives, meanwhile, continued to fume that Ivana was siphoning gamblers from the company's other properties in Atlantic City instead of attracting new customers.

At the same time, some of those executives felt sympathy for Ivana, having learned that Trump was having an affair with Marla Maples, an actress and model in New York. In the end, Trump removed Ivana from the casino and dispatched her back to New York to run his newly acquired Plaza Hotel. It was a bittersweet moment for Ivana. At a good-bye ceremony at the Castle, she sobbed as she thanked her colleagues and told them she'd miss them. Then her husband addressed the employees: "Look at this. I had to buy a $350 million hotel just to get her out of here and look at how she's crying. Now that's why I'm sending her back to New York. I don't need this, some woman crying. I need somebody strong in here to take care of this place."

TRUMP FACED NEW QUESTIONS about his plans to take Resorts private and gain control of the Taj. At a hearing in mid-February 1988, Casino Control commissioner Valerie Armstrong expressed frustration, saying Trump's testimony about his Resorts takeover was "laced with hyperbole, contradictions, and generalities that make it difficult to evaluate" his fitness for licensing as the company's owner. She wondered whether Trump had a hand in driving Resorts' stock price down so he could take the company private.

"While it might be possible to conclude that the events of the past eight months resulted from happenstance, impulse, fate, and/or events beyond Trump's or Resorts' control, it is also just as easy, perhaps easier, to conclude that many of the events leading to Mr. Trump's current [takeover] proposal have been carefully staged, manipulated, and orchestrated," Armstrong said at the hearing. But she eventually joined the rest of the commission in backing Trump after he provided assurances about his plans.

A few weeks later, just as Trump's plan to take Resorts private was set to go through, Merv Griffin, the television host and producer, made a competing, top-dollar offer. Griffin said he would pay $245 million for Resorts if Trump would vote for Griffin's takeover and can-

cel Trump's services agreement. Trump declined, and the two fought
a highly publicized battle for weeks. In May, they agreed to a complicated settlement that split the company and its assets. Griffin got the
existing Resorts casinos in Atlantic City as well as one in the Bahamas.
Trump received a substantial payment to release Resorts from his services agreement. More important, Trump got the Taj.

"Our compromise, which gave me $12 million and the unfinished
Taj Mahal, turned out to be one of the best deals I ever made," Trump
wrote in *Trump: The Art of the Comeback.* "At the time, I thought his
chances of making Resorts successful were about as good as [Grif-
fin's] chances of getting [actress] Sharon Stone pregnant." Within days,
Trump formed a company, Trump Taj Mahal Funding, to seek money
for the construction. All the promises that Trump had made to the
commission about bankers practically banging on his door with hundreds of millions of dollars couldn't be fulfilled. He could not line up
loans at the prime rate as he had expected. He seemed to have only one
option: the junk bonds that he had so stridently derided. A company
that used junk bonds was junk, he had said. Now he saw them as his
only solution. As he put it decades later, "I was able to put a tremendous amount of junk bonds on properties that I had in Atlantic City,
and, therefore, take out money. . . . In fact, I wanted X dollars, and
they said, 'How about if we give you twice as much?' I said, 'I'll take it,'
but I also knew that if you do that, there'll be problems down the road.
But I was able to take a lot of money out of Atlantic City."

In November 1988, Trump agreed to a deal with Merrill Lynch
Capital Markets, which agreed to issue and sell $675 million in junk
bonds, set to pay an interest rate of 14 percent, 5 percent above prime.
That would give Trump the money he needed to build the Taj, but he
would have to pay about $95 million a year in interest, not counting the
debt from his other casinos and holdings. Undeterred by the burden,
Trump wanted his trophy, and his costs kept escalating. "The Taj was
going to be the biggest and the best and greatest," recalled Paul Rubeli,
former chief of gaming operations for the Tropicana in Atlantic City.
"As Donald would say, 'It was going to be huge.'" Trump's Taj Mahal
was going to be bigger and costlier than anything its original developer
had envisioned. The complex would include 1,250 hotel rooms, feature

a 120,000-square-foot casino, and employ about 5,800, a major boost to the local economy.

Trump charged ahead despite growing concerns about Atlantic City. In July 1989, Roffman, the market analyst, issued another gloomy report for investors. Its headline: "Atlantic City, New Jersey—Top Heavy in Debt—Houses of Cards." Roffman's message was stark. Five years earlier, the city's nine casinos had recorded almost $169 million in profit on winnings of almost $1.8 billion. By 1988, total profit had dwindled to under $15 million, even though winnings had soared to $2.7 billion. The problem was debt. "The Taj itself looks like a big gamble," Roffman wrote.

In the midst of his dealmaking, Trump took a moment to call Roffman. "Marvin, didn't I do a fantastic deal?" Trump asked, as the analyst recalled.

"I think you made a mistake, Donald," Roffman said. "Why own three casinos?"

Trump brushed it off. "This is going to be a monster property."

8

Cold Winds

The morning of October 10, 1989, dawned bright and sunny, a perfect day for flying. That seemed like good fortune for Stephen Hyde, Trump's confidant and president of his Atlantic City operations, even if the boss was grumpy about the Manhattan news conference where Hyde and two other top casino officials would join Trump. At first, Trump had dismissed the importance of Héctor "Macho Man" Camacho's upcoming boxing match against Vinny Pazienza at the Atlantic City convention center. "It's not going to be a big fight. The public doesn't care about this. I'm not coming," Trump said. "I can't be attending every shitty little press conference. It's not dignified." Hyde, however, persuaded Trump that an appearance by the boss himself was especially important for this, the first fight promoted by a subsidiary called Trump Sports and Entertainment. Trump agreed and went all in, arranging a media spectacle to hype the match.

The trio of Trump executives from Atlantic City buckled into the Sikorsky helicopter for the trip to Manhattan. Hyde had much on his mind, and not just about the upcoming opening of the Taj. The forty-three-year-old was considering how much longer he would stay with Trump. The stress of the work and its impact on his family had been intense. He had to put up with Trump's tirades while shielding others from the boss's wrath. Hyde had recently talked with a friend about leaving in a couple of years, moving to the West, the land of his childhood.

The second executive in the helicopter was Mark Grossinger Etess, thirty-eight, a descendant of the family that built Grossinger's resort in the Catskill Mountains north of New York City. His job in the Trump empire was crucial; as president and chief operating officer of the Taj casino and hotel, Etess was under great pressure to make sure its opening went perfectly. The third man, Jonathan Benanav, thirty-three, had a compelling family history. His grandmother had died in a Nazi concentration camp and his father barely escaped, hiding in the Romanian woods for six months before being liberated by Russian troops. His father left with six hundred Jews on a boat to Turkey. He met a woman on the refugee vessel and, three days later, married her. He became an officer in the Israeli army, and later they moved to the United States, where he and his wife raised their children, including Jonathan. Now Jonathan was executive vice president of Trump Plaza Hotel & Casino. He had recently bought his girlfriend an engagement ring, but had not yet given it to her. The trio had little to contribute at the promotion for the fight, other than a few words of predictable hype. But they went, expecting to smile for the cameras, meet briefly with Trump, and return to Atlantic City by early afternoon.

The press conference at the Plaza Hotel went according to script and attracted little coverage, but the three executives got delayed by their meeting with the boss at Trump Tower. They missed their ride back to Atlantic City on the Sikorsky. Hyde found a substitute flight via a charter company he had never before used. The helicopter, too, was a new experience, an Agusta, manufactured in Italy, instead of the usual Sikorsky. It was known as a comfortable, safe chopper, and Hyde, Benanav, and Etess made their way to a heliport on East Sixtieth Street for a 1:00 p.m. flight.

Unbeknownst to the three Trump executives, one of the helicopter's rotor blades had a nearly undetectable two-inch scrape, which had grown like an untreated wound.

NORMA FOERDERER, TRUMP'S LONGTIME aide, rushed into the boss's office on the twenty-sixth floor of Trump Tower. The helicopter that carried the three executives had gone down. Agonizing minutes went by. Then a New Jersey police official called with the news: no survivors. Three of Trump's most trusted aides, including the ones most responsible for opening the Taj, had perished, along with the crew of two. Trump would later learn that the scrape on one of the rotor blades had expanded during the flight, the result of metal fatigue. Over the pinelands of New Jersey, at an altitude of twenty-two hundred feet, a portion of the blade broke, the helicopter's aerodynamics went askew, and the aircraft split apart in midair, raining wreckage on the Garden State Parkway.

Trump was devastated. He asked if the families had been informed. As an aide watched, Trump sat in his office overlooking Central Park and called the families of the three men. "I have terrible news," he said into the phone, again and again. As word spread through the office, aides in the anterooms burst into tears, wailing loudly. Trump said years later that he learned what it is like when the military informs "the soldiers' families when they're gone. It's a very tough thing to do. I mean, the response was, like, horrible."

A few hours later, Trump took a call from John "Jack" O'Donnell, president of the Trump Plaza Hotel & Casino. O'Donnell already held a key position in Trump's life and business, and now his role grew exponentially. A tragic twist had saved his life. O'Donnell would normally have been on that helicopter trip. He had been close friends with Hyde and Etess and accompanied them to press conferences like today's. Compounding his grief, O'Donnell felt responsible for Benanav's being on the helicopter: he had asked his young associate to go to the press conference in his stead because O'Donnell was competing in a triathlon in Hawaii. For many years, O'Donnell would feel guilty that it was Benanav and not he who had died that day. But there was little time to think of all that; O'Donnell's job now was to commiserate with Trump and get back to Atlantic City as quickly as possible.

"Jack, this is awful," Trump told O'Donnell. "This is the most awful thing. We've been sitting here praying it wasn't true. I still can't believe it." The two talked again a few hours later, and Trump seemed even more shaken. Trump saw no choice but to board a helicopter to go to Atlantic City. The thought of retracing the flight taken by his executives left him rambling and musing about life. He seemed in disbelief. "I'm getting on a helicopter in an hour and I'm going down to see the families," Trump told O'Donnell. "A helicopter. Isn't it crazy? I guess life goes on. . . . You have to keep getting on planes, getting on the helicopters." O'Donnell later said Trump sounded, uncharacteristically, as if he was seeking reassurance: "For the first time since I had known him, I heard fear and uncertainty in his voice."

The Taj opening was looming and Trump's key executives were dead. O'Donnell temporarily picked up much of the responsibility. Now he saw Trump from a closer vantage. Privately, he was developing concerns about his boss.

THE DAY AFTER THE crash, Trump met with more than a hundred of his managers in an Atlantic City conference room. The loss of his three executives, and especially his friend Hyde, was sinking in. "I had my upper management wiped out," Trump recalled. (Thirty-five years after the crash, he still considered the loss of the three men one of the most important and difficult days of his life aside from the deaths of his parents and his brother Fred Jr.) As he sought to steady himself in the days after the accident, he offered an idea that was classic Trump. He would build a monument to them, "something just incredible."

Trump could not stop thinking about the crash. He wondered aloud to O'Donnell if the executives had been murdered by competitors. Then he dismissed his thoughts of sabotage after realizing that the three had booked an alternative flight at the last minute. A federal investigation concluded that the crash was accidental, caused by a "manufacturing-induced scratch in the spar of the blade." Something happened in the factory to make a barely detectable mark that led years later to catastrophe.

In Atlantic City, a place marketed as an escape from reality, the sudden tragedy seemed especially out of place. Trump was bereft, seeking support and sympathy, variously suggesting that he had almost boarded the helicopter or might have boarded it or could have. There were conflicting reports at the time about whether Trump was supposed to have been on the flight. Months later, on CNN, he said, "I was going to go. From the standpoint that they said, 'Do you want to come with us?' And I said, 'I think so, but maybe I'm just too busy.' I mean, it was that close. It would have been, like, a fifty-fifty deal." Trump's comment angered O'Donnell, who believed Trump was trying to shift attention to himself.

Trump served as a pallbearer for Etess, whose funeral was attended by a thousand people and was held in Northfield, New Jersey. The next day, Trump attended Benanav's funeral in Mount Vernon, New York. There, of all places, the messiness of Trump's love life played out before the mourners. Ivana accompanied her husband to the service. As Ivana emerged from the chapel, she saw Marla Maples. It was the first time some people had seen her. For months, Maples had stayed at Trump properties, often in Atlantic City. Ivana had learned about her husband's infidelity, but the women dueling for his affection had usually been kept apart. Now O'Donnell saw Ivana glare at Marla. "I was sure she was going to throw a punch at any moment," he later wrote. "Marla stood there petrified." Trump pulled Ivana away.

Last of all, Trump attended Hyde's funeral—which, like Etess's, was held in Northfield, New Jersey—before Hyde was buried in his hometown in Utah. Hundreds of mourners snaked outside the funeral home. Trump stared at Hyde's photograph and shed a tear, a lonely, shell-shocked look on his face. "For the first time, I saw sadness in it, profound sadness," O'Donnell recalled. Then, composure. The funerals were complete, the page turned. Trump's focus quickly returned to business. O'Donnell wrote later that he wondered whether Trump "cared about anyone other than himself, or if he harbored a sincere emotion." The Taj was supposed to open in a couple of months, although that would be delayed. The magnificent memorial would come one day. O'Donnell was, as Trump later put it, the only one "still standing." Trump turned to O'Donnell's wife and told her he had a lot riding on her husband. "Now," Trump said, "it's his turn."

O'DONNELL WAS AN ASTUTE observer of the way people take risks. He knew what loss was like: his parents had died when he was young; he was then adopted by his uncle, who had headed Bally Manufacturing, the gaming company. O'Donnell grew up inside the company, enthralled by the manufacture of slot machines. He worked in Las Vegas in his early twenties, then moved to Atlantic City, to a casino owned by Steve Wynn. Hyde hired him away to the Trump Plaza Hotel & Casino, where he was now president. O'Donnell had spent most of his adult life observing people gamble with their money, from senior citizens on buses to Trump's wager on Atlantic City. As a casino executive, his job was, in effect, to entice people to part with their hard-earned cash, on the chance that they might profit even if the odds were against them. His job, in part, was to sell the casino experience as theater.

Few casinos profit by attracting only the super-rich. As much as Trump focused on the high rollers, he needed the masses, the storekeepers, hourly workers, and retirees who took charter buses to the Jersey shore and fed coin after coin into slot machines, emboldened by the thrill and sparkle of it all. The attraction wasn't necessarily the long-shot bet that they could get rich; it was that they could, in this version of a reality show, *feel* rich, however briefly. Inevitably, a number of gamblers likely were compulsive, no more able to control the urge to bet than an addict seeking the next high. Trump himself cared little about the psychology of gambling, which had surprised O'Donnell. He learned over time that Trump had a simple mind-set, winners versus losers, and that his chief motivation was winning, even when he didn't need the money.

O'Donnell was frustrated that Trump put his name on buildings to attract customers but sometimes disdained interacting with most of them. "This is bullshit," Trump told O'Donnell one day as they walked to a meet and greet with gamblers. At the event, Trump complained about a gambler who had won big—meaning Trump lost. The boss left the reception after a short stay, saying, "That's it, I'm going." O'Donnell believed Trump needed more patience. It was simple math: the longer gamblers remained at the table, the more likely they were to lose. Trump just didn't like to see what happened in the interim. He couldn't stand being beat.

ON MARCH 20, 1990, two weeks before the Taj was slated to open, analyst Marvin Roffman's concerns about the casino market became big news. He was quoted in a *Wall Street Journal* story about the Taj, and the impact was immediate. The story said the casino-hotel had to gross up to $1.3 million or more every day to pay its bills and loans—more than any casino had ever taken in. "When this property opens, he will have had so much free publicity he will break every record in the books in April, June, and July," Roffman predicted. "But once the cold winds blow from October to February, it won't make it. The market just isn't there. . . . Atlantic City is an ugly and dreary kind of place. Even its hard-core customers aren't coming down as much."

On the morning that the *Journal* story was published, Roffman was scheduled to meet with Robert Trump, who was overseeing final preparations for the Taj's opening day. With the loss of the three executives, and the decision to send Ivana away from Atlantic City, Robert's role had deepened, and he faced added pressure as one of the few insiders Donald trusted. Robert—soft-spoken, cerebral, and empathetic—was a graduate of Boston University, a financial whiz. He lacked Donald's charismatic showmanship, and he was happy to leave the bravado to his brother, but he could show flashes of Trump temper. As Roffman arrived for his meeting with Robert, the gaming analyst didn't yet know that the *Journal* story had been published. He drove up to the Taj, looked over its extravagant features, and thought, "So this is what a billion dollars can buy."

Roffman found Robert Trump and extended his hand for a shake. Robert exploded. He said Roffman had stabbed the bondholders in the back. "Get the fuck off the property," Robert screamed. "Good-bye."

Roffman hustled away, rattled by the accusation that he had hurt bondholders. "I mean, every word out of his mouth was a four-letter word," Roffman recalled. He called his office and was told to return as soon as possible. Donald Trump had already faxed over a letter: "You will be hearing shortly from my lawyers unless Mr. Roffman is immediately dismissed or apologizes." Trump also phoned Roffman and urged him to "write me a letter stating that the Taj is going to be one of the greatest successes ever, and I'm going to have it published."

Roffman had risen to vice president of research. He loved his job. Yes, he had spoken bluntly, but he believed he had a fiduciary duty to do so. He was a gaming industry analyst, and at a time when some derided his profession for too much cheerleading, he took pride in making tough calls that proved accurate. Confronted by his company's chairman, Roffman declared that he believed the junk bonds that Trump relied upon "would fail." The chairman, according to Roffman, responded that he wasn't concerned about that judgment, but was very concerned about the analyst's comment that "Atlantic City is an ugly and dreary kind of place."

The chairman called Trump, who demanded that the *Journal* be told that Roffman had been misquoted, and that Roffman actually believed "the Taj Mahal is going to be the greatest success story ever." Roffman's boss drafted a letter of retraction, and Roffman felt he had no choice but to sign it. Yet Roffman could not sleep that night. The next morning, he told his bosses that he wanted to issue a recommendation that Taj bonds be "sold immediately" because he feared they would fall in value. But Roffman's firm wouldn't let him go public with that opinion, so the analyst wrote a letter in which he said he "basically canceled" the retraction he had signed. Roffman's bosses had had enough. Facing the threat of a Trump lawsuit, the company fired Roffman.

The story might have ended there, with Trump triumphant. But Roffman decided he had been right all along and fought back, saying his dismissal was unjustified. He entered an arbitration proceeding in which he got a $750,000 settlement from his firm. He also sued Trump, eventually agreeing to an undisclosed settlement. Years later, Trump said he could not recall reading any of Roffman's reports. He described Roffman's remarks in the *Journal* as a "vicious attack" and "not a nice thing on a human basis," but he said in a deposition that he had never intended to get Roffman fired. Trump said he only wanted Roffman to withdraw remarks that "were totally inappropriate."

EVERYTHING WAS NOW SET for the grand opening of the Trump Taj Mahal. Aside from some modest architectural echoes, it could not have been more different from its namesake, the ornate seventeenth-century marble mausoleum in India that the United Nations had declared "the jewel of Muslim art" in that country. Trump's Taj was grandiose, fanciful, outlandish, like nothing Atlantic City had ever before seen. Some called it cartoonish. The 120,000-square-foot casino, a low-slung building stretched along the boardwalk, sat across from the whirling amusement rides of the famous Steel Pier. Topped by dozens of minarets and onion domes in bubble-gum shades of pink, blue, and green, the Taj featured a forty-two-story hotel tower, though Trump numbered the top floor as the fifty-first. On each of the tower's four façades, at the highest point, Trump's name stood tall in red capital block letters.

The Taj's doormen, wearing purple robes and feathered turbans, guided guests through a lobby featuring Carrara marble imported from Italy. Deeper inside, the theme continued with restaurants such as the Bombay Café and New Delhi Deli and walls adorned with Indian murals. Above the baccarat tables, massive crystal chandeliers dangled from vaulted, mirrored ceilings. In the luxury suites, guests enjoyed marble and bronze statues and a sunken Jacuzzi tub surrounded by gold Greek columns.

For the moment, the dire warnings, the extraordinary debt, and the marital crisis were all overshadowed by a weeklong parade of opening events. These first nights were crucial: tens of thousands of gamblers were waiting to pour their dollars into Trump's hands, and he needed to make a perfect impression so they would return. The chrome had been polished, the employees were in place. But on the second morning, April 3, Trump learned that state regulators had ordered that the slot machines remain closed. The reason: a mysterious accounting discrepancy. Trump went ballistic. He phoned O'Donnell, Trump Plaza's president, and pleaded with him to handle the emergency at the Taj. "Jack, I'm at the Taj," Trump said, by O'Donnell's account. "I got big fucking problems over here. . . . I've been in meetings with the state all morning. They're not going to let me open. I've got a bunch of fucking idiots down here. . . . You have to come down here and straighten this out. . . . I'm going to fire all these assholes."

O'Donnell rushed to the Taj, where Trump was waiting. O'Donnell said he needed time to figure out the problems. Every minute was costing Trump thousands of dollars in profits. "What the fuck is going on?" he asked. One thing that was going on was that Trump had, six months earlier, received a warning from Deno Marino, the deputy director of New Jersey's Casino Control Commission. Marino had told Trump and his top managers that, with the Taj planning twenty-nine hundred slot machines—the most on any Atlantic City gambling floor—the casino needed a bigger "hard count room," the secured back area where, at the end of each day, coins and tokens are sorted, tallied, and readied for the next day's gamblers. "The place is already built," Trump had replied, by Marino's account. He was not about to move walls made of cinder block over quarter-inch steel.

Now, after the first night of the Taj's soft opening, the ripple effect of his failure to heed that advice was plain. The count-room workers were in a frenzy, unable to keep up. The room was unbearably hot. Marino, on the premises that night, made an exception to the rules, allowing a heavy steel door to an inner hallway to be opened to let cooler air flow in. When the count was finished, the tally was $220,000 less than an initial count from the slots themselves. Under state law, unless the amounts were in balance, regulators couldn't let the slot machines open the next day. In the eleven casinos he had opened before the Taj, Marino had never seen this kind of mess.

Marino broke the news to Trump, and the slots stayed closed all that day and most of the next. Finally, late on the third day of opening week, a worker on his way into the count room stubbed his toe. When he looked down, he saw that the steel door was propped open with a large, heavy canvas bag—the $220,000 in missing tokens. Trump couldn't believe it. Within days, the outer wall was knocked out so the room could be enlarged. O'Donnell recalled that during the same period "we found an entire room full of coin that no one knew about."

To the press, Trump was all smiles, insisting that the only problem the Taj had was that he was making so much money "we couldn't count it fast enough." (A headline in the *New York Times* echoed that view: "Taj Mahal's Slot Machines Halt, Overcome by Success.") Privately, Trump's tone was starkly different. He told O'Donnell he should "fucking fire people" to solve problems. "Don't leave here, Jack," Trump said, as O'Donnell recalled it. "Don't leave me."

Trump headed back to New York as O'Donnell scrambled to fix the problems. After some agonizing hours, the state agreed to let customers into the casino. In O'Donnell's mind, the opening was already a "colossal failure." But the public continued to know little of this. Most of the publicity was about the spectacular setting, the casino floors that went on seemingly forever, the length of three football fields. The halls echoed with the sound of coins clinking and dice falling and music playing and customers laughing, joyful melodies that meant money was being made, although not nearly enough in Trump's estimation.

Late that night, while O'Donnell was still working through problems at the Taj, Trump called him, wondering if the casino would have suffered such problems if Steve Hyde and Mark Etess had not been killed in the helicopter crash. O'Donnell responded that the two would have foreseen the problems and prevented a crisis. "I think these are Hyde's people in here, and I think that Hyde's people are responsible for this problem," Trump told O'Donnell. O'Donnell had long since concluded that Trump knew little about running casinos. A crop of stellar executives led by Hyde had been crucial to Trump's success. Now O'Donnell was upset that Trump seemed to be blaming their deceased colleagues for problems that O'Donnell believed were Trump's fault. O'Donnell concluded that Trump's style was to lash out when things weren't going well.

O'Donnell had seen the same kind of reaction when Trump once launched into a tirade against an accountant who was black. "I've got black accountants at Trump Castle and at Trump Plaza—black guys counting my money!" Trump said, according to O'Donnell's memoir, *Trumped!* "I hate it. The only kind of people I want counting my money are short guys that wear yarmulkes every day. Those are the kind of people I want counting my money. Nobody else. . . . Besides that, I've got to tell you something else. I think that the guy is lazy. And it's probably not his fault because laziness is a trait in blacks. It really is; I believe that. It's not anything they can control." O'Donnell admonished Trump not to talk that way, but he said Trump ignored him. (Years later, O'Donnell hired the accountant at his own business, testament to his belief that Trump had been wrong. Trump, asked about O'Donnell's memoir, said in 1997 that it was "probably true," but years later Trump said it was "fiction," even as he acknowledged, "I didn't read his book." Separately, Trump said, "I'm the least racist person that you've ever interviewed.")

Two days after the casino reopened, Trump flew in his helicopter from New York to Atlantic City, landed on the roof of Trump Castle, and made his way to the Taj for the grand conclusion of opening week. To the public, the imagery was spectacular: Trump had arranged for one of the biggest stars on the planet, Michael Jackson, to tour the Taj, and the two strode through the hotel and casino, an odd couple connected by wealth and celebrity, trailed by the media and mobbed by guests. Publicists made sure the media knew that Jackson was impressed with the $10,000-a-night Alexander the Great suite. More than one hundred thousand people toured the hotel, gawking at the glorious excess and the 167 gaming tables. This was to be one of the proudest moments of Trump's career. Hordes crowded him wherever he went.

As opening week came to a close, however, Trump met with his remaining management team. O'Donnell listened intently as Trump again said he wanted to fire anyone who had caused the problems: "I want the assholes out of here. I want people who are going to kick some ass. I want pricks. What I need are more nasty pricks in this company. Warriors." At yet another meeting, O'Donnell was with a group of executives, including Robert Trump, when Donald walked in. Donald shouted about a series of mishaps, saying, "We're going to lose a fortune!"

Robert spoke up: "Donald, you know there's just no way to predict these things."

"Robert, just never mind!" Trump replied, as O'Donnell recounted it. "I'm sure as hell not going to listen to you in this situation. I listened to you and you got me into this." Soon after that exchange, O'Donnell learned that Robert was gone. "He told his secretary to get some boxes," an executive told O'Donnell. "He said, 'I'm getting out of here. I don't need this.' And he got on a helicopter and went home." (In an interview for this book, Donald Trump disputed O'Donnell's account, saying his brother "never quit" and did a "really good job" at the casinos.)

In public, Trump spoke with pride to the crowds that had gathered to celebrate the grand opening. At once brash and eloquent, he praised the executives who had died in the helicopter crash, and he said opening week at the Taj had exceeded "my wildest expectations." He rubbed the giant Aladdin's lamp, and the image of a genie appeared. Laser lights and fireworks filled the sky, and customers rushed in. Publicists called the Taj the "Eighth Wonder of the World." Trump's former rival Merv Griffin predicted that the Taj would lift up Atlantic City. Television personality Robin Leach, speaking on his show, *Lifestyles of the Rich and Famous*, said just what Trump wanted to hear: "Donald's biggest gamble is turning up aces!"

9

The Chase

Ivana Trump moved along the line at Bonnie's, a popular cafeteria-style spot for skiers, midway up Aspen Mountain, celebrated for its apple strudel, hot spiced wine, and shockingly reasonable prices. In the same queue for food stood Marla Maples, the model and actress who was Donald's mistress. The Trumps—Ivana, Donald, and their three children—were spending the 1989 winter holidays in the postcard-perfect Colorado village. Not everything was copacetic between Donald and Ivana, however, especially after she overheard a conversation in their suite at the Little Nell, a five-star hotel that opened that year. "I did pick [up] the phone in the living room, and Donald did take the phone in bedroom," Ivana recalled. "He was talking about Marla. And I really didn't understand. I never heard a name like that in my life. And I came to Donald. I said, 'Who is Moola?'"

"Well, that's a girl which is going after me for last two years," Ivana recalled her husband saying.

At Bonnie's, Ivana saw Donald speak to a woman she believed was a friend of Maples's. In the queue, Ivana stepped up to the woman and told her, "I understand from my husband that you have a friend which is after my husband for last two years. Will you give her the message that I love my husband very much?" Ivana, an expert skier, returned to the slopes without a clue that Maples had been standing right behind her friend "because I never met her, I had no idea." Now, Maples came after Ivana—"just charged right behind me," Ivana recalled. In front of the Trump children, the mistress declared, "I'm Marla and I love your husband. Do you?"

"Get lost," Ivana snapped. "I love my husband very much." Her husband, rarely at a loss for comment, said "not anything, nothing," Ivana recalled. The tabloids reported he took to his skis and schussed away.

WOMEN HAVE DEFINED TRUMP as much as any project or property. The Trump brand's primary product line was a menu of ways to fulfill the workingman's vision of a titan's lifestyle, and Trump sold his products—casinos, hotels, condos—in part by surrounding himself with symbols of the high life, most especially beautiful women. The image Trump cultivated had no place for subtlety. He cared about how things looked, and he carefully created pictures, elegantly staged tableaux of beauty, positioning his dates, his girlfriends, his wives, and his children as avatars of wealth, all dressed and posed to impress the common man. At his public appearances, Trump would have seemed naked without gorgeous women by his side. And he loved a certain sort of woman: models, pageant winners, would-be actresses—most of them stereotypically feminine, long legged, ample chested, with big hair. His wives—Ivana, Marla, and, years later, a Slovenian model, Melania Knauss—were all New York City outsiders with distinctive accents, two from Eastern Europe and one from a small town in Georgia. None had been born to privilege. As Trump grew older, the age gap grew bigger. Publicly, the women grew quieter, too.

Trump believed that the celebrity image he cultivated in the media did more to polish his reputation than any investigations by government officials or skeptical journalists might diminish it. "You know," he said, "it really doesn't matter what they write as long as you've got a young and beautiful piece of ass." He embraced, cultivated even, a playboy image. His marriages imploded in public, spilling boldfaced muck all over the tabloids. The excruciatingly public battle that Ivana and Marla, two former models with tabloid-perfect names, waged over Trump was a real-life version of *Dynasty*, the prime-time soap that mirrored the decade's excesses. The ordeal was an emotional horror show by any measure, seemingly the height of embarrassment, and a costly fight, too, yet it also established Trump as a prize, an object of beautiful women's desires. He spoke publicly about his relationships, as if his randy reputation would enhance his popularity. He used the media, the courts, and his lawyers to help manage his former wives. But beyond the parties and the sightings with models and actresses, despite the screaming headlines, his relationships with women rarely seemed romantic or even libidinous. With Trump, his friends said, women were always the object of a chase, a quest. The actual relationship seemed secondary. In everything he does, said former Trump executive Louise Sunshine, "He's in pursuit. It's such a turn-on. 'Life with Donald must be a ball.' People are drawn to his magnetism. There's no ho-hum. He's, like, 'Oh my God.' You go along for the ride. He's so stimulating."

Trump saw his very public love life as a service provided both to his potential customer base—creating an aspiration for people who craved more fabulousness in their lives—and to a few lucky women. "I create stars," he said. "I love creating stars. And, to a certain extent I've done that with Ivana. I've done that with Marla. I've really given a lot of women great opportunity. Unfortunately, after they're a star, the fun is over for me. It's like a creating process. It's almost like creating a building. It's pretty sad."

In his bestselling books, Trump cast himself as the irresistible lust object, never the groper, always the gropee. "If I told the real stories of my experiences with women, often seemingly very happily married and important women, this book would be a guaranteed best-seller (which it will be anyway!)," he contended in his 1997 memoir, *Trump: The Art of the Comeback*. In his telling, Trump was hounded by lustful women. He described one encounter with an unnamed married "lady of great social pedigree and wealth," whose husband was seated at the same dinner table: "All of a sudden, I felt her hand on my knee, then on my leg. She started petting me in all different ways." With Trump as the passive object of that desire, the woman was said to have insisted, "Donald, I don't care. I just don't care. I have to have you, and I have to have you now." When Trump gave a limousine ride to another "truly great-looking and sexy" wealthy woman who was about to get married, "within five seconds after the door closed, she would be jumping on top of me wanting to get screwed."

Women desired him, Trump often said, yet he held them at a distance, suspicious of what he saw as their crafty, cunning antagonism. "Women have one of the great acts of all time," he wrote. "The smart ones act very feminine and needy, but inside they are real killers. . . . I have seen women manipulate men with just a twitch of their eye— or perhaps another body part. . . . There's nothing I love more than women, but they're really a lot different than portrayed. They are far worse than men, far more aggressive, and boy, can they be smart. Let's give credit where credit is due, and let's salute women for their tremendous power, which most men are afraid to admit they have."

As much power as women might wield, however, Trump rarely let the opportunity pass to proclaim his own virility. Asked for his view of Viagra, Trump once boasted that he never needed such assistance. What he really needed, he said, was an "anti-Viagra, something with the opposite effect. I'm not bragging. I'm just lucky."

THE FIGHT OVER DONALD on Aspen Mountain was more than a tabloid sensation. It marked an evolution of Trump's image, from flashy, brash real estate man to a different kind of celebrity, a showman who deployed his wife not as a business partner, but as a symbol of the glamour he was selling in ventures that would stretch from casinos to clothing and perfume lines. Ivana had been a top manager in the family firm, his contemporary, the woman credited with the over-the-top opulence of his real estate holdings. She had helped establish the signature Trump look—a sort of Vegas meets Versailles that detractors found gaudy, nouveau riche, even absurd. Marla, by contrast, projected *youth*. As Trump turned forty-five, with his empire rapidly expanding yet facing financial strains ("Trump in a Slump," said a headline in the *New York Daily News*), he went public with a far younger woman. Marla generated buzz and heat yet didn't play any role in the family business. If Ivana had enhanced Trump's portfolio and helped Donald shift his image toward being a successful family man, now Marla expressed a different aspect of his personality—his desire to keep business and romance separate, as his father had done. "They are completely different from each other," Trump observed of his first two wives. "Ivana is a tough and practical businesswoman; Marla is a performer and actress. . . . I have come to realize these two exceptional women represent the extremes of my personality."

The two women's midmountain meeting seemed inevitable. Trump had assiduously kept the two women apart for more than two years. In Manhattan, Marla—often installed at the St. Moritz Hotel, three blocks from the family triplex in Trump Tower—was sometimes shielded by his security detail. Trump arranged for her to appear at public events in the company of other men who posed as dates, sometimes even when Ivana was in attendance. The subterfuge allowed Trump to be at once secretive and boyishly brazen about his mistress. Maples was spotted at a 1988 Mike Tyson fight when Trump flew a gaggle of celebrities, including Kirk Douglas and Jack Nicholson, to Atlantic City on his Sikorsky helicopter. On that trip, she was accompanied by Thomas Fitzsimmons, a close friend and former cop who many believed to be her boyfriend. Now, the two women entered the fevered orbit of tiny Aspen at the height of the Christmas season. How were they *not* going to run into each other?

The Aspen meltdown forced Maples into hiding—she moved to Guatemala for some weeks to work for the Peace Corps—as the Donald-Ivana divorce played out in the tabloids and the lawyers' offices. The divorce negotiations were toxic, the publicity relentless. Both sides tackled the case as if it were a military campaign. At one point, with TV cameras rolling, Trump's attorney, Jay Goldberg, stood on the courthouse steps in lower Manhattan, waving a $10 million check that Donald proposed to give Ivana to end their dispute.

The public squabbling got supremely ugly: Ivana alleged in a deposition that Trump had raped her after they argued over a painful medical procedure to remove Donald's bald spot. Ivana had recommended the cosmetic surgeon, and Trump wasn't happy with the result. Ivana said in the deposition, according to Harry Hurt III's book *Lost Tycoon*, that Donald pinned back her arms, pulled hair from her scalp, tore off her clothes, and forced her to have sex with him. In 1993, after Hurt's book was published, a note to the reader from Ivana was appended to the flyleaf at the insistence of Trump's lawyers: "During a deposition given by me in connection with my matrimonial case, I stated that my husband had raped me." On "one occasion during 1989, Mr. Trump and I had marital relations in which he behaved very differently toward me than he had during our marriage. As a woman, I felt violated, as the love and tenderness, which he normally exhibited towards me, was absent. I referred to this as a 'rape,' but I do not want my words to be interpreted in a literal or criminal sense." Trump vigorously denied that either the incident or the surgery ever happened. The allegation was, a Trump spokesman said, "a standard lawyer technique, which was used to exploit more money from Mr. Trump especially since he had an ironclad prenuptial agreement." During a contentious meeting in 1990, the judge urged the two sides to settle for an amount Trump considered "inappropriate," Goldberg recalled. Trump stood up and said to the judge, "You are full of shit. I am leaving." Trump took his coat and left.

TRUMP ALWAYS MADE IT clear who was boss in his marriages. He and Ivana never had "tremendous fights" because, he said, "ultimately, Ivana does exactly what I tell her to do." Trump came to regret having had her work for him, running hotels and casinos: "My big mistake with Ivana was taking her out of the role of wife. The problem was, work was all she wanted to talk about. When I got home at night, rather than talking about the softer subjects of life, she wanted to tell me how well the Plaza was doing, or what a great day the casino had. . . . I will never again give a wife responsibility within my business." He didn't.

As Trump's private life merged with his public identity, he came to see his marriages as something that either boosted his image and therefore his business's reputation, or as a hindrance. "My marriage, it seemed, was the only area of my life in which I was willing to accept something less than perfection," he said during divorce proceedings with Ivana. Maples would pose far less of a threat. She wasn't one to challenge him, except for continually pressing him to wed her. This time, there would be no talk of a marriage of equals. In wealth and celebrity, experience and worldliness, he clearly bested her. "It had obviously been a torrid affair, but I didn't see it lasting," Goldberg said.

Whereas Ivana maintained a busy social calendar that Trump openly disdained, with Maples, Donald became the social director. "Once we started going out in public, an image was expected," Maples recalled. "The hair and the makeup and the designer dresses, and you become a caricature of yourself. And I think what he loved about me the most was that I wasn't part of that world. But once we were together publicly, he wanted to change me into that social animal." Years later, she recalled that "putting on gowns and going out hosting events and having Harry Winston put jewelry on my hands was always uncomfortable for me—that was me playing a role. I felt that's what the job called for."

Her job was to turn heads. The tabloids dubbed her the Georgia Peach. Maples grew up in Dalton, Georgia, which called itself the Carpet Capital of the World. Her father was a real estate developer. After Marla's parents divorced, her mother married a carpet-plant manager. Blond with blue-green eyes, Marla was eager from an early age to act, on Broadway and in Hollywood. She competed in pageants—and won several, including the Miss Resaca Beach Poster Girl contest—but didn't enter some of the more prominent beauty contests because they had a talent component. Friends knew her as sweet and generous; she made jams and jellies and gave them away. At Christmas, she surprised friends with homemade sweaters and baskets. She arrived in Manhattan in 1985 and soon landed bit parts in B movies and a larger role in a workout video. In the Stephen King 1986 science fiction horror movie, *Maximum Overdrive*, her unnamed character was pummeled to death by a truckload of watermelons. She and Trump met soon after she got to New York, and Maples knew immediately that "we had this connection, but it wasn't appropriate timing. So we'd spend a lot of time on the telephone with each other without ever being out together in public. By '88, I knew I truly loved this guy."

For three years after the Aspen incident, Trump and Maples's love life became a running tabloid soap opera. They were on. They were off. Spat. Rinse. Repeat. All of it chronicled in the gossip pages and on TV. In 1990, shortly after Ivana argued that her husband's adultery had violated the terms of their marital contracts, Maples went on ABC to be interviewed by Diane Sawyer at an Atlantic City house that a friend of Trump's owned. "He hated the fact that I felt like I had to be in hiding," the twenty-six-year-old told a national TV audience of more than 13 million. Maples refused to discuss Aspen, instead paying her rival a barbed compliment: "I think she's an absolutely beautiful woman. I think she was before surgery. And, I mean, now she's very, very gorgeous." Maples could dish, but she was also often portrayed cruelly in the press. A *Vanity Fair* story said, "Getting to know Marla Maples is akin to pressing your thumb on an aerosol can and watching mountains of Reddi-wip flow out."

In July 1991, Trump gave Maples a 7.5-carat diamond ring—which for a time he contended was not meant to imply any engagement. Maples said she hoped to be married by winter. But she would wait two more years. In the meantime, she appeared as "Ziegfeld's Favorite" in the Broadway production of *The Will Rogers Follies*. Trump packed the house with guests, including singer La Toya Jackson, TV newsman Mike Wallace, and TV talk show host Maury Povich. Trump threw an after-party at the Plaza, which his first wife had helped redecorate.

Once again, Trump insisted on a prenup, and Maples went on TV to talk about it: "I've always told Donald that I will do whatever I need to do. I will sign, so your bankers will feel good. But I don't want to call it a prenuptial agreement. I'm willing to give him my word on paper that I'm not going to interfere with his business dealings, if it ever came down to that." The wedding, in December 1993, was planned in ten days. Maples wore a $2 million diamond tiara on loan from a Fifth Avenue jeweler. A thousand guests joined the couple in the Grand Ballroom of the Plaza. Their daughter, Tiffany, had been born two months earlier. At the wedding, football star O. J. Simpson voiced doubts about the marriage: "I think everybody in the country believes if *their* relationship can work, then anyone's relationship can work." (Six months later, Simpson was charged with killing his ex-wife Nicole Brown Simpson and was ultimately acquitted.)

Maples, who had spoken of wanting a quiet, simple wedding, shimmered in a Carolina Herrera gown as she cut the six-foot-tall cake in front of guests from politics, sports, and entertainment, including Liza Minnelli and Howard Stern, who said of the happy pair, "I give it four months." (It lasted six years.) Seventeen television crews and close to a hundred photographers documented the event. "There wasn't a wet eye in the place," the *Times* reported. Trump said the caviar alone cost more than $60,000. But his conquest paled next to the adrenaline rush of the chase. "I was bored when she was walking down the aisle," Trump recalled later. "I kept thinking, 'What the hell am I doing here?'"

That sense of anticlimax was evident to people around the couple, too. "Once married, they seemed distant and their behavior was often at odds with one another," Goldberg said. Trump was annoyed by Maples's entourage of relatives. Within a few years, Trump was publicly airing their problems. In *Trump: The Art of the Comeback*, he described a typical day in the marriage: "6:30 p.m. I leave the office and go to my apartment. Marla is waiting for me with dinner, and while I really appreciate it, I realize that this is a marriage coming to an end. It just doesn't seem to be working out. Maybe it's my schedule, and probably it's my fault. But you've just got to really look forward to going home, and if you don't, something is critically wrong."

Trump had made sure he could get out at a low cost. If the marriage proved to be brief, the prenuptial contract strictly limited the amount Maples could collect. She received $5 million or less. Trump, Goldberg observed, "had his eye on the clock." He also had his eyes on other options.

ALMOST AS SOON AS he had crossed the bridge into Manhattan after college, Trump found ways to deploy beautiful women in service of his financial success. In Trump's vocabulary, a superlative man is *successful*; a superlative woman is *beautiful*. He joined Le Club because it was, he said, "the hottest club in the city and . . . its membership included some of the most successful men and the most beautiful women in the world." He started attending high-voltage parties, accompanied by photogenic women whose company he obtained by calling modeling agencies and asking for help filling out his guest list. He became a regular in the front rows of New York fashion shows, showing up in tabloid and fashion publications, surrounded by statuesque women with leonine hair and plenty of lip gloss.

In 1985, Trump found a way to create his own clubhouse, featuring the blend of success and beauty that he wanted his brand to embody. He bought Mar-a-Lago, a historic Palm Beach estate built in 1927 by one of the world's richest women, Marjorie Merriweather Post. She had donated the 128-room mansion to the US government in 1973 for use as the winter White House. But President Jimmy Carter's administration turned the property, just off the Atlantic Ocean on perhaps the ritziest stretch of beachfront in Florida, over to the private Post Foundation, saying it was too expensive to maintain. Trump wanted it and offered $28 million. Not enough, the foundation said. Trump didn't raise his offer; he lowered it. He decided to play hardball. Through a third party, he bought the beachfront property directly in front of Mar-a-Lago and threatened to erect a hideous home to block the Post estate's ocean view. "That drove everybody nuts," Trump said. "They couldn't sell the big house because I owned the beach, so the price kept going down and down."

In the end, Trump bought the landmark for a bargain $5 million for the house, plus $3 million for Post's antiques and lavish furnishings. He converted the estate of more than seventeen acres into a private club (in 2015, new members paid a $100,000 initiation fee plus annual dues of $14,000), available to rent for weddings and events. In Palm Beach, a tiny village of cloistered estates and private beaches where blue bloods and billionaires relished their privacy, Bentleys and Rolls-Royces slipped off South Ocean Boulevard and into estates hidden behind high hedges. At Mar-a-Lago, Trump had the hedges chopped down to give passersby a clear view of his castle. And he invited celebrity guests such as Michael Jackson to stay overnight, drawing paparazzi. The local newspapers took Trump to task for floating rumors that Princess Diana, Madonna, and other big names were joining his club, all part of his effort to build buzz around Mar-a-Lago. Trump also added a Louis XIV–style ballroom with forty-foot ceilings and $7 million worth of gold leaf on the walls (actually, Ivana was in charge of the redesign). Trump spent $100,000 on four gold-plated bathroom sinks near the ballroom.

Appalled by Trump's ostentatious behavior, the Palm Beach town council handed him a list of restrictions it was imposing on membership, traffic, party attendance, even photography. But Trump refused to be hemmed in. He took his battle to the court of public opinion. His lawyer sent every member of the town council copies of two classic movies about discrimination—*Gentleman's Agreement*, about a journalist who pretends to be Jewish to expose anti-Semitism, and

Guess Who's Coming to Dinner, about a white couple's reaction to their daughter's bringing home a black fiancé. The point was clear and painful: the town's political leaders for decades had condoned rules by which the established private clubs in town excluded Jews and blacks, and now they wanted to slap Trump with tough rules on his club, which was open to anyone who could afford the steep fees. Council members insisted that their only concern was that Trump was turning a quiet, demure stretch of beachfront into a noisy party attracting a lot of outsiders. No matter: Trump's tactic worked. Over time, he got most of the restrictions lifted.

The parties Trump hosted were designed to draw exactly the attention that the town council abhorred. Many of the guests were models from Miami, who floated around the patio and pool. Trump insisted on at least a three-to-two ratio of women to men at his bashes. "There's a hundred beautiful women and ten guys," recalled Roger Stone, his longtime adviser. " 'Look, how cool are we?' I mean, it was great."

BEFORE AND BETWEEN HIS marriages, Trump played up his image as a ladies' man. He arranged to be photographed with beauty queens in skimpy outfits, in limos with models, visiting Hugh Hefner's Playboy mansion. Trump blended his interest in certified beautiful women with his expanding empire, diving into the beauty-pageant and modeling businesses. "What I do is successful because of the aesthetics," Trump said. "People love my buildings and my pageants." The pageant industry raised Trump's international profile, taking him around the globe, to countries large and small where he would pose with Miss Wherever at his side at ribbon cuttings or announcements of Trump real estate and hotel projects. Foreign political and business leaders were eager to join him at events that featured beauty queens as well as a little commerce. Trump saw pageants as a welcome diversion from blueprints and environmental impact meetings, a chance to "mix it up" in his investment portfolio, as well as entrée to a large national and international television audience.

Trump's investment in pageants began with the American Dream Calendar Girl Model Search contest, which had started in 1966 as a joint venture between a men's toiletries company and a motor-sports-calendar business that wanted to add scantily clad women to its pages. In 1992, Trump entered into a partnership with the Florida couple who owned American Dream. George Houraney and Jill Harth hoped the Trump brand would lend buzz to their contests and calendars featuring women posing in bathing suits next to fast cars. The relationship did not last long. After the 1993 pageant at Trump Castle, Houraney and Harth sued for breach of contract, claiming that the venture lost them $250,000 and as much as $5 million in future revenue.

In a tangled legal battle that stretched on for years, Harth accused Trump of groping her. She sought $125 million in damages, alleging in a deposition that Trump made aggressive and unwanted sexual advances at a 1993 party at Mar-a-Lago. "When we got to the dinner table, Donald started right in on the groping under the table," she said. Later that same night, by Harth's telling, Trump brought her to a bedroom ordinarily used by his then eleven-year-old daughter, Ivanka. There, Trump "kissed, fondled, and restrained" Harth from leaving the room, she alleged. Harth and Houraney left the estate in the small of the night. Trump vehemently denied that any of that happened. Rather, he cited a 1997 *National Enquirer* account of the incident that quoted an unnamed Trump friend saying it was Harth who was obsessed with Trump. Harth said, however, in a deposition that Trump had been going after her ever since she and Houraney first met with him, even after Houraney made it clear that he and Harth were married. "Basically, Donald Trump stared at me throughout that meeting," she recalled under oath. "He stared at me even while George was giving his presentation."

Harth also alleged that Trump "directed that any black female contestants be excluded" from his Mar-a-Lago parties; Houraney said Trump systematically eliminated black women from the pile of photos he was sent to choose contestants for the finals of the calendar competition. Trump consistently denied the couple's claims; his attorneys called Harth "delusional" and said her allegations were "clear evidence of mental instability." Years later, an attorney for Trump said, "There is no truth to the story at all," and that Harth "was a pawn in a lawsuit that was created by her ex-husband." In 1997, Trump settled the breach-of-contract case with American Dream; Harth at the same time dropped the suit in which she alleged the sexual misconduct. Houraney told the *Boston Globe* that he received a payment from Trump but was not allowed to reveal its amount. Harth said she dropped her case as a condition for settlement of Houraney's suit, but she said her allegations were accurate.

Around the time he was dealing with those lawsuits, Trump had already stepped up to a grander stage in pageantry, to what he called "the triple crown of beauty." In 1996, he bought a controlling share of the Miss Universe pageants, which included the Miss USA and Miss Teen USA competitions. At the time, he said he paid $10 million for his stake in the organization; years later, he said he had spent only $2 million. Miss Universe started out in 1952 in Catalina, California, as a swimsuit competition, without the academic component that the Miss America contest boasted of. Miss Universe had a reputation as the racier of the two popular pageants, and Trump set out to make it sexier. As a result of his leadership, he said, "The bathing suits got smaller and the heels got higher and the ratings went up." (Actually, the ratings sank over time. When Trump bought the pageant in 1996, Miss Universe's Nielsen ratings had already declined, from about 35 million viewers in 1984 to about 12 million. The pageant never regained those higher numbers, and in 2013, two years before Trump sold it, fewer than 4 million people tuned in.) Trump's management of pageants became a family affair: his daughter, Ivanka, hosted Miss Teen USA one year; his second wife, Marla, herself a former beauty contestant, cohosted Miss Universe and Miss USA; and his third wife, Melania, would serve as a judge at the Miss USA pageant. Although pageant executives traditionally tended to be men, Trump promoted women, including Maureen Reidy, an accountant in the Trump Organization whom he named the first female president of the Miss Universe organization in 1997, when she was twenty-seven.

Trump was actively involved in the pageants. After Miss Universe Alicia Machado, a Venezuelan, gained considerable weight in 1996, Trump publicly excoriated her. He staged a photo op to show Machado exercising at a Manhattan gym. In front of about eighty reporters and photographers, Trump said, "When you win a beauty pageant, people don't think you're going to go from 118 to 160 in less than a year, and you really have an obligation to stay in a perfect physical state." Machado called the photo op an ambush designed to humiliate her.

"He had his triumphant entry," she recalled, "and I got to feel like a hamster on a wheel for an hour. I was his first Miss Universe when he just bought the company. Unfortunately, this also meant that I experienced, firsthand, his rage and racism and all the misogyny a person can demonstrate." Trump wrote years later that he did what he did to protect her from being fired: "God, what problems I had with this woman. First, she wins. Second, she gains fifty pounds. Third, I urge the committee *not* to fire her."

Trump kept close tabs on pageant contestants. Carrie Prejean, who was Miss California in 2009 and first runner-up in that year's Miss USA contest, said Trump "inspected us closer than any general ever inspected a platoon." In front of fellow competitors, Prejean recalled, Trump asked Miss Alabama who was the most beautiful contestant. When Miss Alabama suggested that Miss Arkansas was "sweet," Trump responded, "I don't care if she's sweet. Is she *hot*?" Trump posed the same question to several contestants, and then, Prejean said, "motioned those girls he liked over to one side, leaving the discards to one side of the stage." Trump said he had to step in because "the judges didn't know what they were doing. . . . They wouldn't pick the women that should've been in the finals. . . . So I developed a system where everybody would be on stage . . . with numerous people from CBS. . . . I'd be on stage and I'd talk. We would pick the top fifteen smartest, most beautiful women. Once I got involved . . . it became very successful. . . . Look, it is a beauty pageant, okay? It's about beauty. We can't be ashamed of it."

A few years after investing in Miss Universe, Trump branched out into another aspect of the beauty business—modeling. His new agency, originally conceived as Trump Models Inc., ended up with the name T Management after protracted negotiations between Trump and a veteran of the industry, Annie Veltri, a part-owner of the company. Known for its "legends"—older models—T Management was otherwise an "inconsequential agency," said James Scully, a prominent casting director in the fashion industry. T's models were generally not household names. It was "a way to funnel beauty-pageant contestants somewhere," Scully said. Some of the bookers at Trump's modeling business were also pageant judges, and favored pageant contestants would score modeling contracts with the agency. Although Trump wasn't involved in day-to-day management of the modeling business, he approved major decisions, and some models said they got their contract offers directly from Trump.

The modeling business introduced a different culture to Trump's empire. Initially housed in Trump Tower, the model bookers eschewed the uniform of suits and dresses that was the rule in the Trump Organization's offices. The modeling culture was far less formal than what the boss generally enforced. "They were all, 'Mr. Trump,' 'Mr. Trump,' 'Mr. Trump,'" said John Bassignani, who worked at the agency. "And we were, 'Hey, Donald,' 'Hey, Donald,' 'Hey, Donald.'"

THE SUBJECT WAS MARIAH CAREY, the singer. "Would you bang her?" Howard Stern asked on his nationally broadcast radio show. Trump replied, "I would do it without hesitation." On another morning, the host of the daily raunch-fest asked the same question, this time about Princess Diana, then one of the most famous and most admired women in the world. "Without hesitation," Trump said. "She had the height, she had the beauty, she had the skin. . . . She was crazy, but these are minor details."

Starting in the nineties, Trump appeared about two dozen times on Stern's popular morning talk show, which grew ever more explicit through the years. Stern and Trump developed a rollicking patter on the air, rating women's tops and bottoms, debating the merits of oral sex, and egging each other on about whether they would like to go to bed with famous women from Cindy Crawford to Diane Sawyer. Trump seemed to love the game. On one show, the shock jock asked, "Is oral sex important to you? Man to man, and I've had this discussion with many men." Trump replied, "No, it's not important to me."

Another morning, Trump considered the assets of Nicollette Sheridan, an actress on the nighttime TV soap opera *Desperate Housewives*: "A person who is very flat chested is very hard to be a ten." Trump turned the tables and asked Stern about Sheridan's costar: "Would you go out with Marcia Cross or would you turn gay, Howard?" The two guys traded barbs about all manner of female celebrities, mainly focusing on whether they'd be worth having sex with. Trump's guest appearances, which stretched from 1990 to 2005, included his judgments on reality TV star Kim Kardashian: "Does she have a fat ass? Absolutely!" and "Her boob job is terrible. They look like two light posts coming out of a body."

Trump talked on one show about how taken he was with Princess Diana. After her marriage to Prince Charles broke up in 1992, Trump began sending her flower arrangements. He seemed to believe they could have dated. "You could've gotten her, right?" Stern asked Trump soon after Diana was killed in a car crash in 1997. "You could've nailed her."

Trump thought for a moment, then replied, "I think I could have."

Trump's comments about his sexual desires were not limited to theoretical cases. Calling in to the show in 2000, he talked about his girlfriend, Melania Knauss, then handed her the phone. "We have incredible sex once a day," she told Stern's listeners, "sometimes even more." A few years later, when Donald and Melania were married, Stern asked if Trump would stay with his wife if she emerged from a car accident disfigured, with her arm and leg damaged, and with "one hundred stitches on her face."

"How do the breasts look?" Trump asked.

"The breasts are okay," Stern said.

"That's important," Trump said.

FOR ALL OF TRUMP'S salacious chatter on the radio and carefully staged appearances with models and other beautiful women, those who spent lots of time with him through the 1990s described not an overheated Casanova, but rather a workaholic and something of a homebody, a savvy business operator who was keenly aware of the value of being perceived as a player. Goldberg, the attorney who was often by Trump's side during those years, said many of his client's much-ballyhooed associations with famous women and top models were mere moments, staged for the cameras. "Give him a Hershey bar and let him watch television," Goldberg said. "I only remember him finishing the day [by] going home, not necessarily with a woman but with a bag of candy. . . . He planned his next project, read the blueprints, met with the lawyers, never raising his voice, never showing off, never nasty to anybody in the office, a gentleman. . . . I never heard him speak romantically about a woman. I mean, I heard him speak romantically about his work."

Kate Bohner, who cowrote *Trump: The Art of the Comeback*, said the public perception of Trump as a serial womanizer and a glamorous night crawler was a calculated effort to add gloss to the brand, and nothing more. "There were times when I'd see him chatting up a bevy of gorgeous creations, and I can see how an outsider might think he was in it to win it, so to speak," she said. "But never did I feel that it was anything other than part of his shtick to fuel the Trump brand. I saw Mr. Trump being more paternal toward women than playboy."

Trump often said he wouldn't have had time to breathe if he had truly consorted with all the women he was credited with dating. People "may be surprised that my life is much less glamorous than they thought, including every story about a supermodel," he said. His wives were all good people, he recalled, "but I'm married to my business. It's been a marriage of love. So, for a woman, frankly, it's not that easy in terms of relationships." In his book *Trump: Think Like a Billionaire*, Trump attributed his success, like that of "Jeff Bezos, Steve Jobs, and Ted Turner" to an "unrelenting focus [on] achieving their dreams, even if it's sometimes at the expense of those around them. . . . Narcissism can be a useful quality if you're trying to start a business. A narcissist does not hear the naysayers. At the Trump Organization, I listen to people, but my vision is my vision." To think like a billionaire, Trump said, never take vacations ("I love relating to [my kids] just the way my father related to me—through a passion for work well done"), "have a short attention span," "don't depend on technology" ("I don't even have an ATM card—I've never used one in my life" and "email is for wimps"), don't overthink things ("The day I realized it can be smart to be shallow was, for me, a deep experience"), and "think of yourself as a one-man army. . . . You must plan and execute your plan alone."

DESPITE THE TURBULENCE IN their marriages, his former wives never disparaged Trump publicly after their divorces. Trump made sure of that. The consummate negotiator, he had his wives sign confidentiality agreements, and he held the ultimate leverage: the kids.

Trump often said he was not the kind of father who spent much time hanging out or playing ball with his children, but when they were old enough to learn the business, they spent far more time with him, especially at the office. Ivana had gone public with her allegation that "the children are all wrecks" from the turmoil surrounding the divorce—Donny Jr. had been teased at Buckley, his Manhattan private school, and Ivanka was often in tears at Chapin, her girls' school on the East Side—but all three children from the marriage with Ivana would come to work by their father's side at the Trump Organization. All three told of difficult times with their father—Donald was so competitive that when he and Eric were skiing, the son said "he would try to push me over, just so he could beat his ten-year-old son down the mountain," and during the divorce battle, Donald Jr. went a year without speaking to his father. But they came to admire him as a businessman and as a parent who loved them in his own way and deeply wanted them to work together with him. "My parents . . . had their own thing, and it was public," Eric Trump said, "and naturally kids get dragged into it because of the media. But my parents were so solid at keeping us away from it. And I think boarding school was their subtle way of also doing that, in a certain way." The frenzy around his parents' divorce nonetheless defined a period of Eric's life: "Everybody, that's all they want to talk about is this, because this is the biggest story in the world, hands down. And yet when you're ten years old, your mind's still developing and you're trying to grow up as a little man . . . and you gotta be able to develop as a kid." The solution was work, according to Eric and his siblings. As his father had done, Donald brought his children to construction sites and had them do hands-on labor.

How his ex-wives might describe the family's inner life remained uncertain, as Trump managed to hold their public comments in check. In January 2000, ReganBooks, a division of HarperCollins, announced plans for a book by Maples entitled *All That Glitters Is Not Gold*. The "remarkably candid memoir," the press release stated, would be "the story behind the headlines" about "loving a man whose greatest passion was the empire he built." Maples worked with literary agent Susan Crawford on what she described as "a cautionary tale" about being married to Trump. Crawford recalled taking Trump Tower's service elevator up to meet Maples in the private suite, where she would share stories of her roller-coaster affair with Trump, the scandal on the ski slopes, their clandestine meetings and eventual wedding. "It would have been very sensational," the agent recalled.

The book never appeared. Two years after it was to be published, in 2002, "Marla called and said, 'Susan, I can't do it,' " Crawford said. It was unclear whether Maples didn't want her daughter, Tiffany, to read about her mother's love life in a bestselling book, or if Maples, who had a newfound commitment to spirituality, had had a change of heart, or if Trump quashed the project. Trump later said he was "not unhappy" about the turn of events. "She signed a confidentiality agreement," he said. Earlier, he had set his attorneys on Ivana, after she granted a May 1991 television interview with Barbara Walters. Trump threatened to terminate her $350,000 annual alimony payment and $50,000 annual housing allowance, arguing that she had violated the terms of their divorce settlement.

Once again, Trump sought to control the story. The divorce agreement, signed in 1991, barred Ivana from publishing or broadcasting "any diary, memoir, letter, story, photograph, interview, article, essay, account or description or depiction of any kind whatsoever . . . concerning her marriage to Donald or any other aspect of Donald's personal business or financial affairs . . . without obtaining Donald's written consent in advance." Ivana did publish a memoir, but it carefully steered clear of any personal account of the marriage. She didn't even offer her take on the infamous fight on Aspen Mountain, quoting instead from the *New York Post*'s version of what happened between her and Maples.

Long after the marriage collapsed, Ivana and Donald remained friends, they both said. "Donald took the divorce as a businessman," Ivana said. "He had to negotiate and he had to win. Once the financial part was settled, we're friendly." He attended her fourth wedding in 2008, held at Mar-a-Lago. Looking back at what he called his "three shots at being a husband," Trump called them all "good women. Very good women. But my thing has always been I've been a worker. I have always been working, and it was always all-consuming." Asked about his wives, he praised his company and its "great locations" and "very little debt." Donald the husband? "I built a great company. The company is a great company with some of the greatest assets in the world, and you don't do that by working five hours a day."

10

A League of His Own

When the leaders of the nascent United States Football League gathered in New Orleans in January 1984, most of the team owners revered Donald Trump as the one man who might bring them into the promised league, the NFL. That would soon change. The business model for the USFL was simple: play America's most popular sport in the spring, when there was no competition from the NFL or colleges. The USFL's first season in 1983 had been a modest success. The television ratings were decent, some teams drew solid attendance, and some even had enough money to lure fringe NFL players and topflight college talent away from the dominant league. But the owners believed the eighteen-team USFL still wasn't being taken seriously, or at least it hadn't been, until September 1983, when the soft-spoken, aging Oklahoma oil baron who owned the New Jersey Generals sold the team to a thirty-seven-year-old New York real estate developer who had just opened a soaring fifty-eight-story tower in Manhattan with his last name emblazoned in gold above the entrance.

As the owners' meeting began in the grand ballroom of the Hyatt Regency Hotel on that January morning, Trump looked at the men seated around him. Some were on his level of wealth and ambition, he thought. There were a few other real estate moguls, a former US ambassador to Switzerland who also was part-owner of a large savings and loan, and the new owner of the Los Angeles team, the mercurial, eccentric Bill Oldenburg, who went by the nickname Mr. Dynamite and had an employee at his San Francisco mortgage firm ring a gong every time the company made another $1 million. The night before, Oldenburg had arrived at his first USFL owners' dinner with an entourage that included singer Wayne Newton. Later in the meal, Oldenburg tore open his shirt and declared that his new team would "beat the shit" out of anyone else's.

Trump had his doubts about some of the other USFL owners, though. A few were just doctors and lawyers, guys who probably qualified as rich but lacked the wealth to compete with the NFL's owners. A few were probably content for the USFL to remain inferior to the NFL. They didn't see what Trump saw: an opening created by the NFL's shortsighted, arrogant ownership. To maximize this opportunity, Trump argued, the USFL had to act, and quickly. His impatience was starting to nag at some of his fellow owners. They loved the attention he brought to their league, but some had started griping about things Trump said and did. And Trump didn't appreciate their complaints.

He let them know that the league had been "heading very rapidly downhill" until he'd bought the Generals four months before. In those few months, Trump alone, by his own account, had orchestrated a complete flip in the perception of the USFL among fans, reporters, and the people who controlled the purse strings at major television networks. A series of high-profile negotiations between Trump and star NFL players and coaches had generated a crush of media coverage. Network presidents were finally taking this league seriously, Trump said. He was tired of reading that some owners were concerned about his spending habits. He was particularly angry with Myles Tanenbaum, the shopping mall developer who owned the Philadelphia Stars. "Myles comes up to my office about a month ago to see me," Trump told his fellow owners gathered in New Orleans. "The next day I read about this goddamn confidential meeting in the newspaper where he's saying everything that I'm talking about. I write him a letter, a somewhat nasty letter—oh, good, Myles, I'm glad you're here." Trump interrupted himself as Tanenbaum entered the room. "And I say the next time you want to get publicity, don't do it at my expense. . . . I'll have the goddamn camera crews waiting for you. . . . If you want to play the game, I can play it myself. I don't like having you talking about

Trump, the guy that's just throwing around money. The money that I throw around is for the good of the league. . . . It's given the league credibility."

That morning in New Orleans, Trump reiterated his plan for the USFL's success: move the games to the fall and compete head-to-head with the NFL for big television money and overall supremacy. The NFL had just vacated New York City proper—the New York Jets had moved out of Shea Stadium in Queens to join the New York Giants in the Meadowlands of New Jersey—presenting Trump with the opportunity to move his Generals into the city, giving the USFL the only major football team in America's media capital.

Trump had allies in the room: several other owners also wanted to move to the fall. The NFL was dealing with significant labor strife and had just had a players' strike in 1982. Its television ratings had dipped for the first time in years. Some network officials, meanwhile, bristled at the exorbitant rights fees the NFL demanded, and they liked the idea of a little competition in professional football. But in an all-out war with the NFL, the USFL would be massively outgunned—the average NFL team got roughly $14 million a year from the league's television contracts; the *entire* USFL made about $14 million from ABC per season.

Still, Trump saw a path to victory. "I guarantee you folks in this room that I will produce CBS and I will produce NBC and that I will produce ABC, guaranteed, and for a hell of a lot more money than the horseshit you're getting right now," he said. "Every team in this room suffers from one thing: people don't want to watch spring football. . . . You watch what happens when you challenge the NFL. . . . I don't want to be a loser. I've never been a loser before, and if we're losers in this, fellows, I tell you what, it's going to haunt us. . . . Every time there's an article written about you, it's going to be you owned this goddamn team which failed . . . and I'm not going to be a failure." In the worst-case scenario, Trump said, the USFL could sue the NFL for antitrust violations and either win a massive judgment or force a merger. What he didn't say was that a merger would be a game of musical chairs: not every USFL team would get a spot in the NFL. Some owners would inevitably be left standing when the music stopped.

A week later, Tanenbaum—the Philadelphia owner—wrote to a fellow USFL team owner who had missed the New Orleans meeting:

ever since, a concern had been "gnawing at me virtually every day. That concern has to do with Donald Trump's grand plan for the USFL."

IN TRUMP'S ZERO-SUM WORLD of winners and losers, sports had always held a special place. As a child in Queens, he was a fan of both the Brooklyn Dodgers and New York Yankees, and a fanatical collector of baseball cards. In school, he and his childhood friend Peter Brant were caught several times listening to baseball games in class on their transistor radios. At New York Military Academy, Donald had excelled at sports, and especially at baseball—he played first base and was a star hitter. And in college, at Fordham, Trump had played football, until an ankle injury sidelined him, and then squash. As a young man in Manhattan in the 1970s, he had mingled with celebrities at Le Club and developed a friendship with George Steinbrenner, the imperious owner of the New York Yankees and a master at winning publicity (and notoriety). In the early 1980s, Trump had flirted with team ownership several times. He unsuccessfully bid $20 million for the New York Mets, and when the Cleveland Indians were up for sale, Trump went as high as $34 million. That deal fell through over Trump's reluctance to promise to keep the team in Cleveland. Trump had had preliminary talks with Robert Irsay about the NFL's Baltimore Colts before Irsay decided to move the team to Indianapolis.

Trump's worth and liquidity were already topics of constant debate, and buying an NFL team required both deep wealth and verifiable cash. In 1983, the going rate for an NFL team was about $70 million. After Trump bought the Generals for about $6 million, he told anyone who asked (and some who didn't) that he could have bought an NFL team, but chose the USFL because it presented more of a challenge: "I feel sorry for the poor guy who is going to buy the Dallas Cowboys. It's a no-win situation for him, because if he wins, well, so what, they've won through the years, and if he loses . . . he'll be known to the world as a loser."

TRUMP WENT ON A spending spree to convert his new football team into one of the USFL's best. The atrium at Trump Tower became the stage for a series of press conferences where Trump held court about his war with the NFL.

In the Generals, Trump had purchased a team with one bona fide (and expensive) star: Herschel Walker, the Heisman Trophy–winning running back. In an era when the NFL forbade teams from drafting underclassmen, Walker had bucked tradition by leaving the University of Georgia as a junior for a three-year contract with the Generals that paid $5 million, then the richest deal in football history. In the USFL's inaugural 1983 season, Walker led the league in rushing yards, but the team around him sputtered to a 6-12 record. Trump went to work surrounding Walker with talent, but first he needed a new coach.

Trump set his sights high, trying to lure Don Shula—one of the winningest coaches in NFL history—from the Miami Dolphins. Shula made about $450,000 a year, so Trump offered him $1 million. But the coach apparently asked for a deal-sweetener. Trump went on CBS's *NFL Today* show to discuss his ongoing negotiations with the coach. The deal was almost done, Trump said, but for one hang-up: Shula wanted an apartment in Trump Tower, and the developer wasn't certain he could offer one. An infuriated Shula—who had publicly entertained the notion of jumping to the USFL for weeks—announced the next day that he had broken off talks and would stay in Miami. Trump claimed he, not Shula, ended the talks. "I could not give up an apartment in Trump Tower," Trump said. "Money is one thing, gold is another."

Spurned by Shula, Trump turned to someone who would be popular with New York football fans—Walt Michaels, a former coach of the Jets. Next, the mogul raided several NFL rosters to build his new coach a winning team. Trump plucked quarterback Brian Sipe—a former NFL Most Valuable Player—from the Cleveland Browns, among other NFL players. Trump marveled at how much more press he got for routine football transactions than he did for his usual business dealings: "I hire a general manager to help run a billion-dollar business and there's a squib in the papers. I hire a coach for a football team and there are sixty and seventy reporters calling to interview me."

The player who probably generated the most publicity for Trump's team never actually suited up for the Generals. One day, Jim Gould, the man Trump hired to be president of the Generals, was sitting in

Trump's office. Lawrence Taylor, the fearsome linebacker for the New York Giants, had recently been in the news over his displeasure with his contract. "Maybe we oughta sign Taylor," Gould suggested. Trump agreed; certainly Taylor would sell tickets. There was one problem: Taylor was signed to play with the Giants through 1987. Gould and Trump came up with a plan.

That day, the Giants star got an unexpected phone call: "Mr. Taylor, please hold for Mr. Trump." A few hours later, one of the greatest players in football history arrived at Trump Tower, in a car Trump had sent. Gould greeted Taylor and told him that Trump insisted he first watch an eight-minute slide show. The promotional presentation heaped praise on Trump Tower and its "visionary builder": "This is Manhattan through a golden eye, and only for the select few. . . . Any wish, no matter how opulent or unusual, may come true." Taylor was still uncertain why he was there. He wasn't interested in a condo. He was, however, very interested in what Trump had to say a few minutes later.

Trump offered Taylor a $1 million bonus to sign a contract guaranteeing he'd play for the Generals after his deal with the NFL's Giants expired. If Taylor signed *that day*, Trump offered to wire him the $1 million immediately. "He had me call my bank, and sure as shit, thirty minutes later he wired a million dollars into my account," Taylor recalled. "I was like, 'Thanks, Don.' I respected that he put his money where his mouth was." Before Taylor even got back home that night, word leaked to the press about the deal, and there was little mystery about who had leaked it. Trump dealt coyly with questions about Taylor in a *New York Times* story. (The *Times* reporter, Ira Berkow, was also made to sit through the promotional video before he could meet Trump.) "No one knows if we signed him—actually, only three people know, that's Lawrence, his agent, and me," Trump said.

The "futures contract" Trump used to lure Taylor outraged Giants management, but they weren't willing to let the public drama go on long. The Giants essentially bought out Taylor's contract with the Generals, giving him a new deal with the Giants and a hefty raise, and paying Trump back the $1 million he gave Taylor, plus another $750,000. (Technically, Taylor bought himself out of the contract by giving Trump $1.75 million from the Giants. This spared the NFL team the indignity of having to pay Trump directly.) The deal made Taylor a lifelong Trump fan: "He has certainly always known how to use the media. It was a brilliant publicity stunt."

On the field, Trump's mad-scientist off-season paid off. The Generals went 14-4 in 1984, made the playoffs, and lost in the first round. But off the field, some other USFL owners were having second thoughts about their new colleague. Trump had effectively become the face of the league, and his mouthing off did not sit well with other team owners. Trump casually told reporters that he thought the USFL should fold at least four of its eighteen teams, the ones with "weak ownership." Then came a steady drumbeat of stories citing anonymous "USFL sources" saying, falsely, that a switch from spring to fall play was imminent. After a *Times* story trumpeted a move to a fall schedule based on information from two "prominent USFL executives," league commissioner Chet Simmons was apoplectic. Simmons, a former president of ESPN, was trying to keep the peace between owners who wanted to switch seasons and those who didn't, and now it appeared that one owner was trying to tip the scales by placing anonymously sourced news stories. Simmons had a pretty good idea who that was.

The day after the *Times* story, Simmons sent a memo to all owners: "To air the league's business in the press is unwarranted and unconscionable and to distort the truth is malicious." He called Trump, who neither confirmed nor denied being the source. Trump reacted calmly to Simmons's scolding, but got his revenge later that week. A column in the *Los Angeles Herald Examiner* was headlined, "Trump to Simmons: You Are Useless . . . You Just Sit There," which Trump purportedly told Simmons after the commissioner's angry call about the *Times* story. (Trump told Simmons he'd never said those words.) A few months later, when Simmons developed a pinched nerve, doctors told him the ailment was likely stress related. He took to calling it his "Trump nerve."

The fight over whether to switch to the fall boiled down to an argument chiefly between two men: Trump and John Bassett. A Canadian film producer previously involved with the failed World Football League, Bassett owned the Tampa Bay Bandits, one of the few USFL teams to turn a profit. Like Trump, Bassett had a flair for the dramatic; he enlisted Hollywood star Burt Reynolds as a celebrity part-owner and ran halftime events at games, including bikini contests and mortgage burnings. Bassett liked Trump at first. At that early 1984 New Orleans owners' meeting, Bassett said Trump had boosted the league's credibility. But Trump's needling of his opponents changed Bassett's opinion. In August, he sent Trump a sternly worded letter: "Dear Donald: . . . I have listened with astonishment at your personal abuse of the commissioner and various of your partners if they did not happen to espouse one of your causes or agree with one of your arguments. . . . You are bigger, younger, and stronger than I, which means I'll have no regrets whatsoever punching you right in the mouth the next time an instance occurs where you personally scorn me, or anyone else, who does not happen to salute and dance to your tune. . . . Kindest personal regards, John F. Bassett."

A few weeks later, USFL owners gathered to hear the results of an important study by the consulting firm McKinsey, which the league had paid $600,000 to determine its best financial course forward. The consultant, Sharon Patrick, realized that no matter what season it played in, the USFL was in trouble. Seven of the eighteen owners told Patrick they could not stay afloat over the next two years based on the league's current television revenue, and four more said they'd be able to keep playing only with "great difficulty." Trump's plan to boost television income by moving to the fall assumed a series of events the consultant couldn't foresee happening. Moving to the fall before 1987 would violate the USFL's contract with ABC. And Patrick hadn't heard anything to convince her that a move would result in a better contract for the USFL. NBC told her it had no interest in the USFL, period. CBS said it wouldn't be interested until 1987, and then only if the league's ratings improved. If the USFL tried to move before 1987, Patrick said, the league could end up without any major-network contract.

She recommended cutting costs, launching an ad campaign to improve ratings, and remaining a spring league through 1986. Only after that, when the NFL's TV contracts would be up for renewal and the USFL would be a free agent, should a move to the fall be considered. Trump termed Patrick's report "bullshit." Eddie Einhorn, the new owner of the USFL's struggling Chicago franchise, agreed, saying he doubted network executives would speak candidly with a "girl" from a consulting firm. Einhorn was convinced he could get two major networks into a bidding war for a fall USFL. If that didn't work, Einhorn and Marvin Warner, another owner, agreed the next step should be an antitrust lawsuit against the NFL. The owners voted to ignore Patrick's recommendations. Fourteen of the sixteen owners present backed Trump's drive to move to the fall. Commissioner Simmons told reporters, "We're going to take the NFL on head-to-head beginning in the fall of 1986."

Before the 1985 season, Trump made another splashy, impulsive signing. A year after throwing $800,000 at quarterback Brian Sipe, Trump drafted Heisman Trophy–winning quarterback Doug Flutie out of Boston College, signing him to a five-year deal worth up to $7 million. At a press conference, a humble Flutie said he was unsure he was ready to start and looked forward to learning from the veteran Sipe. Trump had different plans, declaring, "Doug Flutie will be the Joe Namath of the USFL." A few weeks later, according to a fellow owner, Trump asked him to have his team take it easy on Flutie, an idea that the fellow owner rebuked. Trump denied having made the request. When Flutie struggled early in the season, Trump suggested that other USFL owners reimburse him for the quarterback's contract. Trump conceded he had overspent, but said he was selflessly generating publicity for the league. (USFL officials noted a name they didn't recognize speaking on behalf of Trump in news coverage of that incident—John Barron, the fictitious spokesman Trump occasionally pretended to be.)

Trump's Generals again finished with a winning record, 11-7, and again were bounced in the first round of the playoffs. But off the field, the USFL, without a new television contract, faced great uncertainty. As the consultant had predicted, NBC and CBS didn't appear interested, and ABC was furious that the USFL intended to break its contract. It became increasingly clear the league's only chance of survival would come in the courtroom. USFL owners voted to sue the NFL, and again Trump stole the show. As USFL executives were about to fly to Florida for a league meeting, Simmons got a message: Trump planned to hold a surprise press conference the following morning, speaking on behalf of the USFL about its case against the NFL. By his side would be the lawyer Trump had picked for the case, without consulting anyone else: Roy Cohn. (Years later, Trump biographer Harry Hurt would report that Trump had promised Cohn the case as partial payment for his work renegotiating a prenuptial agreement with Ivana.)

The *USFL v. NFL* trial was scheduled for late spring of 1986 in New York federal court. Many sportswriters viewed the lawsuit as a desperate move by the USFL. But lawyers for the NFL knew that an internal NFL document would significantly bolster the upstart league's case that its established rival had broken federal law in an effort to put its competition out of business. And a secret meeting that had taken place between Trump and NFL commissioner Pete Rozelle in 1984 would rock the trial—depending on who was telling it straight and who was cheating the truth.

SPORTS ILLUSTRATED'S MANAGING EDITOR, Mark Mulvoy, was playing a round of golf with Trump on Long Island one morning when the skies opened. When the rain let up and the men returned to the green, Mulvoy noticed a ball ten feet from the hole that he didn't remember seeing before the storm. "Who the hell's ball is this?" Mulvoy said.

"That's me," Trump said, according to Mulvoy.

"Donald, give me a fucking break," Mulvoy replied. "You've been hacking away in the . . . weeds all day. You do not lie there."

"Ahh, the guys I play with cheat all the time. I have to cheat just to keep up with them."

After college, after Trump mostly gave up his personal athletic interests, he came to view time spent playing sports as time wasted. Trump believed the human body was like a battery, with a finite amount of energy, which exercise only depleted. So he didn't work out. When he learned that John O'Donnell, one of his top casino executives, was training for an Ironman triathlon, he admonished him, "You are going to die young because of this."

But Trump continued to play golf through the years, often touting his skill at the game as evidence of his athleticism. Trump claimed eighteen club championships, which he said were "really like majors for amateurs," referring to the most important, prestigious tournaments for professional golfers. Many experienced golfers who hit the links with Trump found him to be talented, albeit with an unorthodox swing, but stories of Trump's cheating became legion. "When it comes to cheating, he's an eleven on a scale of one to ten," said sportswriter

Rick Reilly. In one afternoon of golfing with Trump, Reilly said, he witnessed the developer write down phony scores, award himself close putts by raking balls into the hole, and call a gimme—usually reserved for shots two feet or closer to the hole—when his ball was at least a few yards away. "He took the world's first gimme chip-in," Reilly said. Despite repeatedly taking do-over balls, Trump told Reilly to "make sure you write that I play my first ball. You don't get a second ball in life." (Trump steadfastly denied any shenanigans: "I've never cheated in golf." And he disputed Reilly's recollection: "I absolutely killed him, and he wrote very inaccurately. . . . I never took a gimme chip shot.")

When Trump bet big on Atlantic City, sports played a vital role in bringing people to his casinos. In 1989, acting on an idea pitched to him by college basketball commentator Billy Packer, Trump sponsored the Tour de Trump, a bicycle race billed as America's answer to the Tour de France. The race covered 837 miles through five states, ending in the shadow of Trump Plaza in Atlantic City. Trump sponsored the race for two years—it eventually became the Tour DuPont—and many cyclists were happy that a prominent American businessman was investing in their sport. Powerboat racers were less thrilled when Trump waded into their sport. Traditionally held in sunny Key West, the World Powerboat Championship races were moved to Atlantic City in 1989 after Trump put up $160,000 to host the event, beating bids from groups in Key West and Honolulu. Almost immediately, some racers questioned the logic of holding a race off the New Jersey coast in October, when the waters can be much choppier than off South Florida. Those concerns proved prescient. Rain and high seas forced cancellation of multiple days of racing. When the boaters did race, the results were disastrous: several boats sank, and accidents caused one driver to break his back. On another day, when the waters were calm, a racer was killed when his boat flipped over.

One of the few who didn't complain about the weather that weekend was Trump, who crowed to reporters that the rain only ensured that the racers spent more time in his casinos: "From a truly cynical financial standpoint, I walked through the [Trump] Castle today and it's Boomtown, USA. The worse the weather, the better for business."

One sport above all others helped Trump rake in millions in Atlantic City: boxing. Trump's move into Atlantic City coincided with the emergence of one of the most electrifying fighters in the sport's history, a Brooklyn native with a distinct lisp and a knack for delivering knock-out blows with blinding speed. In 1986, twenty-year-old Mike Tyson became boxing's youngest heavyweight champion, and Trump tried to ensure every big Tyson fight happened at one of his properties. For a while, Trump nearly single-handedly relocated America's boxing capital from Las Vegas to Atlantic City, culminating in Tyson's June 1988 fight against Michael Spinks. Trump put up $11 million to host the fight, a record price. Tyson knocked out Spinks in ninety-one seconds, less time than it took to introduce Trump's family and many celebrity friends who were ringside that night. Still, the fight was a windfall for Trump and other casino owners. Trump Plaza grossed more than $18 million that weekend, and the combined gross from the city's twelve casinos topped $40 million. Trump's competitors took out a full-page ad in the local paper: "Thank you, Mr. Trump."

Trump took more than a passing interest in Tyson's career, trying to act as his personal financial adviser, even offering marital advice when Tyson was about to divorce the actress Robin Givens. When Tyson was convicted of raping eighteen-year-old Desiree Washington in 1992, one of his first calls was to Trump. A few weeks later—before Tyson was sentenced—Trump held a press conference to put forth an unusual proposal: Tyson should not be incarcerated for his rape conviction, but rather should be allowed to remain free and fight, with the proceeds going to benefit victims of sex crimes and Desiree Washington. The proposal was, not surprisingly, resoundingly criticized, with many people pointing out that Trump's plan would let him continue to benefit financially from Tyson's career. Tyson was sentenced to six years in prison. Years later, one of Trump's biographers would notice a boxing championship belt in his office. The belt had belonged to Tyson, Trump explained, and was payment for an unexplained debt.

TRUMP AND HIS FELLOW USFL owners had every reason to be optimistic. The first few weeks of the trial in Courtroom 318 at the federal courthouse in lower Manhattan had belonged to the underdog league. Its new attorney—Harvey Myerson, who had replaced the ailing Cohn at Trump's behest—made a strong case alleging that the NFL's antitrust violations had cost the USFL hundreds of millions of dollars. The jury of six—one man, five women, none football fans—listened as the bombastic Myerson, who often reeked of his omnipresent cigars, hammered away at the NFL. He produced two internal NFL exhibits: a document titled "Spending the USFL Dollar," which advocated that NFL teams poach lower-priced USFL players, forcing the cash-strapped league to spend more; and a slide show in which a Harvard Business School professor urged the NFL to use tactics inspired by Sun Tzu's military-strategy classic, *The Art of War*, such as dissuading ABC from keeping its contract with the USFL, surreptitiously encouraging unionization in the rival league, and luring away the most "influential USFL owners with promises of NFL franchises."

When Trump took the stand on June 23, 1986, testimony focused on a secret meeting between him and Rozelle in March 1984 at a suite in Manhattan's Pierre Hotel. Now the two men could agree on only three facts about their meeting—the date, location, and who paid for the room (Trump). According to Trump, he and Rozelle had been friends for years—Trump had attended parties at Rozelle's home and knew his wife well—but when rumors circulated that Trump might buy a USFL team, Rozelle strongly discouraged him from getting involved. After Trump bought the Generals, Rozelle treated him "like I had the plague."

In Trump's version, Rozelle promised that if Trump did all he could to keep the USFL from switching from spring to fall and prevented the USFL from filing an antitrust lawsuit, he'd get an NFL franchise. Trump testified he couldn't possibly take that deal: "I had some very good friends in the United States Football League; . . . there is no way that I am going to sell out people."

When Rozelle took the stand, he directly contradicted nearly everything Trump had said. "He was an acquaintance," the commissioner testified. "He was not a friend. He was not even on my Christmas card list." By Rozelle's account, Trump informed him that he was bringing two new owners to USFL franchises in Miami and Chicago: strong, wealthy men. "Then he said, 'But I don't want to do these things,'" Rozelle testified. Rather, what Trump really wanted was an NFL expansion team in New York, and Trump offered to arrange for a new stadium to be built for that team. Rozelle continued, "And he said, and I quote him directly, 'I would get some stiff to buy the New York Generals.' . . . Then he said, and again I quote him exactly, 'If I were to leave the United States Football League, it would be psychologically devastating'" for the USFL.

Rozelle supported his account with a summary of the meeting he had typed up immediately after it happened. Trump had no notes from his discussions with Rozelle. "I would have considered notes to be a very unnatural thing to do," Trump explained. "People don't go around making notes of conversations in my opinion."

Trump's testimony marked a turning point in the trial. A few days later, Frank Rothman—the NFL's reserved, grandfatherly attorney— argued that the USFL's financial struggles were its own fault. The league had lost its television contract when it moved to the fall at the behest of one owner—Trump—who wanted to force his way into the NFL. Rothman introduced the posthumous testimony of John Bassett, Trump's rival owner who had fought to keep the league in the spring. Bassett had succumbed to brain cancer the week the trial started, but in a deposition, he said the fall move for the USFL was premature, and it was all Trump's idea.

When the six jurors started to deliberate, it quickly became clear there was an even split. Two jurors thought the NFL had obviously harmed the USFL, which deserved hundreds of millions of dollars in damages. Two other jurors thought the NFL had done nothing wrong, and that the lawsuit was a desperate ploy by a rival struggling to stay alive. The two remaining jurors fell somewhere in between. Patricia Sibilia, like the rest of the jury, knew little about football or television contracts. She concluded that the NFL had acted as a monopoly and was guilty of predatory action toward the USFL, but she also thought the USFL's owners had overspent, moved teams from city to city seemingly at random, and prematurely lurched from spring to fall in violation of their TV contract. Sibilia decided she didn't like Trump, whom she'd barely heard of before the trial. "He was extremely arrogant and I thought that he was obviously trying to play the game," Sibilia recalled. "He wanted an NFL franchise. . . . The USFL was a cheap way in."

After thirty-one hours of deliberation, the jury reached a verdict. Sibilia helped broker an unusual compromise. As the forewoman started to read the verdict on July 29, 1986, the USFL owners initially thought they had won a startling, historic victory. The jury ruled the NFL was a monopoly. But the forewoman kept reading: "Damages: one dollar," which the court would triple to $3. Sibilia's compromise had been to call the NFL a monopoly, but absolve it of blame for the USFL's financial struggles. NFL officials celebrated. Without significant damages, they knew their rival was doomed. "We're lost now," said one USFL executive. "We're dead."

Myerson promised his clients he'd win them damages on appeal, but that never happened. The case was held up in appeals court for years over the USFL's legal fees, more than $5 million, which the NFL ultimately had to pay. The USFL never played another game. A few stars—Walker, Flutie, Steve Young—were immediately snatched up by the NFL, but most players from the disbanded teams either retired or tried to catch on with teams in the NFL or even the Canadian Football League. In Trump's book, *Trump: The Art of the Deal*, he came close to expressing regret: "I bought a losing team in a losing league on a long shot. It almost worked, through our antitrust suit, but when it didn't, I had no fallback. The point is that you can't be too greedy. If you go for a home run on every pitch, you're also going to strike out a lot." He laid much of the blame on his fellow owners: "If there was a single key miscalculation I made with the USFL, it was evaluating the strength of my fellow owners. In any partnership, you're only as strong as your weakest link."

Although the USFL's demise was one of Trump's first major public failures, the story faded over time amid the ceaseless torrent of Trump's subsequent ventures. Despite the league's ignominious end, his USFL adventure gave Trump, already a celebrity in New York, his first extended run of national attention. His first national newsmagazine profile came in *Sports Illustrated*, and his first national television appearance came on Sunday NFL pregame shows. To much of America, Trump was now the successful young developer from New York City who had taken on the NFL.

Some USFL alumni blamed Trump for the league's collapse and said the NFL was able to paint Trump as the villain because he was one. "Only Donald Trump could somehow turn the behemoth of the NFL into an underdog," said Michael Tollin, who ran a production company that made USFL highlight videos. Trump's involvement with the

USFL was all about "self-aggrandizement, narcissism, and his efforts to find a way to get a team in the National Football League." In 2009, Tollin directed the ESPN documentary *Small Potatoes: Who Killed the USFL?* To Tollin, the answer was simple: Trump. The documentary's climactic scene was an uncomfortable interview at Trump Tower: "I don't even think about the USFL anymore," Trump said. "It was a nice experience, it was fun, we had a great lawsuit." When Tollin asked if the move to the fall happened too quickly, Trump replied, "We had owners that were dying, we had owners that couldn't pay their bills. And when you have that, you have to act a little bit quickly. . . . A couple more questions and then I want to get out of here. I've had enough of this." Tollin then presented Trump with the result of the trial: the damages award from the NFL, a check for $3.76. (The seventy-six cents was interest.) Trump looked at it awkwardly, then quickly handed it back and ended the interview: "Well, that's very good. You can have it. Okay, thank you very much. Good luck, fellas."

Trump lost an estimated $22 million on the New Jersey Generals. The Dallas Cowboys—the team Trump said he considered buying in 1983 but wouldn't because you could only succeed "laterally" in the NFL—were sold in 1984 for $85 million. That ownership group flipped the team in 1989 to Jerry Jones, for $170 million. In 2015, *Forbes* declared the Cowboys the most valuable sports franchise in the world, worth an estimated $4 billion.

Trump flirted with buying an NFL franchise a few times after the USFL. In 1988, he discussed purchasing the New England Patriots, but ultimately bowed out. In 2014, he made a $1 billion bid for the Buffalo Bills, but was beaten by a $1.4 billion bid. In early 2016, he was asked about losing out on the Bills. For once, Trump was content with defeat. Running for president, he said, was "more exciting. And it's a lot cheaper."

11

The Great Unraveling

The air was cool and the fog thick over the Atlantic City boardwalk on the morning of June 16, 1990, as people gathered on risers outside the Trump Taj Mahal hotel and casino. Ten weeks had passed since its troubled opening, and Donald Trump was due to arrive for a surprise celebration of his forty-fourth birthday.

The two thousand or so Trump employees and their families stood across from the slate-gray ocean, on a stage erected for the occasion. Doug Cox, a motivational speaker Trump admired, warmed up the crowd. A wiry man with a white beard, Cox had run team-building workshops for nearly every employee of the mogul's casinos over the prior four years. Cox had been in California, attending his son's high school graduation, when he got an urgent call from a Taj manager, asking if he could get to Atlantic City to host the birthday rally. Cox took a red-eye to Philadelphia, where a driver whisked him to the rally. He directed the crowd to play imaginary trombones in the air while he led the vocals on James Brown's "I Feel Good."

Some in the crowd understood just how much Trump needed cheering. News reports had disclosed his casinos were in trouble. His buying spree, his astonishing accumulation of debt, and his affair with Marla Maples now threatened a great unraveling of his mystique and his empire. Trump's cash was in such short supply that, on the day before the rally, he had, for the first time, missed a payment on one of the casinos—$43 million due on the Trump Castle Hotel & Casino. Two days before, on June 14—Trump's actual birthday—an accounting firm that he had retained completed a devastating review of his finances. The confidential analysis by Kenneth Leventhal & Co. said that of Trump's twenty-two assets—the casinos, the yacht, Manhattan's Plaza Hotel, and all the rest—only three were running a profit. He had piled up a remarkable $3.2 billion in debt. The monthly cash balance from all his businesses was tumbling into the red. His net worth: negative $295 million.

By the time Trump boarded his helicopter for the twenty-minute hop from New York to Atlantic City, his financial troubles—his missed payment, and the specter of losing control of the Castle casino if he couldn't conjure up the money within ten days—had jolted many of his employees. On this morning, the lead headline in the *Press of Atlantic City* was "Trump Skips Payment on Castle Bond."

Trump was running late. It was close to noon by the time his Super Puma helicopter landed on the Castle's roof. A limo ushered him down Huron Avenue to the Taj. The fog had lifted as Trump glimpsed the balloons and signs that his workers held aloft. A band struck up "Happy Birthday." The crowd yelled, "We love you, Donald!" An Asian high roller presented him with a rug, a needlepoint of Trump's visage. No one mentioned the negative headlines. But as Trump stood on the stage in blazer and red tie in front of a banner that said WE'RE BEHIND YOU 400% DONALD, the bad news seemed to weigh on his mind. "Nobody wants to write the positives," he shouted to the crowd. "Over the years, I've surprised a lot of people. The largest surprise is yet to come."

TRUMP HAD, INDEED, MADE a career out of surprising people. He had created an empire greater than his father's, assembling stellar properties in Manhattan, his trio of casinos in Atlantic City, even an airline. He prided himself on buying or building the very best, sometimes overpaying out of faith in the Trump name and an ever-expanding market. His propensity for purchases that played to his ego had been especially evident in his acquisition of one of New York's most storied properties, the Plaza Hotel. Trump often had gazed at the château-style Plaza from his office at nearby Trump Tower—and decided he must have it. To trumpet his 1988 purchase, he took out a full-page advertisement in *New York* magazine and made a startling confession about his deal for the nineteen-story landmark hotel he called his *Mona Lisa*. "I can never justify the price I paid, no matter how successful the Plaza becomes," he wrote under the title, "Why I Bought the Plaza."

The price—$407 million—was not the point, Trump suggested. The hotel was etched into American culture. Scenes in F. Scott Fitzgerald's *The Great Gatsby* were set in the Plaza. The architect Frank Lloyd Wright lived in a second-floor suite while he designed the Guggenheim Museum. The Plaza was the home of Eloise, the fictional six-year-old who carried out escapades while living with her nanny on the "tippy-top floor."

Trump had installed his wife, Ivana, who had overseen the Trump Castle in Atlantic City, as president of the Plaza, authorizing her to make it into "New York's single great hotel, perhaps the greatest hotel in the world." The restoration—gleaming chandeliers, a new Japanese restaurant, the ballroom returned to its original splendor—cost $50 million, more than twice what Trump had intended. Trump obsessed over how the remodeling was done. Once, while touring the hotel, he became livid about a slab of cut-rate Chinese marble that he had initially approved, saying it looked too cheap and was the wrong shade of green. "He was mad about it and he blamed me for it," said Barbara Res, who supervised the Plaza reconstruction. "He was very, very angry, saying, 'This is shit, this is no good. . . . You're making a fucking fool out of me, you and Ivana.'" Res and Trump had sparred before, but she had never before seen him so furious.

The Plaza's financial underpinnings, never sturdy, weakened. Trump's purchase—a record price for a US hotel—was tens of millions of dollars more than the next-highest bid. He had borrowed the money, including $125 million backed by his personal guarantee, without collateral—a risky move. To make interest payments, the Plaza needed to fill all of its 814 rooms every night of the year at a rate of $500—more than twice what the hotel was charging.

Trump began to search for someone to invest in half of his cherished Plaza. He traveled as far as Japan to sit down with the wealthy Japanese who had been eager to put cash into Trump Tower. But they were put off by his debt, as well as his contention that Japan had been "taking advantage" of US military protection—a statement some perceived as anti-Japanese. Trump came home, no investor in sight, the Plaza's debt mounting.

AS THE PLAZA'S FINANCES worsened, so did those of one of Trump's most unlikely visions: a new airline, the Trump Shuttle. The same year he bought the hotel, 1988, he paid $365 million for the aircraft and northeastern routes that had belonged to bankrupt Eastern Airlines—a price many analysts deemed too high. Trump's plan was to retrofit each of Eastern's twenty-one worn-out Boeing 727 airplanes into a Trump-worthy "diamond in the sky." He hired a company to advise him on a logo, and after the first plane came out of the paint shop, he seemed satisfied with a red TRUMP emblazoned on the fuselage. But the *T* on the tail was a problem. He wanted it bigger. He sent the plane back to be repainted.

As with the Plaza, Trump had borrowed money to make the purchase, leaving the airline so burdened by debt that, to turn a profit, it would need an unrealistically high number of passengers. As soon as the Trump Shuttle took flight in June 1989, it became another drain on his finances.

Trump didn't know much about running an airline. Moreover, he discounted the advice of his own customers. Passenger surveys found that business travelers cared about little other than getting on-time service between New York, Washington, and Boston. Trump couldn't believe that was enough. He insisted on installing leather seats, chrome buckles, and bird's-eye maple paneling. The bathrooms were faux marble with gold-plated sinks.

Some of this luxury was impractical as well as unnecessary. Trump insisted on burgundy carpeting so plush that flight attendants had trouble navigating their meal and beverage carts. Trump's solution? He told them to push harder.

All this added luxury had a cost—about $1 million for each plane. As the airline's losses deepened, Trump came up with ideas that sometimes mystified his executives. He directed them to give every passenger a chip to one of his casinos, not realizing that his airline's business travelers did not frequent Atlantic City. Only two chips were redeemed. Seeking to cut costs, Trump suggested that the cockpit crews be reduced from three people to two. The shuttle's president, Bruce R. Nobles, pointed out that Federal Aviation Administration safety regulations required a pilot, a copilot, and an engineer.

BY SPRING OF 1990, Trump oversaw an empire at risk of collapse. It was in "severe financial distress as a result of cash flow shortages," a Casino Control Commission report found. The Trump Shuttle lost $34 million during the first half of the year, and Trump was trying to sell it, along with his yacht. The opening of the Taj initially brought a windfall—which wouldn't last—but the Taj was cannibalizing business from his other Atlantic City properties. A fading economy worsened matters, and threatened to make George H. W. Bush, who had succeeded Ronald Reagan, a one-term president. Suddenly, it seemed, Trump had neither the cash nor the credit he needed. The Trump Castle's bond payment was due in mid-June. A $63 million loan payment was due the following month on stock Trump had bought in Alexander's department store, a struggling, middlebrow retailer whose land he hoped to use someday for developments of his own.

Desperately in need of cash, Trump came up with an audacious act.

AS BANKERS ACROSS THE country tightened their lending practices, Trump still had a $100 million line of credit at Bankers Trust. Worried that his bankers would try to block any large transfer, Trump learned that they were going on vacation. He waited until they were gone; then, in a single day, withdrew virtually the entire $100 million. "I said, 'Draw it down.' . . . I took everything out of the bank," Trump said in an interview for this book. When the bankers realized what had happened, Trump said, they were shocked. One "went absolutely berserk." To Trump, the move seemed ingenious. His bankers thought it was reckless. Yet even the $100 million would not be enough. The possibility of personal bankruptcy loomed.

• • •

TRUMP TOOK A SEAT at a long conference table on the twenty-fifth floor of Manhattan's General Motors Building, a Georgian-marble-and-glass skyscraper that occupied a full block between Fifth Avenue and Madison Avenue. Trump was used to being in charge, but on this spring 1990 morning at the law firm of Weil, Gotshal & Manges, he was surrounded by nearly thirty bankers united by a shared goal: to prevent Trump's tottering financial empire from tumbling over the precipice—and taking their money with it.

It was the first face-to-face meeting between Trump and the group of bankers who, since the mid-1980s, had been lending him the money to buy most of his businesses and large-scale luxuries. These loans had now become a source of angst for a sprawling network of seventy-two banks. The biggest stakes lay with seven premier financial institutions—including Citibank, Chase, and Bankers Trust—but some had, in turn, sold parts of the loans to banks in Britain, Germany, and Japan.

Trump had borrowed from the banks during a time of easy money, which was coming to an end as the economy cooled. Only now had the bankers compared notes. Trump would later say the negotiations had been his idea. But with so much of his empire losing money—and so many loan payments coming due—bankers had their reasons for wanting to sit down with Trump. What the bankers discovered worried them. The arithmetic showed that Trump owed them, collectively, two-thirds of his $3.2 billion debt. Complicating the situation further, many of his loans provided that if he defaulted on any one such financing agreement, other bankers who had also lent to Trump could swoop in and demand payment on their loans.

To avert mutual destruction, a few of the lead bankers decided that their best hope would be to negotiate jointly with Trump. They would rein Trump in but leave him at the helm of his businesses. "He was basically worth more alive than dead," said Alan Pomerantz, a Weil, Gotshal real estate attorney who represented Citibank.

Which is why, on this morning, Trump came to the conference table to start negotiating. The group process was unorthodox, and no leader had been chosen. One of the few women in the room, Ann Lane, seized the moment. Lane, in her midthirties, was a Citigroup managing director for corporate debt restructuring, representing the bank with the most at risk. Lane blended a demure appearance with a take-charge manner. The bankers had to figure out just how much trouble they and Trump were in, she said, and find a solution acceptable to all. Trump had his own reasons for going along. Without borrowing more money, he would be unable, for starters, to cover his mid-June bond payment on the Castle casino or $28 million due the same day to Manufacturers Hanover Trust bank.

Trump's troubles at his casinos had, meanwhile, multiplied. He had clashed with his top managers after the deaths of the three executives in the 1989 helicopter crash forced him to play a more direct role in his Atlantic City holdings.

John O'Donnell, the president of Trump Plaza Hotel & Casino, regarded Trump's behavior as unsettling. He grew increasingly incensed at what he saw as Trump's effort to blame two of the dead executives, Stephen Hyde and Mark Etess, for his financial problems. "I'm fucking sick of you treating these people this way," O'Donnell told Trump, according to O'Donnell's memoir.

"You're fucking sick of it?" Trump responded. "Well, I'm fucking sick of the results down there."

"Donald, you can go fuck yourself!"

O'Donnell dictated a letter: "Dear Donald: Effective immediately, I resign my position as president and chief operating officer of Trump Plaza Hotel & Casino. Jack." (Years later, Trump gave a different version, saying he fired O'Donnell.)

Other departures further decimated Trump's team. He fired the vice president for human resources who had built the Taj's workforce. He demoted the president of the Taj casino, invoking what would become one of his favorite put-downs: the executive was a low-key "Type C personality." The growing crisis led to more stories about Trump's possible downfall. In June, Trump went public with his strategy of blaming others, including Hyde, who had overseen all of Trump's casinos. "Steve was my great friend, but I just saw things that I frankly wanted changed because I wasn't satisfied," Trump said. It was only after the helicopter crash, he bluntly acknowledged, "when I started getting involved and watching the operation in Atlantic City."

Through it all, Trump clung to his billionaire image. "It's ridiculous," he said of suggestions that he lacked the cash to pay contractors who had built the Taj. "I have a lot of money." Behind the scenes, however, Trump was frantically negotiating with his bankers. At any instant, they could call in many of the loans, demanding repayment. Trump kept reminding them that, unless they gave him relief, they all would suffer together.

BY THE LAST WEEK in June, Trump and the bankers had a tentative plan to restructure his loans. The bankers would provide $65 million, deferring interest payments on about $1 billion in loans for up to five years. In exchange for that breathing space, the bankers would assume control of vast chunks of Trump's empire. They would place liens on many of his most prized possessions, including his three casinos, the yacht, and his personal plane. They would compel him to sell off much of what he owned. In a particular indignity, they would place him on a personal spending leash—a budget of $450,000 a month at first, dropping within two years to $300,000—a fortune for most people, but a substantial curb on Trump's habits. Trump needed to keep up appearances, the bankers reasoned, to be in position to sell off his assets. Still, an obstacle remained. Some of the foreign banks balked, protesting that the deal was too easy on Trump. Finally, only two holdouts remained, both in Japan, a culture in which unpaid loans are a source of shame, even suicide. One night, Robert McSween, a Citigroup managing director who dealt with the foreign banks, realized that only one solution remained. At 11:00 p.m., he was still in his office when he called Trump at home: "Donald, you gotta come over and talk to these guys." McSween remembered Trump sounding miserable, dejected, as if he were almost crying: "Why bother? There's no way this is getting done. It's all over."

McSween said he persuaded Trump to get dressed, get in his limo, and drive the five blocks to Citibank headquarters. McSween, Lane, and a few other bankers escorted him into a conference room with a speakerphone. They dialed the Japanese bankers, who had gathered in a Tokyo office. At first, Trump was hunched over, downcast. He apologized to the bankers in Tokyo. McSween motioned for him to pick up the pace. Trump, the pitchman, found his cadence. Once the loans were restructured, he promised, the money would grow. It would all be great. Within thirty minutes, the bankers half a world away said they would sign the agreement.

On August 21, Trump was back in Weil, Gotshal's offices, seated this time at the head of the conference table. Pomerantz, the attorney representing Citibank, was to his left, handing him document after document to sign. "Donald, this is the lien on your house," Pomerantz told him. "This is the lien on your boat. This is the lien on Mar-a-Lago." The agreement was complex—two thousand pages in all. When the document signing was complete, Trump's bankers would hold the keys to a shriveling empire.

Trump, however, portrayed his humbling before the bankers as a victory. "It was the greatest deal I ever made because I saw the world collapsing, and instead of waiting a year, I took my pride and I said the hell with it," he recalled years later. "I'm telling you, six months later the banks were in such trouble they couldn't have given you ten cents." He had barely escaped. Yet, during the document signing, an aide arrived with stacks of books. Trump opened the cover of each one, inscribed "Thank you" in his bold, angular autograph, and handed out copies of his fresh release, *Surviving at the Top*.

THE BANKERS DEMANDED THAT the Trump Organization put its financial house in order and hire a chief financial officer and create a fiscal plan. Trump found his man by happenstance. He picked up a copy of a finance magazine that featured on its cover thumbnail photos of nearly a dozen chief financial officers. Trump asked a visiting investment banker to tell him which CFO was best. The banker pointed to one he knew, Steve Bollenbach, who was working in Memphis for a hotel-and-gaming company and was eager to return to New York. Trump had never met him but offered the job, and Bollenbach accepted. But when Bollenbach asked for a significant signing bonus, he got his first glimpse of the situation close-up. His boss-to-be had no cash for a bonus. They devised a plan: Trump persuaded Citibank to release its lien on unit 11A in Trump Parc Condominium, the former Barbizon Hotel on Central Park South. Thus Bollenbach came to own a twenty-eight-hundred-square-foot apartment with commanding views of the park.

Before long, Bollenbach was in the witness chair in the Casino Control Commission's main office, at a hearing on Trump's deal with the bankers. Bollenbach was asked how much Trump was worth. "Well, he tells me he's worth $3 billion," Bollenbach responded. The answer was technically true; Trump had, indeed, told him that. But Bollenbach did not yet know how much money his new boss had. He had worked at the Trump Organization for one day.

When Bollenbach began delving into the organization's finances, he got a surprise. The small staff on the twenty-sixth floor of Trump Tower included three accountants. Each knew about pieces of the fraying empire—the casinos, for instance, or the condos. But no one knew the overall picture; there were no consolidated financial reports. The Trump Organization seemed to Bollenbach less like a company than like one guy making investments. Bollenbach put together the organization's spreadsheets, listing each asset, its likely earnings, its debt, and its anticipated losses—basic figures that businesses routinely calculate.

Around this time, a confidant of Trump's became alarmed at the way his life seemed to be coming unglued: his financial mess, the drawn-out divorce fight, the humiliation. "I don't know how to say this nicely, but at times I was wondering, you know, would somebody put an end to themselves with the pressure?" said the confidant, who revealed his thoughts twenty-five years later on condition that he not be named. Far from anything dire, the confidant saw that Trump "showed up every morning at eight a.m. . . . tie tied, suit pressed, focused, and moving forward, and asking, 'What do we do now?'"

Trump continued to act like the billionaire he still told people he was. He failed to make payments on his yacht, yet he convinced the bank to pay for insurance; the bank reluctantly went along after Bollenbach pointed out that, for the bank to protect its own interest, the boat had to be insured and its owner couldn't afford to do it. Trump missed so many payments on his five helicopters that bankers clamored to claim them; he hid the choppers somewhere in New York for days before finally divulging where they were. The banks got the helicopters.

Trump nonetheless still radiated star power. When he and Bollenbach were in Atlantic City, they strolled now and then, with Trump's perpetual trio of security guards, a mile along the boardwalk from the Taj to his Plaza Hotel & Casino, to get some lunch. Crowds followed along, eager to get close, talk to him, touch him. The more time Bollenbach spent with Trump, the more he was struck by Trump's unshakable faith that his empire would endure intact. Bollenbach, however, recognized that the bankers' rescue plan was only a partial solution. It had not addressed $1.3 billion in debt on the three casinos, including the $675 million in high-interest junk bonds that Trump had used to buy the Taj. Although the Taj was breaking records for Atlantic City's gambling earnings, interest rates on the bonds were so high that the casino's income couldn't cover the bond payments. The first was due in mid-November, and Trump was in danger of missing that one, too.

So, late in the summer, Trump began another round of negotiations, trying to restructure the debt on the Taj bonds. Trump was so anxious to save badly needed dollars that he negotiated even when it seemed there was nothing to discuss. One day, Ken Moelis, an investment banker recommended by Bollenbach to help restructure the Taj debt, arrived at Trump's office. If he succeeded, Moelis's fee would be $8 million. "That's crazy," Trump responded, demanding a $1 million reduction. Moelis stood firm. After a half hour of discussion, Trump fished a coin out of his pocket and said they should flip for the difference. Moelis made sure the coin had a head and a tail, then tossed it in the air. He watched in dismay as it landed on the table, then bounced on the floor, landing near Trump. Moelis leapt across the table, trying to see the coin before Trump picked it up. It was too late. "Heads, I win!" Trump declared, and the price was shaved by $1 million. (Years later, asked whether he had really won the toss, Trump responded with a smile: "Only God knows. And me, I guess.")

By the time the negotiations began, the bonds' market value had sunk to as low as thirty-three cents on the dollar, and many had been sold by their original owners to investors specializing in distressed assets. A steering committee of Taj bondholders met with Bollenbach and other Trump representatives in New York at the Plaza. The talks centered on how much equity in the Taj the bondholders would extract if they lowered the interest rate on Trump's 14 percent bonds. Offers and counteroffers seesawed. Tempers flared. Two days before Thanksgiving, when Trump's bond payment was due, he proposed to lower his interest rate more than in his earlier offers; bondholders rejected the idea and prepared to force him into bankruptcy. That evening, the talks broke off.

The next night, however, the two sides were back at the Plaza. Behind the scenes, an idea had emerged from two men pivotal to the talks: the head of the bondholders' steering committee, Hillel Weinberger, who had bought a large bloc of the distressed Taj bonds for his employer, Loews Corp.; and the billionaire financier Carl Icahn. A Queens native like Trump, Icahn had built his reputation in the 1980s as an investor and corporate raider. He held the controlling interest in Trans World Airlines, stripped its assets, and took it private, leaving the airline in debt and prompting its former chairman to call Icahn "one of the greediest men on earth."

Like Trump's bankers before them, Icahn and Weinberger reasoned that the Taj—and their investment—would retain the greatest value if they kept Trump in charge. Pushing him out of the Taj or into involuntary bankruptcy would frighten away gamblers, force a search for a new casino operator, and require a new gaming license. The other casinos in town would, like vultures, hire away the Taj's first-rate hosts and lure the casino's prized high rollers.

Television crews camped along Forty-Fifth Street, outside the bankruptcy lawyers' office where Trump's people and the bondholders haggled. Midnight came and went. Trump defaulted on his bond payment. The talks shifted to the phone, with Trump doing his own negotiating, until 2:00 a.m., when the parties hung up, deadlocked.

At daylight, the bondholders scheduled a midday press conference to announce that there would be no deal. At midmorning, the bondholders' lead negotiators decided to try again. By noon, they and Trump had an agreement. Trump got what he wanted at the Taj—whisker-thin majority ownership: 50.5 percent of the stock and control of the casino's board. The deal was folded into a new kind of legal tool, a "prepackaged" bankruptcy—in which the two sides would dip briefly into court to ratify their agreement—instead of a drawn-out traditional bankruptcy that would leave the fate of the Taj, the bankers, and Trump himself in the unpredictable hands of a judge. When the bondholders' leaders shared these details with the larger group, some were angry. They had wanted to exact revenge against Trump, not rescue him. Icahn, the billionaire with the most bonds, got on the phone and argued that the agreement was the best they could get. "We're both on a life raft now, and it's sinking," he told a dissident bondholder. "We have to do something to save ourselves."

Late in the afternoon, Trump stood in a gilded conference room at the Plaza and cast the blame far from himself. "The Taj Mahal," he told the crush of reporters, "is caught in a huge recession—maybe the word is *depression*."

The tentative agreement that day was not the end of the drama. Four months later, in April 1991, Trump again faced New Jersey's casino regulators, needing them to renew the Taj's license. The commission approved licenses only if casino owners could show they were financially stable. The commission staff's report on Trump's financial condition painted a dark scenario. Despite the deal with the bankers, Trump could be expected to "exhaust his available financial resources in July" and "cannot be considered financially stable."

Nevertheless, when commission members convened in Atlantic City three days later to vote, they became the latest group to give Trump a break. There was more to consider than his fragile finances, they reasoned. If the commission withdrew his license and the Taj failed, what about all the employees who would lose their jobs, the vendors who would be cut off from Atlantic City's biggest casino, the taxes that New Jersey and the city would forfeit? With one dissenting vote, the commission let the Taj stay open for another year.

ONE STORY FROM THIS era is emblematic of the pressure Trump faced. The week before Christmas 1990, Trump's father, Fred, dispatched a lawyer to the Castle casino, with its crimson and gold neon crowns over the front door. The lawyer, Howard Snyder, approached the casino cage and handed over a certified check for $3.35 million, drawn on Fred's account.

Snyder then walked over to a blackjack table, where a dealer paid out the entire amount in 670 gray $5,000 chips. The next day, the bank wired another $150,000 into Fred's account at the Castle. Once again, Snyder arrived at the casino and collected the full amount in 30 more chips.

Neither Fred Trump nor his attorney nor anyone else used any of the $3.5 million in chips to gamble. The gray chips were yet another emergency strategy to funnel cash to Fred's hard-pressed son. Nearly a decade after Fred had lent his son $7.5 million to help pay off debts, Donald Trump, in his midforties, was again relying on his father as a financial crutch. In this instance, Fred stepped in because, six months after his son had missed the first Castle bond payment, another was coming due, and casino executives warned that they couldn't pay the full amount. Trump's father, they learned, could provide $3.5 million in cash, but there was a catch: if he simply gave the money as a gift, it would be siphoned off to the Castle's many creditors. Depositing the cash into a gambling account was a way to sidestep them. Sure enough, the Castle made its bond payment the day Fred's lawyer bought the first batch of chips.

By then, the Castle was Donald's most endangered casino. He had missed three loan payments. The newer, fancier Taj was draining away customers. As 1991 began, the bleeding continued. For the first three months of that year, Castle gambling revenues dropped nearly one-third. For the year, it lost $50 million.

Years later, Trump contended that propping up the Castle with millions in his father's chips had been Fred's idea. "My father said, 'Oh, let me do it, it's easy with the chips,'" Trump said.

New Jersey casino regulators griped that, in reaching a settlement with the Castle, the state's Division of Gaming Enforcement had agreed to shield the identity of the person who dreamed up the scheme. "I don't think there is anyone in this room that doesn't know how this came down," commissioner Frank J. Dodd said. "Fred Trump didn't wake up in the middle of the night and say, 'I feel like buying three and a half million dollars' worth of chips.'" As unprecedented as the episode was, commissioners concluded that it had violated only a rule intended to keep organized crime out of Atlantic City. Under the rule, anyone who lends money to a casino must be approved as a qualified "financial source." Because Fred was an unauthorized source, the commission unanimously voted to fine Trump Castle $65,000—more than the Gaming Enforcement Division had recommended, but less than 2 percent of the money that Fred had handed to his son's casino. Neither Fred nor his son nor anyone else was ever personally punished.

The lifeline from the chip purchases didn't last. Trump's mountain of debt eventually compelled him, in March 1992, to put the Castle and the Plaza Hotel & Casino into the same kind of bankruptcy arrangement that had barely preserved his ownership stake in the Taj. Trump had now put all three of his casinos into bankruptcy. He survived thanks to a principle that had served him well: his creditors believed his name still had enough value to keep him in charge.

A FEW YEARS EARLIER, when he was first widening his lens beyond Manhattan to the possibilities in a down-and-out gambling mecca, Trump had told the Casino Control Commission that he only wanted what was best for Atlantic City. Many years later, he revealed a different perspective. The bottom line, he said, was that "for myself these were all good deals. . . . I wasn't representing the country. I wasn't representing the banks. . . . I was representing Donald Trump. So for myself, they were all good deals."

The small-fry contractors who'd placed their faith in Trump and built his gambling palaces learned about his priorities the hard way. Mark Cutler thought he was hitting the big time when, in 1989, his Pennsylvania business won the contract to create the neon-red TRUMP TAJ MAHAL sign that would sparkle against Atlantic City's skyline. Cutler, whose business dated to his father and uncle's struggle to make a living during the Great Depression, went twice to Trump Tower in New York to make a deal with Trump. The casino magnate pounded his large desk, demanding the best of everything—the best materials, best finishes, best fabrication techniques, a sign that would last. Trump was demanding even about the metal edges of the sign's twenty-foot-tall letters, insisting that they be red. It took some doing, but Cutler finally persuaded him that black edges would make each letter stand out more vividly against the night sky.

At first, it seemed a dream job—Cutler Industries won a contract for about $2.5 million. Payments came as soon as invoices were sent in. A couple of months before the Taj opened, however, something changed. A delay, then more delay. Soon, Cutler was waiting for Trump to pay him $303,000. He banded together with four dozen other subcontractors who had worked on the Taj but hadn't been paid—Trump owed them $54 million in all. Marty Rosenberg, the co-owner of Atlantic Plate Glass Co., had installed the shimmery reflective glass on the Taj's exterior. Now Trump owed his company more than $1 million.

Trump offered to pay each contractor one-third of what was due. For the rest, he would issue bonds that gave him nearly a decade to pay the full amount. Cutler couldn't absorb the loss. It was a challenging economic time. His business was in turmoil. He couldn't make payroll for his fifty employees. He couldn't pay on time for the materials he needed to make signs. He took money from his daughter's college fund. Still, it wasn't enough. "It was devastating," Cutler said years later. "Financially devastating and mentally devastating." This was his company, his family's heritage. He had built up its skill and reputation, finally winning the job at the Taj, which seemed like the biggest plum of all, and now it had knocked him down. In May 1991, Cutler Industries filed for bankruptcy. Seventeen months later, a judge gave permission to sell off the parcel of land that had been the company's home.

FOR MONTHS AFTER TRUMP worked things out with his bankers, he was required to meet with a group of them every Friday morning to report what he had spent and what progress he had made in unloading the *Trump Princess* and other possessions. Then, on a July afternoon in 1991, bankers saw Trump on television alongside Marla Maples. She held up her left hand to display a 7.5-carat, emerald-cut diamond ring. The best woman, Trump said, deserved the best.

The next Friday, when his bankers saw Trump, they were enraged. Where, they demanded to know, had he gotten the money for the $250,000 ring? Trump skated past their ire. The ring, he said, was on loan, borrowed from the jeweler Harry Winston in exchange for free publicity. This was Donald being Donald, his bankers figured. It wasn't the first time they had had to deal with the messy intersection of his personal life and his finances. A few months earlier, without his bankers' permission, Trump had handed Ivana a certified check for $10 million as part of their divorce settlement. The bankers had advanced him the money to keep his casinos and other businesses afloat, not to help end his marriage. Bollenbach, his chief financial officer, was astonished when he learned about the check after the fact, and he told Trump he shouldn't have done it. Trump gave a familiar reply: What are they going to do? Trump's affair with Marla, the fallout from his divorce from Ivana, the was-he-or-wasn't-he links to other beautiful women—all distracted him from his faltering businesses. Over the years, he had blamed problems on his underlings, a weak economy— anything but himself. But in an interview for this book, he said: "I did take my eye off the ball, and part of that was because of the difficulty I had with the marriage, of course." He acknowledged that he didn't "focus as much as you would if things were going swimmingly."

The first president of Trump Shuttle, Bruce Nobles, heard from women that they were shunning the airline because of its owner's womanizing. Nobles was chairman of the New York chapter of a net-work of young chief executives, and even a male CEO approached him at one meeting and said he wouldn't fly on the Shuttle and wouldn't let his employees use it. The reason? He didn't approve of Trump.

Nobles called his boss and urged him to get his sex life out of the headlines: "Look, businesswomen in particular are tending to avoid us because they don't like what they're reading about you in the paper."

Trump chuckled. "Yeah, but the guys love it."

DESPITE THE TROUBLES, TRUMP had kept talking up his Shuttle with customary bravado. As late as September 1991, he asserted that, with falling fuel prices and a seasonal influx of passengers, the airline was gaining value. "There is no pressure to sell," he said. What Trump left unsaid was that, a year earlier, he had begun defaulting on the Shuttle's loan payments, prompting Citibank, in tandem with other financial institutions, to take over the airline. As a technicality, they left Trump as owner, but the banks called the shots, requiring him to keep the planes flying to protect the airline's value as the banks searched for a buyer. The situation, the bankers reasoned, was unlike that of the casinos, where the Trump name added luster and generated business. Trump was a real estate guy, not an airline expert, and in this case his brand wasn't much of a boost to its value.

It took another year and a half before the bankers found a buyer,

US Airways. In March 1992, the banks took nominal ownership away from Trump. He blamed the economy, not his own widely questioned decisions, for the Shuttle's problems. "If the economy stayed good or went better, it would've been a good deal," Trump said years later. "But the economy didn't go good, and I got out of the airline without any damage. I mean, it worked out fine. You have to understand, those were the go-go days where the banks would give you more money than you needed."

In April 1992, workers stripped the giant *T*s off the tails of Trump Shuttle's Boeing 727s, the very ones Trump had sent back to be repainted with bigger logos. Now they were vanishing. The Shuttle, which had never made money, would no longer bear his name. It was the latest ignominy after what industry insiders regarded as a string of miscalculations.

THIS WAS NO ORDINARY Saturday night at the Trump Taj Mahal. Upon arrival in the grand ballroom, each of eight hundred friends, relatives, and gamblers got a Donald-on-a-stick, a life-size mask. Free drinks flowed. Dinner was lobster-wrapped veal. After dinner came the impersonators—an Elvis crooning "My Way," a faux–Marilyn Monroe singing, in Trump's honor, "Happy Celebration to You." Billed as a comeback party, "Against All Odds" was intended to spotlight the improving circumstances of Trump's Atlantic City holdings. It was November 1992, eight months since the Castle and Plaza casino bondholders had agreed to lower Trump's interest payments in exchange for nearly half his ownership. As with the Taj before them, a judge had quickly approved these tidy prepackaged bankruptcies.

Waiting in the ballroom for their host, his guests watched a large-screen video of Trump's earliest days in Atlantic City and his recent gains in gambling revenues. The most notable new fact about the Trump empire, however, was conspicuously missing from the evening. Just three days before the party, Trump's most cherished property—his *Mona Lisa* opposite Central Park, the Plaza Hotel—became his fourth to slip into bankruptcy. Trump had worked out yet another deal in which creditors would lighten his loan payments. In exchange, they would take nearly half his stake in the hotel—and win the right to sell it if it fetched a nice enough price. Of everything remaining in his empire, Trump wished most passionately that he could keep the Plaza.

Thus had the first three years of the decade left him presiding over an empire in tatters: Four corporate bankruptcies. An airline repossessed by his bankers. His Alexander's department store stock in the banks' hands. His 282-foot yacht sailing, on bankers' orders, from port to port around the globe in search of a buyer, until a Saudi prince picked it up for one-third less than Trump had paid.

Yet there was seemingly no room for melancholy that Saturday night in the Taj ballroom. At 9:00 p.m., Trump was about to make his appearance. He stood behind a ceiling-high paper mural, decorated with rising stock prices and headlines celebrating his comeback. His hands wrapped in red boxing gloves, Trump punched through the paper and stepped through, revealing a bright silk robe and matching boxing shorts over his tuxedo.

The *Rocky* theme song played over the sound system. An announcer cried out, "Let's hear it for the king!" But the king, if that is what Trump was, would need yet another magic act if he was to survive.

TRUMP HAD TAPPED LINES of credit, issued bonds, and even relied on his father to raise money. He retained control of the three casinos that had fallen into bankruptcy. By 1995, he believed it had all been worth it. The economy was improving, and increasing numbers of gamblers were filing into Trump's Atlantic City properties. Still, he faced huge debts. So Trump seized upon a new strategy, based on one of the oldest tools in capitalism. He created a publicly traded company, which owned the Trump Plaza Hotel & Casino and was expected to operate Trump's new casino ventures. Investors could now own a piece of the Trump brand, under a ticker symbol composed of Trump's initials: DJT.

The plan worked, at least at first. Trump's company raised $140 million from investors at $14 a share. He combined some of that cash with a sale of $155 million in new casino junk bonds to pay down $88 million of his debts. Shares soared to $36 in 1996, and Trump's stake in the company grew to about $290 million, restoring him for the first time since 1989 to the Forbes 400 list of America's wealthiest people.

(Unsatisfied, he called the editors from his plane to argue that his net worth was "probably over $2 billion," four times higher than *Forbes*'s estimate.)

Less than a year after Trump's company went public, it paid premium prices for two of Trump's deeply indebted, privately held casinos, the Trump Taj Mahal and the Trump Castle. In essence, he was both buyer and seller, able to set whatever price he wanted. The company bought his Castle for $100 million more than analysts said it was worth. Trump pocketed $880,000 in cash after arranging the deal. By the end of 1996, shareholders who had bet on a rosy Trump future suddenly found themselves saddled with $1.7 billion of his debt. The company spent much of its cash on interest payments. The share price plunged to $12 in 1996, about one-third of its peak price. The company paid Trump $7 million that year, including a $5 million bonus.

For years, details of Trump's dealings had been kept private. But now, since public companies must disclose performance data, the gap between his projections and reality was revealed to all. Trump said in 1996 that his new riverboat casino in Gary, Indiana, would generate $100 million a year in revenue. In fact, it logged $82 million in revenue that year, and cost $80 million to run. In March 1997, when the stock was trading at one-quarter of its price ten months earlier, Chase securities analyst Steve Ruggiero said the company wasn't "forthcoming with all the analysts," which he said "raises suspicions."

In 1998, the US Treasury fined a Trump company $477,000 for failing to file transaction reports designed to guard against money laundering. In 2000, Trump and his partners paid $250,000 to settle a New York case in which they were accused of secretly funding an ad blitz against the opening of new casinos in the Catskill Mountains. In 2002, federal securities regulators cited the casino group for having used a type of financial reporting that was designed to downplay negative results.

While Trump was chairman, the company lost more than $1 billion and was in the red every year between 1995 and 2005. During that time, the company's share prices plunged from a high of $35 to as low as 17 cents. A shareholder who bought $100 of DJT shares in 1995 could sell them for about $4 in 2005. The same investment in MGM Resorts would have increased in value to about $600. Holders of the company's

stocks and bonds lost more than $1.5 billion during Trump's manage-
ment. In 2004, stock-exchange officials froze trading in the public
company as word spread that it was filing for bankruptcy—the fifth
such corporate action of Trump's career. Its reorganization plan would
reduce shareholders' stake in the company from roughly 40 percent to
5 percent, with much of the difference given over to bondholders owed
money by Trump.

Trump would also see his share reduced, but he would stay on
as chairman—and, for his leadership, be granted a $2 million annual
salary, a $7.5 million tract in Atlantic City, and a minority stake in
the Miss Universe pageant, which the company co-owned with NBC.
Shareholders sued, calling the plan a "basket of goodies" for Trump.
Trump settled, agreeing to pay the stockholders $17.5 million and pro-
ceeds from an auction of the land. Sebastian Pignatello, an Atlantic
City investor who bought 150,000 shares of the company beginning
in the late nineties, said shareholders lost tens of millions of dollars because of what he called Trump's use of the company as a personal piggy bank. Pignatello started buying when shares were around
$3 each and sold when they were worth pennies. He recovered some
of his money in the settlement, but said he still lost tens of thousands
of dollars on the investment. "He had been pillaging the company all
along," Pignatello said. "He has no qualms about screwing anybody.
That's what he does. He still made out great."

Indeed, the company was a good deal for Trump. During his time
as the company's chairman, from 1995 to 2009, including five years as
its chief executive, he was paid more than $44 million. Between 2006
and 2009, the company bought $1.7 million of Trump-brand mer-
chandise, including $1.2 million of Trump Ice bottled water.

Trump's casinos struggled every year. His publicly traded company had bought the Castle (later renamed Trump Marina) for $525
million in 1996, and sold it for just $38 million in 2011. Trump had no
regrets over his company's performance: "Entrepreneurially speaking,
not necessarily from the standpoint of running a company but from
an entrepreneur's standpoint, [the stock offering] was one of the great
deals." The entrepreneur, of course, was Trump himself, and the implication was that he had profited even as shareholders did not. Trump

had managed to rebuild his finances, and even the skeptical analysts at *Forbes* said in 2004 he was worth at least $2.6 billion.

Once again, Trump saved himself by selling himself. The image, he'd always said, was at least as important as the underlying product. Now that image was about to catapult his personal brand to a new, nationwide stage, one where he wouldn't need to build anything other than his reputation. A fellow "survivor," one of the nation's most prominent TV producers, was looking for the right billionaire to star in a reality show.

12

Ratings Machine

Just when the Trump brand was teetering on the edge of no longer being the gold standard, along came a British-immigrant TV producer who was only a few years removed from selling $18 T-shirts on Venice Beach. By 2002, that shirt seller, Mark Burnett, had transformed himself into the creator and chief architect of *Survivor*, the biggest of the TV reality shows. One of the nation's most durable ratings power-houses, *Survivor* was a glamorous bit of TV catnip that attracted viewers by the millions to watch beautiful people compete in exotic spots such as the Australian outback and the Polynesian islands. The ratings zoomed from the start, but Burnett's newfound millions couldn't mask one bit of unhappiness at the center of his life: he had little kids at home in New York and he was hardly ever there. On one visit home from filming the show, Burnett's son, ten years old at the time, told his dad he'd forgotten what he looked like.

"There has to be a way to do a successful show in an American city," Burnett thought. The way home, he realized, was through Donald Trump. Burnett's lightbulb moment came when he was filming the finale of *Survivor: Marquesas* in New York's Central Park, at Wollman ice-skating rink, which Trump operated, having famously renovated it in a jiffy and under budget after the city government had spent six years and $12 million failing to fix it. Burnett was fed up with being stuck in the jungle, "with crocodiles and ants and everything that could kill you." He decided that his next show needed to be set in a different kind of jungle, made of asphalt, "and what I needed was someone larger-than-life, very colorful," a character who could carry this new urban *Survivor*, who would be likable, tough, and fascinating enough to interest an audience for a full season.

Wollman Rink put the idea right in Burnett's face: TRUMP was plastered all over the Zamboni and the walls of the rink. Burnett took the hint and went to see Trump at his office in Trump Tower. Burnett's notion for a new show had struck him on one of his visits home, when he watched ant colonies swarming around each other; it looked like a battle. Burnett let the image tumble around in his mind and it morphed into teams of competing job-seekers—the premise for *The Apprentice*. Burnett's meeting with Trump lasted an hour. Burnett explained that the show would showcase Trump's whole empire—Trump Tower, the casinos, the hotels, the helicopter and the jet, the opulent apartment, and the splendor of Mar-a-Lago. Trump would be the main character, the arbiter of talent, the boss—judge, jury, and executioner in a weekly winnowing of young go-getters desperate for a chance to run one of the mogul's businesses.

Trump didn't watch reality TV and didn't much like what he'd heard about it. "That was for the bottom-feeders of society," Trump said. And he was worried that the show would take too much of his time. Burnett assured Trump that he could devote just a few hours to each episode, and the show could be made entirely inside Trump Tower. Despite his concerns about time, Trump was immediately taken with the show's potentially enormous promotional value. "My jet's going to be in every episode," he said. "The Taj is going to be featured. Even if it doesn't get ratings, it's still going to be great for my brand." Trump saw the show as a bridge to a new market, a new audience, and especially to young people. Burnett pressed Trump on the power of TV to shape reputations: Trump had been famous for more than a generation, but a TV show of his own would allow him to mold his image as never before, giving Americans the chance to see him in a way they perceived as unmediated. Without a show of one's own, Burnett believed, a celebrity is but a product of editors' headlines and journalists' takes. Being the star of a show would let Trump remake himself as he saw fit.

The pitch was an instant hit. Burnett walked out of that first meet-.

ing with a handshake deal to make *The Apprentice*. Trump secured not only a starring role on a show made by TV's hottest producer but also 50 percent ownership of it. Trump had consulted no one, done no research. He liked the idea; he bought it. It was a classic Trump moment, an example of the gut-instinct decision making that he had proudly touted throughout his career. Buy a show. Win an audience. Burnish an image. "It's very easy," Trump said.

But first, the show needed a home. And a Trump TV show struck many in Hollywood as a pretty dumb idea. Even Trump's own agent told him *The Apprentice* was a loser—business shows never work on TV, he said. (Trump said he fired the agent shortly thereafter: "If I would have listened to him, I wouldn't have done the show.") Burnett made the rounds of the networks, pitching *The Apprentice*. Fox passed on the show, concluding that it was too elitist—Trump didn't seem like a TV star, and the contestants were too highbrow, products of fancy educations, and therefore too difficult for average American viewers to connect with emotionally.

ABC had once tried to recruit Trump to a different reality show, in which cameras would follow him around as he made deals with politicians and contractors. Trump hated the idea; he thought it was too much of an intrusion into his business and wouldn't make for good TV. Now, ABC executives liked the pitch for *The Apprentice*, but negotiations bogged down over price. Burnett knew how much money he needed per episode and wasn't about to chip away at the concept. CBS wanted the show, too, but Trump was angry at the network for deciding not to pick up the option on the Miss USA and Miss Universe beauty pageants, which he owned until 2015.

NBC wanted *The Apprentice* even before Burnett made the pitch—not because of Trump, but because of Burnett's success with *Survivor*. To the network's decision makers, Trump was just one more iconic businessman. He'd be fine on the show, but so would moguls such as Richard Branson or Mark Cuban. But two key executives—Jeff Zucker, then president of NBC Entertainment, and Jeff Gaspin, who ran reality programming for the network and was later chairman of NBC Entertainment—were longtime New Yorkers who had watched firsthand as the city's tabloids developed covering Trump into a symbiotic, profitable industry. They shared the belief that there was more

Friedrich Trump, Donald's grandfather, immigrated to New York City at sixteen and moved West, where he prospered in the gold rush before returning to New York to raise his family.

After Donald's rambunctious behavior got him in trouble at his private school in Queens, his father sent him to New York Military Academy, a boarding school where he was promoted during his senior year to captain of A Company (Donald, front center).

Fred Trump made his fortune building middle-class apartments in Brooklyn and Queens, but the home he built for his family was a twenty-three-room Georgian mansion equipped with an intercom system and staffed with a cook and chauffeur.

Donald's mother, Mary, was a Scottish immigrant who sought a better life in America. His father, Fred, made a fortune in New York real estate.

Donald learned the real estate business from his father, Fred, who built a massive housing complex called Trump Village, pictured here. Donald became president of his father's company, Trump Management.

Trump won his first major political battle when he got New York City and State officials to support tax breaks for his renovation of Manhattan's Commodore Hotel into a Grand Hyatt. In 1978, Governor Hugh Carey points to a rendering of the Hyatt. Joining Carey were (left to right): Trump, Mayor Ed Koch, and Robert Dormer, executive vice president of the Urban Development Corp.

Lawyer Roy Cohn (left) defended Trump (right) in a racial bias case brought by the Justice Department and became a key adviser, advocating that an opponent be counterattacked with all possible force.

In the 1980s, Trump developed his signature property in Manhattan, Trump Tower, built on the site of the old Bonwit Teller department store. He hired hundreds of undocumented Polish immigrants to demolish Bonwit Teller. Historic preservationists were outraged when the building's famous friezes were destroyed in the process.

Trump already owned two hotel-casinos in Atlantic City in 1990 when he opened the massive Trump Taj Mahal, which was supposed to be his capstone. But the Taj entered a gambling market already hit by hard economic times, and Trump eventually put all three of his casinos through corporate bankruptcies because of massive debts.

Trump spent nearly three decades in and around the beauty pageant business. He owned the Miss Universe contest for nearly twenty years. Here, Trump poses with contestants in the Miss USA pageant on his yacht in Atlantic City in 1988.

Trump's businesses were facing considerable pressure when TV producer Mark Burnett asked Trump if he would star in a reality show about a Manhattan real estate mogul picking his apprentice by putting contestants through a series of challenges. For fourteen seasons, Trump played a decisive manager with an opulent lifestyle on *The Apprentice* (here, contestants from the show's offshoot, *Celebrity Apprentice*).

Trump's marriages and divorces were the stuff of tabloid drama. He married Czech skier Ivana Zelníčková (top) in 1977 and they divorced, after much controversy, in 1992. Trump then married model and actress Marla Maples (right) in 1993; they divorced in 1999. He married his third wife, Slovenian model Melania Knauss, in 2005.

In 2010, Trump visited the construction site of a golf course his company was building near Aberdeen, Scotland. Trump said the development, which had faced local opposition, would be the "greatest golf course in the world."

Trump announced his candidacy for the Republican nomination for president in June 2015 in the lobby of Trump Tower. From left to right, members of his family include Eric Trump, Lara Yunaska Trump, Donald, Barron Trump, Melania Trump, Vanessa Haydon Trump, Kai Madison Trump, Donald Trump Jr., Donald John Trump III, Ivanka Trump, Jared Kushner, and Tiffany Trump.

Trump, wearing his signature "Make America Great Again" ball cap, visits the Iowa State Fair in Des Moines on August 14, 2015, as he campaigned ahead of that state's caucuses. Trump lost the Iowa vote to Senator Ted Cruz but prevailed against a field of sixteen opponents to become the first major-party nominee since Dwight Eisenhower who had not previously held elective office.

to Trump than people outside the New York area might know. And if they were wrong about Trump, they figured, *Apprentice* might survive anyway. The concept NBC bought envisioned Trump as host for only one year. The idea was to have a different mogul as the star each season. Trump was to be followed by Branson, Cuban, and Martha Stewart, the home-furnishings billionaire who had not yet been convicted and imprisoned for obstructing justice and lying about a stock sale.

That notion fell by the wayside during the taping of the first episode. The script for *The Apprentice* called for the host to play a relatively modest role. The show was about the contestants—and more than 215,000 people had signed up to become one of the first sixteen candidates on the show, living in a faux-apartment set that Burnett had built on the same floor of Trump Tower as the boardroom set (the elevator that contestants would be seen taking "up to the boardroom" was just one more piece of showbiz). Trump was to introduce the challenge that contestants faced at the start of each episode, then appear in a brief boardroom scene at the end, when he would decide which contestant had performed poorly and would not return the next week.

Trump took to his TV role as if he'd spent his life preparing for it. The taping went on for nearly three hours, well longer than planned. A couple of days later, when NBC executives screened rough cuts of the boardroom scenes, they were unanimous: the show's script needed to be revised. Trump's scenes were gold. "After the first episode," Gaspin recalled, "we said we want more Trump." So did the viewers, 20 million of whom tuned in to the first episode—an audience that would build to 27 million by the end of that first season. The show was built as a virtually nonstop advertisement for the Trump empire and lifestyle, complete with an opening montage that contrasted Trump in his limo with an image of a homeless man on a bench. "I'm the largest real estate developer in New York," Trump's voice-over boasted. "I own buildings all over the place. Model agencies, the Miss Universe pageant, jetliners, golf courses, casinos, and private resorts like Mar-a-Lago. . . . I've mastered the art of the deal and have turned the name Trump into the highest-quality brand. And as the master, I want to pass along some of my knowledge to somebody else."

What would become the show's catchphrase, "You're fired," was not scripted. Although TV reality shows generally follow a detailed outline, Trump made clear from the start that he intended to just wing it. He didn't like the idea of memorizing lines. He would read the outline for the episode ahead of time, but once the camera was rolling, he would improvise his part, just as he always had at speaking engagements. In the first boardroom scene, when it came time for Trump to decide which finalist would not return the next week, he blurted, "You're fired." Backstage, the production crew immediately cheered the line, cementing its place in future episodes.

But although "You're fired" became a symbol of Trump's blunt toughness, he didn't deliver the line in a sneering or gloating fashion. In fact, Trump often seemed to find it difficult to summarily oust a member of the cast. He would pause uncomfortably and soften his voice just before he sacked a contestant, and he frequently consulted with the two managers he had at his side in those scenes, often accepting their advice even when his own views ran in a different direction.

Trump's performance style on the show evolved quickly. During the filming of the first episode, he seemed to know in his gut which contestant should be fired and saw little reason for a prolonged discussion. But an immediate ouster did not make for compelling television, so producers asked their famously impatient star to slow down and let the drama play out between the contestants battling for the grand prize of a one-year, $250,000 job with the Trump Organization. Trump took the advice and quickly learned to milk the contestants, letting their anguish and embarrassment in the moment of decision play out in extended scenes that viewers found impossible to stop watching. "Trump used no teleprompters, no cues," said Andy Dean, a contestant during the second season who went on to become president of Trump Productions.

Over fourteen seasons as the show's host and executive producer, Trump got plenty of practice honing a blunt speaking style accentuated by short, declarative sentences; delivering taunts—sometimes playful, sometimes searing—of the finalists; and captivating the audience with a theatrical sense of timing. Trump took pride in his stage skills. "I've never had lessons," he said. He traced his knack for theater to his mother, who he said had a natural talent for performance. "I've always felt comfortable in front of a camera. Either you're good at it or you're not good at it."

The show's first seasons featured sixteen to eighteen contestants, selected after in-person interviews, standardized testing, and psychological and medical evaluations. The contenders saw Trump mainly when he assigned them tasks and later in the wood-paneled boardroom, where the showdowns were every bit as tense off camera as they appeared to be on TV. In those scenes—two or three hours under the unforgiving heat of TV lights and the eye of the man whose patronage they sought—the contestants saw a talented performer who was deeply concerned with how he was perceived by others. Trump was as consumed by ratings as he would later be about campaign poll numbers. "He is obsessed with metrics, polls and data," said Sam Solovey, the first-season contestant who, upon being fired, delivered a searing glare that became a pop sensation. On a morning after *The Apprentice* lost the ratings race to a rival Fox show, *American Idol*, Solovey visited Trump to introduce him to his fiancée—and found the usually ebullient businessman slumped at his desk. "It was the only time I saw him totally downcast and dejected," said Solovey, who soon after that meeting signed on with the Trump Organization to help rally *Apprentice*'s ratings and bolster Trump's brand by appearing on *The Oprah Winfrey Show*, promoting the Miss Universe pageant, and hustling Trump's latest book.

When Elizabeth Jarosz, a second-season contestant who later became a brand strategy consultant, once stood near Trump as he finished a press interview, she was surprised when he turned to her and asked, "How did I do? Was that okay?"

"Wow," Jarosz thought. "He was very insecure." Another time, Jarosz sat with Trump at a bar as he explained his view that "all publicity is good publicity. . . . When people get tired of you is when you do more publicity, because that's when you become an icon."

Although NBC marketed Trump's *Apprentice* character as tough and ballsy, the show's producers and Trump's public relations advisers saw a character emerging on the show who artfully blended his love of power with a glimmer of humility, a touch of self-deprecating humor, and an unexpected willingness to cede to the expertise of others. NBC public relations chief Jim Dowd, who later handled publicity for Trump directly, spent many hours with Trump during the show's first weeks and watched as the star crafted a new public persona: "He was tempering himself and didn't want to come across as a villain. He always says everything he does is *yuuge, yuuge, yuuge*. But his feet were on the ground on this. He was nervous about the ratings. He kept asking, 'Is this going to work?'"

The line between Trump the character and Trump the person had been fuzzy for decades. Writing in the *New Yorker* years earlier, Mark Singer had portrayed Trump as a "hyperbole addict who prevaricates for fun and profit," the proprietor of a long-running, glittery, but ultimately dishonest and empty show. Singer concluded that Trump had "achieved the ultimate luxury, an existence unmolested by the rumblings of a soul." Trump didn't like Singer's harsh critique, but often referred to himself as a "ratings machine." Trump's image-molders now saw *Apprentice* as a chance to present him as a more authentic, nuanced person than the glitz-obsessed, ego-first character Americans knew from tabloid headlines and TV cameos. Trump himself initially saw the show as a brand extension and took advantage of his *Apprentice* success to plaster his name on ties, suits, fragrance (Success by Trump), water, lamps, and a credit card. "Donald calculates the brand awareness," Burnett said. "He's a showman."

"Donald does everything for a reason," Dowd said.

The success of his TV show renewed questions about which aspects of Trump's public persona reflected his true self and which were pure showmanship. Trump sometimes scoffed at the idea that he'd created a separate or different character that he played on the public stage, and he sometimes insisted that things he said on TV were intended just to provoke or entertain. In *Time to Get Tough*, a book he published in 2011, Trump wrote that he did *The Apprentice* "not for the money, mind you, but because it creates such a powerful brand presence and is a lot of fun to do." But Trump later said he decided to do the program for a simple, mercenary reason: because "it's lucrative, even if you're rich. It's an amazing thing, you never get tired of that." (Trump started out making $100,000 per episode for his performance; of course, he also owned half of the show.)

Whichever motivation was more important to him, Trump believed that *The Apprentice* let Americans see him as more humane, more complicated than just his crumbling marriages, gold-plated surroundings, and constant promotion of his name and identity. The show made Americans realize that "I'm highly educated," Trump once said, "which until *The Apprentice* most people didn't know. They thought I was a barbarian."

"I do have great feelings for people," Trump said. "But I became more popular by being on a show where I fire people. It's weird. I am an honest person. People understand you have to do what you have to do. Michael Douglas said I'm the best actor on television. I said, 'I'm not acting. This is who I am.'"

Apprentice changed Trump's trajectory almost immediately. On the morning after the premiere, Dowd accompanied Trump as he made the rounds of Manhattan TV studios for nine interviews promoting the show. Dowd witnessed the making of a star: "People on the street embraced him. He was mobbed. And all of a sudden, there was none of the old mocking, the old *New York Post* image of him with the wives and the parties. He was a hero and he had not been one before. He told me, 'I've got the real estate and hotel and golf niche, I've got the name recognition, but I don't have the love and respect of Middle America.' Now he did. That was the bridge to the [2016] campaign."

As *The Apprentice* gained audience, Trump became more involved in both the production of the program and its promotion. With each passing week, he grew more serious about the show, devoted more time to it, and became a close student of its audience demographics. "He really ate it up," Gaspin said. "He didn't necessarily take it seriously at first, but when he gets traction, he puts everything into it. . . . He just loved, loved being a TV star." The show's audience diminished sharply in later seasons, especially when the network added a version of *Apprentice* starring Martha Stewart (her show premiered six months after she was released from prison). When Stewart's *Apprentice* was canceled after one season, Trump wrote her a nasty note: "Your performance was terrible. . . . Be careful or I will do a syndicated daytime show, perhaps called 'The Boardroom,' and further destroy the meager ratings you already have!"

As soon as *Apprentice* hit the top ten in its first season, Trump was in demand on talk shows as never before. Dowd booked Trump on Don Imus's morning radio gabfest every week for a year and a half. The appearances were initially meant to promote the TV show, but almost immediately, Trump started talking politics. The people who made

The Apprentice with Trump didn't think he would ever really run for office, but they recall his drawing a direct line from the show's success to the possibility that he'd shoot for the nation's top job. Burnett said, "Donald mentioned a number of times, 'Maybe I'll run for president one day.'"

The Apprentice turned Trump from a blowhard Richie Rich who had just gone through his most difficult decade into an unlikely symbol of straight talk, an evangelist for the American gospel of success, a decider who insisted on standards in a country that had somehow slipped into handing out trophies for just showing up. Before Trump, the rule book for reality shows said that TV should be positive and inspiring, not negative. But Trump changed those rules, Gaspin said. Trump, like *American Idol*'s Simon Cowell, could be simultaneously inspiring and negative—a politically incorrect truth teller. "Donald was about honesty; he was tough but truthful," Gaspin said. "He wasn't saying you were good at your job when you weren't." And although the show's loyal viewers delighted in Trump's blunt, decisive style—and in the way he humiliated some losing contestants—fans of *The Apprentice* also saw Trump as a billionaire with a heart, at times playful and unexpectedly willing to change his mind.

Above all, *Apprentice* sold an image of the host-boss as supremely competent and confident, dispensing his authority and getting immediate results. The analogy to politics was palpable, and Burnett saw it in action as the show's format was franchised to several dozen other countries around the world. Increasingly, the hosts of the foreign editions of *Apprentice* were celebrities with political aspirations. "Nobody is missing this," Burnett said. The show's creator came to believe that if Trump ever ran for president, it wouldn't be a result of *The Apprentice*, but without *The Apprentice* there could be no candidacy: "People want to hear the unvarnished, that same style that he showed on *The Apprentice* . . . the ability to speak his mind clearly and not tone down his voice in a politically correct, TV way."

Trump initially resisted the idea that *The Apprentice* played an important role in inspiring both his decision to run and the electorate's interest in his campaign. He noted how well-known he was before the show premiered. Unprompted, he reeled off his ratings on other TV shows, the magazines whose covers he'd graced, the bestselling books he'd written. But then he pivoted and said that the reality show "was a different level of adulation, or respect, or celebrity. That really went to a different level. I'm running to really make America great again, but the celebrity helped, that's true."

At the least, *The Apprentice* fed Trump's hunger for public recognition. Gaspin saw "some sort of huge need for public validation" from his star. "He would call me every day: 'How are the ratings?' He's fueled by it." Looking back years later, some of the show's top executives saw Trump's move toward elective politics as an effort to re-create those heady first months of public adulation that followed *Apprentice*'s premiere. "The show was magic, and that's what he's trying to recapture," Dowd said.

As *The Apprentice*'s numbers soared, Trump explored ways to extend his TV brand. In 2007, Fox announced that Trump would be executive producer of a show to be called *Lady or a Tramp*, a reality competition in which "rude and crude party girls" would be sent to charm school to get a strict reeducation on manners. In the wake of Britney Spears's shaving her head and Lindsay Lohan's and Paris Hilton's snaring headlines for all the wrong reasons, Trump would reprise his *Apprentice* role as judge, evaluating the contestants' progress. The show was never made.

Trump also proposed that a network create a dramatic series based on his life and work. To be called *The Tower*, the idea was for it to be *The West Wing* of the real estate development world, with a main character who aspires to excellence, craves winning, and is out to build the tallest building in the world. Gay Walch, a Hollywood TV writer hired to create a pilot for the series, wrote a character who was larger-than-life and had a complicated family, with two adult children and an ex-wife all working for him. She borrowed scenes from Trump's books, including the clever ruse he once deployed in Atlantic City to impress potential investors by having a crew move dirt around to make an idle construction site look active.

When Walch met with Trump about *The Tower*, he didn't object to any of her work, not even when the Trump-like character was less than scrupulous. "He was very respectful of my creative process," she said. "It wasn't like things had to be his way. He was a confident listener, acutely listening." Trump gave the writer only one note: he wanted the main character's last name to be Barron. No problem, Walch said. *The Tower* would be the story of John Barron—the name Trump had used for years when he called news outlets with tips for stories about Donald Trump. *The Tower* was never produced—it just wasn't great, network executives said.

In 2015, when Trump was fourteen years into the run of *The Apprentice*, NBC announced that it was removing him as host of the program "due to the recent derogatory statements by Donald Trump regarding immigrants." (In reply, Trump blasted the network, saying it was "so weak and so foolish to not understand the serious illegal immigration problem.") Even after he became a presidential candidate, Trump loved the idea of retaining a regular presence on primetime TV. He said he'd still like to make *The Tower*. "Depending on what happens with this thing, I'd like to do that," he said in 2016. "Of course, if this goes all the way, I can't do it. I won't have the time. And it wouldn't be appropriate." Trump clearly relished talking about *Apprentice*, but he had to get on a plane. Before he got off the phone, though, he had a question for the reporter on the other end of the line. "So Schwarzenegger's going to do *The Apprentice*," Trump said. "You think he'll be good? I hope he's good. He was in politics. So maybe he can do this, too."

Going back to his first appearances on Page Six of the *New York Post*, on *The Howard Stern Show*, and on Barbara Walters's celebrity interviews, Trump always took pride in knowing how to win attention for himself, knowing how to feed the media's insatiable appetite for stories about wealth, sex, and controversy—and ideally, all three blended together. Dabbling with investments in Broadway shows and making cameo appearances on TV sitcoms and in movies seemed like novelties, good for a quick injection of celebrity juice. *The Apprentice*, however, was a sustained development of a character, a powerful mainline into the American consciousness, an essential bridge on the journey from builder to politician. It was only a matter of time before he would use his showmanship not only to sell condos and fill hotel rooms, but to expand his brand into a dazzling array of fields.

13

The Name Game

Donald Trump built his reputation selling real estate, but the thing he had always wanted to sell was Donald Trump. His career as a reality television star would finally make Trump into a household brand—and he was determined to cash in. He started before *The Apprentice* had even debuted. In mid-2003, Trump laid out his vision for Mark Hager, a minor figure in the world of clothing licensing. Hager had once done a clothing deal with the rapper Nelly, but his experience with celebrity labels was limited. Still, Hager shared a lawyer with Trump, so he worked his connection to secure a meeting to propose a joint business venture. As Hager's taxi wound its way through Manhattan's clogged streets, he was mentally reviewing his presentation when he got a call from his lawyer friend. There had been a last-minute change: Trump no longer had any interest in the business Hager wanted to discuss. Instead, Trump had a proposal of his own.

Hager found Trump in an expansive mood. Trump talked up his role as the central character in the new show, predicting *The Apprentice* would be a ratings smash hit. He envisioned that companies would pay to put his name on products showcased on the program. He told Hager that he would start with menswear—shirts, ties, and suits with the classic American executive look that had been his own uniform for decades. Then he would move to fragrance and water and anything else that could be sold under the Trump brand.

Trump offered Hager a broker's fee if he could persuade a big-name clothing company to make the first of what would eventually become more than twenty licensing deals. Hager accepted the challenge, but he found the clothing industry did not immediately share Trump's vision. Shortly after *The Apprentice* premiered in January 2004, Hager's deputy Jeff Danzer pitched the idea to Phillips–Van Heusen, the apparel industry heavyweight that manufactured clothing for Calvin Klein. The company's head of licensing laughed. The clothing executive, Danzer recalled, saw Trump not as the powerful titan of the boardroom that he played on TV, but as what he had been in the 1980s and 1990s—the tabloid playboy known for his bluster in the face of bankruptcies at several of his businesses. Who would want to dress like him?

Undaunted by the brush-off, Danzer sent the Phillips–Van Heusen executive a copy of a *New York Post* story headlined "*Apprentice* Buzz Likely to Mint Trump a New Fortune." Explaining that the show provided a "priceless" boost to Trump's brand, the story quoted advertising honcho Donny Deutsch: "The Trump name always had a premium veneer to it, but it lacked the personable, likability factor that we get to see now on the show. The brand was always top-shelf; now it's top-shelf with a smile."

By April, after the season finale of *The Apprentice*, no one laughed at the idea of Trump-branded shirts, ties, cologne, water. Trump's success emboldened him to set up an in-house licensing division instead of outsourcing it to Hager. "Everything that goes into this business, everything that goes out of the business, everything having to do with my image"—everything having to do with his brand—"everything we do here is under my thumb," Trump said, as Danzer recalled their conversation. "I do everything. I will manage my own license, thank you."

Trump created a new position of executive vice president of global licensing and gave the job to Cathy Hoffman Glosser, who had worked in licensing for two decades, including merchandising for Marvel Entertainment, where she had gotten Spider-Man on kids' pajamas. Now she would get *Trump* on vodka and soap. But a complication arose. Danzer was still negotiating with Phillips–Van Heusen, and Trump wanted a deal with the industry heavyweight to produce his shirts and ties. The company was wary because it had just discontinued a Regis Philbin line that had petered out quickly, despite the popularity of his TV show *Who Wants to Be a Millionaire*. So Trump employed his strongest tool: himself. In August 2004, Trump announced he wanted a meeting with the company's executives. Instead of summoning them to Trump Tower, his usual practice, he offered to visit the shirt manufacturer's Garment District headquarters. "I was taken aback," said Mark Weber, the company's CEO at the time. Sure enough, Trump arrived at the company's offices looking just as he did on television, and full of flattery for his future business partners.

"I really respect and love Regis," Trump told Weber. "However, I'm a brand. I'm building a brand. Everything I do, I do with the best quality, the finest taste. That's why I want to do business with your company." The more insistent Weber was that the deal just wasn't going to work, the harder Trump pushed back. Both companies will make money. This will work, Trump told him. As the meeting concluded, Trump looked at Glosser, his newly hired licensing director. "Make it happen," he ordered.

Despite the demands of his TV show, Trump put in extra time to pump his new product. When the clothing company unveiled a tiny showroom in its headquarters to showcase its new Donald J. Trump line, Donald and Melania surprised Weber by showing up, shaking hands, and signing autographs. The event was an internal company party—the only reporter who had even been invited was from the industry trade publication *Women's Wear Daily*. Weber recalled asking, "Donald, why are you doing this?"

"Because I want to win, and I'll do whatever it takes to win," Trump responded.

For eleven years, Phillips–Van Heusen manufactured clothing for Trump, contracting with factories in China, Honduras, Bangladesh, and other countries, where low-wage workers stitched Trump's name into the collars of thousands of shirts. Trump put up no money. The clothing company paid him a percentage of sales, amounting to more than $1 million a year.

• • •

TRUMP MENSWEAR MADE AN appearance, of course, in an episode of *The Apprentice*. So did Trump Ice, a new brand of water, and Trump Success, a new fragrance. Riding the popularity of the show, Trump licensed his name to clothes, ties, home furnishings, eyeglasses, wallets, even mattresses. All sold well for years. Trump-branded products were on prominent display at Macy's, which catered to middle-class shoppers seeking a bit of style. By 2016, Trump was receiving income from twenty-five different licensing deals, and he reported ownership interest in dozens of other companies that appeared to have been set up for licensing around the world, a sign of the scope of his ambition. Trump's branding theory was that anything that could be sold, could be sold under his name—for a fee. That led to some unusual gambits. A venture to sell Trump Steaks at the Sharper Image, a high-tech-gadget store found in many suburban shopping malls, fared poorly.

By licensing his name without putting up money, he could often make significant profits, even when the ventures failed. The new model let Trump weather even worldwide economic collapse. Initially, his licensing deals captured the easy money flowing during the economic boom of the first decade of the new millennium, when consumers had ready money to spend on seemingly luxurious Trump-brand goods and banks were eager to finance high-priced real estate developments. Under his new strategy, he profited from the wreckage of the bust that followed as well. At worst, licensing let him walk away from deals that collapsed in the downturn, having pocketed hefty fees. Trump's crucial insight was to turn away from building one business at a time and expand his ambition to create an empire—a series of entities that bore his name, but didn't rely on his cash. His business was the brand. It was like owning a casino—when run properly, the house wins. The gamblers would be those who paid him for the rights to his name. Trump couldn't lose.

Few of his branded ventures received as much notice as, or created more controversy than, Trump's effort to educate the masses in his style.

• • •

ON A DAMP SPRING day in 2005, Trump summoned reporters to a press conference at Trump's Bar, located on the ground floor of Trump Tower, close to Trump Grill, just steps away from Trump's Ice Cream Parlor and the Trump Store, which was then pushing a new cologne for men called Donald Trump, the Fragrance. At the news conference, Trump unveiled Trump University, a branded product with an ostensibly noble purpose: "I would say that if I had a choice of making lots of money or imparting lots of knowledge, I think I'd be as happy to impart knowledge as to make money." At the time, the housing market was booming, and many ordinary people saw investing in real estate as an easy path to riches. Trump promised his university would show them the way. "At Trump University, we teach success. That's what it's all about—success," he said in a promotional video. Not long after his new university opened, the real estate market softened, then tanked. Rather than close shop, Trump's university pivoted. Now it would teach people how to make money in a depressed market. "Learn from Donald Trump's handpicked experts how you can profit from the largest real estate liquidation in history," read one Trump University ad that ran in a San Antonio newspaper in 2009.

Sales pressure was intense. It began at free seminars such as one hosted at a Holiday Inn just outside Washington, DC, in 2009. A placard outside the ballroom read TRUMP, THINK BIG. Inside, aspiring real estate investors heard the theme song from *The Apprentice*, the O'Jays' classic "For the Love of Money." Then a Trump University instructor took the microphone and yelled, "All right, you guys ready to be the next Trump real estate millionaire? Yes or no?" The crowd responded with lackluster enthusiasm, so the instructor tried again: "Let's blow the roof off this building. You guys are the best in the world. So, you guys ready to be the next Trump real estate millionaire, *yes* or *no*?!"

"*Yes!*"

Five hundred Washingtonians attended the free seminars offered during that September week in 2009. They listened to speakers and watched videos as the Trump sales team promised to reveal ways to profit from the real estate downturn. "Find it, flip it, forget about it," instructors told potential students at a free seminar on investing in property with little or no money down. "You don't have to own real estate; you just have to control it." Again and again, students at these events heard about Trump's personal involvement in hiring professors and developing the curriculum.

Behind the scenes, the staff was taught to build interest and "set the hook" for customers who might sign up for pricey classes. Instructions on running the events came in employee "playbooks" that detailed how to pressure students to choose the most expensive courses. The playbooks suggested how to persuade attendees of free seminars to buy a $1,495 ticket to a three-day workshop: "Let them know you've found an answer to their problems and a way for them to change their lifestyle." The playbooks urged the sales team to push further by suggesting that students who bought the $1,495 course upgrade to classes with a mentor that could cost between $9,995 and $34,995. Students filled out forms detailing their personal assets, ostensibly to provide each with targeted recommendations for investment. But the confidential playbooks revealed that the real purpose of getting the students' financial details was to determine which customers were good targets for the $34,995 program. In the evenings, after the first day of seminars had concluded, staff members were to use the financial data to rank each participant according to assets they had available to spend on more Trump University programs. "If they can afford the gold elite," the playbook advised, "don't allow them to think about doing anything besides the gold elite."

Bob Guillo, a retiree living on Long Island, was one of nearly six hundred people who paid $35,000 for the Trump Gold Elite package, charging the program to his credit card at a New York seminar. He later said he was left with little more than feel-good class certificates and a photo of himself with a cardboard cutout of Trump. "I really felt stupid that I was scammed by Trump," said Guillo, who earned Trump's personal ire by appearing in ads sponsored by an anti-Trump group. "I thought that he was really legit."

He was not alone. Guillo and other former students filed two class action lawsuits in California. In 2013, New York attorney general Eric Schneiderman filed a $40 million suit against Trump and Trump University, alleging that Trump had defrauded more than five thousand people through a program that called itself a university but failed to meet New York State's requirements to be classified as an educational institution. (After resisting for years, the company dropped *University* from its name, rebranding itself as the Trump Entrepreneur Initiative shortly before closing its doors in 2010.)

The plaintiffs claimed that much of what Trump had said about his university was not true. From its first days, Trump had described the faculty he assembled as "the best of the best," with "professors and adjunct professors . . . who are going to be handpicked by me." The promotional material touted Trump University as "the next best thing" to being Trump's apprentice. Trump and his sales team attracted customers by insisting Trump was not even intending to profit from the expensive classes. "He does not need your fifteen hundred dollars," said one instructor whose pitch was recorded.

Trump promised to give profits from his university to charity, but none were donated. (Alan Garten, Trump's lawyer, said Trump had intended to pass the proceeds to charity but instead spent the money defending against lawsuits.) Trump University president Michael Sexton would later say that Trump did not pick the instructors. Sexton also said he could remember no special Trump methods that were taught, other than the investment opportunities presented by foreclosures. Former students who sued alleged that their trainers had little real estate knowledge.

Trump repeatedly denied any wrongdoing, citing surveys showing that students, including Guillo, reported they were highly satisfied with the lessons. The students "were provided a substantive, valuable education," Trump said later. Trump also argued that he had lent his name to the courses but had little to do with their daily operation. Told by a lawyer for the plaintiffs that 25 percent of Trump University attendees had requested refunds, Trump compared the university to the Home Shopping Network, which had generous refund rules and therefore also a high refund rate: "You go to the Home Shopping Network, whatever it's called, the refunds are unbelievable. The people use the product, wear the product, and then they send it back. I shouldn't have given their money back. I gave back millions of dollars because I'm an honest guy." As they did across Trump's expanding branded empire, his representatives insisted that the truth about the seminars was available to any savvy consumer. Classes, after all, were held in hotel ballrooms.

• • •

THE APPRENTICE HAD DEBUTED during the rapid expansion of the country's real estate bubble. Trump tried to cash in not only with his university but with a new foray into Trump-licensed developments.

The show's 2007 season concluded with a live broadcast from the Hollywood Bowl. Perched behind his now familiar boardroom table, Trump sounded uncharacteristically humble as he noted that he was in a setting where Frank Sinatra had once performed. Trump presented a choice of prizes to the person he would name the season's winner: his new apprentice could oversee construction of a Trump luxury resort in the Dominican Republic or a forty-seven-story condominium project that Trump bragged would reshape the skyline of downtown Atlanta.

As Trump narrated video of construction cranes looming over a Caribbean beach and the streets of Atlanta, he didn't note that he neither owned the properties nor was primarily responsible for their construction. Trump had merely licensed his name to the developers. Both of the projects he hawked on the *Apprentice* finale that year eventually faltered. Trump Towers Atlanta went into foreclosure in 2010. The lot where the project was once slated to rise stood empty for years.

Trump's Dominican partners also struggled to make their luxury resort a reality. "Like most second home real estate developments, our cash situation over the last year and a half can only be described as precarious on the best of days and more akin to bungee-jumping than textbook cash management," one of the partners wrote to Trump's son Eric, begging for more time to remit licensing payments. "You are being paid sooner and faster than ANY of our senior secured lenders." Though Donald Trump had been paid millions for the project, including a $4 million payment when the deal was signed, he sued in 2012, alleging the Dominican project owed him $14 million more. The suit was settled in 2013.

Ultimately, lawsuits proliferated across Trump's licensing empire. Trump was sued by people who lost down payments at failed projects in Baja, Mexico, and in Tampa. After each failure, Trump and his representatives said the billionaire had merely lent his name to the project and had no responsibility for development. Garten, the attorney, said Trump's role in such endeavors was clear to anyone who read the legal documents. But several licensing agreements included confidentiality contracts, barring his partners from revealing the details, or even existence, of the licensing deal. At times, Trump and son Eric also said they had made equity investments in projects in which they had not. "This building is largely owned by me and being developed by me," Trump wrote about the Trump International Hotel & Tower in Waikiki, Hawaii, in a letter to the *Wall Street Journal* in 2007. Trump did not own the building, largely or otherwise. Nor was he developing it. Asked about the discrepancy, Trump declared in a sworn deposition that he held "such a strong licensing agreement that it's a form of ownership."

A few months after his father was confronted with this statement, Eric Trump announced at a news conference in Puerto Rico that his family would make a "very substantial equity contribution" in a golf course and resort project on the north coast of the island. But documents filed when the project went bankrupt in 2015 showed that Trump held no equity in the project. Eric Trump later said the family had planned to buy units at the resort, but "deals can change over time."

Still, the benefits to the Trumps were enormous. The deals were thick with contract provisions that redounded to Trump's favor. If the project failed or the developer went bankrupt, Trump could walk away. The same was true if construction lagged or if Trump decided a project was not living up to his high standards. He was allowed to demand changes—higher ceilings, larger windows—to meet these standards, with the partners footing the bill for modifications. Trump typically agreed to attend a handful of marketing events for his branded buildings, but his contracts ensured that the cost of his first-class accommodations would be paid by someone else.

IN FORT LAUDERDALE, A new Trump-branded condominium building launched in early 2005 would ultimately reveal the full range of the Trump real estate experience. It started with bravado, high hopes, and high prices. But the optimism ultimately fell victim to the real estate recession and seemingly endless claims and counterclaims in multiple courtrooms.

J. Michael Goodson seemed like the kind of person who'd be immune to inflated marketing pitches. A high-powered lawyer and businessman, Goodson decided in 2004 that he wanted to invest in a part-time home in South Florida, where his high-tech, New Jersey–based plastic-welding company, Crest Ultrasonics, had established a rapidly growing Southern base. Late that year, he met one of his classmates from Duke University School of Law for dinner at the Trump International Hotel & Tower in Manhattan, near Columbus Circle. The classmate had bought a condo in the Trump building and was pleased with the investment. As they enjoyed the fine cuisine and impeccable service at a restaurant in the hotel, the friend urged Goodson to take a look at Trump properties.

On his next trip to Florida, Goodson visited the beachside site of the planned 298-room Trump International Hotel & Tower in Fort Lauderdale. The building was designed as a hotel-condominium, in which owners could rent out their units like hotel rooms when they weren't using them. It seemed perfect for Goodson, who planned to live in Florida a few months of each year. Soon, Goodson, back home in Princeton, New Jersey, began receiving promotional material from the Fort Lauderdale project. An elegantly boxed package of information included a signed letter from Trump calling the planned tower "the finest and most luxurious experience I have created." Trained as an accountant before going to law school, Goodson had worked on Wall Street deals. He studied the polished sales literature, which touted Trump as the project's developer. "It is with great pleasure that I present my latest development, Trump International Hotel & Tower, Fort Lauderdale," read another promotional letter that Trump signed.

Goodson had his eye on a unit on the same level as the planned outdoor pool, overlooking the beach. Goodson believed Trump's name, associated with high standards, would command top dollar. So in 2005, he wrote a check for $345,000 to reserve his new Trump residence. Trump's reputation and the Fort Lauderdale tower's luxury design attracted other high-end investors, including savvy real estate consultants. It drew working-class and middle-class buyers, too. A used-car dealer from Maryland, Michael Leo Rousseaux, made a down payment after bringing home marketing material to show his mother, Sheila, an eighth-grade special education teacher. Rousseaux couldn't afford an oceanfront condo, but he wanted to own in a Trump building, his mother later said, and thought he could manage a more modest unit, facing the street. When Michael was killed a few months later in a dispute with a former customer, his parents and siblings decided to honor his dream and continue making payments on the Trump condo.

A condo at the Hotel & Tower was also a stretch for Naraine Seecharan, who owned a small Coral Springs, Florida, air-conditioning firm and had previously managed McDonald's restaurants in the Washington, DC, area. Seecharan dreamed of getting rich through smart real estate investments, just as Trump had done. So he took out a private equity loan against his home and four rental properties he owned to make a $289,000 down payment on a unit in the Fort Lauderdale building. Seecharan said he and his wife were comforted by the letters from Trump, and a silver key ring from Tiffany's adorned with the Trump name, which they received after making their second payment. "You can't lose," Seecharan thought to himself. After all, the sales agent told him repeatedly throughout 2005 that his developer was Donald Trump.

In April 2006, a crowd celebrating the Fort Lauderdale project gathered around Donald Trump and his son Don as they arrived in a black limousine at the historic Bonnet House, a Caribbean-style mansion on the Intracoastal Waterway. The Haitian-born rapper Wyclef Jean entertained the several hundred real estate agents, contractors, and buyers. Jean said he was eager to learn from Trump: "He's real tough when it comes to business. I'm like a sponge right now. I know I can pick up things from him." The rapper, who would a decade later denounce Trump's comments about immigrants, wrote a few desultory lines for the guest of honor and sang them before Trump and his entourage came to the microphone: "I'm at the Trump International, in Fort Lauderdale. Yo! I landed in Fort Lauderdale. I gave Donald Trump a call." Applause and cheers rippled through the audience as Trump took the stage and said, "We are celebrating tonight with the people that purchased, with the brokers, with everybody who has made the job such a success."

But the saturated Florida condo market was already showing signs of trouble. A development official took the microphone to announce that the next agent to sell three units in the Trump International Hotel & Tower would receive a special incentive—diamond cuff links just like the ones Trump wore that night.

Within three years, the lavishly promoted project would grind to a halt amid a thicket of lawsuits and recriminations. The actual developers, SB Hotel Associates, had been struggling to pay the $139 million construction loan they had secured in December 2006, just as the market had begun to slide. The lender, Corus Bankshares of Chicago, failed in 2009 in part because the institution had made so many loans in South Florida, which saw the worst of the nationwide real estate recession. Construction on the partially completed Trump Tower stopped in 2009, after Corus Bankshares went under. A successor company, Corus Construction Venture, bought the unfinished building in 2012 at a foreclosure auction, assuming the project's $166 million debt. Work on the project resumed, but slowly; it was not scheduled to open to hotel guests until early 2017. Trump's response was familiar to buyers at projects around the country that had failed during the recession: he distanced himself, saying he had merely licensed his name to the building and held no ownership stake—or responsibility for its failure.

"The world is ending for me," Seecharan thought when work on the project stalled.

"I panicked," recalled Sheila Rousseaux.

Garten, Trump's lawyer, advised complainers to contact the developers. After all, he explained, that was the entity from which buyers had agreed to purchase their units. Formal documents never indicated they were buying from Trump. Condo buyers learned all kinds of details about their investment that hadn't arrived with their Tiffany key chains. Not only was Trump not the project's developer, but a local ordinance prevented condo owners in hotel buildings from using their units for more than ninety days a year. And one of Trump's partners—a member of the building's actual development team—had pleaded guilty in a major Wall Street fraud case involving Mafia crime families. That partner, Felix Sater, was a Russian immigrant who was once convicted of stabbing a man in the face with the stem of a broken margarita glass. In 1998, he pleaded guilty to involvement in a penny-stock fraud scheme orchestrated by the mob. But Sater was spared prison time in recognition of "extraordinary cooperation" he provided to the FBI in a series of secret operations. Sater was a top executive in the New York development firm Bayrock Group, which had first pitched the Fort Lauderdale project to Trump. But his criminal past was not revealed to partners and condo buyers. Trump said he, too, had no idea Sater had been convicted in the mob scheme; the conviction had been kept under seal by federal authorities to protect Sater's status as a cooperating witness. Trump said he barely knew Sater when he agreed to join forces. "If he were sitting in the room right now, I really wouldn't know what he looked like," Trump said.

But in a 2008 deposition in a libel suit, Sater claimed he and Trump were "friendly" and that he frequently went to the tycoon's office, located two floors above Bayrock's in Trump Tower, to discuss possible development projects from Los Angeles to China. "Anybody can come in and build a tower," Sater remembered explaining to potential investors. "[But] I can build a Trump Tower because of my relationship with Trump." Sater said Bayrock had a one-year exclusive deal to get a Trump Tower project going in Moscow, where he worked with Trump on a proposal to build on the site of a shuttered pencil factory. Sater said the relationship was so close that Trump asked him to accompany Donald Jr. and Ivanka around Moscow on their 2006 trip to the Russian capital. (Garten, the Trump lawyer, said Sater met up with the adult Trump children simply because they were both traveling to Moscow, and that Trump only had a business relationship with Bayrock. He was adamant that Trump did not have a relationship with Sater, only with his company, Bayrock.)

More than a hundred buyers at the Fort Lauderdale hotel filed suit, arguing that Trump had defrauded them by failing to disclose key information about the project. Many investors were angry that Trump could walk away, pocketing millions in fees while never having invested his money in the deal. "We were all screwed in this deal, but he made out," Seecharan said.

The litigation revealed Trump's aggressive style with critics, complainers, and even former collaborators. When the Fort Lauderdale case began, Trump signed an agreement with the developers, SB Hotel Associates, to jointly defend the project if it became the target of lawsuits. In late 2012, SB Hotel Associates, representing the two firms that developed the project, negotiated a settlement with buyers, reimbursing a portion of their initial down payments, minus legal fees. Trump refused to join the settlement, filing suit to block it and to penalize the SB Hotel group for breach of contract. In one Broward County, Florida, case, a circuit court jury found in 2014 that Trump had not defrauded the buyers, and most other cases were settled by 2016, as Trump shrugged off the last remnants of the historic real estate crash.

IN 2006, TRUMP HAD been filled with optimism about the housing market. Residential real estate prices had been soaring across the country for years, as properties were flipped and reflipped, many snatched by buyers with mortgages they should never have been granted. Many borrowers had taken subprime loans with low teaser rates designed to escalate after a few years—a disaster in the making for borrowers with stagnant incomes. So, on April 6, 2006, Trump announced at a press conference that he was betting on a real estate boom. He had created a lending company he believed would transform the industry and sweep the country: Trump Mortgage.

As tourists snapped photos from Trump Tower's atrium escalators, Trump declared that his new company had "what a lot of people are saying is the hottest brand in the country—in the world." Trump's son Donald Jr. had arranged for an acquaintance, E. J. Ridings, to be chief executive. Ridings boasted that the new company would "own New York" and expand to all fifty states. Trump said he expected business to be great. "If it's not, E.J., you're fired," he said, echoing his famous line from *The Apprentice*. It all sounded great to Jan Scheck, the company's national sales director. As Scheck stood onstage alongside Trump, he felt lucky to be working with "somebody who is a god in the real estate industry," he recalled years later. "Everybody wanted to be Donald Trump. Donald was putting his name on buildings all over the country."

Trump appeared on CNBC to hawk his new product, and anchorwoman Maria Bartiromo sounded skeptical. During the interview, the network showed graphics illustrating uncertainties in the market that Trump was entering. The first graphic showed good news: "Existing

Home Sales Rose 5.2 Percent in February." The second was downright alarming: "New Home Sales Fell 10.5 Percent in February; Biggest Drop in 9 Years." Trump scoffed at the numbers: "I always get a kick when I watch the great economists talking about where rates will be in a year from now and two years from now. And they have no idea what's going to happen. . . . Assuming rates stay where they are and even go just a little bit higher as opposed to a lot higher, we're in very good shape. . . . It's a great time to start a mortgage company."

Trump Mortgage offered residential loans with promises of quick approvals. It recruited aggressive salesmen and set up several satellite offices. Trump gave the business a floor of his building at 40 Wall Street, part of which was a boiler room where salesmen hawked subprime loans; another wing was dedicated to what were known internally as "boutique" sales, targeted at better-qualified, high-income borrowers. A photo of Trump appeared atop the company website with the instruction "Talk to My Mortgage Professionals Now!" Seeking synergy across his business empire, Trump wrote language into the deal for at least one of his licensed properties—a vacation complex in the Dominican Republic—requiring the project's developers to urge buyers to try to get a Trump-related mortgage.

Trump could not have been more wrong about the housing market. He had created his mortgage company just as the market was starting to crash. Within eighteen months of Bartiromo's warnings, the experts' worst fears came true and home prices plummeted. Trump Mortgage closed, leaving some bills unpaid. In its first year, the venture brought in less than a third of the $3 billion that the company's CEO initially had predicted.

Seven million Americans would lose their homes during the Great Recession, which overlapped the presidencies of George W. Bush and Barack Obama. The financial crisis reverberated for years, resulting in an economic dislocation that would become a major issue in the 2016 presidential campaign. (Trump said years later that he had known that the housing market "was a bubble that was waiting to explode. . . . I told a lot of people. And I was right. You know, I'm pretty good at that stuff.") The blame for Trump Mortgage's failings lay elsewhere, Trump insisted at the time. "The mortgage business is not a business I particularly liked or wanted to be part of in a very big way," he said, explaining that he had put his name on a mortgage operation managed by others.

His handpicked CEO, Ridings, had inflated his résumé, overstating his Wall Street experience, according to a 2006 story in *Money* magazine. Ridings had described himself as a "top professional" in one of Wall Street's most prestigious investment banks, but the magazine reported that he had actually worked in the brokerage division of Morgan Stanley for just a few months.

Trump wasn't done with the lending industry, but his next move signaled a shift in his financial vision. When a company named Meridian Mortgage asked for his backing in 2007, he agreed to let it be renamed Trump Financial. "We think [Meridian] will do a better job," he said at the time. The deal gave Trump a licensing fee without risking his money. The company, like Trump Mortgage, soon ceased operations. But, thanks to the fees he collected, it was not a failure for Trump.

IN 2009, TRUMP LICENSED his name to a program he said would let other people "opt out" of the recession, too. In that year, he launched Trump Network, bringing a new name to an ambitious multilevel marketing organization previously called Ideal Health, which specialized in selling a vitamin-supplement regimen based on a purchaser's urine test. Many employees at Trump Network thought Trump would play a significant role in the organization, but in fact he again received a large fee for use of his name and occasional promotional activities.

"Oh my God, people cried when they heard it was him," recalled Jenna Knudsen, who worked as a high-ranking saleswoman for Ideal Health when Trump entered the picture. "They cried and looked at each other and said, 'We're going to be millionaires!'" Trump received a hero's welcome when he addressed the organization's convention in Miami in late 2009. As he strode to the podium, a giant screen captured his florid face and pastel-yellow tie. "When I did *The Apprentice*, it was a long shot. This is not a long shot," Trump said as more than five thousand attendees roared their approval. Trump said he was a fan of so-called multilevel marketing, a business structure that has drawn criticism for rewarding salespeople based on how many customers they get to join the sales force. Consumer activists and government prosecutors have accused some other multilevel marketing programs of being thinly disguised pyramid schemes, in which early investors become wealthy, but many people lower down the chain lose money or at best break even.

The flagship product of Ideal Health and the Trump Network was a specially tailored multivitamin. Customers took a urine test, which was analyzed to produce a vitamin combination based on their perceived health profile. Consumers paid $139.95 for the urine analysis and $69.95 a month for the vitamins, plus $99.95 for additional testing every six months. Former salespeople praised the product, saying it helped customers live healthier lives. To hear Trump tell it, he wasn't selling pee-based vitamin protocols. He was selling a golden parachute to a soft landing in the economic downturn. "The Trump Network wants to give millions of people renewed hope . . . with an exciting plan to opt out of the recession," Trump told prospective network salespeople in a promotional video. "Let's get out of this recession right now with cutting-edge health and wellness formulas and a system where you can develop your own financial independence. The Trump Network offers people the opportunity to achieve their American dream."

But within three years after Trump agreed to lend his name, some of the once-ebullient participants at the Miami convention expressed regret, filing complaints with the Federal Trade Commission about the multilevel marketing program. Health experts at universities expressed concerns about the legitimacy of the health care products, warning about the value of the costly tests and the related health claims for the vitamins.

At the end of 2011, Trump's licensing contract ended and he withdrew from Trump Network. Early the following year, the company was sold to another firm, Bioceutica. Some salespeople who invested thousands of dollars to buy and market Trump Network products felt abandoned. "They devastated thousands of people, and no one ever apologized," Knudsen said. Garten, the Trump lawyer, gave a familiar response when complaints later arose about the supplement-marketing company. He said Trump was not involved in its operation. He simply licensed his name.

DESPITE HIGH-PROFILE DISAPPOINTMENTS, Trump's licensing empire also had striking examples of success. Trump Hollywood in Florida, a luxury condominium project between Miami and Fort Lauderdale with ocean views, was a sold-out project, with an infinity pool, cigar humidors, wine lockers in the lobby, and an on-site movie theater.

It hadn't always been that way. When construction was completed in 2009, after the Miami condo market had crashed, the building's original developers could find few takers for apartments that started at around $2 million. A year later, the bank that had financed the building's construction foreclosed on the property—and Trump quickly pointed out that the failure was not his. "I was a little surprised at the timing myself," he said about a project he had once championed. He said the Miami-based developer "took a big chance" on constructing a $355 million condo high-rise at the edge of a housing collapse. By Thanksgiving 2010, the building was an empty shell. It was fully staffed but had only two occupied units, whose buyers had secured their apartments amid the downturn, recalled Ken Grossman, a Chicago hedge fund manager who bought in the building at the time.

A new developer stepped in. He bought Trump Hollywood out of foreclosure and slashed prices. At a flashy party in 2011 designed to draw new attention to the project, a cigar roller offered eight hundred guests handmade stogies, a five-piece jazz band entertained by the pool, and models strolled the grounds adorned with Ivanka Trump–brand jewels. Posing for pictures, Trump once again happily touted the project. "A fantastic relaunch for a phenomenal building on the ocean," he declared.

Within fifteen months, all the units in the building were sold, with Trump receiving an undisclosed percentage of each sale. Suddenly, the building was full. A thick book of Trump's standards remained in the concierge office years after Trump was paid all his fees and his formal involvement with the building had concluded. The volume guided the staff's behavior in minute detail. (Fingernails: short, neat. Underwear: always worn. All visitors are to be greeted by staff with eye contact at ten feet and a verbal "hello" at five.)

To Daniel Lebensohn, the successful new developer, the experience showed that doing business well meant doing business aggressively: "Otherwise, you're going to get crushed. Your name won't be there. They won't know who Donald Trump is." On a project that once looked to be a failure, Trump had made between $10 and $20 million, Lebensohn estimated.

Having figured out how to profit from branding, whether or not projects succeeded, Trump was ready to take on the world.

14

Empire

About thirteen hundred miles southeast of Moscow, in Baku, the capital of Azerbaijan, on the shores of the Caspian Sea, a gleaming thirty-three-story building rose like a massive copper-colored sail in the heart of downtown. The sign at the building's elegant peak said, in English, TRUMP TOWER. Down at ground level on a spring day in 2016, however, the structure was only a shell, with a broken window and a section of stone façade chipped out like missing teeth. At night, the building was completely dark but for the glowing white lights of the TRUMP sign.

A couple of security guards and a sleepy caretaker kept an eye on the place, its grounds overgrown with weeds. A huge globe that announced TRUMP sat in a fountain filled with sand and litter, near the locked-up front entrance and another huge sign proclaiming TRUMP INTERNATIONAL HOTEL & TOWER. Inside, the massive lobby—finished in lovely sand-colored tiles with black and gold trim, with mirrored ceilings, and a chandelier sporting a dreamy ribbon of golden bulbs—was covered in construction dust. Reception desks stood sealed beneath plastic wrap. A huge circular staircase remained sheathed in plastic and cardboard. On the second floor, a pool finished in copper-colored tiles awaited water. Next to a sauna that smelled of fresh cedar, a gym was equipped with exercise machines still in cardboard boxes.

A caretaker leading a tour pointed the way with the flashlight app on his phone, stepping around loose wires hanging from unfinished fixtures in a basement passageway because there was neither electricity nor water in this Trump Tower, a huge construction site frozen in time.

BY THE EARLY 2000S, when *The Apprentice* launched him from New York household name into a national phenomenon, Donald Trump was already looking well beyond the Atlantic and Pacific horizons. He gazed north, south, east, and west and saw a world that needed Trump. In late 1999, developers broke ground on six Trump World residential towers in South Korea; the next year, Trump promoted a nearly $900 million Trump Tower in Berlin that he called "a bridge between New York and Berlin." In 2003, Toronto's City Council approved a seventy-story Trump International Hotel & Tower, which would have been the city's tallest building. Later that year, Trump unveiled plans for villas around a golf course in the Grenadines in the Caribbean. In the first decade of the new century, he announced projects including hotels, condos, offices, and golf courses with the big gold TRUMP stamp in Dubai, Israel, Panama, Scotland, Mexico, the Dominican Republic, and Turkey.

In 2007, he created the Trump Hotel Collection, a luxury brand targeting the richest 5 percent of global travelers. With his three oldest children now full-fledged executives in the business, the Trump Organization not only added properties in major American cities from Fort Lauderdale to Waikiki, but sharply accelerated its global expansion. Between 2011 and 2015, Trump announced deals in more than a dozen countries, including two projects in Indonesia in 2015, when he was already running for president. Several Trump projects were located in countries where the United States had important economic and national security concerns—such as Turkey, Indonesia, the United Arab Emirates, and Azerbaijan.

In almost all cases, Trump's only involvement in the overseas projects was to license the Trump brand to local partners for fees that reached millions of dollars, and sometimes to manage the hotels when they opened. The Trump name proved in some instances to be a hugely successful draw. In others, the name didn't deliver buyers as promised. But as happened with some of his US deals, when Trump projects overseas went bust, he still got paid, reaping millions even if his local partners ran into financial problems or went bankrupt.

In 2012, Trump boasted that the former Soviet republic of Georgia was "booming" and "unbelievable" and "going to be one of the great places of the world within four or five years." He announced a $300 million project there: "I'm doing a big development there. And it's been amazing." Nothing was built. Trump's attorney, Alan Garten, said the global recession that started in 2008 forced the cancellation of many projects. "A lot of developers lost their entire portfolios and fortunes," he said. "Mr. Trump came through that as well as anyone." By mid-2016, at least seven of Trump's foreign projects were completed and opened, another eleven were still under construction, and more remained in the planning phase. Other projects never got past the initial announcement. Some were pared down. In Dubai, his promised Trump Tower was never built, but two Trump golf courses were under construction in 2016.

Whatever their ultimate fate, the projects benefited from the Trump treatment, an effusive display of promotional bravado. But sometimes Trump's charm wore thin and he and his overseas partners got into legal brawls, mainly focused on Trump's use of complex contracts. In Toronto, angry apartment buyers lashed out at Trump after they found themselves making less money on their investments in Trump buildings than they said they'd been told to expect. Trump contended that he'd acted entirely within his rights as spelled out in the fine print, and he often prevailed in such cases.

Sometimes, Trump teamed with smaller local developers who had never before built anything on the scale of their Trump projects. In other cases, Trump made deals with characters of questionable backgrounds or with developers who lost their passion for the Trump style. In Dubai in 2015, Trump's comments about Muslims caused a partner to pull the Trump name off a golf course project (he put it back up days later). And in Turkey, the manager of a Trump-branded shopping mall in Istanbul condemned Trump and said he "does not understand Islam."

Trump's global ambitions nonetheless remained powerful, and some deals grew out of other, unrelated aspects of his business empire.

• • •

WHEN TRUMP TRAVELED TO Moscow in 2013 to open the Miss Universe pageant at an opulent seventy-three-hundred-seat concert venue called Crocus City Hall, the beauty contest provided a chance to get closer to a prominent oligarch who was interested in building a Trump Tower in Russia. Before the pageant got under way, Trump joined about a dozen Miss Universe contestants in filming the music video for "In Another Life," the latest single by Emin Agalarov, a hugely successful pop star in Russia who was an executive in his father's real estate company, which was also Trump's business partner in Russia.

"I said, 'Mr. Trump, would you be in my video?'" Emin recalled. "He's like, 'What am I supposed to do?' I said just be part of it. He said how long would it be? I said ten minutes."

Trump responded, "Okay, seven a.m. at my hotel lobby."

In the video, Emin daydreams about being surrounded by Miss Universes in bathing suits before he finally wakes up to find himself at a boardroom table being barked at by Trump: "Wake him up, right now! . . . What's wrong with you, Emin? Emin, let's get with it. You're always late. You're just another pretty face. I'm really tired of you. You're fired!"

Emin's director wanted to shoot a second take, but Trump would have none of it: "No, it's perfect, stop." Off Trump went. The shot was done.

Emin got his start in property development through his wealthy father, Aras Agalarov, and was often seen in public in the company of beautiful women. Emin was sometimes called the Donald Trump of Russia. Early in 2013, Emin was looking for a gorgeous woman to star in the video for his new single, "Amor." He contacted the Miss Universe organization and asked about hiring Olivia Culpo, an American who had won the 2012 Miss Universe contest. They worked out a deal and shot the video, and that's when Emin and his father decided to try to bring the pageant to Moscow. Eventually they were led to Trump, and father and son traveled to Las Vegas in June to work out the deal.

There, Trump blew the Agalarovs away with his seductive

charm—and home-court advantage. Aras, the father, met Trump for the first time in the lobby of the superglitzy Trump Hotel. When Aras walked in with his wife, daughter, and Emin, Trump was entertaining a group of people in the lobby. Cameras flashed and suddenly Trump pointed at Aras and shouted, "This is the most honest person in Russia!"

"He's very, very charismatic," Agalarov said. "I really liked him. I really like him a lot." The Agalarovs stayed at the Trump Hotel for three or four days, dined at fine restaurants, and took in Vegas shows. Trump appeared with Emin and Aras for the launch of the "Amor" video and posed with Culpo. "He's the American Dream," Emin said. The deal, and the friendship, were sealed.

Aras Agalarov had come a long way from his first brush with storybook American settings such as Las Vegas; he had started his business career pirating movies—he said his first big success was editing down *The Godfather* to fit on illegal bootleg videotapes. Born in 1955 in the former Soviet republic of Azerbaijan, Aras moved to Russia and made his fortune organizing trade fairs and developing high-end real estate, including the mall complex where Trump would bring the Miss Universe contest. Agalarov also had impeccable relations with the government of President Vladimir Putin. Putin selected Agalarov's Crocus Group to build the Far Eastern Federal University near Vladivostok, where Putin and Secretary of State Hillary Clinton attended a conference together. Shortly before the Miss Universe pageant, Putin presented Agalarov with the Order of Honor, one of Russia's highest civilian awards.

Trump and Agalarov seemed like a natural fit. They both dreamed and built big. They both had showy taste. Agalarov's Crocus complex featured a massive shopping mall called Vegas, a neon dream of a place featuring Russia's largest movie theater. Agalarov also liked to put his name on his buildings. And their interests converged: Trump had found a synergy between his Miss Universe pageant and his development business. Trump would dangle the pageant, with its glamour and huge global television audience, like a baited hook. Dozens of countries bid to host the pageant every year, and sometimes Trump would land a big-fish development partner from among his foreign alliances in the pageant business. Agalarov said he paid about $14 million to put on the pageant, about half of which went to licensing Trump's Miss Universe brand.

But the deal wasn't all about bathing beauties: Trump and the Agalarovs planned to do big business together, bringing the big gold *T* to Moscow. They signed a preliminary agreement to explore building a Trump Tower and an Agalarov Tower side by side on Agalarov's property in Moscow. Trump met with father and son and other Russian businessmen to discuss the proposal, which Emin said would have involved Trump's actually investing in the project, not simply licensing his name.

As early as 1987, Trump had expressed interest in building a Trump Tower in the Soviet Union. That year, on a visit to Moscow and Leningrad—now St. Petersburg—he said Soviet officials had asked him to consider building luxury hotels there. "There are not too many ideas that I become attracted to, but that is one I think would interest a lot of people," Trump said at the time. "Not purely from an economic standpoint, either." In 2008, Donald Trump Jr. said the Trump Organization was keen to build in Russia, noting that Russian nationals made up a "disproportionate" percentage of buyers at Trump projects in New York, Dubai, and elsewhere. But he said Russia was a "scary place" to develop property because of problems with the legal system, government control and corruption, and "whose brother is paying off who, etc."

At the Miss Universe Pageant in Moscow in 2013, Trump the father said he was in serious talks about building a skyscraper in Moscow. Trump made a series of complimentary comments about Putin, whom he had been scheduled to meet on the day before the pageant. Putin canceled at the last minute to meet instead with a foreign king. "Putin sent him [Trump] a letter, like a friendly letter, saying that he's very grateful for this event in Russia," Aras said. "And he also sent him a Russian box, a Fedoskino box. I gave him this box and the letter, so he was leaving with very warm feelings."

Trump would express admiration for Putin's leadership, despite his record of prosecuting and persecuting journalists and political opponents. Still, no Trump Tower rose over Moscow. Emin said the plans were on hold, largely because the residential development market in Russia had weakened. Trump's decision to shift his focus didn't sour his relationship with the Agalarovs: "Every time I'm in New York and when Trump is also in New York, I go visit him," Emin said. In their last conversation before Trump announced his candidacy, "he was criticizing the United States government for not being able to be friends with Russia. . . . He thinks America, instead of fighting Russia, should bond and be friends and have common goals with Russia. . . . This could be an amazing breakthrough if he becomes president and actually becomes friends with Putin. . . . Our family vote definitely goes to Mr. Trump." Emin said Trump's run was likely good for business: "Even if he never becomes president, if he just capitalized his brand, probably he'll triple its value, right?"

FOR A WHILE, IT appeared Trump was going to have much better luck in Azerbaijan, the Agalarovs' home country. Although Azerbaijan became an independent nation after the Soviet empire collapsed in 1991, the Agalarov family managed to rekindle the connection with something of a post-Soviet royal wedding between two powerful families. In 2006, Emin Agalarov married Leyla Aliyeva, the glamorous daughter of Azerbaijan's president, Ilham Aliyev. By marrying into the Aliyev family, the handsome and clean-cut Emin became part of a family well known for its disregard for human rights and repression of free speech, including the jailing of journalists who investigated the regime. Ilham Aliyev had ruled the country since 2003, when he took over from his father, Heydar Aliyev, who had been the dominant political force in Azerbaijan stretching back to the late 1960s.

The Aliyevs ruled the country politically and economically. They were also reputed to be fantastically rich. Although the president's annual salary was slightly more than $200,000, he controlled lavish properties and businesses. A magazine headline called the family "The Corleones of the Caspian," a reference to a US diplomatic cable comparing Aliyev's administration to the powerful mob family in *The Godfather* movies.

Azerbaijan had long posed a delicate balancing act for the United States, as Washington weighed its security and energy interests against the Aliyev regime's record on corruption and human rights. The secular, predominantly Muslim nation of 9 million people, bordering Iran and Russia, positioned itself as a pro-Western counterweight to Tehran and Moscow. It was also a major oil- and gas-producing nation and a crucial link in the $45 billion Southern Gas Corridor, a twenty-one-hundred-mile pipeline from Baku to Italy designed to bring Caspian Sea gas to Europe. For Trump, the country seemed ripe for a business deal.

In November 2014, right around the time Trump was sending birthday wishes to his pal Emin Agalarov in Moscow, he announced he would do a hotel deal in Baku with Anar Mammadov, a prominent young Azeri billionaire. Trump would join a project by Mammadov's company, Garant Holding, to develop the Trump International Hotel & Tower Baku, a sail-shaped structure with 72 "ultra-luxury residences" and 189 hotel rooms. Trump would license his name to the project, which had already been under construction for several years. Trump would also eventually manage the hotel. "When we open in 2015, visitors and residents will experience a luxurious property unlike anything else in Baku—it will be among the finest in the world," Trump said in a 2014 news release.

Mammadov was a kind of Azeri royalty, a scion of one of the most powerful families in the country. His father, Ziya Mammadov, the country's longtime transportation minister and a close confidant of President Aliyev's, was one of the richest men in Azerbaijan, thanks largely to what the US State Department called "corruption and predatory behavior by politically-connected elites."

Anar Mammadov attended American InterContinental University in London, where he earned a bachelor's degree in 2004 and an MBA in 2005. Then, almost overnight, he became a billionaire. In the secretive, kleptocratic world of post-Soviet republics, the meteoric rise of the son of an inexplicably wealthy government minister was unsurprising. President Aliyev's three children owned $75 million worth of real estate in Dubai, including nine waterfront mansions purchased in a two-week period in 2009 in the name of the president's then eleven-year-old son.

And Anar Mammadov's companies, or companies related to him, were reported to have profited from contracts worth more than $1 billion for projects related to his father's transportation ministry.

In 2011, Azerbaijan's old guard decided that Anar Mammadov was

the man the country needed to project modernity and vitality to the
world. He started the Azerbaijan Golf Federation and built the country's first course. He spoke English and was comfortable in Europe and
America, so he became the public face of a massive lobbying effort in
the United States. Mammadov founded the Azerbaijan America Alliance, which swept into Washington in 2011 like a hurricane of cash. In
the next five years, the alliance spent more than $12 million lobbying,
wining, and dining Washington policymakers in an effort that Baku's
critics called "caviar diplomacy."

The alliance held three massive annual gala dinners in Washington
to showcase Azeri culture. The first drew almost seven hundred people, including Speaker of the House John Boehner. Mammadov met
with dozens of lawmakers, including Boehner, former Speaker Nancy
Pelosi, and Senator John McCain, the Arizona Republican. In a push
for gravitas in the capital, the alliance hired former congressman Dan
Burton, a Republican from Indiana, as its US chairman.

Any concerns about Azerbaijan's regime currying favor in Washington or cracking down on critics at home did not deter Trump from
making his deal. Human rights groups and others had spent years
reporting on widespread corruption in Azerbaijan, and the prominent
role of Mammadov and his family in the ruling clique turned up in any
Google search, but Garten, Trump's attorney, said the Trump Organization did "due diligence" on Mammadov and the principals in his
company before making the deal, "and there was nothing" suspicious.
Garten said the licensing agreement between Trump and Garant was
signed in May 2012—more than two years before the project was publicly announced. Asked about press reports raising questions about the
sources of Mammadov's wealth, Garten noted they were all from 2013
and 2014. "All of this came to light after the deal had been signed," he
said. Now that the Trump Organization was aware of the reports about
Mammadov, Garten said, "These are things that are going to have to
be discussed."

Critics of the Azeri regime saw Mammadov's role in the Trump
deal as tacit approval from the government, and they argued that the
property's success hinged in part on good relations with the country's
top officials. Ganimat Zahid, who was editor of one of Azerbaijan's
main opposition newspapers before he was jailed and then moved to

live in exile in Paris, said Trump's partnership with Mammadov was deeply troubling, if a smart business move: "In the best case, we can say that Donald Trump had to work with one of these guys" to get a deal in Azerbaijan. "But in the worst case, he knew these people were [corrupt] and he didn't care."

When Trump announced his hotel deal with Mammadov in November 2014, the same month as the Azerbaijan America Alliance's third annual gala in Washington, still-booming Azerbaijan looked like a good bet. Garten said Trump was approached by "an intermediary known to both sides" and was "intrigued" by Azerbaijan because it was in "a region that was trying to establish itself." Marriott, Hilton, Four Seasons, and other luxury hotel chains were investing there, so "that's something that's going to be on your radar," Garten said.

At the time, Baku was a blazing center of development fueled by oil profits. The massive and futuristic Heydar Aliyev Center, designed by the late, renowned architect Zaha Hadid, had opened in 2012, followed by the Flame Towers—three stunning office, hotel, and apartment buildings each shaped like a candle flame—and a massive new airport terminal building featuring a "caviar and champagne" bar.

The Baku Hotel appeared on the Trump website, which promised a 2015 opening. Then, nothing. After about a year, the hotel disappeared from the Trump site. The general manager Trump had hired left for a job in Prague. Construction crews were sent home and the hotel was locked up tight. "We have had an interruption in the construction," said Khalid Karimli, chief financial officer for Mammadov's company. He noted that Azerbaijan's economy was devastated when oil dropped from more than $100 a barrel in 2014 to as little as $30 a year later. The Azeri currency, devalued by the government, dropped to about half of its previous value.

The once-booming city skyline turned into a tableau of blight, with idle cranes perched atop half-finished buildings. Businesses shuttered, thousands lost jobs, and luxury hotels along the waterfront offered five-star rooms at three-star prices. Karimli said construction was about 90 percent complete when the site shut down; he said the hotel would "maybe" open in 2017.

The only key player who did not lose money on the project was Trump. His deal was not being renegotiated and his fees would not be reduced, said Karimli and Garten, neither of whom would disclose how much Trump was being paid. (On his campaign finance disclosure forms, Trump reported $2.5 million in income from the project between January 2014 and July 2015, and another $323,000 in management fees in the subsequent months.)

At about the same time that the Trump Hotel project in Baku came to an abrupt halt, Mammadov virtually disappeared. Friends said he was living mainly in London. He stopped paying some of his bills. The Azerbaijan America Alliance didn't hold its annual gala in Washington in 2015. In March 2016, Burton resigned, saying he hadn't been paid in a year. The next month, after queries from the *Washington Post*, the alliance's website was quietly taken down. The Trump Hotel remained "on hold," Garten said. "Hopefully it will restart, but we don't know."

Karimli said Mammadov initially licensed Trump's name because it was known among political and business leaders in Azerbaijan as well as international businessmen who would be attracted to a five-star hotel in Baku. But now that Trump was running for president, Karimli said, Trump's name was even more valuable for the Baku hotel project. "It was a good investment and unexpected," he said with a laugh. "We hope Trump will be elected president."

ON JULY 6, 2011, Trump flew to Panama City to inaugurate his Trump Ocean Club International Hotel & Tower, his first overseas property to open its doors. "Whoever said less is more never had more," boasted the marketing material for the seventy-story complex of hotel rooms, condos, restaurants, offices, and a casino—all part of the tallest, most unapologetically Trumpian building in Central America. Trump beamed for the paparazzi in a dark suit, white shirt, and fireball-red tie, with a beauty queen on each arm—on his left, Miss Panama 2011, and on his right, Justine Pasek, a Panamanian beauty who had taken the crown at Trump's Miss Universe pageant in 2002.

Trump's appearance said all the right things about a steamy tropical nation whose primary claim to relevance had always been its narrowness, which allowed for construction of the fifty-mile Panama Canal connecting the Atlantic and Pacific and revolutionizing ocean shipping in the Western Hemisphere. To Panamanians yearning for a world-class capital, a big gold TRUMP etched on a sail-shaped tower on the waterfront meant that Panama City, increasingly known as the fast-living Miami of Central America, had arrived.

Now Trump stood beneath the hotel's soaring ceilings, fawned over by beauty queens and dancers in traditional Panamanian costume. President Ricardo Martinelli—a supermarket tycoon who would flee a few years later to Miami amid allegations of vast corruption—thanked Trump for selling Panama the five letters it craved. Trump had warm words for Martinelli, too, suggesting that Panama's newfound glitz could bring even greater rewards: "Maybe the president will get us to bring Miss Universe back here."

But as the ceremony ended, the skies opened and the entire Punta Pacifica neighborhood—notorious for its chronic poor drainage—flooded. Trump was stranded for nearly an hour. The president was called. Cars were stuck in the flooded streets. Finally, someone sent a big SUV to rescue Trump. Nothing was going to be easy for the Panama hotel.

The hotel on the Panama City waterfront was meant to be Trump's springboard into the world of international real estate development. "This building is a very important bridge for us as we begin to expand internationally," Ivanka Trump said on a tour of the property in 2011. The Trump family had first noticed Panama's possibilities, she said, when Panama City hosted the Miss Universe Pageant in 2003. Developer Roger Khafif, who had immigrated to Panama from Lebanon three decades earlier, invited Donald Trump to join the Panama City project. Before the Trump deal, Khafif had done a few successful projects, but mainly, he said, property development "was a hobby." In about 2002, he paid $2.7 million for three acres of newly created land along the Panama City waterfront. Khafif saw it as his chance for the kind of score he'd never had: a massive complex with hotel, 630 condominium units, office space, retail shops, and casino. Over the next couple of years, he had plans drawn up, evoking the sail shape of the famous Burj Al Arab hotel in Dubai.

To land the $230 million or so in financing required to build the complex, Khafif needed a name, a brand as big as his ambitions. "In those days," he said, "Trump was the brand." So Khafif wrote a letter explaining his project and sent it to Trump's New York address. No response. Khafif said that the letter "probably went to the trash," and that Trump was likely asking himself, "What the hell is Panama?" But Khafif didn't give up. In 2005, through a friend of a friend, he finally landed a meeting with Trump.

Khafif flew to New York and went to Trump Tower, carrying his drawings, market analysis, financial projections, and a short video about Panama and the project. Khafif argued to Trump that Panama was the perfect, safe, US-friendly environment to attract well-heeled American retirees, and that Trump's brand would be a huge draw. "He asked the questions," Khafif said. "We showed him the drawings. We talked about Panama. We showed him a little movie." Ivanka Trump joined the meeting. Khafif said he was not asking Trump to invest, just to let him purchase the rights to call it a Trump project. The Trump name, Khafif was sure, would get him the financing he needed.

Trump thanked him for coming in, and Khafif left. The next day, in Miami, Khafif's cell phone rang. The caller asked if he would hold for Trump. Khafif thought a friend was playing a joke on him, until he heard Trump's voice. "Roger, I'm excited. I really love that thing," Trump said. "I want this for Ivanka." Then just twenty-four, Ivanka was taking a bigger role in the company, and Trump wanted the Panama project "to be her baby." The timing was perfect: Trump wanted to expand outside the United States. And the Panama project promised to be huge, the largest of its kind in Central America, "a Trump-sized project," as Khafif put it.

With the Trump name attached, Khafif went to Bear Stearns in New York and landed a $220 million bond deal. Without Trump's name, he said, he would never have been able to get that money. Trump's name also allowed Khafif to raise the price of his apartments to more than $3,000 per square meter—more than three times what nearby condominiums were charging.

Khafif and two other people in Panama familiar with the details of the project said the original deal gave Trump about $75 million from licensing fees and a share of each condo sale. In addition, Trump's organization would earn a fee for managing the hotel. By 2016, Trump had earned about $50 million on the Panama deal, according to two people with knowledge of the project. Trump himself reported revenue of "over $5 million" in royalties and more than $896,000 in management fees from the Panama project between January 2014 and July 2015. In the nine months thereafter, he reported revenue from the Panama deal of between $1 million and $5 million in royalties and another $1.28 million in management fees.

The money kept flowing, even as the Panama property generated a powerful wave of bickering and litigation. Problems started almost immediately after Trump's flashy ribbon-cutting in 2011. Within two years, Khafif's company had filed for Chapter 11 bankruptcy protection, and a court approved a debt-restructuring deal. Khafif said the global economic downturn had caused condo sales to dive. Buyers who had already paid deposits couldn't afford to close their deals as mortgages became harder to find. Although about 90 percent of the condominium units had been under contract, Khafif said more than half of those buyers couldn't complete their deals and had to forfeit their 30 percent deposits—a total of about $50 million.

Even after the bankruptcy deal, problems persisted, boiling over in 2015. Trump managed not only the hotel, but also the condominium portion of the building. There, Trump's company paid $100 for Room 1502, a 170-square-foot storage closet on the fifteenth floor, which was used mainly for utilities. Under Panamanian law, that tiny foothold made Trump's managers eligible to serve on the condominium's board of directors. In 2015, members of the condo board who were not in Trump's employ revolted over what they called mismanagement by Trump's local managers. The owners claimed Trump's managers had overspent the condo board's budget, given themselves undisclosed bonuses, and improperly mingled the finances of the condo and the hotel to make the hotel look more profitable. The Trump Organization consistently denied those allegations.

Khafif and two other sources said Trump's managers proposed imposing a onetime levy of more than $2 million on the condo owners' association to cover the budget shortfall. Angry board members refused to apply the fee and demanded the resignation of Trump's top official in Panama, Mark Stevenson. After the meeting, Stevenson quit as board president, and the other owners took charge of the board. The new board demanded the return of more than $2 million they alleged had been improperly spent. Trump's lawyers responded by demanding that the unit owners pay Trump a $5 million termination fee. Then Trump filed a claim of at least $25 million against the owners, saying they had fired his management team illegally. Trump, already a candidate for president, tried to keep the claim quiet by filing it with a confidential, Paris-based arbitration court, but the case was disclosed by the Associated Press.

Outgunned, the board backed down and settled the case. Two people familiar with the resolution said both sides agreed to walk away from their claims. People on both sides said they were forbidden from disclosing details, but Garten said that the case ended "amicably" and "I don't think anyone was bullied; we had the right to protect our interests and we did." The settlement included another frequent Trump tactic: the nondisclosure agreement. A condo owner said restrictions in the agreement prevented him from speaking publicly and that he feared that Trump might sue him for a sum that could ruin him. Stevenson, Trump's former top manager in Panama, declined to comment because he had signed an agreement not to talk publicly for at least a year. He said violating that agreement could cost him substantial amounts of money that Trump still owed him.

Most key players in the Panama City deal suffered losses when the economy crashed and the project stalled. In the bankruptcy agreement, most of the bondholders accepted a significant "haircut"—a reduction in the return on their original investment. As for Trump, instead of making $75 million on hardly any investment, he had made $50 million as of 2016, according to people with knowledge of the deal. The way Trump structured the deal, the "worst thing that can happen is he's still going to make money," Khafif said.

Even after all the troubles, Khafif believed he got a good deal from Trump. After the debt restructuring and with a recovering global economy, the hotel's business was improving, the condominiums were nearly all sold, and Khafif kept his yacht anchored just off the hotel's pier.

"He did what he had to do, and we did what we had to do," he said in an interview at the Trump Ocean Club tower. "If not, we would not be sitting here in this office, on this floor, because there would be nothing on top of it."

• • •

IN EARLY 2006, RUMORS began to circulate in northeastern Scotland: Trump was thinking about expanding his golf empire to Europe, to Scotland—birthplace of the sport and of his mother, who grew up in a tiny village on the island of Lewis. Trump already owned several golf courses, mostly in warm resort areas of the United States. Now he set his eyes on creating a course that could host the British Open golf championship. A frenzy of expectation broke out in the Scottish press about the potential for a big boost to the country's economy.

In late March, Trump confirmed the rumors: after considering more than two hundred locations in Europe, he had fallen in love with an eight-hundred-acre shooting estate along the North Sea, about twelve miles north of Aberdeen, where he now proposed to build "the greatest golf course anywhere in the world" on top of majestic sand dunes. Trump envisioned investing more than $400 million and creating at least four hundred new jobs as part of a project that included two golf courses, a 450-room luxury hotel, and a gated community with hundreds of villas and condos. It was supposed to be the greatest thing to happen to the region since oil was discovered in the 1970s. Even Sean Connery was rumored to be coming. The *Aberdeen Evening Express* gushed about the possibilities: "Property prices will rocket, millions of pounds will be pumped into the local economy and celebrities will descend."

But some local residents proved to be as craggy as the Scottish coastline. Part of the dunes, which shifted with the winds, were protected from development, and environmentalists argued that a big project would irreparably damage the habitat of many local birds and animals. The complications kept coming: an experimental wind farm was already planned for just off the coast, and its turbines, as tall as Big Ben, threatened to ruin Trump's perfect ocean view. And a handful of neighbors who lived in the footprint of the development weren't happy to hear that the Trump company wanted them to move if the golf resort was built.

Trump pronounced himself unfazed by these challenges, yet he warned that if the project became too complicated, he would abandon it. Although the project was widely popular, some skeptics puzzled over why Trump would build a golf course in a spot regularly shrouded in a cold fog. The plan was "fabulous news for the area," a local columnist wrote, "and also for knitwear manufacturers, who will make a killing when the world's top players step out on the first tee and feel as though their limbs are being sawn off by a north-east breeze that hasn't paused for breath since it left the Arctic."

That spring, Trump's private Boeing 727 landed in Aberdeen, greeted by a bagpiper playing "Highland Laddie" and a swarm of reporters. Some thought it odd that Trump kept referring to himself as being not Scottish but "Scotch," like the whisky; still, most local officials fawned over their ancestral son and did what they could to smooth the way toward approval of his project. The wind farm was scaled back from thirty-three turbines to twenty-three, and Trump scaled up his plans, tripling the budget to nearly $1.5 billion and expanding the development to include a conference center, employee housing, a turf-grass research center, the hotel and spa, thirty-six luxury villas, and more than a thousand residences, all in an area without the infrastructure to handle a big influx of newcomers. A Trump official later promised more than twelve hundred permanent jobs at the resort, plus thousands more playing support roles. Locals were told to expect their property values to go up 20 percent. Construction would be completed by 2012, officials said.

But in 2007, the local planning council turned down the plan, in a close vote decided by a council member who said Trump's application didn't back up his grand promises of economic prosperity. Scottish law allowed Trump to appeal the decision or revise and resubmit his plans. Instead, he threatened to move the project to Ireland. Scottish officials quickly rushed to calm the waters, announcing that the national government would handle the application and hold an extensive public hearing.

By the time the public inquiry started, in June 2008, the US recession had hit, but although the collapse of the real estate market eventually forced the Trump Organization to delay or cancel several projects, Trump stuck with the Scotland plan. On his way to testify at the hearing, Trump stopped for about three hours on Lewis, where his mother was born and lived until she was eighteen and moved to New York in search of work. The visit was Trump's first since he was a toddler, and cheeky reporters at a press conference near a castle peppered him with questions about whether his visit was just a clumsy case of pandering to the locals. His older sister, Maryanne Trump Barry, came to his defense: "My mother would be so proud to see Donald here today. She would be so proud to see what he's done, all the good he's done and the TV star that he is. I'm here not because of these things, but because he's my brother. I love him. He's never forgotten where he comes from and he comes from here. This is a man I revere. He's a nice guy and he's funny, too."

The next day, Trump testified for several hours. "The world is in chaos," he said, and the housing portion of the development might have to wait until after the economy recovered, but he promised to see the project through. He claimed to know more about the environment than his consultants did, though he admitted he had not read their reports. "In life, you can only read so much," he said. He promised to preserve the dunes, but when the councillor who had cast the deciding vote against his permit accused Trump of failing to understand the property or its environmental fragility, Trump snapped back, "Nobody has ever told me that I don't know how to buy property before. You're the first one. I have done very well buying property. Thanks for the advice."

In November 2008, Trump got the green light. But he still had to win over neighbors who thought he was trying to shortchange them. The largest parcel was owned by Michael Forbes, a farmer, fisherman, quarry worker, and jack-of-all-trades who lived with his wife in a farmhouse surrounded by a collection of outbuildings. "He lives like a pig," Trump said at one point. Forbes refused to sell—the words NO MORE TRUMP LIES appeared on the side of one of his farm buildings— and Trump began to pursue using compulsory purchase, a process, similar to eminent domain in the United States, by which he could force some neighbors out of their homes. Trump said he didn't want the views from his luxury hotel "obliterated by a slum."

Scots had a centuries-long history of fighting against compulsory purchase, and they took after Trump with a vengeance; a group of activists purchased a piece of Forbes's land and piled their names onto a deed, complicating efforts to seize the property. Although elected leaders had bent to Trump's demands in the past, they stood firm against kicking Scots off their own land to make way for a private business. It appeared the two sides would be forced to live alongside one another—and not peacefully. Outside the home of David and Moira Milne, who resided in a converted coast guard station on a hill above the golf course, Trump's staff planted a row of trees in front of the sea-facing windows, blocking the family's views. When the first stand of trees died, the staff ripped them out and planted a second batch. The Trump workers also blocked in Susie and John Munro's cottage, constructing a two-story-high hill in their front yard, then adding a fence and locked gate. Whenever it rained, their yard filled with water and their steep dirt road turned into a mudslide.

Despite the skirmishes over land, construction of the golf course proceeded apace, and when it opened in 2012, even critics admitted it was beautiful, meandering through the stabilized sand dunes with sweeping views of the coastline and North Sea. Trump considered it his masterpiece, comparing it to a treasured multimillion-dollar painting. But he had halted work on the resort itself in protest of the wind farm, which was still moving forward. Trump warned that the wind turbines were ruinous, and he took out ads in the local press criticizing the project. He traveled to Scotland again to testify at a hearing, accusing the Scottish government of luring him into investing in their country on the false promise that the turbines would never be built—an assertion the officials denied. In 2013, Trump sued the Scottish government and watched his popularity plummet in a country that had once embraced him as one of its own.

The legal battle went on until late 2015, when England's highest court ruled against Trump. The resort, named Trump International Golf Links, would be completed—with the wind farm. Any good feeling once attached to the Scottish development seemed sharply diminished as Trump's statements about Muslims and immigrants during his presidential campaign led to protests and petitions against him in Scotland. Robert Gordon University in Aberdeen rescinded an honorary degree it had given Trump in 2010. When a petition that called for Trump to be barred from Great Britain collected more than half a million signatures, the highest concentration of signatories lived in the Aberdeen area. When Trump broke off his campaign in June 2016 to preside over the ceremonial opening of his second resort in Scotland, Trump Turnberry, the country's first minister declined to attend.

Trump continued to insist that the people of Scotland loved him. Indeed, he said, his golf course near Aberdeen was a blueprint for how he would operate as president: "When I first arrived on the scene in Aberdeen, the people of Scotland were testing me to see just how serious I was—just like the citizens in the United States have done about my race for the White House. I had to win them over—I had to convince them that I meant business and that I had their best interests in mind. Well, Scotland has already been won—and so will the United States."

15

Showman

Money, money, money!" the singer wailed as Donald Trump strutted down a runway and climbed into a ring at the center of a throbbing mass of eighty thousand wrestling fans in Detroit. Pumping his fist, Trump raised his chin and pursed his lips, a proto-gladiator in white shirt, light pink tie, and blue suit. His glazed hair, swept into its familiar blond swirl, glistened beneath the arena's bright lights. After more than thirty years in the public realm, a journey that had taken him from real estate to global fame, Trump was still cultivating new audiences. When he wasn't hawking condos or casinos, he was busy building his own celebrity, the unique persona of a billionaire who could poke fun at himself, a plutocrat with a penchant for popular appeal. In addition to television and movie roles, he went on the lecture circuit, earning $100,000 per appearance at motivational seminars hosted by Tony Robbins. Trump advised a crowd in St. Louis that paranoia was crucial to success. "Now that sounds terrible," Trump said. "But you have to realize that people—sadly, sadly—are very vicious. You think we're so different from the lions in the jungle?" He told another group, "When a person screws you, screw them back fifteen times harder."

To reach the millions of Americans hooked on the comic-book fantasy world of professional wrestling, Trump agreed in 2007 to costar in a garish showdown entitled "Battle of the Billionaires." Choreographed by a team of scriptwriters, Trump and Vince McMahon,

WrestleMania's impresario, were to duel for a prize that defined the outer reaches of the absurd: the right to shave the other's studiously curated coiffure. Neither man would actually fight, leaving that, for the most part, to two proxies. Trump's was Bobby Lashley, an African American with mountainous shoulders and a head as smooth as a cue ball. McMahon's representative was a tattooed muscle mass known as Umaga, who called himself the Samoan Bulldozer.

The alliance with McMahon began in the late eighties when Trump hosted WrestleMania IV and V at Trump Plaza in Atlantic City. Trump loved the big crowds and overwrought pageantry and posed for photographs with the wrestlers Hulk Hogan and André the Giant. "Battle of the Billionaires" was an opportunity to merge huge audiences from *The Apprentice* and WrestleMania, and McMahon and Trump delighted in promoting the moment. In the weeks before their duel, the two businessmen staged several appetite-whetting encounters, the first of which occurred as McMahon honored himself at an over-the-top "Fan Appreciation Night" in Dallas.

High above the arena, Trump's face suddenly appeared on an oversize screen. "You claim that you tell your audience what they want, what they like, and all that nonsense," Trump bellowed. "They want value. Who knows more about value than me, Vince?" In the next moment, money fell from the ceiling—a shower of dollar bills—fluttering into spectators' outstretched hands. "Look up at the sky, Vince, look at that!" Trump shouted as the crowd screamed. "Now that's the way you show appreciation!" McMahon, his face twisted in feigned rage, growled, "Donald, you embarrassed me!"

In Portland, on another night, before another rabid crowd, two curvaceous brunettes accompanied Trump into the arena, where he and McMahon signed a "contract" to duel. McMahon said he would win because of the size of his own "grapefruits," an apparent reference to his testicles. "Your grapefruits are no match for my Trump Towers," Trump replied. The crowd roared. "You want some, Vince?" Trump snarled. He pushed McMahon over a conference table, catapulting him into a backward somersault. The crowd cheered as the announcer shouted, "Donald Trump just shoved Mr. McMahon on his billionaire butt!"

During another appearance, Trump ratcheted up the rhetoric:

"I'm taller than you, I'm better-looking than you, I'm stronger than you. . . . I will kick your ass." At their final joint appearance before the match, Trump smacked McMahon in the face after the promoter playfully touched Trump's cheek. "I gave him a wallop," Trump boasted afterward, promising that their upcoming clash would "escalate." Trump relished his role, following the commands of the scriptwriters and producers as he navigated a new audience. "He was working crowds who weren't going to take kindly to an outsider," said Court Bauer, who wrote the script for "Battle of the Billionaires." "He had to win them over, and he did, very effectively and very quickly. He knew how to read a crowd and manipulate them. You're trying to convert them from viewers to customers, to get them to buy the ticket, to buy pay-per-view."

Trump's success with WrestleMania's audience, Bauer said, was propelled by his ability to speak the language of an average American while evoking vast wealth: "What Donald stands for is aspirational, and that's what it is for wrestling fans—'I can't do it at work, but I can do it vicariously through the wrestlers.' Donald talks blue collar, but he has the world. He's been selling people on that dream for a long time." Trump also won over the audience with his willingness to play his role to the max. In Detroit, he jumped on McMahon and, after they tumbled to the ground, punched him in the face. "The hostile takeover of Donald Trump on Vince McMahon!" the announcer shouted. When "Stone Cold" Steve Austin, a retired wrestler who was the event's referee, performed his signature Stunner move on Trump, kicking him in the stomach and decking him, Trump "was game to do it all," Bauer said. "He exceeded all expectations. We never thought he'd do any of that stuff."

The "Battle of the Billionaires" culminated with Lashley mauling Umaga, giving Trump the right to scalp McMahon at the center of the ring. His lips twisted in a fiendish grin, Trump performed the procedure with both an electric shaver and a razor and shaving cream. The following morning, McMahon appeared on the *Today* show, bald and with a black eye, purportedly the result of a Trump punch. Feigning humiliation, the promoter articulated what was perhaps the showdown's single undeniable truth: "Donald Trump is a great entertainer."

• • •

THE DOORBELL RINGS AND a butler announces the famous couple's arrival: "Sir, it is my esteemed pleasure to introduce Mr. and Mrs. Donald Trump!" Donald and Marla Maples step through the doorway, surprising the studio audience and millions of viewers watching the television sitcom *The Fresh Prince of Bel-Air*. "It's The Donald! Oh my *God*!" a character exclaims before fainting. Another grabs Donald's hand and gushes, "You look much richer in person!"

By 1994, when he appeared on *Fresh Prince*, the comedy that launched Will Smith's acting career, Trump's fame as a real estate developer and bestselling author had made him a coveted novelty in Hollywood. Producers clamored for Trump to lend their shows and movies a moment of authenticity by performing as himself, the world's best-known tycoon, a boyishly handsome showman of outsize wealth and ego. Instead of new skyscrapers and casinos, Trump was selling only himself in cameos in movies such as *Zoolander* and *Home Alone 2*, and on sitcoms such as *The Drew Carey Show* and Fran Drescher's *The Nanny*. His earliest appearances included a role in *Ghosts Can't Do It*, a film in which he tells the character played by Bo Derek, "In this room, there are knives sharp enough to cut you to the bone, and hearts cold enough to eat yours as hors d'oeuvres."

Derek removes her glasses. "You're too pretty to be bad," she purrs.

"You noticed," Trump replies, his lips forming his famous pout (this performance won him a Golden Raspberry Award for Worst Supporting Actor).

Trump the mogul wanted the world to see a hard-nosed, almost imperious businessman, but Hollywood experienced Trump the actor as an eager, cooperative performer who learned his lines, did not require much direction, and was "particular about his hair," said Shelley Jensen, who directed him in *Fresh Prince*. The cameos allowed Trump to poke fun at his reputation for cartoonish vanity while advertising his brand, at no cost, to millions of Americans. If he came off as thin-skinned in interviews and in his business relationships—he spoke often of suing his critics—this was his opportunity to present himself as a good sport, able to withstand barbs and even lampoon himself. "If you were going to pick a real estate mogul for a show," said Jensen, "he was one of those guys you'd go after because he was one of the few who would actually do it."

Four years later, Trump appeared as himself in another sitcom, *Spin City*, which starred Michael J. Fox as an adviser to fictional New York City mayor Randall Winston. With their topical scripts, the show's producers liked to create bit parts for prominent New Yorkers such as Mayor Rudolph Giuliani, Senator Alfonse D'Amato, and Yankee pitcher Roger Clemens. In one episode, the fictional mayor experiences writer's block as he tries to craft his memoir, which leads Fox's character to invite Trump to City Hall.

"Mr. Trump here wrote *Art of the Deal*," Fox's character tells the mayor, "then he wrote a new bestseller, *Art of the Comeback*."

"Wow," the mayor responds, inviting Trump to take a seat. Ignoring the chair reserved for guests, Trump instead takes a seat behind the mayor's desk, prompting guffaws from the audience. "Must have been tough getting started," the mayor says of Trump's writing.

"First day, nine chapters," comes the casual reply.

Walter Barnett, a *Spin City* producer, said Trump's aide had warned, prior to taping, that his boss "was shy, didn't like to shake hands, and was germophobic. I was expecting this crazy, paranoid guy." When Trump arrived on the set, Andy Cadiff, the episode's director, braced for a "nightmare" because "you had an image of him that he could be difficult and demanding. Frankly, I remember him being delightful. He was having a good time. He was totally cooperative and game, he seemed genuinely happy to be there. I usually remember the pricks and assholes who came on the show, and he was not one of them."

On a 1999 episode of *Sex and the City* entitled "The Man, the Myth, the Viagra," Trump played himself at the Plaza Hotel, which he owned at the time. "A cosmopolitan and Donald Trump—you just don't get more New York than that," Sarah Jessica Parker's character, Carrie Bradshaw, says as viewers see Trump finishing a business meeting at a table inside the hotel's Oak Room. "Look, Ed, I've got to go—think about it. I will be in my office at Trump Tower," he says. When Victoria Hochberg, the show's director, handed Trump a sheet with his lines, Donald looked them over and promptly handed back the script. "Donald, don't you want to study them?" Hochberg asked.

"Nope, I've got it," he replied, causing the director more than a few anxious thoughts, including "Oh, dear, it's going to require, like, twenty takes." But then, Hochberg said, "he got it on the first try. One-take Donald."

In 2000, Trump threw himself into a more risqué role. At New York's Inner Circle show, an annual production featuring satirical sketches by City Hall reporters and the mayor, Trump, as himself, made a pass at Giuliani, who was playing a woman shopping at a department store. "You know, you're really beautiful," Trump told Giuliani's character, who wore a dress and blond wig. When the mayor's character sprayed a sampling of perfume on herself, Trump buried his face in Giuliani's neck and breasts. "Oh, you dirty boy—Donald, I thought you were a gentleman!" Giuliani shrieked.

Elliot Cuker, the show's director, was inspired to create Trump's role because he knew Trump from New York's social circuit, where their typical conversation involved assessing female beauty. "We would always talk about women; what do you think about this one or that one; it was like he was a traveling judge," Cuker said. Asking Trump to "come on to Rudy" did not seem like a stretch: "I gave him the idea of what was going to happen—Rudy is an attractive woman, you're going to have a love scene. You want to kiss her. Go with it. I did not tell him to kiss his breast. He did that himself. He was spontaneous and open to it, and those are the earmarks of a real showman."

Trump did have his limits, though. Hosting *Saturday Night Live* in 2004, he rejected writer T. Sean Shannon's proposal that he play a tattoo artist who inks only customers' faces because all other bodily locations have grown passé. "He was, like, 'No, I'm not doing that. What's next?'" Shannon said. The writer came up with another sketch based on *The Prince and the Pauper*, in which Trump played a janitor and Darrell Hammond was his identical twin, who was a tycoon. As the janitor, Trump told his double that his office "looks like the Liberace museum" and that his comb-over "looks like you killed a squirrel . . . and put it right on top of your head." But Trump asked that Shannon tweak the sketch so that the prince and the pauper were not siblings. "Just don't make it my brother because I don't want people to think I'm making fun of him," Trump told Shannon.

Trump, Shannon said, "was willing to make fun of himself. He was prepared every day. He wasn't nervous. He was very charming and straightforward. He was always that persona. He was Donald Trump at all times." No more so than in his opening monologue. "It's really great to be here at *Saturday Night Live*, but I'll be completely honest— it's even better for *Saturday Night Live* that I'm here," he boasted. "Nobody's bigger than me. Nobody's better than me. I'm a ratings machine." He then informed the audience that *The Apprentice* was the country's most watched show and that he was the "highest-paid television personality in America. And, as everyone in this room knows, *highest-paid* means 'best,' right?"

At the Emmy Awards the following year, Trump ventured into a new realm as a performer. Before a live television audience, Trump, in straw hat and overalls and carrying a pitchfork, teamed with *Will & Grace* star Megan Mullally to sing a satirical rendition of "Green Acres" that included a plug for Trump Tower. The song was part of *Emmy-Idol*, a send-up of *American Idol*, in which stars performed and the audience voted for the winner. Trump and Mullally won, leading one critic to write, "The Donald's transformation from business tycoon to pop-culture oddity is now complete." The following day, Mullally's cell phone rang. It was Trump calling to say, "Listen, we really needed to win that and we did and you were a big part of that, so I just wanted to say thank you." Performing before 14 million Americans wasn't enough. No matter the venue, Trump needed to win.

On January 22, 2005, Trump starred in another show that was the subject of breathless attention: his wedding to his third wife, Melania Knauss, a five-foot-eleven fashion model who had immigrated to the United States from the former Yugoslavia. Jeff Zucker, then chief of NBC's entertainment division, wanted to broadcast the nuptials live, an idea that intrigued Trump, who thought the publicity could benefit *The Apprentice*. But he passed on the offer. In truth, the Trumps did not need NBC to draw attention to their wedding at Mar-a-Lago. *Vogue* produced a photo spread of Melania in her $100,000 Dior dress, which workers had spent 550 hours decorating with fifteen hundred crystals. Gossip columnists hyperventilated about the guest list, which included Bill and Hillary Clinton, Rudy Giuliani, Barbara Walters, Derek Jeter, and Arnold Schwarzenegger. Paul Anka, Tony Bennett, Elton John, and Billy Joel took turns serenading the couple. Trump used the celebration to show off Mar-a-Lago's new ballroom, its ceilings and bathroom sinks adorned in gold leaf.

At fifty-eight, after two failed marriages, Trump appeared to have found a partner who fulfilled his long-standing desire for a "no-maintenance woman," one who would not steal attention from him. Melania, who was thirty-four when they wed, did not generate headlines or seek to upstage him. Donald's older children referred to her as "the Portrait" because she spoke so little. Born Melanija Knavs in the former Yugoslavia, she grew up in a nondescript concrete apartment building in the hilly village of Sevnica. Feeling stifled under her country's socialist regime, Melania told high school friends that she wanted to escape their town and travel around the world. Modeling was her path. Changing her surname to Knauss, she worked as a fashion model in Milan, Paris, and, starting in the mid-1990s, New York.

Saving her earnings and avoiding Manhattan's nightclub circuit, Melania preferred anonymity. "She was a homebody," said Edit Molnar, a friend and fellow model. Yet, one night in 1998, Melania found herself at the Kit Kat Klub because her modeling agency was hosting a party. Donald, who had recently split up with Marla Maples, was at the event with a date, Celina Midelfart, a beautiful Norwegian heiress. But Trump noticed Melania and asked for her phone number. "She's incredible," Trump told Molnar that night. "I want this woman." Melania resisted, aware that Trump had come to the party with another woman. But Trump was persistent and soon they began going out. He introduced her to celebrities such as Michael Jackson, Céline Dion, Michael Douglas, and Catherine Zeta-Jones. Melania was not altogether impressed. "I was with a celebrity myself," she said, "so it's not something new for me."

On Trump's arm, the brunette with ice-blue eyes and full figure was more of a target for paparazzi than she had been on her own. Trump boasted that his new girlfriend was "a very, very successful model," but her most high-profile moment occurred after their relationship started, when *Sports Illustrated* featured her in its swimsuit edition. In January 2000, she was on the cover of *GQ*'s British edition, lying on a fur throw in Trump's Boeing 747, apparently naked but for a diamond choker and matching bracelets. The headline read, "Sex at 30,000 feet. Melania Knauss earns her air miles." The spread also showed Melania handcuffed to a leather briefcase stuffed with jewels, and perched on an airplane wing, wearing a red bra and thong and pointing a pistol, as if she had stepped out of a James Bond movie.

After her wedding to Trump, Melania sold jewelry on a home shopping channel and launched a line of caviar-infused face cream. Following their son Barron's 2006 birth, the same year that she secured US citizenship, Melania devoted herself primarily to parenting. If Donald was too busy to join his wife and son on vacation, as often was the case, she went ahead with Barron. Her parents helped out with the baby, staying at Trump Tower and Mar-a-Lago, as Donald's former in-laws had with his older children. Trump's absence did not appear to bother his wife. "We are both very independent," Melania said in her halting English (she also speaks Italian, French, and German). "We give ourselves and each other space. I allowed him to do, to have his passion and his dreams come true—and he let me do the same. I believe not changing anybody. You need to understand them and let them be who they are."

For all the freedom she allowed Trump, Melania was no pushover: "I am very opinionated. I'm very strong. I have yes or no. I'm not a maybe person. I know what I like." She bristled when a journalist described her as a woman who exists quietly in Trump's shadow: "I am not shy. I'm not reserved, [but] I don't need . . . to be an attention seeker." She and her husband, she said, embrace traditional roles: "We like the same things. We are both very detail oriented."

To Trump's confidants, his third wife's temperament seemed to best balance his perpetual histrionics. "Of all three women, Melania handles Donald the best," said Louise Sunshine, who for decades served as a close adviser to Trump. "She's very independent. He's very independent. She doesn't hesitate to tell Donald good from bad, right from wrong." As the years passed, Melania was more the stay-at-home mom than the glamorous model. In her view, their lives were defined by bland routine. They awoke at 5:30 a.m. She did Pilates. He read the newspapers. When he was in town, they preferred to eat dinner at home and watch baseball or basketball on television while he monitored his Twitter feed. She tried, not altogether successfully, to discourage him from eating too many desserts: "I tell him my opinions. Sometimes he listens, and sometimes he doesn't."

Donald's view of Melania was similar: "She's a very private person. . . . She's very smart. And there's no games. You know, it's *boom*—it's all business. But a very smart person; and considered one of the great beauties." Trump credited Melania with being his greatest booster, the partner "who grounds me." At last he had a wife who knew how to fulfill her primary duty, serving as Mrs. Donald Trump, smiling, standing by his side (usually his left), strengthening his brand, and creating not a moment of drama to steal the spotlight or distract him from his roiling ambition.

In 2011, Trump's stature as a showman of far-reaching renown was confirmed anew when Comedy Central made him the target of a star-studded roast, a distinction previously conferred upon the likes of Hugh Hefner, Chevy Chase, and William Shatner. With Melania and Ivanka in the audience, Trump grinned and grimaced while *Family Guy* creator Seth MacFarlane, rapper Snoop Dogg, and others made fun of his hair, his multiple marriages, and his vanity. "You've ruined more models' lives than bulimia," said comedienne Lisa Lampanelli. MacFarlane described Trump as "the second-worst tragedy to hit New York," and comedian Jeff Ross said Trump's ego is "so big he videotapes himself masturbating and then masturbates to the video." Trump and Melania, Ross said, "are so compatible they both yell out Donald's name when they climax."

When it was his turn to speak, Trump played to his caricature, telling the audience, "What a great honor it must be to honor me tonight." He also had an answer for the hair insults. "What's the difference between a wet raccoon and Donald J. Trump's hair? A wet raccoon doesn't have seven billion *fucking* dollars in the bank." At a moment when he was contemplating entering the 2012 presidential race, the show was a vehicle for Trump to demonstrate that, for all his riches, he was not above poking fun at himself. Trump had "proved to every American voter that you have thick skin," Ross told the audience, "that you can take a joke, that you are a man of the people."

Despite the veneer of good fun, performers said that Trump had asked in advance of the show that his roasters steer clear of the one subject he deemed off-limits: the true extent of his wealth. "Trump's rule was, 'Don't say I have less money than I say I do,'" said Anthony Jeselnik, one of the comedians who performed that night. "'Make fun of my kids, do whatever you want. Just don't say that I don't have that much money.'"

In 2013, McMahon's World Wrestling Entertainment inducted Trump into its Hall of Fame during a raucous ceremony at Madison Square Garden. After a promotional video introduced him as a "business mogul, bestselling author, reality television show star," Trump walked onstage to a roiling mix of cheers, boos, and chants of "You suck! You suck!" Undaunted, Trump called his induction his "greatest honor of all." He promised a rematch with McMahon, in which he would "kick his ass!" The booing and catcalls persisted, subsiding only when Trump introduced his wife and daughter Ivanka, who were in the audience. "I really do love you people," Trump said as he concluded his speech, "even the ones who don't love me so much."

Two years later, just after his sixty-ninth birthday, Trump declared that he was ready for a far different sort of spectacle. He was determined to prove that the ultimate showman could play on any stage, even the biggest one in the world. This would involve adjustments. He would get out of the beauty pageant business, for example, selling off his shares of Miss Universe for $49.3 million. "I sold it because I'm running for president," he said. He would reconsider the wisdom of some of his more outlandish moments, including the crude remarks about sex he had made on Howard Stern's radio show: "I never anticipated running or being a politician."

16

Political Chameleon

Donald Trump, dressed in a dark navy suit, walked into Marble Collegiate Church on Fifth Avenue, a mile and a half south of Trump Tower. This had been the setting of so many memorable moments: the place where he married Ivana, and where he learned the power of positive thinking from the church's longtime minister, Norman Vincent Peale. Now he was here to say good-bye to his father. Fred Trump had died four days earlier, on June 25, 1999, at ninety-three years old. The first signs of Alzheimer's disease had surfaced five years earlier. Donald and Fred were riding together in a car when Donald proudly told his father that he had just bought the land under the Empire State Building. "That's a tall building, isn't it?" Fred replied. "How many apartments are in that building?"

After that day, Donald had watched his father fade little by little, and now Fred lay in a casket surrounded by white roses. Hundreds of mourners—politicians, developers, and celebrities—filled the church. As late-morning sunlight streamed through the sanctuary's ten stained glass windows, family members shared stories about the elder Trump: how he whistled and bounded up the front stairs as he arrived home at night after working long days, how he taught his grandchildren the value of a dollar, how his favorite poem was "Don't Quit." Mayor Rudolph Giuliani proclaimed that Fred Trump had helped establish New York as "the most important city in the world."

When it was Donald's turn, he reflected upon his father's greatness by listing iconic projects that Donald had built with his father's unwavering support—the Grand Hyatt, Trump Tower, Trump Plaza, Trump Taj Mahal, Trump Castle. It was an irony, he said, that he had learned of his father's death just after reading a *New York Times* story about his latest development, Trump Place, on Manhattan's West Side. It was yet another success, and a testament to the work ethic Donald had learned from his father. Fred had passed down Donald's most treasured asset, the emblem of all his accomplishments: the Trump name. "The name just sells," Donald was quoted as saying.

The burial, Trump said, was "by far the toughest day of my life." His father had been his best friend. His death made Donald take stock of his own life. Trump, rarely introspective, said in an interview for this book that he felt "loneliness and responsibility, because I was really close to my father." He began to see himself differently, not just as the new family patriarch or as a builder, but as someone who could help shape the world.

Trump received a condolence letter from John F. Kennedy Jr., who had been three years old when his father, President Kennedy, was killed by an assassin's bullet. "No matter where you are in life, losing a parent changes you," wrote Kennedy, whose celebrity in New York at the time rivaled Trump's, and who was often urged by Democrats to run for office. On the same day that Trump opened the note, Kennedy, then thirty-eight years old, died when an airplane he was piloting crashed, also killing the passengers: his wife and his sister-in-law. Trump, then fifty-three years old, saw parallels between the Trumps and the Kennedys. Hadn't the glowing obituaries about his father been the kind you'd expect for a major statesman? Years later, Trump would say his father's death was perhaps what "inwardly" pushed him finally to decide he wanted to be president. The decision had been years in the making.

"DO YOU HAVE ANY political connections?" gossip columnist Rona Barrett asked Trump in unaired parts of a 1980 interview, nearly two decades before Fred Trump's funeral.

"I really say no," Trump said. "I absolutely say no." Trump sat on a couch in his Fifth Avenue apartment, wearing a charcoal suit and over-size tie with diagonal stripes. The interview—likely his first on network television—was part of an NBC special, "Rona Barrett Looks at Today's Super Rich." Trump wanted to promote Trump Tower, but Barrett had picked up on something else: Trump's competitive instincts and desire for power. When she asked about his willingness to make controversial decisions, Trump abruptly turned the conversation to what he saw as a lack of leadership in the United States. Gas prices were soaring and inflation was rampant. More than four dozen Americans who had been seized at the US embassy were still being held hostage in Iran while, according to Trump, "we just sit back and take everybody's abuse. . . . I just don't feel the country is going forward in the proper direction."

The interview was taped one month before the presidential election. Trump had donated to President Jimmy Carter while helping his challenger, Ronald Reagan, raise money. Reagan, a former actor, ran for the White House employing a memorable slogan: Let's Make America Great Again. Barrett was taken aback by Trump's pivot to politics. "Would you like to be president of the United States?" she asked.

No, he said. Politics was a "mean life. . . . Abraham Lincoln would probably not be electable today because of television. He was not a handsome man, and he did not smile at all." Trump said he knew people who would be "excellent" presidents because they were "extraordinarily brilliant . . . very, very confident . . . and have the respect of everybody." None of them would seek the office because of the media scrutiny, which he called a tragedy. "One man could turn this country around. The one proper president could turn this country around."

TRUMP WAS NO POLITICAL naïf. He and his father had thrived in New York City's pay-to-play culture for years, in part by cultivating local elected officials. Trump almost always answered political operatives' calls for money. His criterion was simple: he wanted a winner, someone who would be an ally once in office. Sometimes he donated to opposing candidates in the same local race. He showed no concern about a candidate's views or political party. "He wanted someone who was going to continue to climb . . . and someone he was going to have a relationship [with] over that time," said longtime New

York Democratic consultant George Arzt, who over the years asked Trump to support several candidates.

In the late 1980s, Trump's largesse caught the attention of a New York State commission examining possible political corruption. Armed with subpoena power, the commission called Trump to testify in March 1988. Under oath, Trump acknowledged that political donations had been a routine part of his business for nearly two decades. He gave so generously that he sometimes lost track of the amounts. When an attorney for the commission asked him to verify that he had given $150,000 to local candidates in 1985 alone, Trump responded, "I really don't know. I assume that is correct, yes."

The amount Trump donated in 1985 was equal to three times the annual limit for individuals ($50,000), or thirty times higher than the cap for companies ($5,000), under New York state law. But Trump "circumvented" the law, a state commission found, by spreading the donations among eighteen subsidiary companies. Each had a different name—such as Shore Haven Apartments No. 2, Inc., Shore Haven Apartments No. 3, Inc., and Shore Haven Apartments No. 6, Inc.—but Trump had significant control over all of them. He told the commissioners he didn't know "the exact reason" it was done this way; it was how his lawyers had said to do it.

Trump found other ways, too, to give candidates financial help. In June 1985, he guaranteed a $50,000 loan to the campaign of Andrew Stein, a Democrat who was running to be New York's City Council president. Six months later, with the debt still unsettled, Trump paid it off. Trump told commissioners that he had expected Stein's campaign to pay off the loan and only learned that it would come out of his pocket when the loan came due. More than thirty years later, Stein said in an interview that he did not recall the loan, but that developers were close to city officials at the time.

Donald's business expanded beyond New York in the 1980s—and so did his donations. He gave more than $72,000 to federal candidates in 1988, which was $47,000 more than was permitted under federal law. The Federal Election Commission discovered the infraction years later during an audit and fined him $15,000. "We were going to fight it, but it would have cost more money than the settlement," Trump said at the time.

• • •

MICHAEL DUNBAR, A FURNITURE maker in Portsmouth, New Hampshire, recognized Trump's ability to connect to the masses. In the spring of 1987, nearly a year before his state's first-in-the-nation primary, the Republican Party activist was searching for a presidential candidate. Thumbing through the *Wall Street Journal*, Dunbar became fascinated by Trump's business acumen and personality. He sent out mailers encouraging Republicans to "draft Trump." Friends told him the idea was laughable, but Dunbar invited Trump to speak to the local Rotary Club. Trump, intrigued, asked Dunbar to discuss the idea at Trump Tower that summer.

Dunbar marveled at the opulence of the tower's lobby, then ascended to the twenty-sixth-floor office, where Trump offered him a Diet Coke as they discussed Dunbar's pitch: Trump would fly his private helicopter to a New Hampshire airfield, speak to the Rotary crowd at Yoken's restaurant, and hold a press conference. They had a deal.

A few weeks later, Trump took out full-page ads opining on foreign policy in the *New York Times*, *Washington Post*, and *Boston Globe*, which was widely read by New Hampshire voters. "There's nothing wrong with America's Foreign Defense Policy that a little backbone can't cure," Trump wrote in the ads, which cost a combined $95,000. The advertisement provided an early snapshot of Trump's political thinking, with ideas that he would repeat in different forms for decades. He questioned why the United States continued to pay for Japan's and Saudi Arabia's protection: "Tax these wealthy nations, not America. End our huge deficits, reduce our taxes and let America's economy grow unencumbered by the cost of defending those who can easily afford to pay us for the defense of their freedom. Let's not let our great country be laughed at anymore."

The image of the rest of the world laughing at US leaders would become an enduring theme in Trump's political rhetoric. This time, it came in the seventh year of Ronald Reagan's presidency, just weeks before the publication of *Trump: The Art of the Deal*, in which Trump called Reagan "a smooth performer," but questioned whether "there's anything beneath that smile." The slap against the president was a surprise; the Trumps had been Goldwater Republicans, and they had raised money for Reagan. Reagan's approval rating stood at 51 percent, the stock market was booming, and the unemployment rate had dipped below 6 percent for the first time that decade. Yet in Trump's portrayal, the United States was a sucker in a worldwide hustle.

Trump had previously said that he was more than capable of pulling off the kind of nuclear-weapons-reduction deal that would become one of Reagan's proudest achievements. Trump told a *Washington Post* reporter in 1984 that he dreamed of employing his negotiating skills on nuclear disarmament talks with the Soviets: "Some people have an ability to negotiate. It's an art you're basically born with. You either have it or you don't." It didn't matter that Trump was no expert on missiles. "It would take an hour and a half to learn everything there is to learn about missiles. . . . I think I know most of it anyway. You're talking about just getting updated on a situation."

ON THE DAY TRUMP'S foreign policy ad appeared, he announced he would go to New Hampshire, the perfect way to stoke political speculation. Trump was asked whether he was running for office. "There is absolutely no plan to run for mayor, governor, or United States senator," an unidentified spokesman replied. "He will not comment about the presidency." The *New York Times* headline fueled the anticipation: "Trump Gives a Vague Hint of Candidacy."

On the bright morning of October 22, 1987, Trump's helicopter landed at a New Hampshire airfield, where a limousine paid for by Dunbar ferried Trump to Yoken's restaurant. There, a waiting crowd held placards that said VOTE TRUMP FOR PRESIDENT and VOTE FOR AN EN-"TRUMP"-ENEUR. In his talk, Trump reprised themes from his advertisement. As for the presidency, he said, "We have had enough of the men who say, 'Vote for me because I am nice.' I have nothing against nice people, but I personally have had enough of them."

But what Trump said to the assembled reporters made Dunbar's heart sink: "I am not interested in running for president." Dunbar wondered why Trump had even bothered coming to New Hampshire. Was it just a promotional gambit for his book? Dunbar later received a copy of Trump's book, inscribed, "To Michael: I really appreciate your friendship—You've created a very exciting part of my life—on to the future." Dunbar hoped he had planted a seed.

TRUMP'S BRIEF FLIRTATION WITH a run for office was over, but his reputed wealth still attracted politicians from both parties. On November 19, 1987, Frank Donatelli, Reagan's assistant for political and intergovernmental affairs, sent a memo to Tom Griscom, the president's press secretary, warning that Democrats in Congress wanted Trump to serve as chairman of a fund-raiser. "His fundraising prowess is significant and if he accepts, he could considerably increase the Democratic Party prowess next year," Reagan's aide wrote. "It would be most helpful if you would place a phone call to Don Trump *today*. He has a *large* ego and would be responsive to your call."

Trump declined the Democrats' invitation to raise money. Prominent Republicans continued to court him as a donor or future candidate. That Christmas, with the presidential race under way, former president Richard Nixon wrote Trump a letter after his wife, Pat, saw the businessman on *The Phil Donahue Show*: "Dear Donald, I did not see the program, but Mrs. Nixon told me you were great. As you can imagine, she is an expert on politics and she predicts that whenever you decide to run for office, you will be a winner!"

Although he was not a candidate, Trump reveled in the curiosity about his ambitions and emerging political profile. He stepped up his press tour, giving interviews in which he repeated his stance on issues such as trade, inviting questions about his ambitions. "That sounds like political, presidential talk to me," Oprah Winfrey told Trump when he appeared on her popular talk show in the spring of 1988.

"I just don't think I really have the inclination to do it," Trump said. "I just probably wouldn't do it, Oprah, but I do get tired of seeing what's happening in this country. And if it got so bad, I would never want to rule it out totally." If he did run, he added, he would have a "helluva chance of winning."

A few months later, Trump attended his first Republican convention, as George H. W. Bush accepted the party's nomination for the presidency. During an interview on CNN, talk show host Larry

King asked Trump why he was there. Trump said he wanted to see "how the system works." Next came the questions that would follow Trump for decades: How would he classify his politics? King wanted to know if Trump classified himself as an "Eastern Republican" or a "Rockefeller/Chase Manhattan Republican," shorthand for the liberal wing of the GOP.

"I never thought about it in those terms," Trump replied.

"How about a 'Bush Republican'?" King asked.

Trump, who regularly boasted of his great wealth, responded by casting himself as a man of the people: "You know, wealthy people don't like me because I'm competing against them all the time and I like to win. The fact is, I go down the streets of New York and the people that really like me are the taxi drivers and the workers."

"Then why are you a Republican?"

"I have no idea. I'm a Republican because I just believe in certain principles of the Republican Party."

THAT FALL, BUSH BEAT his Democratic opponent, Massachusetts governor Michael Dukakis, in part by portraying him as weak on crime. A pro-Bush political committee ran ads featuring Willie Horton, a black man who had raped a twenty-seven-year-old white woman while on a weekend furlough from a Massachusetts prison when Dukakis was governor. The Bush campaign then ran ads that referred to the issue without mentioning Horton's name. The combination proved powerful. The ads worked, critics said, by fueling racial tension and fear.

Months later, Trump seized on a notorious crime that threatened to divide New York along racial lines. On April 19, 1989, Trisha Meili, a twenty-eight-year-old white investment banker, went for a jog in Central Park. As she made her way from her Upper East Side park entrance north toward Harlem, Meili was attacked, bound with her own shirt, beaten with a rock, raped, and left for dead in a pool of her own blood. Doctors told reporters it was not clear if she would live. If she did, brain damage was a near certainty. The Central Park jogger, as she become known, would remain unconscious for nearly two weeks.

Five boys, four black and one Hispanic, ages fourteen to sixteen, were arrested. Two weeks after the crime, millions of New Yorkers reading the city's four major newspapers—the *New York Times, Daily News, New York Post,* and *Newsday*—were greeted with a full-page ad paid for by Trump. "Bring back the death penalty," he wrote, warning of "roving bands of wild criminals." Trump used the horrific crime as an opportunity to attack Mayor Ed Koch. Trump had been considering running against Koch in the Democratic primary and had long feuded with the mayor over tax abatements Trump wanted for a proposed development. Trump had called the mayor a "moron," and Koch had said Trump was "greedy."

Now, Trump used the Central Park jogger case to further ridicule his rival. "Mayor Koch has stated that hate and rancor should be removed from our hearts," Trump wrote in the ad. "I do not think so. I want to hate these muggers and murderers. They should be forced to suffer and, when they kill, they should be executed for their crimes."

Many blacks saw in Trump's ads not just opportunism, but also racism. The Reverend Al Sharpton, then president of an organization called the United African Movement, called on Trump to apologize publicly for what Sharpton called a "hatemongering ad." The day the ads ran, Trump said in TV interviews that the teenagers arrested for the rape symbolized New York's problems. Trump presented himself as an everyman who had the money and courage to speak freely without fear of economic consequences or damage to his reputation: "You better believe that I hate the people that took this girl and raped her brutally. You better believe it."

Trump insisted he was no racist. With tension swirling around the issue, Trump appeared later that year on an NBC special called the "Racial Attitudes and Consciousness Exam," hosted by Bryant Gumbel. "A well-educated black has a tremendous advantage over a well-educated white in terms of the job market," Trump said on the program. "I think sometimes a black may think they don't have an advantage or this and that. I've said on one occasion, even about myself, if I were starting off today, I would love to be a well-educated black, because I believe they do have an actual advantage." Movie director Spike Lee called Trump's assertion "garbage."

The jogger would survive the brutal beating but suffered permanent damage. The young men were convicted and served six to thirteen years in prison. But years later, a career criminal confessed to the rape, providing a DNA match. The convictions were overturned, and the city paid $41 million to settle a wrongful imprisonment suit that the men had filed. Trump called the settlement "a disgrace," refused to apologize, and said, "These young men do not exactly have the pasts of angels." He said he wouldn't have given them "a dime" and insisted "they owe the taxpayers of the City of New York an apology for taking money out of their pockets like candy from a baby." Decades later, one of the falsely accused men, Yusef Salaam, called Trump "a hateful person" who had rushed to judgment and inflamed tensions in the city. "Donald Trump, he was the fire starter," Salaam said.

Trump didn't run for mayor. Manhattan's borough president, David Dinkins, beat Koch in the Democratic primary and went on to become the first African American to hold the city's highest office.

IN THE YEAR AFTER the Central Park rape, Trump was consumed by his affair with Marla Maples and his struggle to pay off hundreds of millions of dollars in debt. If Trump had any political ambitions, they had been put on hold. In response to rumors that he might run for governor of New York, Trump told Larry King in 1990 that he had "zero interest. . . . Can you imagine me running for office? Wouldn't you say I'm a little controversial for that?"

Trump remained outside the political system, but he continued to influence it through his lobbyists and campaign contributions. Trump spent millions to sway politicians and bureaucrats, especially to guard his Atlantic City casinos from encroaching competitors. And he wasn't shy about employing his signature bravado on Capitol Hill.

In 1993, while testifying before a congressional committee, Trump questioned whether members of a Connecticut tribe operating the Foxwoods casino, which he viewed as serious competition to his Atlantic City operations, were really Native Americans. "They don't look like Indians to me," Trump told the House Native American Affairs Subcommittee. He said the tribe would not be able to keep organized crime out and he predicted "the biggest scandal ever."

The comments echoed a racially charged interview Trump had given months earlier. "I think I might have more Indian blood than

a lot of the so-called Indians that are trying to open up the reservations," Trump had said on shock jock Don Imus's show. Imus referred
to tribes hoping to open casinos as "drunken Injuns," comparing them
to an African-American basketball star: "A couple of these Indians
up in Connecticut look like Michael Jordan, frankly." Trump replied:
"I think if you've ever been up there, you would truly say that these
are not Indians." Representative George Miller, a California Democrat who chaired the congressional hearing, took aim at Trump's comments to Imus and on Capitol Hill: "Mr. Trump, do you know in the
history of this country where we have heard this discussion before?
'They don't look Jewish to me,' 'They don't look Indian to me,' 'They
don't look Italian to me.' And that was the test for whether people
could go into business or not go into business, whether they could get
a bank loan: 'You are too black; you are not black enough.'" Trump
responded that casinos on Indian reservations got unfair, "discriminatory" advantages.

In 2000, when New York was considering expanding Native American casinos in the Catskill Mountains, Trump played a role in a series
of explosive TV, newspaper, and radio ads that accused members of
the Mohawk Indian tribe of having long criminal records and ties to
the mob. The ads showed pictures of cocaine lines and syringes and
asked, "Are these the new neighbors we want?" The campaign against
Indian casinos included an ostensible telephone survey in which
respondents who opposed gambling in New York were transferred to
Governor George Pataki's office to register their complaints. A group
called the Institute for Law and Safety sponsored the ads; the group
was funded by Trump and facilitated by his longtime lobbyist, Roger
Stone. Stone, a Republican operative and fixer, had worked on Richard Nixon's Committee to Re-elect the President in 1972, taking part
in campaign high jinks that emerged during the Watergate scandal.
Stone's role in the affair was minor but colorful: he donated money to
Pete McCloskey, Nixon's rival in the 1972 Republican primary, under
a fake name—the Young Socialist Alliance—then tipped off a newspaper about the rival candidate's supposed communist supporters. Stone
first met Trump while on the hunt for political donations on behalf of
Reagan's campaign in 1980. Stone visited Roy Cohn, Trump's attorney
at the time, and Cohn steered Stone to Fred and Donald Trump. Stone

developed a fondness for the younger Trump and would eventually fill the void left by Cohn's death. Stone teamed up with Paul Manafort (later Trump's 2016 presidential campaign manager) and others to start a lobbying firm in 1981, after Reagan's election. Trump became one of the firm's first clients.

Nearly two decades later, Stone was at the center of Trump's under-the-radar antigambling campaign in New York. Trump had paid more than $150,000 for the ads—on top of more than $300,000 he reported spending to lobby New York legislators over the first half of 2000. But Trump and Stone never reported the ad spending as a lobbying effort, as state law required. They admitted their role only after regulators launched an investigation. The state lobbying commission imposed its largest-ever civil penalty—a $250,000 fine—and Trump agreed to issue a public apology. "It's been settled," Trump told reporters. "We're happy it all worked out nicely." As part of the settlement, the lobbying commission agreed not to refer the case for criminal prosecution. A violation of the state's lobbying act carried the potential for a misdemeanor charge.

Even then, Trump continued to fight the proposed casino in the Catskills, casting upstate gaming as a threat to New York City. "It will destroy the progress that's been made in New York City," Trump said on the day he agreed to the fine. "It will drain money out of the city. Instead of buying cars and apartments, they'll be spending money at casinos." That, of course, was what his business relied on in Atlantic City, but Trump apparently saw no contradiction in fighting against gambling in New York if it helped his interests in New Jersey.

Even as he warned of the dangers of Indian gambling in New York, he pushed for an Indian casino in Connecticut. Trump had a stake in that project, partnering with the Paucatuck Indians. Under a 1997 pact, Trump had agreed to pay for efforts in Washington to get the tribe the federal recognition it needed to operate a casino. He also agreed to provide his expertise. In exchange, the tribe agreed to give Trump a management fee based on a percentage of the future casino's revenues. Trump hired lobbyists at the Miami-based firm Greenberg Traurig to help get the tribe federally recognized. Lobbyist Ronald Platt represented Trump Hotel & Casino Resorts Inc. in 1999 and 2000. The tribe won federal recognition in 2002, but backed out of the deal with Trump shortly afterward. There would be no casino for Trump in Connecticut, but he still owed the lobbying firm more than $600,000.

Trump had been slow in paying, so Platt visited him in Manhattan. The lobbyist got a taste of what happened when Trump didn't win. "I'm here to get us paid," Platt told Trump.

"It should be so prestigious to represent me that you should do it for free," Trump responded, according to Platt.

"Bullshit," Platt answered. Trump then picked up a yellow legal pad, slammed it onto a table, and stormed out of the room, according to Platt. An intermediary chased after Trump and came back with the check fifteen minutes later. Platt left the office and deposited the check as soon as he could—before Trump could change his mind. Trump said later that he didn't remember Platt, but added, "If I held back payment, it was probably because he did a lousy job."

WHILE TRUMP REBUILT HIS empire and his personal life, an epic battle was under way for the presidency. In 1992, a new face on the political scene, Governor Bill Clinton of Arkansas, defeated President Bush and a billionaire independent, Ross Perot. Clinton became the nation's forty-second president in January 1993 and promptly announced that his wife, Hillary Rodham Clinton, would play a major role in his administration, in charge of creating a national health care plan. Three months later, Tony August, the organizer of a gaming industry awards ceremony in Atlantic City, wrote to the White House and invited President Clinton to the event. The invitation was a long shot, but the organizer thought Clinton would hit it off with the guest of honor: Donald Trump. "I'm not a matchmaker," the organizer wrote, "but if you two don't know each other, you should. You have much in common—age, broad vision for the future, and most importantly, the resources and desire to make America bigger and better than it already is." The Clintons didn't make it to the event with Trump, but their social and professional circles began to intersect. Trump, for example, was one of about fifty prominent officials and political fund-raisers President Clinton sat down with during a trip to Manhattan in 1994.

There were limits to the social niceties. In 1996, Clinton's personal secretary floated the idea of sending a letter to Trump on his fiftieth birthday. Three days later, the same secretary sent instructions to the person who handled Clinton's personal correspondence: "Cancel the letter to Donald Trump." Trump, though, was a vocal Clinton supporter in the late 1990s. "I think Bill Clinton is terrific," Trump said on December 27, 1997, on CNN's political talk show *Evans & Novak.* "I think he's done an amazing job. I think he's probably got the toughest skin I've ever seen, and I think he's a terrific guy."

One month later, reports surfaced that Clinton had had a secret sexual relationship with an intern named Monica Lewinsky, beginning when she was twenty-two years old in 1995 and lasting for more than two years. Trump was unperturbed, becoming one of Clinton's most vocal backers. "The best thing he has going is the fact that the economy's doing great," Trump said in August 1998, days after Clinton finally admitted a relationship with Lewinsky. "I've never seen anything like it. You know, they talked about the eighties were good. The nineties are better." When a former Arkansas state employee, Paula Jones, sued Clinton, alleging sexual harassment, Trump called her "a loser." Trump suggested that if he were a candidate, he would face similar controversy: "Can you imagine how controversial that'd be? You think about him with women. How about me with the women?"

Clinton was impeached by the House for lying to a grand jury about the Lewinsky relationship, but the Senate did not convict him, enabling him to complete his second term. Trump, meanwhile, began thinking more seriously about succeeding him. As a new election approached, Stone, Trump's longtime lobbyist, examined the potential field, led by Republican George W. Bush and Democrat Al Gore. Stone said this could be Trump's moment, and that the path forward might be within a third party. The country seemed receptive to candidates from outside the two major political parties. Ross Perot, a Texas billionaire with no political experience, had won 18 percent of the vote in 1992 and was still popular. Trump was particularly familiar with the rise of Jesse Ventura, a professional wrestler Trump knew from WrestleMania who had improbably won the governorship of Minnesota in 1998 on the Reform Party ticket. Ventura had made his name parading in a feather boa and, as a World Wrestling Federation commentator, mocking Hulk Hogan. If Ventura could go from being known as The Body to The Governing Body, maybe Trump could become president.

• • •

MORE THAN THREE MONTHS after his father's funeral, on October 8, 1999, Trump announced on *Larry King Live* that he was leaving the Republican Party to join the Reform Party, which was eligible for federal funds because of Perot's performance in the previous two presidential elections. Fed up with the two-party system, Trump announced that he was forming an exploratory committee to run for president. In little more than a year, Trump's assessment of the Clinton years had made a U-turn. "I think there's a great lack of spirit in this country," Trump told King. "You know, what happened over the last four years is disgusting, and I just think there's a tremendous lack of spirit, and I think the spirit has to be brought back."

Despite joining the Reform Party, Trump said his role model was Reagan, notwithstanding his criticism twelve years earlier of the former president. Trump still wasn't thrilled about Reagan's policies, but he liked the way the former president acted—the very quality Trump had once criticized: "He'll go down as a great president and not so much for the things he did. It's just, there was a demeanor to him and spirit that the country had under Ronald Reagan that was really phenomenal. . . . There is a certain pomposity and there was a certain ribbon-cutting stature that is important for the president." Trump said his main competitor for the Reform Party nomination, Pat Buchanan, was too divisive. Trump insisted he was all about inclusiveness. Who, King asked, would Trump pick as his vice presidential candidate? He named one possibility: Oprah Winfrey, the African-American talk show host who had asked him about presidential ambitions more than a decade earlier.

TRUMP'S SUGGESTION OF AN entertainer as vice president raised questions about whether this was all just one more publicity stunt. But Trump insisted this was a serious endeavor. He called himself a conservative but sounded like a liberal on many issues. In the *Advocate*, a gay-oriented newsmagazine, Trump took issue with how Buchanan talked about "Jews, blacks, gays, and Mexicans. . . . He wants to divide our country." Trump called himself a conciliator, saying he would extend the Civil Rights Act to include protections for lesbians and gays and allow them to serve openly in the military, repealing Don't Ask, Don't Tell, the Clinton-era policy that had lifted a ban on gays in the military, but forbade them from talking about their orientation while in the service. Trump also called for universal health care and the protection of Social Security through a onetime tax on the super-wealthy and new funds generated by renegotiation of trade agreements.

Two weeks after Trump announced his exploratory committee, he appeared on *Meet the Press*, where the moderator, Tim Russert, pressed him on a statement he had reportedly made about Clinton's affair with Lewinsky: "When you say that if the president had had a fling with a supermodel rather than Monica, he'd be a hero—"

Trump interrupted, "But I didn't say that. I said there are those that say that 'if he had a fling with a supermodel, he would be everyone's hero.' I didn't say that I said it."

Trump, who had made countless appearances on friendly television venues, seemed unprepared for a grilling by a famously tough modera-tor such as Russert. Trump said he supported a right to partial-birth abortions, a late-term procedure that results in the death and intact removal of a fetus from the uterus. Stone, Trump's political adviser, accompanied him to the interview. When the two left the studio, Stone said Trump admitted he didn't know what a partial-birth abortion was.

In January 2000, Trump published *The America We Deserve*, which started with a blunt statement: "Let's cut to the chase. Yes, I am considering a run for the presidency of the United States." He said he wouldn't run for "vanity" and said he would only enter the race "if I become convinced I can win." Whatever happened, Trump wrote, he was certain that "nonpoliticians represent the wave of the future." He also addressed his earlier comments to Russert: "When Tim Russert asked me on *Meet the Press* if I would ban partial-birth abortion if I were president, my pro-choice instincts led me to say no. After the show, I consulted two doctors I respect and, upon learning more about this procedure, I have concluded that I would indeed support a ban." But what was his overall view? He said that while he was "uncomfort-able" with abortion, "I support a woman's right to choose."

• • •

TRUMP'S QUASI CAMPAIGN TRAVELED to Minnesota for a January 2000 meeting with the role model Ventura. Trump and his wife-to-be, Melania Knauss, went to the penthouse of the Northland Inn in Brooklyn Park, a Minneapolis suburb, where a dozen members of Ventura's election campaign awaited them. Trump told them he wanted to learn how a man who started at the bottom of the polls, who was deemed a joke by some, ended up as governor. How did he beat well-known politicians such as the mayor of St. Paul?

Dean Barkley, who had chaired Ventura's campaign, advised Trump, "Just be honest. It's not what you say, but how you say it. And talk to the public, not at them." Phil Madsen, who ran Ventura's online operations, told Trump how they used the Internet to solicit donations and spread their message.

Trump asked about the health of the Reform Party, given the fight between Perot and Ventura over its mission. Trump expressed concern about being a member of a party that included Buchanan and David Duke, the former Grand Wizard for the Ku Klux Klan. Trump wondered aloud if the differences were reconcilable. Barkley could offer little assurance that they were.

Later that afternoon, Trump and Ventura appeared at a lunch for the local chamber of commerce. Trump the listener was gone; the showbiz Trump had returned. He mocked the Republican candidates, winning laughs: "Are these people stiffs or what?" But Trump eventually chose not to run. On February 19, 2000, Trump wrote an op-ed in the *New York Times* in which he said that his exploratory campaign was the "greatest civics lesson that a private citizen can have." He was not sure he would be able to win as a third-party candidate—especially one in a party beleaguered by such infighting.

But another seed had been planted. Indeed, although he had already pulled out of the race, Trump's name remained on the Reform Party ballot in Michigan and California. He won both primaries.

WHILE TRUMP PULLED OUT of the arena, another politician was stepping in, in New York. Hillary Clinton was angling to be the US senator from Trump's home state, and he seemed eager to support her. During her campaign for Senate in 2000, the First Lady had agreed to be the guest of honor at a fund-raising event for the New York State Democratic Committee. Judith Hope, the state party chairwoman, asked Trump if he would host the event at his Trump Tower penthouse. He told Hope he would be happy to do it as long as no more than fifty people attended. "No problem," Hope responded.

On the evening of the event, 250 people showed up, crammed shoulder to shoulder, spilling drinks and food on the furniture as they jockeyed for photos with Trump and Clinton. A mortified Hope apologized to Trump, who graciously let it pass. Trump was registered as an independent at the time, but his politics were by now widely recognized as malleable, changing like a chameleon's color to fit the moment. He seemed happy to stand next to Clinton and help out the state Democratic Party. Trump declined to say in an interview for this book whether he voted for Hillary Clinton, but said, "I felt it was an obligation to get along, including with the Clintons and including with a lot of other people. It was very important for me to get along with politicians in my business."

Clinton won the Senate seat, and Trump continued to contribute to her over the next decade. He donated to Clinton's campaigns six times, giving a total of $4,700 between 2002 and 2009. He also invited the Clintons to his wedding in 2005 to Melania. Hillary Clinton sat in the front row at the ceremony at Mar-a-Lago.

As Hillary took her seat in the Senate in 2001, Trump joined the Democratic Party. Years later, he explained the decision: "I said to myself, if I ever ran for anything in New York, which I thought about, you virtually can't get elected as a Republican." Trump gave his first big endorsement after joining the Democratic Party to one of the most liberal candidates running for mayor of New York City. Fernando Ferrer had been the Bronx borough president and was trying to become the city's first Hispanic mayor, positioning himself as a liberal counterforce to outgoing Republican mayor Rudolph Giuliani. Ferrer thought Giuliani's focus on policing and the commercialization of Times Square had come at the expense of the city's lower and middle classes, what he called the "other New York." He campaigned with the Reverend Al Sharpton, rallying black and Latino voters. He supported the right to late-term abortions.

On the eve of the runoff, Ferrer held a press conference with

Trump, hoping the last-minute endorsement would swing the election his way. In the weeks after the September 11 attacks, which brought down the twin towers of the World Trade Center, Ferrer had endorsed a plan to rebuild the lost office space in the outer boroughs. Trump told reporters the plan was "very smart."

Ferrer was surprised to win Trump's support, wondering to himself, "What am I doing here?" This was not what he considered "serious politics." But if it helped him win office, he would take it. Ferrer lost the primary to Mark Green, whom Trump then supported by giving his campaign $4,500. Trump's belief that only a Democrat could win in New York City turned out to be misguided. Michael Bloomberg, a billionaire media mogul, ran as a Republican and won the general election.

Trump continued to help politicians from both parties, notably including a dynamic former prosecutor and Democrat, Eliot Spitzer. Trump had encountered Spitzer in the nineties, when he was vying to become New York's attorney general under the slogan Total Change. "You're a nice kid, but you're never going to win," Trump told him. In 1998, Spitzer won, and Trump sent him a handwritten letter. "I told you that you wouldn't win. You did. Good luck," it said, according to Spitzer. Inside the envelope was a $10,000 check for Spitzer's reelection. Trump would later pledge to help Spitzer raise $250,000 for his successful gubernatorial campaign, including hosting a cocktail party at his Trump Plaza apartment. Spitzer resigned in a prostitution scandal in 2008. In 2013, Trump slammed Spitzer, calling him a "horrible" governor and attorney general "who ruined many good people."

TO TRUMP, POLITICAL DONATIONS were a cost of doing business, suggesting that his practice of politics was transactional, not ideological. "I give to everybody. When they call, I give," Trump said. "And you know what? When I need something from them—two years later, three years later—I call them. They are there for me." Frank Sanzillo, Trump's lobbyist in New York in the late 1990s and early 2000s, said Trump was privately dismissive of politicians: "He laughed about them, like, 'Let's give his campaign twenty-five thousand dollars, that'll shut him up.' And it was our job to translate that to the politician as 'He loves you.'" Trump also was loath to attend political fund-raisers, often asking Sanzillo, "How much more do I have to give not to show up?"

Trump and his major companies gave at least $3.1 million to local, state, and federal candidates from both parties between 1995 and 2016, not including donations that may have flowed through limited liability corporations that Trump controlled. He donated $620,000 to the Republican Governors Association between 2009 and 2014. From 1995 to 2006, he also gave $11,500 to Charles Rangel, the Democratic congressman from New York ("The only thing Donald Trump ever talked to me about was Donald Trump!" Rangel recalled). But Trump said his votes for president were consistently Republican. He voted for Bush in 2000 and said he lost respect for the forty-third president because of his handling of the war in Iraq, which he would later call a "disaster." Trump maintained that he had been against the war from the beginning, but when radio host Howard Stern asked Trump on September 11, 2002, if he supported going to war—six months before the invasion—he responded, "Yeah, I guess so. You know, I wish the first time it was done correctly." (Five days after the invasion began, a *Washington Post* reporter overheard Trump at an Oscars after-party calling the war a "mess.") Still, he voted for Bush again in 2004 because he felt it was important to "carry the Republican line." Recalling the 2004 vote, Trump said he showed his distance from Bush by not throwing fund-raisers for him. He gave the campaign $2,000, according to federal filings.

Trump's public statements sent mixed signals about his political leanings. In 2006, he said that Senator John McCain, who would become the 2008 Republican nominee, could not win because he advocated sending more troops to Iraq. Trump praised the eventual Democratic nominee, Senator Barack Obama of Illinois, for his "wonderful qualities." Nonetheless, Trump contributed $3,600 to McCain during the 2008 campaign and voted for him.

Trump changed parties seven times between 1999 and 2012. After registering as a Democrat in 2001, he switched back to the Republicans in 2003. He became a Democrat again in 2005 and a Republican in 2009. He chose not to be affiliated with any party in 2011. Then he returned to the GOP in 2012, once again stoking speculation that he would seek the presidency. Asked what he would say to critics who saw the constant party-switching as proof that he had no core beliefs, Trump responded, "I think it had to do more with practicality, because if you're going to run for office, you would have had to make friends."

TRUMP'S CELEBRITY STATUS PROMPTLY put him among the 2012 front-runners. An NBC–Wall Street Journal survey among Republican primary voters released in early April 2011 showed him tied for second behind front-runner Mitt Romney. Among Tea Party supporters, Trump led the field. He had bashed Obama with an intensity he had never displayed for Obama's predecessors. He called the president's signature health care law a "job killer!" and "one of the greatest threats our country faces." He drew wide attention for focusing on the long-discredited assertion (though one accepted by at least a fifth of the population) that the president had not been born in Hawaii, but in Kenya, his father's native country. On NBC, Trump expressed "real doubts" about whether Obama was US born, cementing his role as a leader in what became known as the birther movement. Provocatively, he suggested that he had private investigators combing through records in Hawaii: "I have people that actually have been studying it, and they cannot believe what they're finding. . . . I would like to have him show his birth certificate."

Obama had long ignored such taunts. But three weeks later, as Trump prepared to arrive in New Hampshire for an exploratory visit, Obama announced that he had sent a member of the White House counsel's office to Hawaii to bring back a copy of his long-form birth certificate. Obama put the document on public display, explaining, "We do not have time for this silliness." Days later, when Trump was a guest of the *Washington Post* at the annual black-tie White House Correspondents Dinner, Obama ridiculed the real estate mogul: "Now, I know that he's taken some flak lately, but no one is happier, no one is prouder, to put this birth certificate matter to rest than The Donald. And that's because he can finally get back to focusing on the issues that matter—like, did we fake the moon landing?" The audience roared with laughter while Trump looked stone-faced, although he later insisted the jokes were fine and the evening "phenomenal."

Two weeks after the dinner, Trump announced he would not run in 2012, saying, "Business is my greatest passion and I am not ready to leave the private sector." In a later interview, he explained the decision: "My children were younger. I was doing numerous jobs, many jobs, and I really wanted to wrap them up. . . . I had a signed contract with *The Apprentice.*" On February 2, 2012, he endorsed Mitt Romney: "We really have the opportunity to do something great for our country." Trump became an outspoken surrogate for Romney, recording calls that were automatically sent to voters during the primaries, attacking Obama on Twitter, and offering to give $5 million to a charity of Obama's choosing if he released his college transcripts and passport information. Obama ignored the request. On Election Day, Trump went to Boston to attend what was supposed to be a Romney victory party and told the *Boston Herald* he "felt good" about how things would turn out. After the results came in, he was livid at the loss, and he took to his increasingly favored medium, Twitter, to vent his frustration: "This election is a total sham and a travesty." "Let's fight like hell and stop this great and disgusting injustice!" "We can't let this happen. The world is laughing at us." "We should march on Washington and stop this travesty. Our nation is totally divided!" Trump said years later that if Romney had relied on Trump more, he might have won the election. "But they chose not to use my services—which was fine with me because I'm very busy, you know," Trump said.

Twelve days after the 2012 election, Trump filed an application with the US Patent and Trademark Office for a phrase he wanted to be his own: Make America Great Again.

17

The Worth of a Man

I'm really rich." With those words, Donald Trump pointed to what he considered a central qualification for his run for the White House. At Trump's campaign announcement address on June 16, 2015, his aides passed around a document stating that he was worth more than $8.7 billion in 2014—a fortune that would rank him among America's wealthiest people. Trump was hardly the first person of great wealth to aspire to the presidency. President George Washington had overseen a vast plantation made possible by slavery. Mitt Romney, the failed 2012 Republican nominee, became wealthy running Bain Capital, a private equity firm. Few, if any, however, had trumpeted quite so loudly as Trump the notion that building a profitable business was a central qualification. Washington was a general who led the nation to independence; Romney was a Massachusetts governor who won passage of a health care program. Trump had never held public office, and he relied to an extraordinary degree on his carefully crafted image as an astonishingly successful executive. Trump argued, in essence, that his wealth made him uniquely qualified to be president, that he would make America as successful as he was. "I'm proud of my net worth," Trump said. "I've done an amazing job."

But the document highlighted an issue that had trailed Trump from his earliest days as an entrepreneur, real estate developer, and showman: there was no way to verify the bottom line. One month later, his campaign issued another statement that said Trump's "net worth is in excess of TEN BILLION DOLLARS." When Trump's campaign submitted its federally mandated financial disclosure statements to the government, it boasted that the forms were "not designed for a man of Trump's massive wealth." For decades, Trump had made his net worth a major component of his identity as a master dealmaker. He had publicly slammed or sued some of those who questioned his self-valuation. Trump didn't calculate his worth in dollars alone; he also put a value on the perception that he was extraordinarily wealthy. If Trump had his way, no one would question his claims to great wealth. Yet his claims were questioned, time and again.

THE QUESTIONS BEGAN DECADES earlier as Trump emerged as a public figure. In 1976, a *New York Times* profile quoted him saying he was worth more than $200 million. Although net worth and income are different, some skeptics argued that the big number seemed to be at odds with a New Jersey Casino Control Commission report, which showed that he claimed his taxable income in 1976 was $24,594. Trump also received a $6,000 gift from his parents every December, and an escalating series of payouts from family trusts. Questions increased when it turned out that Trump had paid no income tax in 1978 and 1979. Using tax deductions including real estate depreciation, he claimed a negative income of $3.8 million during those two years. The same report showed that he had borrowed $7.5 million from his father, had used his take from the already-indebted Grand Hyatt to back his Atlantic City debt, and had relied on a $35 million line of credit from Chase Manhattan.

By the early 1980s, after Trump had begun construction of Trump Tower, he dramatically increased his estimate of his net worth. He learned that *Forbes* in 1982 was preparing to launch an annual ranking of America's four hundred richest people, known as the Forbes 400. Money, Trump said later, was a way to "keep score" in life. The list was hardly scientific, and staffers had limited time to produce it. They faced a conundrum: How could they estimate Trump's net worth when he ran a private company and offered limited financial documentation? "You couldn't get at Trump's cash flow," said Harold Seneker, then a *Forbes* senior editor in charge of the rich list. That made it especially difficult to pin down the value of his holdings. Editors guessed at what a property might sell for, then subtracted the publicly known debt related to it. Trump told the magazine he was worth about $500 million.

Because of the uncertainty, *Forbes*'s editors decided to offer a combined estimate for Fred and Donald Trump at the time, $200 million. "Our rule of thumb was to divide whatever [Trump] said by three," Seneker said. The *Forbes* list continued to boost Trump's value each year. In 1984, the magazine estimated he was worth $400 million. Then it was $1 billion in 1988. "I'm breaking every record in the history of Atlantic City," Trump said later. Trump carried a lot of debt, but he boasted in 1988 that he was protected from danger: "None of the debt is personally guaranteed. If the world goes to hell in a handbasket, I won't lose a dollar." Behind the scenes, though, Trump was putting his finances in peril as the result of a borrowing-and-spending spree he went on shortly before a collapse in real estate values.

ON NOVEMBER 10, 1988, Trump stepped onto the *Late Night with David Letterman* stage in New York and took his seat next to the TV host. Letterman introduced Trump as a person who knew "everything there is to know about money, finance, economy, budgets, so on and so forth."

"You're worth, like, four billion dollars or something, right?" Letterman asked.

"I hope so," Trump said with a restrained smile.

"Is there any way a guy like you could go broke?" Letterman said, drawing a wave of laughter. "I'm serious. Could you weather any financial storm and come out still a tycoon?"

Trump turned serious. "I would like to think I could weather most. It's a great time to really save as much money in dollars as you can." Trump himself wasn't saving. He had just bought the Plaza Hotel across from Central Park and was launching the Trump Shuttle. Few knew it, but the level of debt behind his empire was soaring. One man who had suspicions about Trump's viability was a little-known real estate specialist named Abe Wallach.

• • •

IN 1989, WALLACH, A senior vice president at a New York real estate firm, appeared on the public television show *MacNeil/Lehrer NewsHour* to speak about Trump's finances. The segment, titled "Trumpty-Dumpty," asked whether the mogul could "keep his financial empire afloat." The situation sounded ominous. Trump faced a $2 billion debt and needed a $60 million loan to keep his business going. "Trump, the cash crunch," a reporter intoned. "Could it really be happening to the symbol of business success in the roaring eighties?" The report transitioned from a scene of a suave-looking Trump to newspaper headlines such as "Banks Squeeze Trump."

After a rundown of Trump's financial woes—highlighted by the contradiction between Trump's prescriptions in *Trump: The Art of the Deal* and his corporate bankruptcies—the program introduced Wallach. Grave and thoughtful-looking, the bespectacled Wallach said Trump could blame some of his troubles on the declining real estate market. But that didn't explain everything. Trump took on too much debt, Wallach said: "The reality is, if you pay too much for properties, and if your ego is as large as his was—is—and you just buy everything in sight, part of the blame has to squarely rest in your own lap."

Trump was incensed. A week after the show, a visitor to Wallach's New York City loft handed him a thick bundle of documents. On a cover sheet were the words *TRUMP vs. WALLACH*. Wallach said the document informed him and his company that they were each being sued for $250 million in damages, alleging slander and defamation of character. Wallach was stunned as he faced the possibility of ruin. (Years later, Trump said he did not recall suing Wallach.) Trump's attorney said he would withdraw the lawsuit if Wallach agreed not to criticize Trump on TV, according to Wallach's account.

Soon afterward, Trump himself called Wallach. "Abe, I hear you are a very smart guy. You don't want to knock me. After all, I am the major real estate force in New York, and knocking me is knocking New York," Trump said, according to Wallach. Trump suggested he wanted to hire Wallach and invited him to Trump Tower. Weeks later, Wallach arrived and described for Trump a Hudson River waterfront project in

New Jersey, featuring thousands of housing units, millions of square feet of office space, and a major mall. Trump, who was intrigued by the waterfront project and impressed by Wallach, eventually offered him a job as a real estate executive for a salary of $175,000; Wallach accepted the offer.

As Wallach settled into the job, Trump's empire was increasingly under siege from bankers and bondholders. Trump maintained that everything was fine. Around this time, he submitted documents to the Casino Control Commission showing assets of about $3.6 billion, including "Real Estate Properties Owned Directly," personal residences, and "Commercial Airlines." Commission officials who factored in Trump's debts calculated his net worth at $206 million. The editors at *Forbes* seized on the commission's report and published a May 1990 story detailing Trump's severe cash-flow problems, "unrealistically optimistic" real estate assessments, and billions in debts. The story concluded, "Trump badly needs an additional source of coin." *Forbes* estimated Trump's net worth at $500 million, down from $1.7 billion the previous year. That knocked Trump off the *Forbes* rich list; he would be absent from it for six consecutive years. Now Trump attacked the list, whose ranking he had previously coveted. It was, he said, a "very inaccurate survey" and "a sloppy, highly arbitrary estimate of certain people's net worth."

Other problems loomed. Two years after Trump said he had not personally guaranteed loans, documents at the Casino Control Commission revealed he had provided personal backing for $832 million in debt. That meant Trump himself was at risk of going down along with his empire. Over the next several years, Wallach watched as Trump repeatedly faced bankruptcy and the prospect of dissolution of his empire. But by negotiating deals, selling assets, and trading away part of his ownership in the casinos, Trump was able to restructure debts and stay afloat. Wallach worked closely with Trump on real estate transactions for the next twelve years, seeing much that he admired, such as Trump's willingness to take big risks. He also recalled that Trump sometimes did not perform due diligence and moved "without thinking about the ramifications of his actions." One day, Trump told a reporter he was worth $1 billion. As Wallach recalled it, Trump rushed back into the office and asked Wallach to generate a financial statement to back up the claim. Wallach took the request to mean he was to generate an informal financial statement that looked as rosy as possible.

As Trump struggled throughout the early nineties, the commercial real estate market continued to sink. That would provide an extraordinary opportunity to boost Trump's fortunes.

WALLACH WAS LOOKING FOR bargains when he came across 40 Wall Street, a seventy-two-story art deco icon completed in 1930 that was the second-tallest structure in lower Manhattan, behind only the World Trade Center towers. In decrepit condition, it had been through a succession of owners, but Wallach saw potential in its more than 1 million square feet of rental space, crowned by a pyramid of copper with a green patina. Wallach persuaded Trump to take a three-hour tour. Trump agreed in 1995 to buy the property, taking advantage of depressed real estate prices. *Bloomberg Business News* reported at the time that the building was 89 percent vacant, that Trump had paid "less than $8 million," and that a prior owner had figured it needed a $100 million rehabilitation.

In the following months, a problem arose with a law firm on some upper floors as Trump sought to clear the building for renovations. As Trump told it, he believed the law firm hadn't been paying the appropriate rent and the matter was in litigation. One day, the lawyers discovered that the heat was off and the elevators had stopped working. Trump arrived to find angry lawyers in the lobby. He told them they would have to walk up sixty flights to get to their offices. Years later, in an interview for this book, Trump recalled the day with an impish smile: "There are those that say that I turned down the heat and that I turned off the elevator. I was in the building because I was very hands-on when I built. I was in the building, I came down, and there were, like, a hundred twenty lawyers standing in the lobby. And I was lucky I was with some very tough construction guys because it was brutal. And I said, 'Fellas, you got to walk upstairs because the elevators are under repair.' And so, there is that story. So, who knows?"

Amid all of Trump's crises—the corporate bankruptcies and shrinking value of his publicly traded company—the deal for 40 Wall

Street was a classic example of Trump tactics and tenacity. Wallach considered the purchase a triumph for himself and Trump. Long after, Trump pointed proudly to the purchase; the building's value had by then risen by one estimate to at least $500 million: "Some people think that's the best deal made in New York in many, many years." The purchase contributed to a long rebound that stabilized the Trump empire. Along with Trump's many licensing deals and income from *The Apprentice*, which Trump said amounted to as much as $214 million over fourteen seasons, 40 Wall Street helped Trump reemerge as the mogul he had always portrayed himself as being.

His reputation was one of his greatest assets, and he protected it fiercely. In 2004, Trump learned that author Robert Slater was researching a book about him. As Slater told it, Trump threatened to sue if the book was published. Trump's lawyer wrote Slater that a lawsuit would be filed if the author wrote the book without Trump's cooperation. Then, in what had become a pattern, Trump did an about-face. He called Slater and said he had heard the writer was "an amazing guy" and agreed to cooperate. As Slater wrote in his resulting biography, *No Such Thing as Over-Exposure: Inside the Life and Celebrity of Donald Trump*, he learned that his subject "wanted to control his image fully by controlling as much as he could what was written about him." Trump told Slater that if he liked the book, he would buy a lot of copies. That was welcome news to the publisher, which agreed to let Trump see the book ahead of its release. Trump, by Slater's account, read the book and persuaded the publisher to take out things he did not like, including a story about how Marla Maples learned he was divorcing her by reading it in the *New York Post*. Trump was also displeased with how he looked on the proposed cover. "The last thing you want to do is make Donald Trump look fat," Slater said in a 2005 speech, explaining how the cover was changed at the "last minute" to please the subject.

AT EVERY STAGE OF his career, Trump tried to punish those who questioned the image he wanted the world to see. Legal threats were as much a part of Trump's business tactics as brash talk, publicity stunts, and the renegotiation of deals. "I'll sue" became the watchwords of his business, just as "You're fired" became the mantra of his television image. Over three decades, Trump and his companies filed more than 1,900 lawsuits and were named as defendants in 1,450 others, according to a *USA Today* analysis. Some of his legal maneuvering was an outgrowth of complex business deals. But some of it was focused on going after those who questioned his wealth or even his taste. He once filed a $500 million defamation complaint against a *Chicago Tribune* critic who described Trump Tower's main hall as "a kitschy shopping atrium of blinding flamboyance." A judge dismissed the complaint. *Fortune* claimed in an article that Trump had once threatened "to sue the ass off" the magazine if one of its writers wrote anything negative about Trump's cash flow.

One of the most revealing lawsuits resulted from an enduring question about Trump: What was he really worth? Timothy O'Brien, a *New York Times* business reporter with a long-standing interest in Trump, coauthored a story in 2004 headlined, "Is Trump Headed for a Fall?" Trump seemed ascendant then, winning national celebrity among a new generation through *The Apprentice*. In one episode of the show, he took contestants to what he called Atlantic City's "number one hotel," the Trump Taj Mahal. O'Brien wasn't so sure about that, writing, "In reality, the Taj Mahal needs all the help it can get—as does the rest of Mr. Trump's increasingly troubled gambling empire. His casino holdings are mired in nearly $2 billion of bond debt that they are struggling to repay. They are aging and overshadowed by flashier competitors, and their revenue and profits have been slumping over the last year." Were Trump's claims based on real numbers, O'Brien wondered, or merely hype from a salesman extraordinaire? Was Trump a success or not?

In December 2004, nine months after his article appeared in the *Times*, O'Brien received a book contract, and Trump agreed to a series of interviews. The men spent hours together in New York, at Trump's Mar-a-Lago estate, and aboard Trump's private jet en route to Los Angeles. O'Brien also spoke with Trump's chief financial officer, Allen Weisselberg, along with other current and former Trump employees, and he examined scores of financial documents laid out for him on a massive conference table at Trump Tower. *TrumpNation: The Art of Being The Donald*, published in the fall of 2005, made light of Trump's showmanship, contradictions, and public persona, but it wasn't the ribbing that bothered Trump. It was a short section in the 276-page book that focused on his net worth. O'Brien wrote about a weekend meeting in early 2005 at which the subject of Trump's net worth came up.

"I would say six [billion]," Trump told O'Brien. "Five to six. Five to six." The exchange perplexed O'Brien. Only a few months earlier, Trump had said the answer was "four billion to five billion dollars." That same day, Trump gave O'Brien a formulation that suggested that Trump's casino holdings were equal to about 2 percent of his wealth. If true, that meant Trump's net worth was about $1.7 billion. About that same time, a brochure for Trump's Palm Beach club said he was worth $9.5 billion. O'Brien wondered, Was it $1.7 billion, or $9.5 billion, or somewhere in between? Could it be less? Baffled by Trump's varied estimates and skeptical about the informal accounting that Trump's people provided him, O'Brien reached out to three "people with direct knowledge of Donald's finances." They told him Trump's net worth was "somewhere between $150 million and $250 million."

A week before *TrumpNation* was published, Trump and his team saw a copy, and they learned that the *New York Times* intended to publish an article adapted from the book. On October 20, 2005, Trump's in-house lawyer fired off a letter to O'Brien's editor, accusing O'Brien of writing "false, defamatory and libelous statements about Mr. Trump." The letter described *TrumpNation* as a "false, malicious and libelous book" and asked the *Times* to provide a prepublication copy of its article "so we can clear up some of the gross misrepresentations and inaccuracies. . . . Mr. Trump's net worth is many billions of dollars," the letter said. The *Times* was undaunted. On Sunday, October 23, 2005, the newspaper published an article under the headline "What's He Really Worth?" The story began, "For decades, Donald Trump, America's most effervescent rich guy, has made his wealth a matter of public discourse. But sometimes his riches are hard to find." Three months later, Trump sued O'Brien and his publishers, Warner Book Group and Warner Books, for $5 billion.

As the lawsuit progressed, O'Brien's lawyers summoned Trump to a law office in midtown Manhattan to answer a litany of questions in a deposition about his claim that O'Brien's book had defamed him. O'Brien's lawyer, Andrew Ceresney, who later became director of the enforcement division of the Securities and Exchange Commission, focused on the uncertainties surrounding Trump's worth and how he calculated it. Under oath, Trump acknowledged that his calculation depended not only on traditional measures such as his balance sheets, stock holdings, and other tangible assets, but also on how he felt at a given moment.

"Now, Mr. Trump, have you always been completely truthful in your public statements about your net worth of properties?" Ceresney asked.

"I try," Trump said.

"Have you ever not been truthful?"

"My net worth fluctuates, and it goes up and down with markets and with attitudes and with my feelings, even my own feelings, but I try."

Asked to elaborate, Trump did: "Yes, even my own feelings, as to where the world is, where the world is going, and that can change rapidly from day to day. . . . So, yeah, even my own feelings affects my value to myself."

Ceresney brought up a *Playboy* interview with Trump in March 1990. The article was built around the notion that Trump was, as *Playboy* put it, a "billion-dollar baby." "Vision is my best asset," the article quoted Trump as saying. "I know what sells and I know what people want." The *Playboy* interviewer noted that *Forbes* reported that Trump was worth $1.5 billion, while "you say $3.7 billion. What's the right figure?"

"I don't say anything," Trump told *Playboy*. "*Business Week* and *Fortune* have numbers much higher than *Forbes*'s."

So *Playboy* got it wrong? O'Brien's lawyer asked.

"I certainly . . . I don't even know where it came from." Trump denied that he had confirmed he was a billionaire: "I don't say anything," Trump told the lawyer. "People can form their own opinion."

TRUMP'S NET WORTH CAME up again and again during the deposition. At one point, Trump was handed a "statement of financial condition" from 2004 that he had submitted to North Fork Bank as part of an application for a line of credit. O'Brien's attorney said that

North Fork had analyzed Trump's statement and other material provided by Trump's organization and "concluded in their estimation that your net worth was actually $1.2 billion instead of $3.5 billion as you claimed. Are you aware of that?"

Trump said North Fork must have missed some assets: "They couldn't have included everything." Trump was asked to look at a net worth report by Deutsche Bank. That number was even smaller: $788 million. "Well, it's incorrect," Trump said, adding that banks don't conduct thorough appraisals. "They have no idea what land in Palm Beach is worth. They have no idea what land in Westchester is worth. . . . They have no idea what most of these assets are worth."

"Didn't you tell Mr. O'Brien you were worth six billion dollars?" Ceresney asked Trump, noting that one financial statement showed a worth of $3.5 billion.

"This doesn't include the value of branding," Trump said, adding that "the value of the brand is very valuable." In accounting practice, brands, even the most well-known ones, are considered a hard-to-measure "intangible asset." Trump was in effect putting a value on his brand that ranged as high as $2.5 billion.

ON MARCH 20, 2009, the court dismissed Trump's suit against O'Brien, saying there was no evidence of malice in the low estimates of Trump's net worth. Trump wasn't finished. On December 16, 2009, he filed an appeal, which gave voice to an underlying logic of his career and his claims: "Critical to Trump's success in business is the fact that he is widely recognized by both the financial community and the public as a skilled, successful businessman, who has financial resources totaling billions of dollars. In the high risk, high reward real estate industry, Trump's ability to close deals and secure financing for his projects depends on investors trusting his reputation and net worth."

O'Brien's lawyers responded by spelling out what they claimed to be long-simmering doubts about Trump's claims to great wealth: "Given the vast uncertainty and exaggeration surrounding Trump's private holdings and debt—much of which Trump has fostered himself and which has been the subject of numerous press reports—it is likely that no statement about Trump's net worth could be defamatory. Indeed, in his deposition, Trump indicated that his net worth fluctuated by the day based on his 'own feelings,' demonstrating some of the inherent difficulties in estimating it."

Trump's appeal failed. In 2011, New Jersey Superior Court Appeals Division Judge Edith K. Payne delivered an opinion that echoed and summarized some of O'Brien's findings: "The largest portion of Mr. Trump's fortune, according to three people who had had direct knowledge of his holdings, apparently comes from his lucrative [family] inheritance. These people estimated that Mr. Trump's wealth, presuming that it is not encumbered by heavy debt, may amount to about $200 million to $300 million. That is an enviably large sum of money by most people's standards but far short of the billionaire's club."

Trump believed he should have won, but he said later that wasn't the point. In an interview for this book, he said he wanted to strike back at O'Brien, whom he called a "low-life sleazebag. . . . I liked it because I cost him a lot of time and a lot of energy and a lot of money. I didn't read [O'Brien's book], to be honest with you. . . . I never read it. I saw some of the things they said. I said, 'Go sue him, it will cost him a lot of money.'"

Trump said he might bring other lawsuits, including against media organizations and against those responsible for this book: "I sued in that case because it was so disgraceful. Now, libel suits are very hard and I may look at that, frankly, if I get elected, because it's very unfair that somebody could write whatever they want to write and get away with it. And I will be bringing more libel suits—maybe against you folks. I don't want to threaten, but I find that the press is unbelievably dishonest."

TRUMP'S LAWSUIT AGAINST O'BRIEN was over. But the turmoil in Trump's empire continued. Trump's public casino company, which had filed for bankruptcy in 2004 and reemerged as Trump Entertainment Resorts, was again struggling with debt. In 2009, Trump was at odds with bondholders who wanted the company to file for bankruptcy again. Rather than fight, Trump resigned. "The company has represented for quite some time substantially less than one percent of my net worth, and my investment in it is worthless to me now," he said at the time. In the bankruptcy proceedings, Trump found himself at odds with Carl Icahn, a man Trump had long called his friend. The billionaire investor had a long history with Trump, watching boxing matches and flying alongside him in helicopters during Trump's early, energetic years in Atlantic City. In the early 1990s, Icahn had championed the deal that helped Trump retain some ownership during his Taj Mahal casino's first brush with bankruptcy.

Now Icahn openly sided with the Trump doubters. Trump Entertainment Resorts was struggling, and it attempted to restructure through bankruptcy. As part of those efforts, Trump allied himself with a hedge fund that sought to buy the company. The hedge fund pledged to give Trump a 10 percent stake if he let the company continue to use his name. Icahn backed a competing deal that would wrest total control of the company, questioning whether Trump's brand signified quality and success. "If the name is so powerful," Icahn said in 2010, "then how come they went bankrupt three times?"

The hedge fund beat out Icahn and took over the company, giving Trump his 10 percent stake, and the casinos exited bankruptcy. But the problems were far from over. In 2011, Trump Entertainment Resorts sold Trump Castle casino (later renamed Trump Marina) for $38 million, one-thirteenth of what Trump's company had paid for it fifteen years earlier. Trump said he got out of Atlantic City at the right time. Trump Entertainment Resorts, which owned Trump Plaza Hotel & Casino and Trump Taj Mahal, filed for bankruptcy again in September 2014. The Plaza closed around the same time, one of four of the city's twelve casinos to close that year. As a result of bankruptcy proceedings for Trump Entertainment Resorts, Icahn reemerged as a corporate suitor, and in 2016, he won control of the company, with the Taj as its primary asset. Though Icahn became a political supporter of Trump, he continued to express doubts about Trump's success in the business world: "I'm not here to say Donald's a great businessman. But I will say he's a great consensus builder, and that's what Congress needs at this time."

• • •

WHEN TRUMP ANNOUNCED HIS campaign for the White House in 2015, questions about his net worth took center stage. Trump offered a valuation of his assets: his "real estate licensing deals, brand and branded development" were worth $3.3 billion. The campaign did not explain how the number was calculated.

In New York City, Trump owned a small collection of properties, including the Trump Building at 40 Wall Street, the commercial floors of Trump Tower, two properties on East Fifty-Seventh Street, and housing co-ops on East Sixty-First Street and East Forty-Third Street. He also held minority stakes in projects such as 1290 Avenue of the Americas, an office high-rise mostly owned by the Vornado Realty Trust. His name was associated with some other projects through licensing deals, not through ownership. Those included Trump International Hotel & Tower, Trump Palace, Trump Park Avenue, and Trump Place.

A month after announcing his net worth, Trump followed up with a ninety-two-page federal filing and a campaign statement valuing his assets at more than $10 billion. But the numbers were not independently audited, and some of the claims appeared at odds with Trump's own estimates. The disclosure valued the Trump National Golf Club, in Westchester County, New York, at more than $50 million, but in a 2015 court case seeking lower taxes, his attorneys argued that the golf club was actually worth only $1.4 million. Alan Garten, the Trump Organization's lawyer, said the values should not be compared because one was used to contend a tax assessment and the other was an estimate of the sales price.

Trump's personal income tax returns could have answered many questions. Every major party nominee of the last forty years had released tax returns. The returns would show how much money Trump made, how much he gave to charity, and how aggressively he used deductions, shelters, and other tactics to shrink his tax bill. Trump went on national TV after launching his presidential bid and pledged to disclose his "very big . . . very beautiful" returns. But then he declined to release them—and had not done so as of mid-2016. He said the problem was that his taxes were undergoing an IRS audit. But he also would not release prior returns on which audits had been completed. He asserted that voters were not interested and said, "There's nothing to learn from them."

Trump had bragged often about his ability to pay as little as possible to the government—a practice he called the "American way." Yet Trump denounced corporate executives for "getting away with murder" by using loopholes to lower their taxes: "They make a fortune. They pay no tax. It's ridiculous, okay?"

JUST AS TRUMP BOASTED of his wealth, he touted his generosity. His company's website labeled him "a deal maker without peer and an ardent philanthropist." At the launch of his campaign, he said he had given more than $102 million to charity between 2011 and June 2015. But the *Washington Post* found that none of the $102 million came from Trump's own cash. Many of his contributions took the form of free rounds of golf at his courses, given away at raffles and charity auctions, the value of which was determined by Trump. He counted as monetary contributions a host of similar donations that involved no cash. One 2015 donation involved the charity of tennis star Serena Williams. Trump gave Williams a ride from Florida to an event in Virginia and counted the trip as a $1,136.56 charitable contribution, according to records shared with the media. Included in his donation was a framed photo of Williams.

Many of the gifts came from the nonprofit charity that bore his name, the Donald J. Trump Foundation, which didn't receive any money from Trump from 2009 through 2014. Trump said he "gives mostly to a lot of different groups." Asked in an interview to cite the beneficiaries, he declined: "No, I don't want to. . . . Why should I give you records? I don't have to give you records."

Separately, Trump had promised in January 2016 to give away $1 million of his own money to veterans' causes—along with millions of dollars raised from the public—but he did not deliver his share of the money until four months later, after a *Post* reporter, David Fahrenthold, pressed him on details of the gift. "You know, you're a nasty guy," Trump told Fahrenthold. "You're really a nasty guy. I gave out millions of dollars that I had no obligation to do." Soon after,

Trump announced that he had given $1 million to the Marine Corps–Law Enforcement Foundation. He held a press conference at Trump Tower at which he announced he had given away the last $1.5 million that other donors had entrusted to him four months earlier, bringing the total to $5.6 million, just shy of the $6 million pledged.

"I wasn't looking for the credit, but I had no choice but to do this because the press was saying I didn't raise any money for them," Trump said. He called the media "dishonest" and "unfair," singled out one TV reporter as a "sleaze," and noted, "I'm going to continue to attack the press."

Self-promotion. Bluster. Litigation. Trump had been open about using all of it and more to protect his image and achieve his ultimate goal: making money. He had bluntly said of his career, "I'm representing Donald Trump." But now, as he pursued the presidency, the self-described multibillionaire would need to convince voters that his value to the country was greater than his net worth, and that he could be a champion of more than himself.

18

"Trump! Trump! Trump!"

Everything about Donald Trump's campaign for the Republican nomination was surreal, starting with the day he announced his candidacy. As he rode down the escalator to the lobby of Trump Tower, he was known as a rich businessman, a developer of high-end properties, a reality TV star, a flamboyant ex-playboy, and a long-running character in the New York tabloids, with a brand name recognized worldwide. He was not known as a politician. He had dabbled with running for president before, only to pull back. Everyone expected the same tease this time. Late-night comics only hoped he would stay around long enough for them to milk his candidacy for a few laughs.

Everyone was wrong. Trump defied virtually every prediction about his campaign. He redrew the rules of presidential politics while upending and dividing the Republican Party. He may have been a novice politician, but he possessed unerring instincts about what was angering so many Americans. His communication skills were ideally suited to the age of round-the-clock cable, the instantaneous reach of Twitter, and the coarseness of the digital media's raucous, often anonymous conversation. He made provocative, often inaccurate comments that no ordinary candidate would dare utter, and aside from providing full-time work to fact-checkers, he mostly got away with it. Along the way, he rendered many of the older, accepted tactics of politics impotent or obsolete. The long battle for the Republican nomination would have many twists and turns, but no day was more significant than June 16, 2015, when everything about the Republican race changed, even if no one—not even Trump—knew it at the time.

THE DAY BEFORE, IN Miami, Jeb Bush had announced his candidacy. The former governor of Florida was the real threat, or so everyone thought. In the previous six months, he had amassed more than $100 million in campaign funds, most of it stockpiled in a super PAC called Right to Rise USA. He hoped to use that super PAC to intimidate and crush his rivals. As the son and brother of presidents, he carried the second most revered name in modern Republican politics after Ronald Reagan. Though he had gone through a season of missteps, and voters were showing signs of Bush fatigue, he was still seen as the favorite.

From the moment Trump announced his candidacy, the standard campaign script was out the window. The crowd gathered in the lobby of Trump Tower turned out to include some people who had been lured with the promise of free T-shirts and other inducements. Campaign manager Corey Lewandowski, with help, had spent the previous weekend writing the announcement speech. He had reviewed it with Trump, emphasizing the main points of the message. The prepared text ran about seven minutes. Lewandowski knew it by heart, and so as Trump's remarks passed the ten-minute mark and then the twenty-minute mark and continued on for a full forty-five minutes, Lewandowski thought to himself, This was going to be a little different.

The previous December, Lewandowski, a Republican political operative from New Hampshire with no experience in presidential campaigns, had met with Trump for thirty minutes. At the end of the meeting, he was hired to manage a campaign that few knew existed, on behalf of a candidate whose positions were very much in flux. Trump would soon disassociate himself from many of the views he had espoused for years. He would oppose abortion rights and gun control. He would advocate the deportation of immigrants, even though he had ridiculed Mitt Romney's "crazy policy of self-deportation, which was maniacal. It sounded as bad as it was," Trump said in 2012, "and he lost all of the Latino vote. He lost the Asian vote. He lost everybody who is inspired to come into this country."

Now, as he began speaking at rallies across the country, Trump dismissed the idea of reading from a script. He regarded prepared texts as little more than outlines. His extemporaneous remarks were replete with memorable lines and narcissistic bravado. He insisted that he would fund his own campaign. He called the country's leaders stupid, disparaged decades of international trade deals as job killers, and warned against threats from ISIS. He said the United States had become "a dumping ground for everybody else's problems." He declared the American Dream dead and promised to "make America great again." He called for decisive action against illegal immigration: "When Mexico sends its people, they're not sending their best. . . . They're sending people that have lots of problems. . . . They're bringing drugs. They're bringing crime. They're rapists. And some, I assume, are good people."

The entire event was treated as a moment of comic relief in the long slog of a presidential campaign. Yet it was a remarkably revealing window onto what was to come. Trump would not and could not be handled. He *intended* to be unpredictable. He was the ultimate improviser, supremely confident of his own gut instincts. He would be politically incorrect, hurling insults at people and groups in defiance of the conventions of politics. His entry into the race brought mostly scorn and dismissal. He was called a political clown. But Trump sensed what ailed and angered many Americans and knew how to speak their language.

Hours after the announcement, Trump flew to Iowa and entered the Hoyt Sherman auditorium in Des Moines to loud cheers and waves of applause. "He's not afraid," said Kathy Watson, who had driven up from Ottumwa with her husband, Don. "He's not a politician." Whatever the party establishment thought of Trump, many voters found him appealing and took him seriously. Steve Scheffler, Iowa's Republican national committeeman and a leader in the social conservative movement, watched Trump and decided he was no joke: "I wouldn't underestimate him at all."

• • •

THE NEXT DAY, A twenty-one-year-old white man opened fire at a historic black church in Charleston, South Carolina, killing nine black people. Hillary Clinton told an interviewer after the shootings that racial violence is often triggered by public discourse. She warned against overheated rhetoric: "For example, a recent entry into the Republican presidential campaign said some very inflammatory things about Mexicans. Everybody should stand up and say that's not acceptable." Trump's aides saw Clinton's comments as the catalyst that generated a wave of anti-Trump protests. Under pressure from their customers, corporations took swift action: Univision, the nation's largest Spanish-language media company, backed out of plans to air Trump's Miss USA pageant in July. NBCUniversal, which had partnered with Trump on *The Apprentice*, ended its relationship with him. The PGA Tour and NASCAR took steps to distance themselves. Chef José Andrés pulled out of plans to open a restaurant in the hotel Trump was building along Pennsylvania Avenue in Washington. Alarmed, Republican National Committee chairman Reince Priebus called Trump and asked him to tone things down.

Facing threats of pickets by anti-Trump protesters, Terry Lundgren, the chief executive officer at Macy's, which carried Trump's branded clothing line, called the candidate—whom he considered a friend— and said he was going to drop the Trump clothing. Trump, who took the call as he prepared to speak to New Hampshire voters, argued that the protests wouldn't last long or have any serious impact. Lundgren disagreed. As Trump was being called onstage, he told Lundgren, "Do whatever you want to do. I don't care." The next day, Macy's announced it would phase out its relationship with Trump because his statements were "inconsistent with Macy's values." The two men did not speak again. "That was blowback like I've never had before," Trump said in 2016. "We had a year and a half before the general [election], and I said, 'Is every day going to be like this?'"

In early July, Trump's staff prepared for its first major rally, booking a ballroom at a luxury resort in Phoenix. When thousands registered for tickets, the staff upgraded to the nearby convention center. On July 11, thousands were lined up outside the center. Inside, more than four thousand screaming fans greeted the candidate. (He would later claim the crowd was fifteen thousand strong.) As he slowly walked along a catwalk cutting through the crowd, he flashed two thumbs up and turned slowly around, looking like an aging rock star on a reunion tour that had unexpectedly sold out. "Wow!" he shouted over the cheers. "This is absolutely unbelievable." That crowd was all the proof Trump needed that he understood Americans' fears and desires better than others in the party. The crowd cheered as Trump declared that illegal immigrants "flow in like water" over the border and that, if he became president, "we'll take our country back." At one point, a man in the crowd shouted, "Build a wall!" Trump's comments that day alarmed Senator John McCain, the Arizona Republican who had pushed for comprehensive immigration reform. "He fired up the crazies," McCain said.

One week later, Trump settled into an easy chair on a stage in rural Iowa before a crowd of evangelical Christians. Moderator Frank Luntz, a Republican pollster, challenged him to defend his past statements, particularly calling illegal immigrants rapists and criminals or labeling McCain a "dummy." "Is that appropriate in running for president?" Luntz asked.

"Crazies!" Trump responded. "He called them all crazy. . . . These people are great Americans." Trump called McCain, the GOP's 2008 nominee, a "loser."

As the crowd laughed, Luntz shot back, "He's a war hero! He's a war hero! He's a war hero!"

Trump scoffed, "He's not a war hero. He's a war hero because he was captured. I like people that weren't captured, okay?"

As Trump came off the stage, Lewandowski met him and asked for a private word: "I closed the door and I said, 'Holy smokes!'" He repeated back what Trump had said onstage and candidly told him just how offensive it was. Trump decided he needed to do a press conference to explain himself. The barrage of questions lasted nearly thirty minutes and was, in Lewandowski's word, "brutal." Trump refused to apologize and accused McCain of not doing enough to protect veterans or strengthen the Veterans Administration.

Most of his rivals had hesitated to attack Trump for his announcement-day comments about illegal immigrants. Now they pounced, sensing that their renegade rival might have made a fatal mistake. Strategist Chip Saltsman was at the event that day with his candidate, former Arkansas governor Mike Huckabee. "I was convinced—like ninety-eight percent of the people—that this was going to be a short campaign [for Trump]," Saltsman said. "The governor said, 'Not so fast.' He said his numbers actually may go up. I said, 'No way.'" Huckabee was correct. By late July, Trump led the field of seventeen GOP candidates. Michael Glassner, newly hired on Trump's team, said the fallout from the McCain controversy forced him to reassess instincts honed during three decades in politics: "That incident is really when I started to understand that a lot of what I thought I knew about political campaigns didn't apply to this one."

THE SUMMER OF TRUMP was now in full bloom. The next test came in early August, when Fox News hosted the first Republican candidate debate. The conservative network put three of its stars on the panel—Bret Baier, Chris Wallace, and Megyn Kelly. For Trump, this was uncertain territory. He was a reality TV star, but politicians were experienced debaters. The heavily hyped event posed a central question: Would Trump get his comeuppance when the campaign turned to issues and the thrust-and-parry of live debates?

As the leader in the polls, Trump won the center position onstage and got to be the target of the first question, from Baier: "Is there anyone onstage, and can I see hands, who is *unwilling* tonight to pledge your support to the eventual nominee of the Republican Party and pledge to not run an independent campaign against that person?" Trump, who had changed parties seven times in fourteen years, knew right away that this was a test of his loyalty to his adopted party. He was the only candidate who raised his hand, clearly a risky move in front of a Republican audience. "The honest answer is what I gave," he said later.

The toughest question of the night came from Kelly. She asked Trump to explain why he had called women "fat pigs, dogs, slobs, and disgusting animals." Trump tried to deflect the question. "Only Rosie O'Donnell," he deadpanned, to the delight of many in the audience. Pressed for a serious answer, he said, "I think the big problem this country has is being politically correct." Trump was furious at Kelly but mostly held his tongue. After the debate, he accused her of trying to sabotage his candidacy: "You could see there was blood coming out of her eyes. Blood coming out of her wherever." The crude remark was widely interpreted as a reference to her menstrual cycle. Trump insisted he had meant her nose or ears. It was another major unforced error. Once again, it seemed not to matter.

THAT SUMMER, TRUMP DOMINATED the news. He was a ratings machine. The Fox debate drew 24 million viewers, the most of any primary debate ever. Cable networks began to carry his rallies live. Anchors read aloud his sporadic statements and tweets, which he sometimes fired off in the middle of the night. Rather than traveling to a studio for interviews, Trump would call in to news programs, even to many Sunday-morning shows that had rarely allowed such interviews. As he sat in his office or traveled in his car, he would dial up reporters to chat.

Though he routinely disparaged the media as "dishonest low-lifes" during his rallies, Trump gave reporters unprecedented access. By doing so, he set the tone and the agenda for his Republican rivals, who had formed their approach to politics under the old rules, with an emphasis on using careful language with the media and a styl-ized, respectful attitude toward their competitors. Trump rules made the old-fashioned ways seem quaint. "Whether you were a candidate running who was mentioned by him or a candidate running who was ignored by him, virtually every question you were asked by the national media had the words *Donald Trump* in them," said Danny Diaz, Bush's campaign manager.

Early on, Trump's campaign strategy called for him to capitalize on his name recognition to slowly improve his favorability ratings, which were negative. His team hoped he could move into the second tier of candidates, then break out later. "Float a little bit under the radar screen, not take all the arrows," Lewandowski explained. That time-table accelerated quickly. Trump's outsider status made him explosively attractive to voters who felt betrayed by both parties. The new strategy would be both simple and radically different. Trump went big instead of small, running a primary campaign that looked more like a gen-eral election operation. He held massive rallies, reacted to the news of the day, dominated the airwaves, and attacked anyone who challenged him. He got so much airtime—$2 billion worth by one estimate—he had no need to spend millions on television ads.

Trump's rallies drew five thousand, ten thousand, even twenty thousand people. He packed fairgrounds, gymnasiums, arenas. "Anybody who says that was not completely eye-opening is kidding themselves," said Mike DuHaime, who was the lead strategist for New Jersey governor Chris Christie's campaign. One August night, Trump drew at least two thousand people to a rally in Derry, New Hampshire. About twenty miles away in Merrimack, Bush spoke to a crowd numbering fewer than one hundred and fifty.

Trump's preference for big rallies rather than retail campaigning also fit with his personal habits. As a committed germophobe, he started out avoiding shaking hands with voters. He kept bowls of hand sanitizer in his office and favored fast-food chains, which he believed were cleaner than restaurants. Despite living in a golden palace high above Fifth Avenue and jetting to rallies in a private jet, Trump pitched himself as the voice of the beaten-down working class. He was completely unlike the Republican Party's recent nominees—a proudly politically incorrect businessman who refused to apologize for anything, even when he seemed to regret his own words. That stubbornness only added to his appeal.

Even Trump's campaign structure defied the laws of politics. Instead of hiring a massive network of consultants, Trump made do through most of the nomination battle with a core staff of five dedicated employees—Lewandowski, Glassner, spokeswoman Hope Hicks, social media director Dan Scavino Jr., and lead advance person George Gigicos—along with a few dozen low-paid state-level workers. Opponents and campaign consultants scoffed at how ill prepared that lean structure would leave Trump. But the candidate boasted of his tiny staff as an example of smart efficiency. The five advisers usually traveled with him and made decisions on the plane as they watched cable television. Lewandowski loved to brag about interviewing major Republican campaign workers for jobs and then turning them down when he learned how much they wanted to charge.

Where other campaigns quietly handed reporters opposition research about their rivals, Trump publicly traded in gossip and dirt.

To prove that he had Senator Lindsey Graham's personal cell phone number, he read it aloud at a rally. He referred to unsubstantiated tabloid stories that accused Ted Cruz of cheating on his wife with numerous women. He repeatedly accused former president Bill Clinton of sexually abusing women. Late in the race, he falsely tried to tie Cruz's Cuban-born father to Lee Harvey Oswald, the man who assassinated President John F. Kennedy. Lewandowski compared the innovativeness of Trump's strategy to Obama's in 2008: "This campaign can't be replicated." On that, there was no disagreement.

ONE BY ONE, TRUMP disrupted all the other campaigns, beginning with that of the presumed front-runner. Trump mocked Bush as "Low-Energy" Jeb, the first of many derogatory labels the branding expert would attach to his rivals. "Little Marco" Rubio and "Lyin' Ted" Cruz were yet to come. "I said 'low energy' and it was interesting," Trump later recalled. "I said it in a speech, and the place went crazy as soon as I said it." The label instantly stuck to Bush, who was proving he lacked his more garrulous brother's comfort on the campaign trail. The damage was apparent to Bush's advisers, but they were paralyzed by a lack of consensus about what to do. Some advocated an aggressive response. Others cautioned against getting "into a pigpen with a pig." So they did nothing, largely ignoring Trump while trying to focus voters on Bush's record in Florida. This misreading of the Republican electorate's frustration turned out to be fatal. Glassner said, "Probably their worst decision was never to change or adapt to reality."

Rick Perry chose to attack. With nothing to lose, the former Texas governor, whose 2012 campaign had ended in humiliation and whose 2016 bid was already struggling even before Trump came along, delivered a slashing takedown of the man who was hijacking the nation's conservative party. He called Trump "a toxic mix of demagoguery, mean-spiritedness, and nonsense" and "a cancer on conservatism." The July 22 attack bounced off Trump without leaving a mark. By early September, Perry was out of the race.

Ten days after Perry quit, Scott Walker followed him to the sidelines. Perry's demise was no surprise; Walker's was. The governor of Wisconsin had become a conservative hero nationally after staring down the unions in his home state and surviving a recall election. Until Trump's entry, he had led the polls in Iowa. But Trump's dominating personality smothered Walker; his poll numbers plummeted and he was a virtual nonfactor in debates. His bland personality could not compete against Trump's showmanship. "If we can't change so that we get more attention, then we don't have a pathway to the nomination," Walker said later. When he bowed out, he urged his fifteen remaining rivals to follow him to open up space for someone with a positive conservative message to confront Trump head-on—to no avail. The big field kept working to Trump's advantage.

The 2016 GOP campaign had become the year of the outsiders, playing out against a backdrop of anger toward the political establishment. Nearly every poll showed a pair of nonpoliticians—Trump and Dr. Ben Carson, a renowned retired neurosurgeon—winning more than 50 percent of the Republican vote. Strategists for other candidates took note and adjusted their messages, but privately most believed that, once voters engaged, the two novices would falter. "We were exactly right about Ben Carson," said Whit Ayres, who was Rubio's pollster, "and we were exactly wrong about Donald Trump."

The hunger for a candidate with no political experience underscored just how disaffected many voters were. Trump's trademarked slogan, Make America Great Again, promised a return to better times—economically and culturally—in America's past. He was offering not an ideology, but a nostalgic journey to a better place. James W. Ceaser of the University of Virginia described the Trump phenomenon as less an "ism" and more a "mood" that struck with impressive force because "they have a leader who can articulate it." Rubio's strategist, Todd Harris, later said, "You had an environment where you had literally hundreds of thousands of people who lost their homes or were upside down, lost their jobs or retirement savings, and saw in their political system that not a damn thing was done about it. . . . At the same time, you had Republicans sweep into power saying they were going to clean up Washington, and nothing changed. . . . The anger was just underneath the surface, and all he needed to do was churn the waters a little bit."

• • •

ON NOVEMBER 13, A Friday night, a suicide bomb went off in a soccer stadium north of Paris. Within minutes, gunmen with assault rifles opened fire at cafés and restaurants and inside a music hall in the city. In less than three hours, three teams of Islamic State terrorists killed 130 people. A few weeks earlier, Trump had called for Syrian refugees to be tossed out of the country and for a ban on any new refugees. That was a marked change from summer, when he had said the United States should "possibly" accept refugees to ease the crisis. The morning after the Paris attacks, Trump opened his rally in Beaumont, Texas, with a moment of silence, then launched an attack on Obama's "insane" plan to allow 10,000 Syrian refugees—Trump claimed the figure was 250,000—into the country. Democrats were shocked to see Paris boost Trump's stature. When a Democratic consultant convened a focus group to hear voters' thoughts on terrorism, the report from the session reflected the group's consensus that Trump was the only candidate with a plan: "While many were troubled by what he had said about Muslims . . . they mentioned his strength, his 'straightforward' approach to 'bombing the shit' out of them, and 'building a wall' to make sure that we take control of who comes into the country. These voters are anxious and feel a loss of control. For many, especially the men, Trump's rhetoric addressed their concerns."

A few weeks later, terrorism hit US soil when a married couple, Syed Rizwan Farook and Tashfeen Malik, opened fire at a county public health training event and holiday party in San Bernardino, California. The attack killed fourteen and seriously injured more than twenty others. Trump and his staff zeroed in on what they considered the root cause of the problem: radical Islam. Their solution: ban Muslims from entering the country. (Farook was a native-born US citizen.) Trump dictated a statement to his spokeswoman, Hope Hicks, who copied it down on a note card.

Trump waited to propose the ban until December 7, Pearl Harbor Day, when he was scheduled to hold a rally aboard a battleship in South Carolina. The campaign released a statement from the candidate calling for a "total and complete" ban, at least temporarily. The backlash was immediate and crushing. Jeb Bush tweeted, "Donald Trump is unhinged." As Trump and his staff flew to South Carolina, some advisers worried that they had completely misread the country's mood. That night, standing aboard the USS *Yorktown*, Trump defiantly read his proposal. The crowd responded with deafening applause. Back in the car, Trump told his advisers, "Well, there's your poll. That's how people feel about this."

Fresh surveys confirmed Trump's instincts, finding that a majority of Republicans agreed with the ban. But some prominent Republicans called the ban a violation of America's core value of freedom of religion. Trump gave no ground: "We're talking about security. We're not talking about religion. We're talking about security. Our country is out of control." At a GOP debate, Bush challenged Trump, saying that "banning all Muslims will make it harder for us to do exactly what we need to do, which is to destroy ISIS."

But by the end of 2015, Trump's rivals understood they were now operating in a world defined by the renegade candidate. They also saw that his followers were absolutely and totally loyal. "We came to the realization that he wasn't just Teflon, that he was titanium, that nothing would stick to him," Rubio's adviser, Harris, said later. "The people who were with him were with him no matter what. There was no new piece of information you could give them." By the time the other candidates realized that, it was too late.

IN SIX SHORT MONTHS, Trump had completely changed the Republican race. But he had yet to face the voters. To Trump, winning was always paramount. "If I don't win, what have I done?" he said in the fall of 2015. "I've wasted time." Iowa, whose caucuses were dominated by religious conservatives, was long seen as Trump's weak spot. The thrice-married Trump had been advised to focus on New Hampshire, with its independent streak and more socially liberal electorate, and South Carolina because of its military ties. "I was told by everybody, 'Do not go to Iowa. You could never finish even in the top ten,'" Trump said later. When Carson pulled ahead of Trump in Iowa polls, Trump responded with angry rants at two rallies in the state: "How stupid are the people of Iowa? How stupid are the people of the country to believe this crap?" But when Carson quickly fell back, Trump faced an even more determined and capable challenger in Iowa, Ted Cruz. The shrewd but polarizing Texan had a message that appealed to religious conservatives; he also claimed to have built a superb ground operation in a state where organization often made the difference.

Barely two weeks before the February 1 caucuses, Trump stood on the set of a western ranch in a museum outside Des Moines, with a mannequin of the late actor John Wayne looming over his shoulder. Reporters pummeled him with questions about his ground game. His operation was a highly guarded secret; his state headquarters was off-limits to prying reporters. "I feel very good about my ground game. We have a great group of people," he said. "Where's Chuck?"

Trump scanned the room for his Iowa state director, Chuck Laudner, an Iowan best known for having helped former Pennsylvania senator Rick Santorum win a surprise victory in the 2012 caucuses. "Chuck!" Trump said. "Get over here, Chuck." Trump wanted his state director to answer the question "because if he doesn't do good—Chuck, you're fired!" Trump laughed.

Cruz took the lead in Iowa in December, but two days before the caucuses, the authoritative Iowa Poll showed Trump up by five points. On caucus night, however, Iowa Republicans delivered a stinging setback to Trump, who finished second to Cruz, barely ahead of Rubio. Embarrassed in his first outing, Trump delivered a subdued concession speech and exited quickly. But he was furious at Cruz and soon went on the offensive, accusing the Texan of dirty tricks, including a last-hour effort to sway votes by telling caucus-goers that Carson was about to quit the race.

The defeat in Iowa left Trump bitter. Even months later, he could not let it go. In interviews after he had clinched the nomination, he repeatedly circled back to Iowa: "I came in a very strong second. I got no credit for it. Marco came in third and they were saying that's great, and I said, 'What about me? I came in second and I've never done this before.'" Lewandowski said Trump's campaign had underestimated the turnout. Trump blamed his Iowa team for the loss: "My team, you know, the people that I had, were not adept, were not good." He said he had learned a valuable lesson, however. "It made me realize that management of an election is very important. [Cruz] had a massive group of people . . . giving lots of false stories of my positions and bringing them over. For whatever reason, I didn't have that."

IN NEW HAMPSHIRE, TRUMP eschewed the state's standard script for retail politics. He thought the conventional strategy of wooing individual voters was silly and inefficient: "You would have to go to these very small meetings with people, sit down and talk to them for two hours, and then maybe go out to dinner in their house." Trump asked his advisers why he should do that, and they told him that was how it had always been done. He mocked that approach: "People would go and have dinner with the voters . . . like, five people, family—the mother, the father, the son, and the daughter—and they'd sit there and have dinner for two and a half hours. . . . If I did that, people would lose respect for me. . . . They'd say this isn't what we want for a president."

But after the Iowa loss, Trump adjusted. He stopped by a shift change at a police station, had breakfast at a diner, and hosted town hall meetings in small venues. Lewandowski, who lived in New Hampshire, and spokeswoman Hicks took over the state headquarters, opening it to reporters to prove they had a real organization. Lewandowski was prepared to resign if Trump lost again. Despite the loss in Iowa, Trump remained the favorite in New Hampshire. But Iowa had changed the dynamics of the race. Rubio was on the move, and a strong finish in the Granite State might let him begin to consolidate establishment Republicans behind his candidacy. Cruz hoped to capitalize on Iowa. Bush was fighting to avoid irrelevancy. Then Rubio hit a wall named Chris Christie in a debate three days before the balloting. Christie, the ex-prosecutor whose candidacy was in deep trouble, hammered Rubio as ill prepared to be president. Rubio stood frozen on the stage, robotically repeating a series of precooked lines about Obama to groans from the audience.

On election night, Trump delivered an overwhelming victory, capturing 35 percent of the vote. Ohio governor John Kasich finished far back in second with just 16 percent, ahead of Cruz, Bush, and Rubio. Trump's victory speech was much more his style. He pointed to Lewandowski: "Does Corey have a ground game or what?" Looking back months later, Trump called the victory a psychological turning point: "The first time I thought I'd win was after I won in New Hampshire."

TRUMP NOW TURNED TO the South with an eye toward demolishing Bush, Rubio, and Cruz. In South Carolina, most of the elected leadership lined up against him. Almost immediately, he veered off course, starting at a debate in Greenville three days after the New Hampshire vote. News of the unexpected death of Supreme Court justice Antonin Scalia prompted Cruz to ask whether Trump, a man of no fixed ideology, could be trusted to appoint reliably conservative justices to the Court. That put Trump on the defensive, but it was the least of his problems that night. Partway through the debate, he attacked George W. Bush over the Iraq War. "They lied," Trump said. "They said there were weapons of mass destruction; there were none. And they knew there were none."

Jeb Bush interrupted, "While Donald Trump was building a reality TV show, my brother was building a security apparatus to keep us safe." Trump hit again: "The World Trade Center came down during your brother's reign, remember that." The audience booed loudly. Trump was told afterward that he had put his victory at risk. But he was unrepentant: "There were people who said, 'You just blew the state.' I said, 'I have to be honest.'"

Trump seemed to be scouring the landscape for controversy. He next got into a scuffle with Pope Francis. Aboard his plane after a trip to Mexico, the pontiff had told reporters, "A person who thinks only about building walls, wherever they may be, and not building bridges, is not Christian." Trump heard the comment and "I immediately thought of the Vatican, with the massive walls, and I said, 'Well, wait a minute, he's got the bigger walls, he's got walls like you couldn't even dream of.'" Trump issued a written response calling the pope's words "disgraceful," adding, "If and when the Vatican is attacked by ISIS, which as everyone knows is ISIS's ultimate trophy, I can promise you that the pope would have only wished and prayed that Donald Trump would have been president."

The night before the primary, at a rally in Charleston, Trump with great flourish told a discredited story about army general John Pershing and how he had dealt with Muslim terrorists in the Philippines early in the twentieth century: Pershing's men lined up fifty captured Muslim prisoners and dipped fifty bullets in pigs' blood. Forty-nine prisoners were shot dead. The survivor was told to go back to his people and describe what had happened. In a state with a military tradition, Trump used the story to project strength. "You gotta be tough," Lewandowski later explained. "This is toughness." The rumor-tracking site Snopes.com had long ago debunked the story, and *PolitiFact* gave Trump's use of the tale its worst rating, Pants on Fire. Asked why Trump used a story that wasn't true, Lewandowski said, "Look, it's an analogy, right?"

Once again, the usual rules didn't seem to apply to Trump. On primary day, February 20, he swept to his second straight victory, carrying the state with 32.5 percent of the vote. Rubio, after his poor finish in New Hampshire, rebounded to second, edging Cruz by three-tenths of a percentage point. Bush got just 8 percent and quit the race that night, having spent more than $100 million through his campaign and its allied super PAC. Rubio adviser Whit Ayres noted that Trump's negatives had doubled after his attacks on Bush and the pope. "Two-thirds of the South Carolina primary electorate voted against the guy," he said, "but the opposition was sufficiently split that he could eke out a win." Trump's rivals now understood the magnitude of the challenge ahead. Cruz adviser Jeff Roe later said, "It was very clear that Trump was going to get thirty to thirty-five percent everywhere, and as long as it stayed a multi-candidate race, it was going to be a problem." Strategists in rival camps came to see that New Hampshire and South Carolina had put Trump on a near-unstoppable path to victory.

THE RESULTS WERE PARTICULARLY troubling for Cruz. All along, Cruz had relied on a Southern strategy, counting on a victory in South Carolina and then a virtual sweep of Southern primaries on March 1 to put him ahead of the field. Instead, Trump now had momentum. After South Carolina, he carried Alabama, Arkansas, Georgia, Tennessee, and Virginia (and Massachusetts and Vermont). Cruz won only Texas, his home state, and Oklahoma.

Trump's sudden clear advantage stirred a powerful backlash within the GOP establishment, led by Mitt Romney. For a party's previous nominee to attack its prospective nominee was unprecedented, but Romney delivered a powerful rebuke to the front-runner, calling Trump "a phony, a fraud," a failed businessman who knew little about the world and was temperamentally unfit for the presidency. Romney encouraged voters to do whatever they could to defeat Trump. Trump had other thoughts. He saw the March 15 primary in Florida as an opportunity to knock out Rubio. The Florida senator had started off with a reputation as a gifted campaigner and the face of a new, more diverse party. As a candidate, he struggled. Now he would prove to be wholly inadequate to the Trump challenge. First, he tried aggression. At a February 25 debate in Houston, he pounded Trump on immigration, trade, and the New Yorker's business practices. Then, he tried sarcasm, calling Trump a "con man" and belittling his appearance. Rubio got into the mud with Trump: at a debate in Detroit, the two candidates traded barbs about Trump's "small hands," an exchange that devolved—incredibly—into a thinly veiled discussion of the man's penis size. Rubio pointed out that Trump's hands were disproportionately small compared to his height: "And you know what they say about men with small hands?"

Trump took the bait: "Look at those hands, are they small hands? . . . He referred to my hands—if they're small, something else must be small. I guarantee you, there's no problem. I guarantee." The coarse banter appeared to do little damage to Trump's momentum; Rubio, on the other hand, soon fell into a downward spiral. He went out with a whimper. Trump won Florida with almost 46 percent of the vote to Rubio's 27 percent. Rubio quit the race. Bush's campaign manager, Danny Diaz, would later say that after Florida "there was no argument for a quote-unquote 'establishment' candidate for the remainder of the Republican primary." Christie adviser Mike DuHaime offered this view: "There was this incorrect thesis that Donald Trump beat the establishment. The establishment sat it out—or got in too late." The others had spent more time attacking one another than taking on Trump.

BEFORE TRUMP ARRIVED IN Chicago ahead of the March 15 primaries, anti-Trump protesters clashed with his supporters outside and inside the rally site. The worst spasm of violence thus far forced

Trump to cancel his appearance. He spent the evening doing phone interviews with cable television anchors, decrying the protesters. The next day, a man was arrested as he tried to jump to the stage at Trump's rally in Ohio. Tensions had been building at Trump's events. The candidate could be abusive—toward opponents, demonstrators, and the media. When protesters disrupted his rallies, they were removed, with Trump's encouragement. "Get 'em out of here!" he'd say. Or: "In the good old days, this doesn't happen because they used to treat them very, very rough." And: "You know what they used to do to guys like that when they were in a place like this? They'd be carried out on a stretcher." He seemed to revel in egging on the crowd: "I'd like to punch him in the face." And this: "Try not to hurt him. If you do, I'll defend you in court." And this: "Knock the crap out of him." Asked whether he had created a tone that contributed to violence at his rallies, Trump responded, "I truly hope not. . . . We have some protesters who are bad dudes. They have done bad things."

BY THE END OF March, Trump was down to just two opponents: Cruz, the anti-Washington antagonist who continued to win some states; and Kasich, the moderate-sounding governor who had won only his home state of Ohio. The stop-Trump forces were clinging to the slender hope that they could deny Trump enough delegates for the nomination and force a contested convention in July. Cruz hoped to give that strategy a significant boost in Wisconsin on April 5. Cruz had beaten Trump soundly in Utah, as Mormon voters, encouraged by Romney, fled from the front-runner. In Wisconsin, Trump found the state's entire conservative apparatus aligned against him. The opposition began with Governor Scott Walker. Though he had fizzled as a presidential candidate, Walker had a tested political organization at home and put it to work for Cruz. And a loose alliance of local talk radio hosts had for weeks broadcast a consistent message: not Trump.

In the week before the primary, more problems erupted. On March 29, Lewandowski was charged with simple battery in Florida, based on an accusation from Michelle Fields, a reporter for Breitbart News, who said he had roughed her up at a Trump rally in Florida. Trump defended his campaign manager and denounced the accuser:

"I can't destroy a man for that." (The charge against Lewandowski was eventually dropped.) The next day, Trump created yet another controversy during a town hall meeting with MSNBC's Chris Matthews. Trump said he would favor punishment for abortions. "For the woman?" Matthews asked. Trump: "Yes, there has to be some form." Hours later, in a rare reversal, Trump recanted the comment, saying only the doctor should be held responsible, "not the woman."

Wisconsin's demographics seemed hospitable to Trump, with a smaller evangelical population than states where Cruz had done best and a preponderance of the white working-class voters who were the heart of Trump's constituency. But Trump could not overcome the combination of a narrower field of opponents and his own gaffes. On Election Day, Cruz captured 48 percent to Trump's 35 percent. Cruz was exultant that night as he delivered his victory speech, but his advisers' joy quickly dissipated when they learned that Fox News had cut away from Cruz's victory address. "Fox cutting away halfway through the speech was stunning," Jeff Roe said later. "We got no bounce out of Wisconsin."

WISCONSIN DID, HOWEVER, FUEL talk of a contested Republican convention. "It gave them a glimmer of hope," Trump said. Cruz now targeted upcoming state GOP conventions to round up delegates who would support him on a second ballot, even if they were bound to Trump on the first. In the complex battle for delegates, Cruz's campaign ran circles around the Trump operation. Trump had won the Louisiana primary, but in the final scramble for delegates, Cruz had gained ground. In North Dakota, where delegates were officially free to vote their conscience, Cruz filled the delegation with far more people partial to him than Trump was able to secure. In Colorado, where delegates were chosen at conventions rather than in a primary, Cruz smoked Trump, leaving the front-runner without a single pledged delegate. Trump blasted the process as "rigged." In truth, Cruz was simply playing the game more skillfully.

In late March, Paul Manafort, a veteran of Republican campaigns going back to Gerald Ford's in 1976, joined Trump for dinner at the candidate's Mar-a-Lago estate. Through a mutual friend, he had offered his services to Trump, whose campaign had impressed him almost from the start. The dinner in Florida brought him into the campaign initially with the title of convention manager (later to become chairman) and a broad portfolio that put him in competition with Lewandowski. Manafort quickly concluded that Trump was on a path to win more delegates than anyone else, but not necessarily the 1,237 he needed for a first-ballot victory.

Manafort developed a new plan designed to maximize delegates and showed the projections to Trump. Tellingly, he did not let Trump keep the piece of paper. He wanted to keep his numbers under wraps. But he made a bold public prediction. Three days after the defeat in Wisconsin, he said, "Our goal is, in the middle of May, to be the presumptive nominee." Trump later said he never doubted that he would sew up the nomination well before the convention: "I felt it was never going to go to a contested convention. . . . When Cruz was trying to get delegates for the second ballot, I said, 'Who cares if he gets it? We're not going to do a second ballot, it's going to be over in the first ballot.'"

AFTER WISCONSIN, THE CALENDAR began to favor Trump with a series of contests in the Northeast and Mid-Atlantic. In New York, he followed a strategy designed to maximize his delegate count, locating his rallies in key congressional districts to boost his margins of victory. He battered Cruz for having derided "New York values" earlier in the race. A limping Kasich, meanwhile, was a virtual nonpresence. On primary day, April 19, Trump won 60 percent of the vote and all but six of the ninety-five delegates at stake. The results instantly reshaped the narrative of the GOP campaign.

Trump sauntered into the Trump Tower lobby to Frank Sinatra's "New York, New York" displaying a new, more sober mien. He delivered his most policy-oriented victory speech yet, promising to bring jobs back from overseas, negotiate better trade deals, block US companies from moving to Mexico, build up the military, care for veterans, and get rid of the Affordable Care Act and Common Core education standards. There was no mention of waterboarding, banning Muslims, building a wall, or any of his other controversial ideas.

But no single appearance could ease the concerns of many party regulars. Appalled by Trump's insults, alienated by his narcissism, frightened by his unpredictability, some Republicans in Congress and in statehouses distanced themselves from the man who would be at the top of their November ticket. In private, Manafort offered assurances that Trump would soon be the kind of tempered candidate GOP leaders wanted. At a closed-door meeting of the Republican National Committee in Florida, Manafort said Trump had been playing a "part" on the campaign trail, but was starting to pivot toward a more presidential "persona." Within days, however, Trump undercut his new adviser, making clear that the "let Trump be Trump" faction knew him better.

A week after New York, Trump swept contests in Pennsylvania, Maryland, Connecticut, Delaware, and Rhode Island. He won every county in each of the states. "I consider myself the presumptive nominee," he told reporters. One more hurdle remained before others would accept that claim—the May 3 primary in Indiana. Cruz knew the Hoosier State was his last stand and tried everything possible to shake up the race. He and Kasich announced a peace pact—they would decide who was strongest in upcoming states and stay out of each other's way where possible. The fragile alliance quickly crumbled. Then Cruz announced former rival Carly Fiorina as his vice presidential running mate, which looked mostly like an act of desperation designed to win a news cycle. Cruz won the endorsement of Indiana governor Mike Pence, and Trump countered with an endorsement from another legendary figure popular for his blunt, unfiltered style— Bobby Knight, the former head basketball coach at Indiana University.

On primary night, Trump won going away. Before Trump could deliver his victory speech, Cruz quit the race. Kasich followed the next day. Four members of Trump's original team posed for pictures at Trump Tower, having pulled off one of the most surprising victories in political history. After the speeches, Manafort and some members of Trump's family celebrated at a cigar bar near Trump Tower. The candidate, now clearly the presumptive nominee, went to bed.

After Indiana, Trump, virtually unopposed, won the last few primaries, in California, New Jersey, and New Mexico, by enormous majorities. He could have pivoted toward the fall election. Instead he found himself mired in controversy. Although many GOP elected officials, driven by fear of a Clinton presidency, endorsed Trump, some prominent Republicans distanced themselves from him. House Speaker Paul Ryan, after offering his endorsement, seemed to squirm almost daily in reaction to something Trump said or did. Romney led the attacks, explaining why he would not endorse Trump: "I wanted my grandkids to see that I simply couldn't ignore what Mr. Trump was saying and doing, which revealed a character and temperament unfit for the leader of the free world." Richard Armitage, Ronald Reagan's deputy assistant secretary of defense and George W. Bush's deputy secretary of state, said Trump "doesn't appear to be a Republican [and] doesn't appear to want to learn about issues." Armitage, a lifelong Republican, said he would vote for Hillary Clinton. Internally, the campaign remained unsettled into the summer; in late June, acting on the encouragement of Trump's three adult children, the candidate fired Lewandowski after a period of feuding between the campaign manager and Manafort.

As Clinton sewed up her own nomination and the July party conventions loomed, Trump seemed determined to settle old scores rather than reach out to a broader electorate. When a gunman who pledged allegiance to ISIS killed forty-nine people at a gay nightclub in Orlando, Trump responded by doubling down on his call to ban Muslims from entering the country. (Once again, the shooter, Omar Mateen, was a native-born US citizen.) Trump insinuated that the president was in league with the country's enemies. (When the *Washington Post*, like many other news organizations, reported on that statement, Trump responded by revoking the newspaper's credentials—a tactic the campaign had used against nearly a dozen other news outlets. Publicly, Trump called the *Post* "dishonest" and "phony," but offstage, his campaign continued to respond to questions from *Post* reporters.) Trump created a firestorm by calling out the federal judge overseeing a class action suit against Trump University, accusing the Indiana-born judge of having a conflict of interest because of his Mexican heritage. Some Republican leaders urged their colleagues to leap off what they saw as a runaway train. Senator Lindsey Graham called Trump's comments about the judge "the most un-American thing from a politician since Joe McCarthy. If anybody was looking for an off-ramp, this is probably it. There'll come a time when the love of country will trump hatred of

Hillary." Ryan did not rescind his endorsement, but did call Trump's attack on the judge "absolutely unacceptable . . . the textbook definition of a racist comment."

Throughout, Trump stood firm—defiant, even. After the Orlando shootings, he put it this way: "I refuse to be politically correct. I want to do the right thing. I want to straighten things out. I want to make America great again." That, he said, was his only motivation. That was why he was willing to deal with the career politicians and the critical press and the close protection by the Secret Service. "It's not like a normal situation," he said of life as a candidate, a life in which even a drive of a few blocks was a precision-choreographed paramilitary operation: "I get into the car, thousands of people. . . . They close the street and thousands of people form on the corner, waving, going crazy, and all this Secret Service. And my wife gets in, and I get in, and she looks at me, and we're in this car with windows that are *this* thick, with steel walls. . . . And she says to me, 'Are you sure this is what you want for the rest of your life?'"

He told her he was sure.

Law and Order

The man who would be president rose from his tall, thickly cushioned leather desk chair, buttoned his suit jacket, and waved his visitors to follow along: "Come on, boys, I have something to show you." He ushered us from his lushly carpeted office in Trump Tower, with its breathtaking view of Central Park and the majestic Plaza Hotel, across the hall to a windowless room, not five steps away. "I just discovered this," he said, pointing at the conference table that took up most of the room. He swept his arm over the table, beckoning us to inspect. Every inch of the table's surface was filled with stacks of magazines. "All from the last four months," he said, and on every cover of every magazine, there he was, Donald J. Trump, smiling or waving or scowling or pouting, but always him.

"Cover of *Time*, three times in four months," he said. "No one ever before. It's amazing." There he was on the *New York Times Magazine*, and on *Esquire* and on *Rolling Stone* and on and on, the man who was about to be nominated as the Republican Party's candidate for president, his success (or his notoriety) emblazoned on magazine after magazine. He was very much impressed. He was all sunshine on this June day, an exemplar of the power of positive thinking, the core of the theology that he'd grown up with in Fred Trump's office and the Reverend Norman Vincent Peale's church. In this moment, Donald Trump was the can-do dealmaker, the tough decider, the ebullient kid who, as his sister put it, was "just a nice boy from Queens." A few moments later, he would switch gears and show us his other side, also a classically American streak, this one darker, with a trace of paranoia and a dash of despair. This was the author of *Crippled America*, the truth teller who told huge crowds, "We don't have a country anymore," the prideful tycoon who now threatened to sue us even as he said how much he was enjoying our interviews. Both aspects of Trump seemed to be the stuff of fiction, of characters who were written to capture the hopes and ambitions of a great, young nation, but also its fears, doubts, and jealousies.

Even after we'd spent hours talking to him—a frequently frustrating process in which he took any and all questions, but often offered disjointed, truncated answers that had nothing to do with the questions—Trump seemed not quite real, a character he had built to enhance his business empire, a construct designed to be at once an everyman and an impossibly high-flying king of Manhattan, an avatar of American riches. Trump was charming, yet forever on the make, like Lonesome Rhodes from *A Face in the Crowd*, the 1957 movie with Andy Griffith as a folksy but ultimately cynical Arkansas traveler who soars from a filthy jail cell to the pinnacle of American celebrity and political power. Trump was a natural-born populist, like Howard Beale, the TV anchorman from *Network*, the 1976 film in which the newsman rallies the nation to open their windows and shout, "I'm mad as hell and I'm not going to take it anymore!" Trump was at times naive yet wise, like Chauncey Gardiner, the dim gardener whose unwitting folk wisdom turned him into a possible presidential contender in *Being There* (1979).

Real people had fascinated Americans in similar ways during trying periods throughout the last century—voices that appealed to the idea that foreigners or The Other were responsible for the nation's troubles: Father Charles Coughlin, the priest who used his nationwide radio show in the 1930s to deliver an America First message laced with assaults on Jews; and George Wallace, the segregationist governor of Alabama who ran for president in the 1960s and '70s as a populist preaching that "there's not a dime's worth of difference" between the Republicans and the Democrats; and Patrick Buchanan, the Washington insider and presidential candidate who encouraged voters in the 1990s to rise up as "peasants with pitchforks" to take their country back from politicians who had failed to stop illegal immigration and the ravages of free trade. These men had appealed to the darker aspect of the American personality, the flip side to Billy Graham's confident theology of good deeds and righteous capitalism, Martin Luther King Jr.'s march to the mountaintop of justice and fairness, and Barack Obama's promise of hope and change.

Trump believed—like so many great Americans real and imagined, such as Steve Jobs or Jay Gatsby—in the unlimited, unequaled power of the individual to achieve nearly anything. And like many other products of the uniquely American machinery of celebrity, Trump believed that his fame and success would catapult him to a level of power that he deserved because he had made so much money. He believed that just by walking into a room, just by reflecting the passions of a crowd, he could shift the course of events. He could, for example, make America great again. "Believe me," he had beckoned crowds throughout the campaign. "Believe me."

IMPROBABLE DIDN'T BEGIN TO describe what he had achieved. Angry outsiders had run for president before, had even collected a respectable protest vote, but now, in Cleveland in July, in the arena where LeBron James had just led the Cavaliers to the city's first sports championship in half a century, Donald Trump was going to be crowned the Republican nominee for president. He remained a polarizing, troubling figure for many—four of the five previous GOP nominees for president had decided not to attend the convention, along with many of the party's most prominent figures—but Trump was determined to put on a show that would break the mold and put him on the road to victory. On the convention's opening night, after a long series of speeches by actors and soldiers bashing Hillary Clinton, by parents whose children had been killed by illegal immigrants, and by black police officials and politicians who declared that it was *blue* lives that mattered, the stage was cleared and Queen's triumphant "We Are the Champions" poured out over the PA system.

Suddenly, a dark opening appeared at the back of the stage, and a silhouette emerged. The big suit, the broad shoulders, the shelf of hair—unmistakably Trump, breaking with tradition, instantly juicing what had been a listless crowd. Trump, not expected until the last night of the convention, walked into the light and basked in the waves of cheers and chants, occasionally nodding, flashing thumbs-up, then promising, "We are going to win *so* big." He had flown in to introduce his wife, the highlight of the first night's program, and Melania dazzled the audience with a creamy white dress, an electric smile, and a game attitude as she pushed through her speech in a thick Slovenian accent. But the warm reception in the hall soon soured, as news spread that key portions of her script had been lifted verbatim from Michele Obama's address to the Democratic convention in 2008. For thirty-six hours, the Trump campaign denied any wrongdoing; only when the media firestorm about the plagiarism would not cease did the speechwriter come forward with a confession and an apology.

The convention that Trump had envisioned as more entertaining, more fun, and looser than the standard dull recitation of political rhetoric instead played out as a series of gaffes and misfires. From the start, the quest for party unity was marred by open rebellion on the floor, as hundreds of delegates tried to force the GOP to hold a roll call vote on rules that prohibited delegates from voting their conscience, requiring them instead to vote as their state's primary results mandated. "Roll call vote! Roll call vote!" they chanted, and their microphones went dead. "Shame! Shame! Shame!" one of the rebellion's leaders, former Virginia attorney general Ken Cuccinelli, shouted. But despite a voice vote that showed the hall nearly evenly divided, there would be no roll call. The managers of the convention turned up the music, silenced the rambunctious delegates, and, after a delay, announced that although enough state delegations had demanded a roll call to satisfy the rules, three of those delegations had just reversed their decisions, and there was now no longer sufficient demand to require an open vote. "Petty, tyrannical politics," Cuccinelli sputtered. "This stunt does not fire up the rank and file."

Some of the rank and file never needed firing up. "Trump is sent from God!" Jamiel Shaw, the father of a young man who was killed by an illegal immigrant, told the crowd. Across town, at an America First rally of truckers, Teamsters, and listeners of white nationalist radio shows, Evan Hubert, a twenty-four-year-old garbage man from Pennsylvania, said, "I'm ready to see somebody really put his foot down. I know Trump will do something about the Islamic religion and the refugee problem."

But many delegates did need convincing. Patty Reiman, a lifelong Republican and a party activist from Wisconsin who spent a break from the convention buying a dress with an elephant pattern, had originally supported Marco Rubio for president, and then Ted Cruz. Now she was, with trepidation, coming around to Trump, "because I want to unify our party." But she still had misgivings: "His personality was a little harsh. He doesn't think before he speaks. All I can hope is that he'll make wonderful appointments. Obviously, I worry."

Lori Hack, a homemaker from Peoria, Arizona, was a delegate for Cruz, but her state's winner-take-all system required her to vote for Trump, the victor in Arizona's primary. She would not. "I have a conscience," she said, and she insisted on the right to be an unbound delegate. She said her state's party chairman disagreed and told her, "You're done." She was stripped of her position and replaced by someone willing to vote for Trump. Now she was in the arena, but only as a guest of a fellow anti-Trump Republican from Texas. "That's fine," she said, "because I have my conscience." Hack, forty-four and a born-again Christian and lifelong Republican, feared that Trump would lead the party to defeat or, if elected, plunge the nation into dangerous confrontations around the world. "He's amoral," she said. "He's a pathological liar. He's a narcissist. If Cruz or Romney had that situation with the [attempted] coup in Turkey [in July], they would think it through. Trump just goes from one view to another, one moment to the next." It had gotten heated on the floor during the battle over the roll call vote, and Hack saw people shouting at one another. It looked as if things might get physical. She didn't like what Trump brought out in people: "It's called a cult. They're so angry that they've lost their judgment. Trump says all the hot things, and it clicks with their anger. But some have woken up to who he really is, I do believe that." Hack could not bring herself to vote for Clinton; she planned to abstain from the presidential election in November.

One of Hack's allies in the battle to stop the Trump nomination, Gary Teal, vice chairman of the Republican Party in the District of Columbia, felt trapped. If he didn't support the nominee, he'd have to resign his party position. Still, "it's not at all clear to me that Donald Trump has the skills to calm and encourage an electorate that is on edge, like it was in the late sixties. I'm still in shock that this happened. I've spent the last four years writing about how it can't happen, don't worry, the American people won't fall for Trump." Teal blamed the news media for Trump's rise, "not because of liberal bias," he said, "but this was simply the media thinking that if they reported everything he said and did, that would kill his chances—people would see who he really is." Instead, he said, Trump seemed to have Kryptonite protecting him against the facts; his supporters would rather denounce those who raised questions than diminish their enthusiasm for the man they saw as a blue-collar billionaire. During the campaign, Teal had supported Christie, then Rubio. Now he needed to decide about Trump: "Usually, you fight for your candidate and you try and then the decision is made and you get on board. But I'm not there yet."

Trump's convention was not designed to get people like Teal there. It was night after night of delectable sweets for true believers. A National Rifle Association executive got a prime-time slot to talk about how "a Hillary Clinton Supreme Court means your right to own a firearm is *gone*." For hour upon hour, the subject was Crooked Hillary, Lying Hillary, Elitist Hillary. One night, the party presented a film titled *Hillary the Horrible*. Each night, the vitriol that poured out against Clinton grew coarser, louder, ever more threatening. The venom and vulgarities being hawked at T-shirt stands on Euclid Avenue in downtown Cleveland—HILLARY FOR PRISON was among the milder slogans—leached into Quicken Loans Arena and morphed into chants of "Lock her up!" Chris Christie played the role of prosecutor, leading the delighted crowd in full-throated verdicts of "Guilty!" as he detailed Clinton's purported crimes—her use of a private e-mail server when she was secretary of state, her support for improved relations with Cuba, her push for a nuclear power deal with Iran. A Montana delegate called for Clinton to be hanged; a New Hampshire state representative and Trump adviser said Clinton should be shot by a firing squad.

Modeled after Richard Nixon's emphasis on law and order at the 1968 convention, Trump's four-evening program presented TV viewers with a vision of a country in deep trouble, unsafe, weak, governed by rigged systems and by people who had dishonest, even evil intentions. Speakers described a country that had lost respect abroad and hope at home, a country nearly at the mercy of what Trump called "barbarian" terrorists. It was a gloomy picture of a nation in decline, a society that had lost its identity. Except for the attacks on Clinton, the approach won a tepid response inside the convention hall: in one delegation after another, the party faithful sat on their hands or folded their arms or shook their heads. This, many said, was not how to win an election. Nor was it the way to make America great again.

The emotional peak of the first night was a series of testimonials by people who had been powerfully affected by the 2012 terrorist attack on Americans in Benghazi, Libya. "I blame Hillary Clinton personally for the death of my son," said Patricia Smith, whose son Sean worked for the State Department at the diplomatic compound in Benghazi. But as Smith spoke, the audience most likely to be moved by her speech, the millions of conservatives who were watching on Fox News, instead heard Donald Trump phone into Bill O'Reilly's show—a programming faux pas that Republican strategists said would never have happened in a better-organized campaign. Even O'Reilly seemed surprised that Trump would preempt his own convention. "I think the strategy is, Donald Trump is it," O'Reilly said.

After Melania's speech, she and Donald flew home to New York. He had, he said, no interest in hanging out with political types.

THE HOME BASE DONALD returned to was his incongruously serene office high above the cacophony of Fifth Avenue. On his desk, a portrait of a confident Fred Trump faced Donald, the father posing for strangers, giving nothing away. The last three presidents had struggled fairly publicly with their fathers. Clinton and Obama wrote and talked about their feelings of abandonment. Their resolve to prove themselves helped propel their meteoric ascents, tempered by a charisma perhaps born of their lifelong need to win the attention and love missing from their upbringing. At a later stage in life, George W. Bush similarly struggled with the shadow cast by the failure of his father's presidency; he, too, chose a road on which he might make right the disappointments of his father's journey. All three of those presidents, to one degree or another, openly carried burdens from their parents' lives. Trump admitted to no such troubles. He had never been very forthcoming about the texture of his home life. His father, he would admit, was sometimes distant—"his life was business . . . a very content person"—but ultimately a loving, strong figure. Trump had reduced his story of his mother, even more of a mystery to outsiders, to less than a sentence: "very warm . . . great sense of pageantry . . . very beautiful." Donald Trump had walled off the pain in his past, hid it behind a never-ending show about himself.

The rest of the desk was devoted to Donald, the stacks of magazines featuring his image, the morning's news clippings about himself. Yet in an office dedicated almost entirely to celebrating Trump's success and performance, nothing spoke to the man's private passions or predilections, nothing to indicate a hobby, an artistic interest, a literary bent, a statement about his credo, his crises, or his dreams. In one of his books, *Trump: Think Like a Billionaire*, he had asserted that visionary business leaders succeed "because they are narcissists who devote their talent with unrelenting focus to achieving their dreams, even if it's sometimes at the expense of those around them." He approvingly quoted a writer who said, "Successful alpha personalities display a single-minded determination to impose their vision on the world."

He had reached the pinnacle of American politics virtually without allies, rising in opposition to the party structure. More than any other major figure in modern presidential politics, he seemed allergic to ideology. He had won the nomination with an impossibly tiny campaign staff, a core of half a dozen loyalists, most of them newcomers to presidential politics. His most valued consultants were his children and their spouses.

He had never really had close friends. As far back as 1980, he had told TV interviewer Rona Barrett, "My business is so all-encompassing that I don't really get the pleasure of being with friends that much, frankly." She pressed him: Whom would you call if you were in trouble and your family wasn't around? "Maybe I'd call you, Rona," he said. Thirty-six years later, asked again, for this book, about his friendships, Trump said after a considerable, unusual pause, "Well, it's an interesting question. Most of my friendships are business related because those are the only people I meet. The people I meet, really, I guess I

could say socially, when you go out to a charity event or something
. . . I have people that I haven't spoken to in years, but I think they're
friends." And he named—he put the names off the record—three men
he had had business dealings with two or more decades before, men
he had only rarely seen in recent years. Trump continued, "I mean, I
think I have a lot of friends, but they're not friends like perhaps other
people have friends, where they're together all the time and they go out
to dinner all the time." But was there anyone he would turn to if he had
a personal problem, or some doubt about himself or something he'd
done? "More of my family," Trump said. "I have a lot of good relationships. I have good enemies, too, which is okay. But I think more of my
family than others."

IN THE DAYS BEFORE the convention, Trump turned to his family for advice: Who should be his running mate? The party brass and
Paul Manafort, his campaign manager, were pressing Trump to choose
an insider, a well-respected officeholder who might win back some
party mainliners who had been scared off by Trump's willingness—
eagerness, it often seemed—to break with party orthodoxies. Trump
was drawn to two men who were more plainspoken, more iconoclas-
tic, more like himself—Chris Christie and Newt Gingrich, the former
Speaker of the House. He'd even floated the idea of choosing a retired
general—also an outspoken, blunt figure. But in the final hours of his
anguished process, Trump asked his children for advice, as if he was
searching for a way out. The children sided with Manafort, who recommended Mike Pence, the governor of Indiana and a former House
member and radio talk show host. Trump seemed unconvinced of
the wisdom of the move and wavered right up to the night before the
announcement. He went ahead with Pence, but at their early appearances together, Trump seemed not quite comfortable. At their first
news conference, Trump introduced Pence, then left him alone on
the stage. In a joint interview on *60 Minutes*, Trump did the bulk of
the talking. The two men had disagreed on trade and waterboarding
and immigration and gay rights, but now they were trying to present a
united front, coming together on Trump's promises to "get rid of ISIS,
big league, and . . . get rid of 'em fast . . . and we're going to declare

war. It is war." On *60 Minutes*, Trump, confronted with the fact that his new running mate had voted for the Iraq War, said, "I don't care. It's a long time ago." (Trump claimed to have opposed the war from the start, but six months before the war began, he told Howard Stern that he favored the attack.)

But haven't you slammed Hillary Clinton for the same votes that Pence cast in favor of the war? reporter Lesley Stahl asked. Pence, Trump said, chuckling, is "entitled to make a mistake every once in a while."

"But she's not?" Stahl asked.

"But she's not," Trump replied.

Clinton pushed back. Her campaign ran a TV ad, titled "Role Models," showing wide-eyed young children watching broadcasts of Trump's coarsest comments, his vulgar language, his insults of women and Mexicans and Muslims and a disabled reporter and the media generally. "Our children are watching," the ad concluded. Clinton went on TV to deliver a midconvention blast against Trump: "No self-discipline, no self-control, no sense of history, no understanding of the limits of the kind of power that any president should impose upon himself."

In classic Roy Cohn style, Trump only accelerated his attack. He had yielded to the party elders on his vice-presidential pick, but this was still his campaign, his convention, and he was determined to keep doing what had worked in the primaries, so the lineup of speakers included reality TV star Willie Robertson of *Duck Dynasty* ("America is in a bad spot. . . . Donald Trump will have your back"), TV actor Scott Baio ("Nothing feels right. . . . We need Donald Trump to fix this"), and the chief executive of Ultimate Fighting Championship— a roll call of just-folks speakers aimed at blue-collar, white America. The convention's entertainment program read like a playlist from a radio station in white suburbia in the 1970s: Lynyrd Skynyrd, Three Dog Night, The Doobie Brothers, and later acts with similar appeal— Kid Rock, Blues Traveler, Rascal Flatts. "Let's make America *America* again," Baio rallied the crowd.

Republican leaders bemoaned the image that the convention was sending viewers at home—a nearly all-white, older group, a picture at odds with efforts over the previous dozen years to invite Hispanics, immigrants, and blacks into the party. Among the 2,472 delegates in Cleveland, there were, according to a Republican National Committee accounting, only about 18 black people, down from 167 at the 2004 convention. Trump still hoped to win over African-American voters, but his history of controversial statements on race haunted him, and he entered the arena trailing Clinton among black voters by 89 percent to 4 percent. All Republicans struggle to win black votes, but this was an extraordinary falloff. In 2004, George W. Bush had won 11 percent of the black vote; it was a key to his victory. Trump had won over a few black delegates, including James Evans, chairman of Utah's Republican Party—a man who knew what it was like to stand out as a black in a mostly white party. Evans had led an effort to draft Mitt Romney, but when that failed, he'd met privately with Trump: "The rest of America has to see the person I sat down with. The Democratic playbook is that if you are a white Republican candidate, you are a racially insensitive candidate. Let's look at the policies of the political left and how they devastated the black community, and you tell me who is more racist."

The Cleveland convention followed hard on a series of violent, frightening days—the attempted coup in Turkey; the terrorist attack on beachgoers in Nice, France; the horrific murders of police officers in Dallas and then in Baton Rouge as well—and Trump's convention reacted by presenting a catalog of horrors, a cavalcade of conspiratorial notions, feeding the sense that an unnerved nation needed definitive, unnuanced leadership. "The world is a dark place, a scary place," Marcus Luttrell, a former Navy SEAL who had been badly injured in Afghanistan, told the delegates. Representative Michael McCaul of Texas said, "Our city on a hill is now a city under siege; . . . it's time to take back our country." The sheriff of Milwaukee County, David Clarke, said movements such as Black Lives Matter were leading the country to a "collapse of the social order. . . . I call it anarchy." Barack Obama was "absolutely" a Muslim, the actor Antonio Sabàto Jr. falsely insisted after his opening night speech.

Trump embraced the narrative of a country bordering on disintegration: "I'll tell you, it is spinning. Our world is spinning out of control. Our country's spinning out of control. That's what I think about. And I'll stop that." But on TV that week in Cleveland, it was the Republican convention that looked to be spinning out of control. When Senator Ted Cruz delivered a prime-time address that pointedly failed to endorse Trump and urged Republicans to "vote your conscience," the convention erupted in waves of boos and chants— "Endorse Trump!" At the peak of the outburst, who should walk into the arena but Trump himself, either in preparation for his son Eric's speech or to upstage his uncooperative erstwhile opponent, depending on whose version you believed. Either way, it caused a strangely electric disarray: thousands of delegates still jeering Cruz off the stage turned to face the back of the hall, and the jeers blended into cheers and chants: "Trump! Trump! Trump!"

HE HAD ONE LAST chance at the convention to make the pivot he'd talked about on that March day in Washington, that day when he'd been under such pressure to show that he could act presidential, that he could be more than the coarse, sneering voice of a frustrated nation. On the last night in Cleveland, with the arena finally full and the internecine party battles silenced for at least one evening, Trump had the attention of 35 million Americans, slightly more than Mitt Romney had drawn four years before. This was no rally in an airport hangar; this was the formal acceptance address, with plenty of pomp and a guaranteed festival of goodwill at the end. So far in the convention, just about the only times the hall had seen anything approaching unity were when speakers ripped Hillary Clinton—the harsher the rhetoric, the lustier the cheers. Now, two biographical films whetted the delegates' appetite for their nominee's big speech. The carefully crafted videos offered a truncated survey of Trump's life and career, presenting images of rising towers, fresh new golf courses, and other symbols of his life as a builder. There was no mention of his Atlantic City ventures, his gambling or beauty pageant businesses, his corporate bankruptcies, his divorces. He was, as the films presented him, a visionary businessman who got stuff done when no one else could. And that made him the right man, the only man, who could save a country in dire shape. "When you have my father in your corner, you will never again have to worry about being let down," Ivanka told the nation as she introduced her father, and Trump, beaming, took the stage, gave his daughter two kisses, tapped her on the hips, and took a long moment to soak in the applause.

"Who would have believed this?" he said. And he said it again. He read the speech off a prompter; this was no time for his usual stream-of-consciousness riffing. He had a case to make, a dark one, a portrait of a wounded and dazed nation, a nation he alone could save. It was a frightened and insecure nation, beset with crime, unnerved by terrorism, disoriented by rapidly swirling economic change. Donald Trump would fix it. "I am," he said, "the law and order candidate." He repeated that phrase throughout the speech, hitting each syllable hard and clear, like a bell tolling for an America that was nearly lost.

"Beginning on January twentieth of 2017, safety will be restored," he announced. He would tell the truth. He would refuse to say what was politically correct. He would be, unabashedly, an "America First" president. He would stop illegal immigrants at the border. He would build that wall. (The crowd burst into cheers on that note; pockets of delegates remained pointedly silent through the seventy-six-minute-long speech, but most found something to applaud in Trump's signature promises.) He would fix bad trade deals. He would crush ISIS—"and fast." And he would beat Hillary Clinton, the perpetrator of "terrible, terrible crimes."

"Lock her up! Lock her up!" the crown chanted, but Trump would not go there. This was a new phase, a different setting. He waved off the chant and broke from his script: "Let's defeat her in November." He wasn't going soft on them—"the legacy of Hillary Clinton," he said, was "death, destruction, terrorism, and weakness"—but he was finding his way toward the right mix of pure Trumpian populism and that certain presidential elevation. He would still rail against the rigged system, and against the illegal immigrants, and against radical Islamic terrorism, and against the feckless media. And he would assert his independence even as he sanded down some of his coarser edges. He promised to protect "our LGBTQ citizens from the violence and oppression of a hateful, foreign ideology—believe me," he said. After those words won a fair amount of applause, he departed from his script to thank the Republicans for cheering a comment supportive of gays. At a convention aimed squarely at the populist base he had assembled during the primaries, he now made a somewhat broader appeal. Yes, he issued the requisite calls to protect gun rights, get rid of Obamacare, and reduce taxes, but he also spoke directly to Bernie Sanders supporters, mostly avoided social issues, didn't use the word *Mexico*, and didn't specifically promise to ban Muslims from entering the country (he did say he'd keep out immigrants from countries plagued by terrorism).

Trump's vision featured no shining city on a hill and offered no details on how he'd make the instant, absolute fixes he promised. He would just do it—and fast. He seemed smoother now—when a lone protester interrupted the speech, Trump said nothing, just stood quietly and waited for her to be removed, though he looked as if he was bursting to let everyone know what he really thought of her. But he was still Trump, still the cocky, blunt kid from Queens, still the guy who would say what others only thought. "I am your voice," he said. "Believe me. Believe me."

WITH THE CONVENTION OVER, there was no rest. The hundred-day blitz of a fall campaign would begin almost immediately—three debates, rally upon rally, a blizzard of charges and countercharges in countless cable TV appearances—and it was already clear this would be a bitter battle between the two least popular, least liked major party candidates in modern political history. At the end of that slog, Trump was certain, the White House would be his. Yet as confident as he was of victory, he said he had not spent much time planning for how he would operate if he won. He would run the country much as he had his businesses, he said, keeping a close eye on everything, insisting on high standards. The difference would be that he'd be doing everything for the country, not just for himself. What exactly that might look like was not entirely clear. He expected his day-to-day work style to be similar to what he'd done for decades. At Trump Tower, he kept no computer on his desk, and he avoided reading extensive reports or briefings. He preferred to be told about issues orally, and quickly. One day in June, he had a visit from a delegation of prominent executives from the oil, steel, and retail industries, and one of the CEOs told Trump that the Chinese were taking advantage of the United States. "He said, 'I'd like to send you a report,'" Trump recalled. "He said, 'I'd love to be able to send you'—oh, boy, he's got a lengthy report, hundreds of pages. . . . I said, 'Do me a favor, don't send me a report. Send me, like, three pages.' . . . I'm a very efficient guy. Now I could also do it verbally, which is fine. . . . I want it short. There's no reason to do hundreds of pages because I know exactly what it is . . . because I have a lot of common sense and I have a lot of business ability."

He had no time to read, he said. As the reality of the nomination had become clear, he'd thought about digging into a biography of a president—he hadn't had a chance to read one—"but I don't have much time," he said. "I never have. I'm always busy doing a lot. Now I'm more busy, I guess, than ever before. . . . I don't have much time. I have so little time."

There would be so much to do now. His daughter Ivanka had promised the nation on that last night of the convention that come January "all things will be possible again." And Donald Trump had told the crowd that since "nobody knows the system better than me . . . I alone can fix it." He alone. His father, who had warned him against being "a nothing," was gone and never got to see this astonishing American journey to its conclusion. His family joined him onstage for the final celebration as red, white, and blue balloons fell and beach balls bounced around the arena. But in that last moment, Donald Trump was on his own. He stuck out his jaw, pursed his lips, and stepped into the dark tunnel behind the stage.

ACKNOWLEDGMENTS

Traditional biographies gestate for years, taking advantage of archives and interviews with people who speak with a freedom born of having attained a measure of distance. We didn't have such luxuries; to produce a work of biographical journalism in time for voters to use this book to learn more about perhaps the least well-examined presidential nominee in modern American history, we had to vacuum up whatever documents we could find and ask sources to speak openly about a man who has gone to great lengths to control his image. The bulk of the work on this book took place over three months in mid-2016; the book would have been impossible without a large team of surpassingly talented, experienced reporters, researchers, and fact-checkers who were ready to work around the clock for many weeks without a break. The *Washington Post* journalists who reported this book are among the best in the business, and a full catalog of their names, along with those of the editors who were vital to this project, appears in the "About This Book" section at the beginning of *Trump Revealed*.

We are extremely grateful to the many people who told us about their experiences working for Donald Trump, competing with him, or otherwise observing him in his youth, his career, and his political and personal pursuits. Many of those people spoke to us on the record, and they are named either in the body of this book or in the endnotes. Many others talked to us confidentially despite having signed nondisclosure agreements with Trump. We also relied on more than a million pages of documents that we obtained from court records, the various state casino control commissions, and other public sources, and from Trump's former executives, associates, competitors, and regulators.

We owe a special debt to the Trump biographers who hacked the first paths through a tricky thicket. Wayne Barrett, one of the most dogged and devoted investigative reporters in the annals of New York newspapering, not only wrote *Trump: The Deals and the Downfall* (1992), but has also maintained one of the largest and most important archives of Trump-related documents, which he graciously shared with us. Gwenda Blair's *The Trumps: Three Generations That Built an Empire* (2000, reissued in 2016 as *The Trumps: Three Generations of Builders and a Presidential Candidate*) is the best guide to the family's journey to America and to more than a century of the Trump experience in this country. Timothy L. O'Brien's *TrumpNation: The Art of Being The Donald* (2005) and Harry Hurt III's *Lost Tycoon: The Many Lives of Donald J. Trump* (1993) well capture Trump's showmanship and business style at crucial junctures in his career. Michael D'Antonio's *Never Enough: Donald Trump and the Pursuit of Success* (2015) is a thoughtful, detailed overview of Trump's life and work. We also consulted the memoir of former Trump Plaza Hotel & Casino executive John O'Donnell, *Trumped! The Inside Story of the Real Donald Trump—His Cunning Rise & Spectacular Fall* (1991).

As Trump is quick to remind those who write about him, he was there first. Working with writers, Trump has published a shelf full of autobiographical and self-help books. Many of them are repetitive of one another, but *Trump: The Art of the Deal* (1987), written with Tony Schwartz, is an essential guide to the man's version of his story, and *Trump: Think Like a Billionaire* (2004), written with Meredith McIver, contains some important insights into Trump's psychology. Although Trump often spoke critically about our book in public, in his direct dealings with us, he was gracious and generous with his time, even in the heart of the campaign. We are grateful to his assistant Rhona Graff for helping to carve out the hours that Trump devoted to talking to us about his life and work.

The true authors of this book are the people who work in the newsroom of the *Washington Post*. We'd like to thank the *Post*'s extraordinarily generous senior editors who lent this effort some of their best reporters for many weeks at a time: Local editor Mike Semel, Investigations editor Jeff Leen, Financial editor Greg Schneider, Style editor Liz Seymour, Sports editor Matt Vita, and Morning Mix editor Fred Barbash. Thanks also to MaryAnne Golon and Bronwen Latimer, who direct the *Post*'s outstanding photo department, for their help arranging the book's visual elements and the Trump-related photography published in the *Post*. Greg Manifold, the *Post*'s design director, and Terri Rupar, the National digital editor, helped usher this work into the *Post* online and in print.

The entire national politics staff of the *Post*—along with dozens of reporters from the rest of the newsroom—has been involved in coverage of the Trump story, and we're indebted to our colleagues, and especially to politics editors Amy Gardner and Dan Eggen. National editor Scott Wilson somehow managed to assemble the extraordinary staff for this book, help us conceive the structure, and read every draft, all while maintaining his cheerful mien and putting out the best national report in the business. In these trying, existentially threatening times in the journalism industry, we are thrilled (and relieved) to be working in the happiest newsroom in the land, a place where ambitious ideas and big plans are not only welcome but are swiftly put into motion. That's a tribute to Marty Baron, the executive editor, who championed the book from the start and ensured that every resource would be available for it. He read every page and made valuable suggestions in every chapter. Along with managing editors Cameron Barr and Emilio Garcia-Ruiz, Marty has established the *Post* as the nation's most vital newsroom, building upon the ambition of past years even as we dive exuberantly into new forms of storytelling. The *Post*'s publisher, Fred Ryan, has fostered a journalism-first environment that makes all of this possible.

Although we have each written several books, neither of us had ever attempted a project of this scope at this speed. To pull that off, someone had to be the enthusiastic, confident, wise, and witty shepherd of the whole thing, and that was Colin Harrison, Scribner's editor in chief and the editor of this book. Colin was calm when we were frazzled. He saw the whole when we got stuck in the parts. He directed traffic, erased crises, and stood tall for the serial comma. And he had the wisdom to team up with Sarah Goldberg, the savvy and unflappable editorial assistant who was the secret ingredient in our ability to hit deadlines. At Scribner, the publisher, Nan Graham, led a team of people who made the impossible look easy. We are grateful to Carolyn Reidy, Susan Moldow, Roz Lippel, and Paul O'Halloran. Brian Belfiglio, Kate Lloyd, Kara Watson, and Ashley Gilliam got the word out about the book in all manner of creative ways. Thanks to the editors—Irene Kheradi, Monica Oluwek, Emily Fanelli, George Turianski, Katie Rizzo, and Steve Boldt—and designers—Jaime Putorti, Jaya Miceli, Janetta Dancer, and Jonathan Bush—who turned our words into a handsome and urgent package. At S&S Audio, our thanks go to Tom Spain, Elisa Shokoff, and Christina Zarafonitis for their work on the audiobook.

We're grateful to the book's agent, David Black, for his good counsel and close reading, and the work of his associates Jennifer Herrera and Gary Morris. The lawyers at the *Washington Post*, Jay Kennedy and Kalea Clark, and at Scribner, Lisa Rivlin and Emily Remes, provided careful and prompt review of a mass of material. The *Post*'s vice president for communications and events, Kris Coratti, and her staff helped shape and execute the promotional plan for the book.

Both of us vanished from our families and friends for a few months, and we're forever grateful to those who had to fend off every invitation, friendly inquiry, phone call, or knock at the door with some version of "No, he's working on the book."

Michael: My wife, Sylvia, who is an English teacher among her many other talents, once again proved to be an invaluable proofreader, pencil in hand, and always a beacon of support. My daughters, Laura and Jessica, are an unending source of inspiration, as is my mother, Allye. My late father, Arthur, was a wire service reporter who long ago graced the pages of the *Washington Post* and many other newspapers, and whose voice and advice forever remain with me.

Marc: The only person who tackled every draft without getting a paycheck for doing so was my constant and unflagging reader, my wife, Jody. She is still, ever, my light. My parents, Helene and

Harwood Fisher, inspired a life of asking questions. I was thrilled that our children, Julia and Aaron, happened to be at home for a good chunk of the time when I was writing this. I wish them times as interesting as these and a life full of characters as fantastic as Mr. Trump.

NOTES

PROLOGUE: "PRESIDENTIAL"

1 *"can't out-top Abraham Lincoln"*: Trump interview with Robert Costa and Bob Woodward, *Washington Post*, April 1, 2016.

3 *"I'm the Lone Ranger"*: Ibid.

4 *"your guard up"*: Filmed interview with Errol Morris, 2002, https://www.youtube .com/watch?v=upC8pX3RY0A.

4 *"making the country better"*: Trump interview with Marc Fisher and Michael Kranish, April 21, 2016.

5 they should be allowed: "Donald Trump: 'Be Careful!,'" *Chicago Sun-Times*, March 23, 2015.

5 noisy jets roaring: "Decade-Old Plan to Extend Palm Beach Airport Runway Revived," Associated Press, March 23, 2015.

5 reversed course: Brian Swanson, *Scottish Express*, March 22, 2015, 31.

5 *"celebrity video cameo"*: "Radio City: Excitement Continues to Build around New York Spring Spectacular," Globe Newswire, March 23, 2015.

5 *"marketing genius"*: *Hardball*, MSNBC, March 23, 2015.

5 *"fictional presidential campaigns"*: Jeffrey Toobin on *The Situation Room*, CNN, March 23, 2015.

5 *"growing swarm"*: Philip Rucker and Robert Costa, "With Cruz In, Race for GOP Right Heats Up," *Washington Post*, March 23, 2015.

5 *"entire year's salary"*: *Up with Steve Kornacki*, MSNBC, March 21, 2015.

5 oddsmakers were betting: "Odds of Ted Cruz Winning White House Sit at 33–1," *Chicago Sun-Times*, March 23, 2015.

6 *"tired of glib talk"*: Joe McQuaid, "Publisher's Notebook," *New Hampshire Union Leader*, March 23, 2015, 1A.

6 *"just a tease"*: Trump, on *The Kelly File*, Fox News Channel, March 23, 2015.

10 *"germs on your hands"*: Trump interview with Fisher and Kranish.

12 *"The part that"*: Paul Manafort, quoted in "Trump Is Playing a Part and Can Transform for Victory," *Washington Post*, April 21, 2016.

13 *"he might be dating her"*: Karen Attiah interview with Marc Fisher, March 29, 2016. Trump made the comment about dating Ivanka if she were not his daughter on the ABC talk show *The View* on March 6, 2006.

13 *boycott the event*: Rosalind S. Helderman, "Rabbis Organize Boycott of Trump's Speech to Pro-Israel Group," *Washington Post*, March 17, 2016.

13 *"like you folks"*: Ibid.

13 *"beautiful Jewish baby"*: Jenna Johnson, "A New Donald Trump Emerges at AIPAC, Flanked by Teleprompters," *Washington Post*, March 21, 2016.

14 *an unscripted "Yeah"*: David Weigel, "AIPAC's Apology for Trump Speech Is Unprecedented," *Washington Post*, March 22, 2016.

15 *"That window is"*: The Old Post Office was built in 1899.

CHAPTER 1: GOLD RUSH: THE NEW LAND

17 *gold-plated sinks*: "Want Your Own Boeing 727? Donald Trump Is Selling His . . . Cheap!," *Flying With Fish*, November 10, 2009; Hibah Yousuf, "Donald Trump to Personal Jet: 'You're Fired!'" *CNNMoney*, November 10, 2009; and Auslan Cramb, "Donald Trump Flies to Western Isles to Visit Mother's Home," *Telegraph*, June 8, 2008. Note: The 727 Trump used in 2008 is different from the 757 used on the campaign in 2016.

18 *"I feel very comfortable"*: Severin Carrell, "'I Feel Scottish,' Says Donald Trump on Flying Visit to Mother's Cottage," *Guardian*, June 9, 2008.

18 *"I have a lot of money"*: "'I'll Be Back,' Says Trump," *Stornoway Gazette*, June 12, 2008.

18 *luxury hotel*: Ibid.

18 *golf resort*: "Trump Golf Inquiry in Full Swing," BBC News, June 10, 2008.

19 *"creel of seaweed"*: "MacLeod," Tong & Aird Tong Historical Society.

19 *Donald Smith*: Kenneth Maclennan, *Tong: The Story of a Lewis Village* (Tong, UK: Tong Historical Society and the *Stornoway Gazette*, 1984).

19 *143,000 pounds*: Roger Hutchinson, *The Soap Man: Lewis, Harris and Lord Leverhulme* (Edinburgh: Birlinn, 2003).

19 *retail shops*: "Mac Fisheries History," Mac Fisheries Shops, http://www.macfisheries.co.uk/page2.htm.

20 *174 men*: Malcolm Macdonald, "*Iolaire* Disaster." Stornoway Historical Society.

20 *Leverhulme died*: "Lord Leverhulme Dead. Founder of Port Sunlight. Great Captain of Industry," *Argus*, May 8, 1925.

20 *HOLD FAST*: Tony Reid, "The Family History of Mary Anne MacLeod, the Mother of Donald J. Trump," Ancestry.com.

20 *boarded the SS* Transylvania: February 17 and May 2, 1930, manifests of the *Transylvania*, "New York, Passenger Lists, 1820–1957," Ancestry.com.

20 *552 feet*: Premal, *Admiralty Ships/Subs Lost 1939 to 1946*, 515.

21 *Klanbake*: Jim Dwyer, "G.O.P. Path Recalls Democrats' Convention Disaster in 1924," *New York Times*, March 15, 2016.

21 *preferred stock*: S. A. Mathewson, "Now 'National Origins' Fix Quotas for Aliens," *New York Times*, June 30, 1929.

21 *lightning knocked out*: "Sudden Storms Follow Summer Heat Here; Lightning Kills Man, Puts Out Liberty's Torch," *New York Times*, May 2, 1930.

21 *Hoover pinned:* special to *New York Times*, "Worst of Depression Over, Hoover Says," *New York Times*, May 2, 1930.

22 *two or three bedrooms:* Visit to the house by Frances Sellers, *Washington Post*, with Roland Paul, director of the Institut fuer pfaelzische Geschichte und Volks-kunde.

22 *created a* Weinstrasse: http://www.deutsche-weinstrasse.de/.

22 *history of emigration:* Interview in March 2016 with Roland Paul, director of the Institut fuer pfaelzische Geschichte und Volkskunde.

22 *Trumpff:* Freund Archive of online genealogical research, compiled by Christian Freund, great-grandson of Elizabetha Trump Freund, retrieved from the Web by Kallstadt mayor Thomas Jarowek on June 27, 2010; and Gwenda Blair, *The Trumps* (New York: Simon & Schuster, 2000), 26.

23 *Tromp-h:* Interview of Simone Wendel, director of Kings of Kallstadt, by Frances Sellers, *Washington Post*, March 2016.

23 *Immigration records:* Freund Archive, "Passenger List," SS *Eider*, October 15, 1885.

23 *illegal emigrant:* Interview with Paul.

23 *main entry point:* Library of Congress, "Rise of Industrial America, 1876–1900."

24 *thin face:* Friedrich Trump application for passport, May 26, 1904.

24 *Poodle Dog:* An account of Trump's travels West can be found in Blair, *Trumps*, 41–93.

24 *"the Arctic":* *Yukon Sun*, April 17, 1900, https://news.google.com/newspapers?nid =3fE2CSJIrl8C&dat=19000417&printsec=frontpage&hl=en.

25 *On June 6:* Freund Archive.

26 *60 Wall Street:* Blair, *Trumps*, 110.

26 *"vicious spies":* "War Hysteria and the Persecution of German Americans," AuthenticHistory.com; and "Wilson Declares Berlin Is Seeking Deceitful Peace," *New York Times*, June 15, 1917.

27 *and soon died:* Blair, *Trumps*, 116. The account of Friedrich Trump's death was given by Fred Trump in a 1991 interview to biographer Blair.

27 *The population of Queens:* US Census figures, http://www.census.gov/population /www/documentation/twps0076/NYtab.pdf.

28 *the Klan remained prominent:* "Four in Klan Riot Held for Hearing on Police Charge," *New York Daily Star*, June 1, 1927; "Warren Criticizes 'Class' Parades," *New York Times*, June 1, 1927; "Two Fascisti Die in Bronx, Klansman Riot in Queens, in Memorial Day Clashes," *New York Times*, May 31, 1927; and "Warren Ordered Police to Block Parade by Klan," *Brooklyn Daily Eagle*, May 31, 1927. Years later, Donald Trump would assert his father was never arrested. The news-paper accounts show that while his father was arrested, the charge was quickly dismissed and thus had no merit.

28 *Jamaica Estates:* "Jamaica Estates Is Active," *New York Times*, March 22, 1931.

29 *seventy-eight homes:* Richard J. Roth, "Trump the Builder Plays Mothers as Ace Cards," *Brooklyn Daily Eagle*, May 14, 1950.

29 *he planned to marry:* Blair, *Trumps*, 148.

30 *"quicker and larger":* "Trump Expects War Scare Will Aid Homes Sales," *Brooklyn Daily Eagle*, April 23, 1939.

30 *"toy balloon fish":* "Show Boat Tells Bathers about Trump Flatbush Homes," *Brooklyn Daily Eagle,* July 16, 1939.

CHAPTER 2: STINK BOMBS, SWITCHBLADES, AND A THREE-PIECE SUIT

31 *blur of humanity:* Interview with Peter Brant, April 2016.

32 *top five hundred corporations:* Ric Burns documentary *New York: The Center of the World.*

32 *"Trump's dumps on stumps":* Interview with Frank Briggs, April 2016.

32 *$60 a month:* Blair, *Trumps,* 168.

33 *ten-speed Italian racer:* Interview with Steven Nachtigall, April 2016.

33 *deal was off:* Interviews with Chava Ben-Amos and her son, Omri Ben-Amos, April 2016.

33 *"going to tell my dad":* "Donald Trump's Old Queens Neighborhood Contrasts with the Diverse Area around It," *New York Times,* September 22, 2015.

33 *throwing rocks:* Interview with Dennis Burnham, April 2016.

33 *"just kept walking":* Interview with Briggs.

33 *becoming a pilot:* Donald Trump with Tony Schwartz, *Trump: The Art of the Deal* (New York: Ballantine Books, 1987), 70.

33 *entitled "Alone":* 1954 Kew-Forest yearbook, 72.

34 *quiet, sensitive:* Blair, *Trumps,* 231.

34 *"end of Robert's blocks":* Trump and Schwartz, *Art of the Deal* (1987), 72.

34 *"We threw spitballs":* Interview with Paul Onish, April 2016.

34 *a clunk on Donald's head:* Interview with Sharon Mazzarella, April 2016.

34 *"headstrong and determined":* Interview with Ann Trees, April 2016.

34 *"terrifying at that age":* Interview with Nachtigall.

34 *"wasn't malicious":* Trump and Schwartz, *Art of the Deal* (1987), 72.

34 *"very forceful way":* Ibid., 71–72.

35 *recall neither the incident nor Trump's ever mentioning it:* Interviews with Peter Brant, Mark Golding, and Irik Sevin, April 2016.

35 *"very rambunctious":* Trump interview with Fisher and Kranish.

35 *"He was a pain":* "Public Lives: Musical M.C. for Silk Stocking District," *New York Times,* February 23, 2000.

35 *"a little shit":* Interview with Peter Walker, Charles Walker's son, April 2016.

35 *pulling his knees up:* Interview with Brant.

35 *"last man standing":* Interview with Chrisman Scherf, April 2016.

35 *an almost Zen-like ditty:* 1958 Kew-Forest yearbook, 93.

35 *wave at President Eisenhower:* Interview with Brant.

36 *"hit the ball through people":* Interview with Nicholas Kass, April 2016.

36 *"guns a-blazing":* Interview with Brant.

36 *too lost in his fury:* Interview with Jeff Bier, April 2016.

36 *cheaper model:* Interview with Brant.

36 *drive them on their routes:* Blair, *Trumps,* 229.

36 *take Donald with him:* Trump and Schwartz, *Art of the Deal* (1987), 74; and interviews with Brant and Briggs.

36 *had enough toilets:* Interview with Florence Boyar, April 2016.

37 *having them mixed:* Tracie Rozhon, "Fred C. Trump, Post-War Master of Housing for Middle Class, Dies at 93," *New York Times,* July 26, 1999.

37 *about catching germs:* Trump interview with Fisher and Kranish.

37 *"king" and . . . "killer":* Harry Hurt III, *Lost Tycoon: The Many Lives of Donald J. Trump* (New York: W. W. Norton, 1993), 13.

37 *urban Davy Crocketts:* Interview with Brant.

38 *eleven-inch blades:* Blair, *Trumps,* 233.

38 *"That's crazy":* Trump interview with Fisher and Kranish.

38 *was stunned:* Interview with Brant.

38 *swim to freedom:* Interview with Vincent Cunningham, April 2016.

39 *Mussolini's dead body:* Michael D'Antonio, *Never Enough: Donald Trump and the Pursuit of Success* (New York: Thomas Dunne Books, 2015), 42.

39 *set up a boxing ring:* "I Showered with Donald Trump at Military School," *Daily Beast,* March 28, 2016.

39 *"fucking prick":* "The Men Who Gave Trump His Brutal Worldview," *Politico,* March 29, 2016.

39 *"At the beginning":* Interview with Theodore Dobias, November 2015.

39 *summer resort hotel:* Samuel J. Rogal, *The American Pre-College Military School* (Jefferson, NC: McFarland, 2009), 10.

39 *A dirty uniform:* "General Order No. 6: Scale of Punishment," New York Military Academy.

40 *white glove:* Interview with Peter Ticktin, April 2016.

40 *enough to lower a grade:* Interview with Wayne Akstin, April 2016.

40 *film included starlets:* Interview with David M. Smith, April 2016.

40 *Fred arrived in a limousine:* Ibid.

40 *Hazing was a part:* Interviews with Michael Pitkow and Lee Ains, April 2016.

40 *"on the ass":* Interview with Michael Scadron, November 2015.

40 *medals for neatness:* The Shrapnel, New York Military Academy yearbook, 1964, 105.

40 *pride in his grades:* Trump and Schwartz, *Art of the Deal* (1987), 74; and interview with Smith.

41 *"going to be famous":* Interview with Jeff Orteneau, April 2016.

41 *wealth doubled:* Interview with Smith.

41 *"He was self-confident":* Interview with Michael Pitkow, November 2015.

41 *"going to the beach":* Interview with Smith.

41 *"beautiful, gorgeous women":* Interview with George White (birth name George Witek), November 2015.

41 *"dog":* Interview with George White, April 2016.

41 *double dates:* Interviews with Ernie Kirk, November 2015 and April 2016.

41 *struck on the backside:* Interview with cadet who was punished, May 2016. Cadet also recounted this incident in an affidavit connected to an unrelated lawsuit.

42 *second-floor window:* Interview with Ted Levine, May 2016.

42 *"Trump swings . . . then HITS":* The Shrapnel, New York Military Academy yearbook, 1962.

42 *"I thought it was amazing":* D'Antonio, *Never Enough,* 46.

42 *"it was the only thing"*: Ibid., 43.

42 *"big, strong kid"*: Interview with Gerald Paige, April 2016.

43 *angry that he left:* Interview with Levine.

43 *concentrate on academics:* Interview with John Cino, April 2016.

43 *"could always go to Donald"*: Interview with Jack Serafin, April 2016.

43 *"You had to have thick skin"*: Interview with Cunningham.

43 *Klan was coming to get him:* Interview with David Prince Thomas, April 2016.

43 *"almost socially accepted"*: Interview with Ticktin.

43 *Barry Goldwater:* Interview with Roger Stone, April 2016.

44 *I LIKE IKE button:* Interview with Brant.

44 *New York's Democratic establishment:* Blair, *Trumps*, 212.

44 *beating him with a stick:* Interview with Michael Scadron, April 2016.

44 *"even-keeled"*: Interview with Ticktin.

44 *shoved a new cadet:* Interview with Lee Ains and another cadet, who asked to remain anonymous, November 2015.

44 *relieved Trump of duty:* Interviews with Lee Ains, William Specht, George White, David Smith, Ernie Kirk, Theodore Dobias, and Peter Ticktin.

44 *"why I got elevated"*: Interview with Donald Trump, December 2015.

45 *Francis Cardinal Spellman:* D'Antonio, *Never Enough*, 43.

45 *"You know what, Ace?"*: Interview with Serafin. Serafin recounted a story told to him by Helen Castellano, the wife of Anthony Castellano.

45 *follow his father:* Interview with Smith.

45 *educational draft deferments:* Selective Service records for Donald J. Trump.

45 *to be closer to home:* Trump and Schwartz, *Art of the Deal* (1987), 77.

45 *$5.7 million:* "Brooklyn Firm Buys Swifton Village," *Cincinnati Enquirer*, April 15, 1964.

45 *"He'd get in there and work with us"*: "From Swifton Village to Trump Tower," *Cincinnati Enquirer*, June 28, 1990.

45 *sunny and cloudless: New York Times*, November 22, 1964.

45 *"Nobody even mentioned"*: "Verrazano Bridge Opened to Traffic," *New York Times*, November 22, 1964.

45 *wealth was evident:* Interviews with Don Robinson and Robert Klein, April 2016.

46 *three-piece suit:* Interview with John P. Cifichiello, April 2016.

46 *Donald's doodles:* Interview with Klein.

46 *eager learner:* Interviews with Richard O'Donnell and Don Robinson, April 2016.

46 *Rich Marrin, a teammate:* Gwenda Blair, *The Trumps: Three Generations of Builders and a Presidential Candidate* (New York: Simon & Schuster, 2015).

46 *golf clubs on the side of the road:* Interview with squash player who spoke on the condition of remaining anonymous, April 2016.

47 *belonged at an Ivy League school:* Interview with Brian Fitzgibbon, April 2016.

47 *without saying good-bye:* Interview with O'Donnell.

47 *blond mop of hair:* Louis Calomaris interview with *Washington Post*, April 2016.

47 *"Perhaps the most important thing"*: Trump and Schwartz, *Art of the Deal* (1987), 77.

47 *first in the class:* William D. Cohan, "Decades-Old Questions about Trump's Wealth and Education," *New York Times*, September 28, 2015.

48 *honor roll printed:* "Wharton Schools Reveal Dean's List for 1967–68," *Daily Pennsylvanian*, October 25, 1968.

48 *"Trump was not":* Interview with Calomaris.

48 *anti–Vietnam War protests:* "Air Force, Penn End Spice Rack," *Daily Pennsylvanian*, September 13, 1967.

48 *university contracts:* Alison D. Graham, "A Brief History of Global Engagement at the University of Pennsylvania: International Crisis, the War in Viet Nam," UPenn Archives, 2007.

48 *"would have gladly served":* Quoted in Craig Whitlock, "Questions Linger about Trump's Draft Deferments during Vietnam War," *Washington Post*, July 21, 2015.

48 *"sniveled every Monday":* Terry Farrell interview with *Washington Post*, April 2016.

49 *looking to buy apartments:* Bill Specht interview with *Washington Post*, April 2016.

49 *"He was wearing":* Maggie Parker, "Candice Bergen Says Her Date with Donald Trump Was 'Short'—but She Does Remember His Burgundy Limo," *People*, February 12, 2016.

49 *"dating guys from Paris":* Matt Viser, "Even in College, Donald Trump Was Brash," *Boston Globe*, August 28, 2015.

49 *"I don't know why":* Greg Stone, "Trump Towers over East; Shies Away from East," *Daily Pennsylvanian*, November 24, 1987.

50 *"next Bill Zeckendorf":* Interview with Calomaris.

CHAPTER 3: FATHER AND SON

51 *They condemned:* "Begin Action to Clear Coney Island Area for Housing Project," *Brooklyn Daily Eagle*, December 2, 1960.

51 *thirty-eight hundred apartments:* Kareen Fahim, "Brooklyn Towers Have Trump Name but No Limos," *New York Times*, April 8, 2010.

52 *shag carpeted:* Philip Weiss, "The Lives They Lived: Fred C. Trump, b. 1905," *New York Times*, January 2, 2000.

53 *"become a nothing":* Fred C. Trump, 1985 Horatio Alger Award Winner video, https://www.youtube.com/watch?v=BaWPTdme2_U.

53 *"my standing and reputation":* Associated Press, "Tenafly Builder Balks at Inquiry," *New York Times*, July 13, 1954.

53 *$1.8 million:* Edith Evans Asbury, "Housing Windfall Yielded 1.8 Million, Inquiry Here Told," *New York Times*, January 27, 1966.

54 *"Old Man Trump":* Will Kaufman, "Woody Guthrie, 'Old Man Trump,' and a Real Estate Empire's Racist Foundations," The Conversation.com.

55 *Hoyt was allowed:* Interview with Sheila Hoyt Morse by Michael Kranish, *Washington Post*; and *United States of America v. Fred C. Trump, et al.*

55 *"immediately rent":* USA v. Trump, "Plaintiff's Answers," March 6, 1974.

56 *Goldweber won a plum spot:* Interview with Elyse Goldweber by Michael Kranish and Robert O'Harrow, *Washington Post*, January 11, 2016.

56 *1 to 3.5 percent:* September 24, 1973, memo to Attorney General Elliot Richardson, from *USA v. Trump.*

56 *"No. 9":* USA v. Trump, "Plaintiff's Answers," March 6, 1974, 8.

57 *Spiro remembered:* Interview with Phyllis Spiro by Robert O'Harrow, *Washington Post;* and *USA v. Trump.*

57 *"absolutely ridiculous":* Morris Kaplan, "Major Landlord Accused of Antiblack Bias in City," *New York Times,* October 16, 1973.

58 *his routine of going to lunch:* Interview with Anthony Russo by Paul Schwartzman, *Washington Post,* April 2016.

58 *"real reason":* Trump and Schwartz, *Art of the Deal* (1987), 78.

59 *rent-control laws:* Wayne Barrett, *Trump: The Deals and the Downfall* (New York: HarperCollins, 1992), 84.

CHAPTER 4: ROY COHN AND THE ART OF THE COUNTERATTACK

60 *"13 princes":* David A. Andelman, "Le Club, Restaurant of the Jet Set, Cited for Health Code Violations," *New York Times,* July 9, 1974.

60 *"beautiful women":* Donald Trump and Tony Schwartz, *Trump: Art of the Deal* (New York: Ballantine Books Trade Paperback ed., 2015), 93–98.

61 *communists had infiltrated:* Sidney Zion, *The Autobiography of Roy Cohn* (Secaucus, NJ: Lyle Stuart, 1988), 47–51.

61 *"from the mob":* Ibid., 60.

61 *prosecution of Julius and Ethel Rosenberg:* Ibid., 77.

62 *"wreck the army":* "The Self-Inflated Target," *Time,* March 22, 1954.

62 *"better cause":* Zion, *Autobiography,* 81.

63 *"don't like lawyers":* Trump and Schwartz, *Art of the Deal* (2015), 93–98.

64 *"hands down":* Ken Auletta, "Don't Mess with Roy Cohn," *Esquire,* December 5, 1978, 41.

64 *"never really knew":* Trump and Schwartz, *Art of the Deal* (2015), 93–98.

64 *"Prospective clients who":* Auletta, "Don't Mess with Roy Cohn," 41.

64 *"two-faced":* Trump and Schwartz, *Art of the Deal* (2015), 93–99.

65 *He sought $100 million:* Barbara Campbell, "Realty Company Asks $100 Million 'Bias' Damages," *New York Times,* December 13, 1973.

65 *"I have never":* Donald Trump affidavit, December 11, 1973, in *United States of America v. Fred and Donald Trump and Trump Management,* Case 75-C-1529.

65 *"these initial headlines":* Roy Cohn affidavit, December 11, 1973, in *USA v. Fred and Donald Trump.*

66 *"The defendants have refused":* USA v. Fred and Donald Trump, US Courthouse, Brooklyn, NY, January 25, 1974, accessed via National Archives.

66 *"hot-tempered":* Roy Cohn letter to Elyse Goldweber, April 17, 1974, *USA v. Fred and Donald Trump.*

66 *he was "unfamiliar":* Wayne Barrett, "Like Father, Like Son," *Village Voice,* January 15, 1979.

67 *"the nature of Gestapo tactics":* USA v. Fred and Donald Trump, October 24, 1974.

67 *find Goldstein in contempt:* Goldstein, who was a California Superior Court judge when the *Post* sought to reach her in 2016, declined comment.

67 *"pay for it?"*: *USA v. Fred and Donald Trump*, June 10, 1975.

68 *"many, many landlords"*: Trump interview with Fisher and Kranish.

68 *Newspaper headlines echoed*: "Minorities Win Housing Suit," *New York Amsterdam News*, July 9, 1975.

68 *"rough piece"*: Donald Trump interview with Marc Fisher and Michael Kranish, *Washington Post*, June 9, 2016.

68 *Fred was livid*: Karen DeYoung, "N.Y. Owner of P.G. Units Seized in Code Violations," *Washington Post*, September 30, 1976.

68 *$3,640 fine*: Prince George's County district court records, May 3, 1977.

68 *"terrible"*: Elizabeth Becker, "Apartment Rentals Halted Until Repairs Are Made," *Washington Post*, October 29, 1976.

68 *he "never knew"*: Trump interview with Fisher and Kranish, June 9, 2016.

69 *"unavailable"*: US v. Trump, "Motion for Supplemental Relief," March 7, 1978.

69 *"tall, lean and blond"*: Judy Klemesrud, "Donald Trump, Real Estate Promoter, Builds Image as He Buys Buildings," *New York Times*, November 1, 1976.

69 *$24,594*: State of New Jersey, Department of Law and Public Safety, Division of Gaming Enforcement, "In re the application of Trump Plaza Corp. for a casino license," report to the Casino Control Commission, October 17, 1981.

CHAPTER 5: CROSSING THE BRIDGE

70 *cost of city services soared*: Barrett, *Trump*, 103.

70 *"hooked on heroin"*: Felix G. Rohatyn, *Dealings: A Political and Financial Life* (New York: Simon & Schuster, 2010), 124.

70 *World War II*: William G. Connolly, "In Hotels, the Key Is Occupancy, and It Is Up a Little," *New York Times*, December 17, 1972.

70 *Trump family business*: Barrett, *Trump*, 103.

70 *sellers in California, Nevada*: Marilyn Bender, "The Empire and Ego of Donald Trump," *New York Times*, August 7, 1983.

70 *invest in Manhattan*: Robert O'Harrow Jr., "Trump Swam in Mob-Infested Waters in Early Years as an NYC Developer," *Washington Post*, October 16, 2015.

70 *with each lot*: D'Antonio, *Never Enough*, 76.

71 *fifty-three banks*: Robert E. Bedingfield, "Penn Central and Banks Reach Loan Pact," *New York Times*, May 25, 1971.

71 *fielded interest*: Youssef M. Ibrahim, "Mideast Bid for 3 New York Hotels," *New York Times*, May 5, 1978.

71 *Multiple offers*: Connolly, "In Hotels, the Key Is Occupancy."

71 *single bid*: Philip Greer, "Penn Central Bids Are Low: Railroad May Seek More Funds," *Washington Post*, October 16, 1971.

71 *have the financing*: Timothy L. O'Brien, *TrumpNation: The Art of Being The Donald* (New York: Business Plus, 2005), 61.

71 *turned the gift down*: Ibid., 261.

71 *"my complete backing"*: Barrett, *Trump*, 94.

71 *initially opposed*: Wayne Barrett, "Donald Trump Cuts the Cards: The Deals of a Young Power Broker," *Village Voice*, January 22, 1979.

72 *without any indictments*: Barrett, *Trump*, 102.

72 *any quid pro quo:* Ibid., 114; and "Behind the Seventies-Era Deals That Made Donald Trump," *Village Voice*, February 1979.

72 *same opportunity:* Wayne Barrett, "Behind the Seventies-Era Deals That Made Donald Trump," *Village Voice*, February 1979.

72 *creating an empire:* Robert D. McFadden, "Penn Central Yards' Sale Is Approved by U.S. Court," *New York Times*, March 11, 1975.

72 *the plan soon collapsed:* O'Brien, *TrumpNation*, 60.

72 *Trump now held the option:* Bender, "Empire and Ego of Donald Trump."

72 *except the candidate's brother:* Howard Blum, "Trump: The Development of a Manhattan Developer," *New York Times*, August 26, 1980.

72 *with DJT plates:* Klemesrud, "Donald Trump, Real Estate Promoter."

72 *blue Cadillac:* Paul Schwartzman, "Trump Left His Mark All Over New York. Some in the City Would Like to Erase It," *Washington Post*, October 7, 2015.

72 *"Donald's credibility factor":* Interview with Louise Sunshine, April 2016.

72 *flexing his connections:* Interview with Peter Goldmark, May 4, 2016.

73 *barely a tenth:* Former deputy mayor Peter J. Solomon, quoted in Blum, "Trump."

73 *Javits Convention Center:* Charles Kaiser, "Koch Said to Have Chosen 34th St. as Site of New Convention Center," *New York Times*, March 31, 1978.

73 *"came to me properly":* Trump, quoted in Blum, "Trump."

73 *Winning the right:* Barrett, *Trump*, 103.

73 *coursed through the subway lines:* Edward C. Burks, "15 Busiest Subway Stations Show Big Decline in Riders," *New York Times*, November 10, 1975.

73 *fleeing to the suburbs:* Ibid.

73 *New York's largest:* Connolly, "In Hotels, the Key Is Occupancy."

73 *business gutted:* Ibid.

74 *Relaxation Plus:* Ibid.

74 *"what the Plus meant":* Olivia Nuzzi, "Trump Lies So Much Less to NY Mega-Rich," *Daily Beast*, April 15, 2016.

74 *in other words, nothing:* Connolly, "In Hotels, the Key Is Occupancy."

74 *at Madison Square Garden:* Glenn Fowler, "Commodore Plan Is Called Unfair," *New York Times*, April 9, 1976.

74 *biggest development headaches:* D'Antonio, *Never Enough*, 56.

74 *"a seat on the* Titanic*":* Trump and Schwartz, *Art of the Deal* (1987), 121.

74 *"best place to live":* Trump and Schwartz, *Art of the Deal* (2015), 102.

74 *venture collapsed:* Barrett, *Deals and the Downfall*, 147.

74 *no hotel in New York:* Alan S. Oser, "Hotel Dispute Focuses on Tax Abatements," *New York Times*, April 27, 1976.

75 *father's company:* State of New Jersey, Department of Law and Public Safety, Division of Gaming, Enforcement Report to the Casino Control Commission, October 16, 1981, PDF36.

75 *not yet secured:* Trump and Schwartz, *Art of the Deal* (1987), 128.

75 *$10 million property:* Ibid., 123.

75 *to hire an architect:* O'Brien, *TrumpNation*, 61.

75 *aging hotel's steel bones:* Robert E. Tomasson, "Deal Negotiated for Commodore," *New York Times*, May 4, 1975.

75 *to pay the $250,000:* Trump with Schwartz, *Art of the Deal* (1987), 134.

75 *deal with Hyatt to closure:* Ibid.

75 *"shove it":* Trump and Schwartz, *Art of the Deal* (2015), 130.

75 *commercial property:* "Estimate Board to Rule on Easing of Tax Allowing Commodore Transformation," *New York Times,* March 3, 1976.

75 *properties tax-exempt:* Barrett, *Trump,* 121.

75 *ninety-nine years:* Charles Kaiser, "Financing Arranged for the Commodore," *New York Times,* December 23, 1977.

75 *forty years:* David Cay Johnston, "21 Questions for Donald Trump," *The National Memo,* July 10, 2015.

76 *walked out of the office:* Interview with Richard Ravitch, 2016.

76 *deserved a helping hand:* Fowler, "Commodore Plan Is Called Unfair."

76 *Commodore would rot:* "3 Lawmakers Are Critical of Commodore Tax Relief," *New York Times,* April 26, 1976.

76 *dirty scrap wood:* D'Antonio, *Never Enough,* 103.

76 *other investors were interested:* Carter B. Horsley, "New Offer Is Made for the Commodore," *New York Times,* April 10, 1976.

76 *"first-class" hotel:* State of New Jersey, Department of Law and Public Safety, Division of Gaming, Enforcement Report to the Casino Control Commission, October 16, 1981, PDF50.

77 *tax credits:* Klemesrud, "Donald Trump, Real Estate Promoter."

77 *"$200 million":* Ibid.

77 *Fred's control:* Harry Hurt III, *Lost Tycoon: The Many Lives of Donald J. Trump* (New York: W. W. Norton, 1993), 84.

77 *that trust alone:* State of New Jersey, October 16, 1981, PDF50.

77 *"to fire you":* Interview with Ravitch. Decades after the difficult meeting with Ravitch, Trump still nursed the grudge. In 2009, when New York governor David Paterson appointed Ravitch as his lieutenant governor, Trump wrote to the governor, calling Ravitch "extremely weak, ineffective and a poor negotiator." Through the years, Ravitch refrained from responding publicly to Trump, he said, because "my guiding principle is you don't get into pissing contests with skunks."

78 *at Roy Cohn's law firm:* Interview with Stanley Friedman, 2016.

78 *uptown from the Commodore:* Klemesrud, "Donald Trump, Real Estate Promoter."

78 *sparse furnishings:* Interview with Scadron.

78 *"each other":* Ibid.

79 *"the top models":* Trump and Schwartz, *Art of the Deal* (1987), 19.

79 *to the West:* D'Antonio, *Never Enough,* 119.

79 *"griping and bitching":* Donald Trump, *The Art of the Comeback* (New York: Times Books/Random House, 1997), 147.

79 *"couldn't have both":* Donald Trump and Charles Leerhsen, *Trump: Surviving at the Top* (New York: Random House, 1990), 53.

79 *"just a nice all-American kid":* Ivana Trump, *The Best Is Yet to Come: Coping with Divorce and Enjoying Life Again* (New York: Simon & Schuster, 1995), 65.

79 *Tiffany diamond ring:* Hurt, *Lost Tycoon*, 104.

80 *as many as four or five contracts:* Barrett, *Trump*, 5.

80 *after the wedding:* Ibid., 137.

80 *"a grave threat":* Zion, *Autobiography*, 236.

80 *"supermodels getting screwed":* Quoted in O'Brien, *TrumpNation*, 53.

81 *"just a lawyer":* Trump interview with Fisher and Kranish.

81 *"his greatest student":* Paul Schwartzman, "How Trump Got Religion—and Why His Legendary Minister's Son Now Rejects Him," *Washington Post*, January 21, 2016.

81 *"our time":* Ibid.

81 *"I never think of the negative":* New York Times, August 7, 1983.

81 *two hundred people attended:* D'Antonio, *Never Enough*, 123.

82 *"next something":* Interview with Friedman.

82 *"pushing the baby carriage":* Trump interview with Fisher and Kranish.

82 *"no idea what to do":* Jonathan Van Meter, "Growing Up Trump," *New York*, December 13, 2004.

82 *"on his terms":* Donald Trump Jr. interview with Dan Zak, *Washington Post*, April 2016.

82 *"It was unheard of for a businessman":* Nikki Haskell interview with Karen Heller, *Washington Post*, April 13, 2016.

83 *the rats survived:* Barbara Res interview with Drew Harwell, *Washington Post*, March 2016.

83 *"Keep records of everything":* Ibid.

83 *dollar each:* Interview with Scadron.

83 *back to his apartment:* Trump and Schwartz, *Art of the Deal* (1987), 123.

84 *"always go":* Klemesrud, "Donald Trump, Real Estate Promoter."

84 *"collecting rents":* Trump and Schwartz, *Art of the Deal* (1987), 107.

84 *the dreary area:* Carter B. Horsley, "In Environs of Grand Central, New Strength," *New York Times*, April 30, 1978.

84 *profit-sharing deal:* Geraldine Baum, Tom Hamburger, and Michael J. Mishak, "Trump Has Thrived with Government's Generosity," *LA Times*, May 11, 2011.

84 *shortchanged the city:* Ibid.

84 *did not remember:* Ibid.

85 *personally guaranteed:* Mark Singer, "Trump Solo," *New Yorker*, May 19, 1997.

85 *"Oh, I love that site":* Interview with Sunshine.

85 *most pivotal blocks:* Trump and Schwartz, *Art of the Deal* (1987), 151.

85 *"anywhere in the world":* Jonathan Mandell, "Raising Trump's Tower: How a Cast of Thousands Built One Man's Answer to the Pyramids," *New York Sunday News*, February 13, 1983.

85 *a 50 percent stake:* "Trump Pursued a 'Vision' of Tower with Tenacity," *New York Times*, August 26, 1980.

86 *"shimmering sides":* Ada Louise Huxtable, "Architecture View: A New York Blockbuster of Superior Design," *New York Times*, July 1, 1979.

86 *public spaces such as atriums:* Anthony DePalma, "Mixed Results Seen in City's Public Spaces Program," *New York Times*, November 2, 1983.

86 *fifty-eight stories:* Huxtable, "Architecture View."

86 *wrote in 1930:* Christopher Gray, "The Store That Slipped through the Cracks," *New York Times*, October 3, 2014.

86 *would cooperate, too:* Interview with Penelope Hunter-Stiebel, 2016.

87 *"destroy them":* Interview with Robert Miller, 2016.

87 *"question of trust":* Interview with Kent Barwick, 2016.

87 *historic preservationists:* Trump interview with Fisher and Kranish.

87 *"were nothing":* Graydon Carter, "Donald Trump Gets What He Wants," *GQ*, May 1984.

88 *"junk":* Lee Wohlfert-Wihlborg, "In the Manhattan Real Estate Game, Billionaire Donald Trump Holds the Winning Cards," *People*, November 16, 1981.

88 *a carved ivory frieze:* David Remnick, ed., *The New Gilded Age*: The New Yorker *Looks at the Culture of Affluence* (New York: Random House, 2000).

88 *wrecking balls or dynamite:* Suzanne Daley, "Bonwit Building Set for the Ultimate Sale," *New York Times*, March 16, 1980.

88 *threatened with deportation:* Dean Baquet, "Trump Says He Didn't Know He Employed Illegal Aliens," *New York Times*, July 13, 1990.

88 *back payments:* Ibid.

88 *He blamed Kaszycki & Sons:* Ibid.

88 *sealed in 1999:* Tom Robbins, "Deal Sealed in Trump Tower Suit," *New York Daily News*, March 8, 1999.

88 *"U.S. taxpayers":* Donald Trump, *Time to Get Tough: Making America #1 Again* (Washington, DC: Regnery Publishing, 2011).

89 *leave a stain:* Interview with Res.

89 *in charge of all construction:* Ibid.

89 *wasn't for women:* Ibid.

89 *was so demanding:* Mandell, "Raising Trump's Tower."

90 *"construction industry in New York":* O'Harrow, "Trump Swam in Mob-Infested Waters."

90 *accommodate the pool:* Barbara Res, *All Alone on the 68th Floor* (CreateSpace Independent Publishing Platform, 2013), 169.

90 *$150,000:* Verina Hixon deposition, September 8, 1989.

90 *deliveries to the building stopped:* Interview with Res.

91 *"invite me":* Verina Hixon deposition, May 8, 1986.

91 *seized her Trump Tower apartments:* D'Antonio, *Never Enough*, 135. Hixon could not be reached for comment.

91 *on track:* O'Harrow, "Trump Swam in Mob-Infested Waters."

91 *"through Roy Cohn":* Ibid.

91 *"real scum":* O'Brien, *TrumpNation*, 70.

91 *$13 million:* William E. Geist, "The Expanding Empire of Donald Trump," *New York Times*, April 8, 1984.

91 *"driving Rolls-Royces":* Tracie Rozhon, "A Win by Trump! No, by Tenants!; Battle of the 80's Ends, with Glad-Handing All Around," *New York Times*, March 26, 1998.

91 *declined the generous offer:* Richard Haitch, "Follow Up on the News; Shelter Game," *New York Times*, May 29, 1983.

91 *ratty tinfoil:* Carter, "Donald Trump Gets What He Wants."

92 *he denied all:* Ron Suskind, "Trump Eviction Dispute Taken to State Hearing," *New York Times*, February 28, 1985.

92 *"low threshold for pain":* Jonathan Mahler, "Tenants Thwarted Donald Trump's Central Park Real Estate Ambitions," *New York Times*, April 18, 2016.

92 *After a five-year standoff:* George James, "Trump Drops 5-Year Effort to Evict Tenants," *New York Times*, March 5, 1986.

93 *burned through people:* Stephen Ifshin, interview with Bob Woodward, *Washington Post*, May 2016. Trump confirmed Ifshin's account in an interview with Fisher and Kranish, *Washington Post*, June 2016.

93 *later renamed Trump Parc East:* Trump Parc East promotional website, http://www.trump.com/real-estate-portfolio/new-york/trump-parc-east/.

93 *thirteenth floor:* Mahler, "Tenants Thwarted Donald Trump's."

93 *family business:* Trump and Schwartz, *Art of the Deal* (1987), 70.

93 *father's first and middle names:* Rozhon, "Fred C. Trump."

93 *joined his father:* D'Antonio, *Never Enough,* 58.

93 *being wasteful:* Gwenda Blair, *The Trumps: Three Generations of Builders and a Presidential Candidate* (New York: Simon & Schuster, 2015), 244.

93 *didn't appreciate him:* Jason Horowitz, "For Donald Trump, Lessons from a Brother's Suffering," *New York Times*, January 2, 2016.

93 *Century speedboat:* Ibid.

93 *"a killer":* Hurt, *"Lost Tycoon: The Many Lives of Donald J. Trump"* (New York: W. W. Norton, 1993), 126.

94 *Fred and Mary:* Horowitz, "For Donald Trump, Lessons."

94 *"driving a bus":* Marie Brenner, "After the Gold Rush," *Vanity Fair*, September 1990.

94 *Brooklyn apartment complexes:* State of New Jersey. Department of Law and Public Safety, Division of Gaming Enforcement, Report to the Casino Control Commission, October 16, 1981, PDF24.

94 *"a good thing for him":* Horowitz, "For Donald Trump, Lessons."

94 *Lutheran cemetery:* FindaGrave.com burial records, http://www.findagrave.com/cgi-bin/fg.cgi?page=gr&GRid=105719907.

94 *"I've been through":* O'Brien, *TrumpNation,* 189.

94 *"one hundred percent":* Barrett, *Trump,* 4.

94 *"out of you":* Wohlfert-Wihlborg, "In the Manhattan Real Estate Game."

94 *sold for a combined $277 million:* Carter, "Donald Trump Gets What He Wants."

94 *join them for a tour:* Interview with Res.

94 *"to the public":* D'Antonio, *Never Enough,* 138.

94 *"sell them a fantasy":* "Sell Them a Fantasy; Says Donald Trump. And Every Day, He Does," *New York Times*, April 8, 1984.

94 *wealthy foreigners:* Res, *All Alone on the 68th Floor,* 164.

95 *in his closet:* D'Antonio, *Never Enough,* 140.

95 *Charles, Prince of Wales:* Albin Krebs and Robert McG. Thomas Jr., "Notes on People," *New York Times*, August 4, 1981.

95 *never showed:* Mandell, "Raising Trump's Tower."

95 *"didn't hurt us":* Trump and Schwartz, *Art of the Deal* (1987), 183–84.

95 *$1 million a year:* Marilyn Bender, "The Empire and Ego of Donald Trump," *New York Times*, August 7, 1983.

95 *middle-American tourists:* D'Antonio, *Never Enough*, 146.

95 *father's help:* Barrett, *Deals and the Downfall*, 299.

95 *"in some years":* Paul Goldberger, "Architecture: Atrium of Trump Tower Is a Pleasant Surprise," *New York Times*, April 4, 1983.

96 *"passing the day":* Res, *All Alone on the 68th Floor*, 161.

96 *mahogany desk:* Interview with Res.

96 *the Plaza and Central Park:* "Donald Trump's Tour of His Manhattan Office," *Wall Street Journal*, September 13, 2015.

96 *at least for a time:* "Sell Them a Fantasy."

96 *marriage fell apart:* Barrett, *Trump*, 5.

96 *blue onyx:* O'Brien, *TrumpNation*, 71.

96 *"darkest Africa":* Ibid., 231.

96 *own elevator:* Carter, "Donald Trump Gets What He Wants."

96 *stayed in Queens:* Interview with Res.

96 *"what people want":* Carter, "Donald Trump Gets What He Wants."

96 *actually paid:* "Sell Them a Fantasy."

96 *"I believe in spending":* O'Brien, *TrumpNation*, 196.

96 *$8.5 million loan:* Christopher Boyd, "Sweet Deal: $2,811 Cash Gave Trump $10 Million Mar-A-Lago," *Miami Herald*, November 9, 1988.

96 *"Every lender was a starfucker":* Interview with Drew Harwell, *Washington Post*, April 2016.

97 *Upper West Side:* Timothy L. O'Brien, "How Trump Bungled the Deal of a Lifetime," *Bloomberg View*, January 27, 2016.

97 *tallest building:* "Trump Planning 66th St. Tower, Tallest in World," *New York Times*, November 19, 1985.

97 *Rockefeller Center:* Ibid.

97 *"grandest plan yet":* Ibid.

97 *hell of a fight:* "West Siders Voice Concern on Plan," *New York Times*, November 19, 1985.

97 *"bid for immortality":* "The Next Trump Tower and Its Shadow," *New York Times*, November 21, 1985.

97 *Opponents lined up:* "Celebrities Open Wallets to Fight Trump's Project," *New York Times*, September 30, 1987.

97 *"piggy, piggy, piggy":* Margot Hornblower, "In the Shadow of the Boom; Recovery Strains New York City's Physical and Social Fabric," *Washington Post*, August 24, 1987.

97 *half the density:* Interview with Robinson, 2015.

97 *"This is brilliant!":* Ibid.

97 *did not respond:* Interview with Roberta Gratz, 2016.

98 *"twice blessed":* Joyce Purnick, "Trump Offers to Rebuild Skating Rink," *New York Times*, May 31, 1986.

98 *outside the rink:* Interview with Henry Stern, 2016.

98 *on the cover:* Thomas Maier, *Newhouse: All the Glitter, Power, and Glory of Ameri-*

ca's Richest Media Empire and the Secretive Man Behind It (New York: St. Martin's Press, 1994), 192.

99 *"lack of shame"*: Jonathan Yardley, "Trump, the Artless Hustler," *Washington Post*, December 2, 1987.

99 *hardcover copies*: Interview with Peter Osnos, 2016.

99 *publicity blitz*: Gwenda Blair, *Donald Trump: The Candidate* (New York: Simon & Schuster, 2007), xiii.

99 *were the best*: Interview with Res.

100 *"job for life"*: Res, *All Alone on the 68th Floor*, 181.

100 *three security guards*: Steve Bollenbach interview with Bob Woodward, 2016.

100 *had stayed open*: Interview with Res.

100 *"chew the fat"*: Ibid.

100 *through a straw*: Barrett, *Trump*, 3.

100 *his executive assistant*: Interview with Res.

100 *"Don't go in there"*: Ibid.

100 *"something else"*: *Savvy Woman* magazine, November 1989.

100 *"have his way"*: Otto Friedrich, "Flashy Symbol of an Acquisitive Age: Donald Trump," *Time*, January 16, 1989.

100 *even Res, the engineer*: D'Antonio, *Never Enough*, 199.

101 *"being a cartoon"*: Interview with Res.

101 *"The show is"*: Singer, "Trump Solo."

CHAPTER 6: "BEST SEX I'VE EVER HAD"

102 *Somewhere in these stacks*: Wayne Barrett interview with Robert O'Harrow and Will Hobson, *Washington Post*, March 2016.

102 *city wracked by corruption*: Ibid.

103 *"Wayne! This is Donald"*: Barrett, "Like Father, Like Son."

103 *"never spoken"*: Interview with Barrett.

103 *carrot and stick*: Barrett, "Like Father, Like Son."

103 *"I'll sue"*: Ibid.

103 *go to the opera*: Interview with Barrett.

103 *"worth it"*: Barrett, "Like Father, Like Son."

104 *damage the reporter had inflicted*: Interview with Barrett.

105 *"effective form of promotion"*: Trump and Schwartz, *Art of the Deal* (1987), 56–58.

105 *Zeckendorf employed*: D'Antonio, *Never Enough*, 48–49.

105 *Trump was flattered*: Bender, "Empire and Ego of Donald Trump."

105 *Judy Klemesrud*: Klemesrud, "Donald Trump, Real Estate Promoter."

106 *"He was an outsider"*: Interview with Paul Goldberger by Will Hobson, *Washington Post*, April 2016.

106 *communist sympathizers*: Nicholas Von Hoffman, *Citizen Cohn* (New York: Doubleday, 1988), 76.

106 *Si Newhouse*: Ibid., 419.

106 New York Daily Mirror: Steven Cuozzo, *It's Alive: How America's Oldest Newspaper Cheated Death and Why It Matters* (New York: Times Books, 1996), 10.

119 *"every hot woman"*: Sue Carswell interview with Will Hobson, *Washington Post*, April 2016.

119 *"anonymous tipster"*: Linda Stasi interview with Will Hobson, *Washington Post*, April 2016.

120 *"three other girlfriends"*: Recording of call from John Miller to Sue Carswell, obtained by *Washington Post*, May 2016.

120 *"the greatest thing"*: Interview with Res.

120 *Donald's mistress*: Barrett, *Trump*, 13.

120 *"a feeding frenzy"*: Interview with Trump Jr.

120 *"irresistible macho guy"*: Interview with Taylor.

121 *"one-day wonder"*: John Taylor, "Trump: The Soap," *New York*, March 5, 1990, https://books.google.com/books?id=bdF9SYJ7hsQC&pg=PA1&lpg=PA1&dq =john+taylor,+trump+the+soap,+new+york+mag&source=bl&ots=HK2eN9m bQh&sig=yU_YGhMQcdwsQ7wAh1Br-A6HyHU&hl=en&sa=X&ved=0ahU KEwic77zD3LzMAhWI7CYKHftQDZwQ6AEIJTAC#v=onepage&q=john%20 taylor%2C%20trump%20the%20soap%2C%20new%20york%20mag&f=false.

121 *"positive effect"*: Neil Barsky and Pauline Yoshihashi, "Trump Is Betting That Taj Mahal Casino Will Hit Golden Jackpot in Atlantic City," *Wall Street Journal*, March 20, 1990, B1.

CHAPTER 7: ALL IN

123 *millions of dollars in profits*: Phillip H. Wiggins, "Casino Operators' Profit Soars in Third Quarter," *New York Times*, November 10, 1978.

123 *bags stashed*: Steven Perskie interview with Shawn Boburg and Robert O'Harrow, *Washington Post*, April 2016.

123 *City dwellers flocked*: Vicki Golf Levi and Lee Eisenberg, *Atlantic City: 125 Years of Ocean Madness* (Berkeley, CA: Ten Speed Press, 1979), 15.

124 *Atlantic City's population*: New Jersey Department of Labor and Workforce Development, US Censuses of Population and Housing. http://lwd.dol.state.nj .us/labor/lpa/census/1990/poptrd6.htm.

124 *thirty-six corporations*: O'Brien, *TrumpNation*, 116.

124 *As Trump pondered*: Rutgers University, Atlantic City Timeline, December 1980, http://governors.rutgers.edu/on-governors/nj-governors/governor-brendan-t -byrne-administration/governor-brendan-t-byrne-issues-atlantic-city/atlantic -city-timeline-1614-2010-2/.

124 *Trump toured*: Paul Rubeli interview with Robert O'Harrow, *Washington Post*, December 2015.

124 *millions in commissions*: Barrett, *Trump*, 156.

124 *At thirty-four years old*: New Jersey Division of Gaming Enforcement report to the Casino Control Commission, October 16, 1981, 29–31.

125 *Trump told regulators*: Ibid., 17.

125 *Trump initially neglected*: Ibid., 85.

125 *When Governor*: Donald Linsky, *New Jersey Governor Brendan T. Byrne: The Man Who Couldn't Be Bought* (Teaneck, NJ: Farleigh Dickinson University Press, 2014), 188.

125 *A review by:* State of New Jersey Commission on Investigation, "Incursion of Organized Crime into Certain Legitimate Businesses in Atlantic City," December 1977, ii.

126 *a violent organization:* Joseph F. Sullivan, "U.S. Lawsuit Says Mob Controls Union in Atlantic City Casinos," *New York Times*, December 19, 1990.

126 *financier for Scarfo:* New Jersey State Commission of Investigation report on organized crime, 1992, 33–57.

126 *with Daniel Sullivan:* New Jersey Division of Gaming Enforcement report, October 16, 1981, 92–95.

126 *FBI informant:* Sullivan obituary, *Philadelphia Inquirer*, October 18, 1993.

126 *In July:* New Jersey Division of Gaming Enforcement report, October 16, 1981, 92.

126 *Trump arranged:* Ibid., 94–95.

126 *He considered them:* O'Brien, *TrumpNation*, 118.

126 *"I don't think":* Ibid.

126 *"organized crime elements":* FBI memo from Supervisor Damon T. Taylor, September 22, 1981, http://www.thesmokinggun.com/documents/crime/donald-trump-worried-about-oc-ac-0#lightbox-popup-1.

127 *Trump paid:* New Jersey Division of Gaming Enforcement report, October 16, 1981, 92; *Albert M. Greenfield and Co. v. SSG Enterprises et al.*, 213 NJ Super. 1 (1986), 516 A.2d 250, decided October 2, 1986; and Barrett, *Trump*, 232.

127 *thirty-nine stories:* Donald Janson, "10th and Largest Casino Opens in Atlantic City," *New York Times*, May 15, 1984.

127 *"People were excited":* Carl Zeitz interview with Shawn Boburg, *Washington Post*, 2016.

127 *less than two:* Donald Janson, "Trump Assured Casino License," *New York Times*, March 16, 1982.

127 *gambling mecca:* "Profits at Casinos Increase after Atlantic City Slump," *New York Times*, August 30, 1982.

128 *"history of the world":* Trump and Schwartz, *Art of the Deal* (1987), 143.

128 *"The [Harrah's] board":* Ibid., 215.

128 *Three weeks later:* Donald Janson, "Trump and Harrah's Feud over Name," *New York Times*, August 13, 1985.

128 *"look at him":* Frank Lundy III interview with Shawn Boburg, *Washington Post*, May 12, 2016.

128 *his first casino, Harrah's:* Trump and Schwartz, *Art of the Deal* (1987), 217; and Janson, "10th and Largest Casino Opens."

128 *"I gave them a Lamborghini":* Janson, "Trump and Harrah's Feud"; Janson, "10th and Largest Casino Opens"; and John O'Donnell interview with Michael Kranish, *Washington Post*, May 2, 2016.

129 *reputed mob lawyer:* Al Delugach, "New Jersey Regulators Cite Ties with Korshak," *Los Angeles Times*, March 1, 1985.

129 *That spring:* Barrett, *Trump*, 254.

129 *"lost my mind":* Trump and Schwartz, *Art of the Deal* (1987), 239–40.

129 *bright lights:* Barrett, *Trump*, 254.

129 *"natural manager":* O'Donnell and Rutherford, *Trumped!*, 29–30.

130 *intracorporate competition:* Ibid., 81.

130 *"I can be a screamer":* Trump and Schwartz, *Art of the Deal* (1987), 242.

130 *cursing him out:* O'Donnell and Rutherford, *Trumped!*, 30–31, 34; and interview with John O'Donnell.

130 *"very sharp":* Trump and Schwartz, *Art of the Deal* (1987), 220.

130 *tight inner circle:* Interview with John O'Donnell.

131 *"truly trusted":* O'Donnell and Rutherford, *Trumped!*, 56–57, 77.

131 *borrowed money:* Barrett, *Trump*, 408.

131 *He spent $70 million:* New Jersey Division of Gaming Enforcement report, Trump Plaza Renewal, April 7, 1987, 33.

131 *he spent about $62 million:* Ibid., 38.

131 *Trump backed off:* Ibid., 40–50.

131 *At an April:* New Jersey Casino Control Commission hearing transcript, April 20, 1987, vol. 1, 52, 123–24.

131 *accused the Trump organization:* Casino Control Commission hearing transcript, Plaza license renewal, April 22, 1987, 240–42.

132 *agreed to settle: United States v. Donald J. Trump*, Civil Action No. 88-0929, Final Judgment, April 11, 1988.

132 *Over the previous:* Lenny Glynn, "Trump's Taj—Open at Last, with a Scary Appetite," *New York Times*, April 8, 1990.

132 *argued against:* Blair, *Trumps*, 389.

132 *worth $700 million:* Ibid., 362–63.

133 *Princess to the Castle:* Harry Hurt III, *Lost Tycoon: The Many Lives of Donald J. Trump* (London: Orion Books, 1994), 228; and David Johnston and Michael Schurman, "Trump's Ship Comes In—to Cheers," *Philadelphia Inquirer*, July 10, 1988.

133 *Northeastern shuttle service:* David Segal, "What Donald Trump's Plaza Deal Reveals about His White House Bid," *New York Times*, January 16, 2016.

133 *" 'too big to fail' ":* Interview with Perskie.

133 *In 1986:* Marvin B. Roffman, "Casino Gambling in Atlantic City," June 11, 1987.

134 *Marvin Roffman saw:* Marvin B. Roffman with Michael J. Schwager, *Take Charge of Your Financial Future: Straight Talk on Managing Your Money from the Financial Analyst Who Defied Donald Trump* (New York: Carol Publishing Group, 1994), vi–xxiii.

134 *In July 1987:* Casino Control Commission, "In the Matter of the Sale of Certain Shares of Class B Stock of Resorts International, Inc.," October 20, 1987, 2.

134 *eight thousand:* O'Donnell and Rutherford, *Trumped!*, 42.

134 *decline in the price:* Marvin Roffman interview with Robert O'Harrow, *Washington Post*, December 2015.

135 *"Only with":* Donald Janson, "Trump Appears before Casino Panel," *New York Times*, February 14, 1988.

135 *Trump replied:* Trump testimony before Casino Control Commission, hearing transcript, February 8, 1988, 273–74.

135 *"Can go wrong":* Ibid., 300–301.

135 *"Don't people"*: Ibid., 346.

136 *"I mean"*: Ibid., 347.

136 *Trump later*: Ibid., 362–64.

136 *reflective exterior glass*: Marty Rosenberg interview with Shawn Boburg, *Washington Post*, April 12, 2016.

136 *"What's wrong?"*: O'Donnell and Rutherford, *Trumped!*, 121.

136 *One reason was*: Ibid., 74.

136 *Ivana resented having*: Interview with John O'Donnell.

137 *felt sympathy for Ivana*: O'Donnell and Rutherford, *Trumped!*, 73–91.

137 *"some woman crying"*: Ibid., 74, 111, 121, 124.

137 *"resulted from happenstance"*: New Jersey Casino Control Commission hearing transcript, February 18, 1988, 469–70.

137 *backing Trump*: Donald Janson, "Trump's Promise Wins Relicensing for Casino," *New York Times*, February 25, 1988.

137 *$245 million*: Andrea Adelson, "The Underestimated Merv Griffin," *New York Times*, April 9, 1988.

138 *In May*: Nina J. Easton, "Merv Griffin's Outrageous Fortune: When Millionaire Griffin Took on Billionaire Trump, They Said It Was a Mismatch. They Were Wrong," *Los Angeles Times*, July 24, 1988.

138 *"Our compromise"*: Donald J. Trump with Kate Bohner, *Trump: The Art of the Comeback* (New York: Random House, 1997), 33.

138 *"'I'll take it'"*: Donald Trump interview with Marc Fisher and Michael Kranish, *Washington Post*, April 21, 2016.

138 *$675 million*: "Trump Taj Mahal Funding in Mortgage Bond Offering," *New York Times*, November 9, 1988.

138 *debt from his other*: New Jersey Casino Control Commission hearing transcript, February 8, 1988, 345–47.

138 *"The Taj was going"*: Paul Rubeli interview with Robert O'Harrow, *Washington Post*, December 2015.

139 *and employ about 5,800*: Casino Control Commission, New Jersey Casino Facility Statistics, 1978–2004.

139 *"The Taj itself"*: Marvin B. Roffman, "Casino Gaming in Atlantic City: A Crisis Ahead," *Industry Update*, Janney Montgomery Scott, June 2, 1989, 2.

139 *"This is going"*: Interview with Roffman.

CHAPTER 8: COLD WINDS

140 *"It's not going"*: O'Donnell and Rutherford, *Trumped!*, 189.

140 *stress of the work*: Ibid., 190–91.

141 *Nazi concentration camp*: Joshua Benanav obituary, http://www.legacy.com/obituaries/hartfordcourant/obituary.aspx?n=joshua-benanav&pid=86966479.

141 *bought his girlfriend an engagement ring*: O'Donnell and Rutherford, *Trumped!*, 190.

141 *1:00 p.m. flight*: Ibid., 193.

141 *two-inch scrape*: National Transportation Safety Board report, NYC90MA009, Accident, October 10, 1989, Lacey Township, NJ.

142 *"terrible news"*: Interview with unnamed Trump aide by Michael Kranish, *Washington Post*, May 4, 2016.

142 *"the response was, like, horrible"*: Donald Trump interview with Michael Kranish, *Washington Post*, May 19, 2016.

142 *would feel guilty*: Interview with John O'Donnell.

143 *"I heard fear and uncertainty"*: O'Donnell and Rutherford, *Trumped!*, 194–95.

143 *"wiped out"*: Trump interview with Kranish.

143 *"something just incredible"*: O'Donnell and Rutherford, *Trumped!*, 195.

143 *wondered aloud*: Ibid., 197.

143 *"manufacturing-induced scratch"*: National Transportation Safety Board report, NYC90MA009.

144 *"a fifty-fifty deal"*: Donald Trump interview with Larry King, CNN, July 27, 1990.

144 *shift attention*: O'Donnell first made this assertion in *Trumped!* and repeated it in interviews with the *Washington Post* in May 2016. Trump, asked in a May 19, 2016, interview with the *Washington Post* whether he might have gone on the helicopter, responded, "I don't want to go into it, about me potentially being on that helicopter, because people are going to say—so I don't really want to get into it. But it was just one of those things."

144 *"Marla stood there petrified"*: O'Donnell and Rutherford, *Trumped!*, 198–200.

144 *"still standing"*: Trump interview with Kranish.

144 *"it's his turn"*: O'Donnell and Rutherford, *Trumped!*, 204–5.

145 *"This is bullshit"*: Ibid., 64–65.

146 *"ugly and dreary"*: Neil Barsky and Pauline Yoshihashi, "Trump Is Betting That Taj Mahal Casino Will Hit Golden Jackpot in Atlantic City," *Wall Street Journal*, March 20, 1990.

146 *"So this is what a billion dollars"*: Roffman with Schwager, *Take Charge of Your Financial Future*, xiii.

146 *"four-letter word"*: Marvin Roffman interview with Robert O'Harrow, *Washington Post*, November 16, 2015. Roffman also recounted his experience in his memoir, *Take Charge of Your Financial Future*.

147 *"sold immediately"*: Interview with Roffman, November 16, 2015.

147 *Roffman decided*: Roffman with Schwager, *Take Charge of Your Financial Future*, xi–xxiii; and interview with Roffman, November 16, 2015.

147 *"were totally inappropriate"*: Robert O'Harrow, "Trump's Bad Bet," *Washington Post*, January 18, 2016; and interview with Roffman.

147 *"Muslim art"*: Taj Mahal, United Nations, World Heritage website, http://whc .unesco.org/en/list/252.

148 *forty-two-story*: O'Donnell and Rutherford, *Trumped!*, 289.

148 *"fire all these assholes"*: Ibid., 272–73.

148 *"going on"*: Ibid., 287–88.

149 *$220,000 in missing tokens*: Deno Marino interview with Amy Goldstein, *Washington Post*, April 2016.

149 *"full of coin"*: Interview with John O'Donnell.

149 *"Overcome by Success"*: Tim Golden, "Taj Mahal's Slot Machines Halt, Overcome by Success," *New York Times*, April 9, 1990.

149 *"fire people"*: O'Donnell and Rutherford, *Trumped!*, 279–83.

149 *"colossal failure"*: Ibid., 284.

150 *"Hyde's people are responsible"*: Ibid., 287–89.

150 *lash out:* Interview with John O'Donnell. O'Donnell expressed similar feelings in his memoir.

150 *"black guys counting my money"*: O'Donnell and Rutherford, *Trumped!*, 148; and interview with John O'Donnell.

150 *"ever interviewed"*: Trump interview with Kranish; Trump interview with Fisher and Kranish, June 9, 2016.

151 *Hordes crowded him:* Interview with Perskie.

151 *"Warriors"*: O'Donnell and Rutherford, *Trumped!*, 298–99.

151 *"he got on a helicopter"*: Ibid., 293–94.

151 *"never quit"*: Trump interview with Kranish. Trump was asked in the interview to make his brother Robert Trump available to discuss O'Donnell's recollection of this event. Donald Trump said he would not do so: "I could call up my brother, who I speak to all the time. But I don't want to waste a lot of time in this thing. Does that make sense to you?"

151 *"wildest expectations"*: Daniel Heneghan and David J. Spatz, "Trump Opens Taj with Flourish," *Press of Atlantic City*, April 6, 1990.

151 *Merv Griffin predicted:* Ibid.

151 *"turning up aces!"*: Robin Leach, host, *Lifestyles of the Rich and Famous*, April 1990, https://www.youtube.com/watch?v=GGWjUYWatTo.

CHAPTER 9: THE CHASE

152 *In the same queue:* Ivana Trump interview, *Primetime Live*, ABC, May 10, 1991.

152 *"I did pick [up] the phone in the living room"*: Ibid. Ivana Trump and Marla Maples declined requests for interviews for this book.

153 *"piece of ass"*: Harry Hurt III, "Donald Trump Gets Small," *Esquire*, May 1991.

154 *"He's in pursuit"*: Louise Sunshine interview with Frances Stead Sellers, April 20, 2016.

154 *"I create stars"*: Trump interview with Nancy Collins, *Primetime Live*, ABC, March 10, 1994.

154 *"If I told the real stories"*: Trump with Bohner, *Comeback*, 116.

154 *"have to have you now"*: Ibid., 117.

155 *"get screwed"*: Ibid.

155 *"women have one of the great acts"*: Ibid., 117–18.

155 *"I'm not bragging"*: Donald Trump interview with David Hochman, *Playboy*, October 2004.

156 *"represent the extremes"*: Trump with Bohner, *Comeback*, 118.

156 *shielded by his security:* Barrett, *Trump*, 19.

156 *moved to Guatemala:* Michael Gross, "Marla Maples: Tabloid Life," *New York*, April 6, 1998.

156 *$10 million check:* Jay Goldberg interview with *Washington Post*, April 2016.

157 *took his coat:* Ibid.

157 *"tremendous fights"*: Trump, on *Oprah*, April 25, 1988.

157 *"give a wife responsibility"*: Trump with Bohner, *Comeback*, 137–38.

157 *"less than perfection"*: Trump and Leerhsen, *Surviving at the Top*, 47.

157 *"see it lasting"*: Interview with Goldberg.

158 *"going out in public"*: Gross, "Marla Maples."

158 *"job called for"*: "Marla Maples Opens Up," *People*, April 19, 2016.

158 *a talent component*: Elizabeth Sporkin, "Ooh-la-la Marla!," *People*, March 5, 1990.

158 *"had this connection"*: Gross, "Marla Maples."

159 *"very, very gorgeous"*: Marla Maples interview with Diane Sawyer, *Primetime Live*, ABC, April 19, 1990.

159 *"mountains of Reddi-wip"*: Maureen Orth, "Talking to Marla Maples," *Vanity Fair*, 1990.

159 *diamond ring*: James Barron, "The Donald Is to Marry!," *New York Times*, July 4, 1991. Maples auctioned off the ring in 2000.

159 *"interfere with his business"*: Maples on *Today*, NBC, July 26, 1993.

159 *A thousand guests*: Todd S. Purdum, "In This Plaza, I Thee Wed," *New York Times*, December 18, 1993.

159 *"relationship can work"*: Megan French, "O. J. Simpson Made Awkward Comment at Donald Trump's 1993 Wedding to Marla Maples Months before His Arrest: Watch," *Us*, April 6, 2016.

159 *"give it four months"*: Georgia Dullea, "It's a Wedding Blitz for Trump and Maples," *New York Times*, December 21, 1993.

159 *"wasn't a wet eye"*: Ibid.

159 *the caviar alone*: Trump with Bohner, *Comeback*, 140.

160 *" 'What the hell' "*: O'Brien, *TrumpNation*, 7.

160 *entourage of relatives*: Interview with Goldberg.

160 *"critically wrong"*: Trump with Bohner, *Comeback*, 210.

160 *received $5 million*: Bruce Weber, "Donald and Marla Are Headed for Divestiture," *New York Times*, May 3, 1997.

160 *"eye on the clock"*: Interview with Goldberg.

160 *"the hottest club"*: Trump with Schwartz, *Art of the Deal* (2015), 94–95.

161 *erect a hideous home*: Interview with Trump, November 2015.

161 *gold-plated bathroom sinks*: Mary Jordan and Rosalind S. Helderman, "Inside Trump's Palm Beach Castle and His 30-Year Fight to Win Over the Locals," *Washington Post*, November 14, 2015. Trump made $15.6 million from Mar-a-Lago in 2014, according to financial disclosures he filed as part of his presidential campaign.

162 *restrictions lifted*: Ibid.

162 *" 'how cool are we?' "*: Roger Stone interview, April 4, 2016.

162 *"What I do is successful because of the aesthetics"*: Bob Morris, "A Night Out With: Donald J. Trump; Previewing the States of Beauty," *New York Times*, January 10, 1999.

162 *raised Trump's international profile*: During his 2016 presidential campaign, Trump occasionally claimed to have a strong familiarity with Russia because he had held a "major event in Russia"—the Miss Universe contest, which he called a "big, big, incredible event."

162 *"mix it up"*: Trump with Bohner, *Comeback*, 96.

163   *breach of contract:* Matt Viser, "The Pageant of His Dreams," *Boston Globe,* April 17, 2016.

163   *"When we got to the dinner table":* Ibid.

163   *"kissed, fondled, and restrained":* Ibid.

163   *obsessed with Trump:* Ibid.

163   *eliminated black women:* Ibid.

163   *"pawn in a lawsuit":* Trump attorney Michael Cohen, quoted in Rachel Stockman, "Inside the $125 Million Donald Trump Sexual Assault Lawsuit," *LawNewz,* February 23, 2016.

164   *dropped her case:* Ibid. Harth said in 2016 that she considers Trump a friend and she supported his campaign for president.

164   *"triple crown of beauty":* Trump with Bohner, *Comeback,* 96.

164   *paid $10 million:* Ibid., 102.

164   *only $2 million:* Interview with Mary Jordan, April 2016.

164   *"The bathing suits got smaller":* Judy Bachrach, "What's Behind Donald Trump's Obsession with Beauty Pageants?," *Vanity Fair,* January 13, 2016.

164   *promoted women:* Reidy interview with Frances Stead Sellers, May 2016.

164   *"When you win a beauty pageant":* "Weight of the World," *People,* February 10, 1997.

165   *"hamster on a wheel":* Alicia Machado interview with Janell Ross, April 30, 2016.

165   *"God, what problems":* Trump with Bohner, *Comeback,* 106.

165   *"leaving the discards":* Carrie Prejean, *Still Standing: The Untold Story of My Fight against Gossip, Hate, and Political Attacks* (Washington, DC: Regnery, 2009), 68. After news reports in 2016 recounted Prejean's stories about Trump that had appeared in her book, Prejean gave several interviews in which she praised Trump, saying, for example, "I have nothing but positive things to say about Donald Trump."

165   *"It's about beauty":* Trump interview with Marc Fisher and Michael Kranish, June 9, 2016.

165   *Trump Models Inc.:* Kate Kelly, "Fashion Café's Tommaso Buti Schemes to Skim Rent from Guccis," *Observer,* April 5, 1999.

165   *"inconsequential agency":* James Scully interview with *Washington Post,* April 2016.

165   *"a way to funnel":* Ibid.

166   *day-to-day management:* Interview with Jim Dowd, who ran a public relations firm where he represented Trump, May 2016.

166   *"'Hey, Donald'":* John Bassignani interview with Frances Stead Sellers, May 4, 2016.

166   *a rollicking patter:* Mary Jordan, "From Playboy to President? Trump's Past Crude Sex Talk Collides with His White House Bid," *Washington Post,* May 10, 2016.

167   *"Her boob job":* *Stern* show quotations from Andrew Kaczynski and Nathan McDermott, "Donald Trump Said a Lot of Gross Things about Women on 'Howard Stern,'" *BuzzFeed,* February 24, 2016.

167   *flower arrangements:* Josh Glancy, "Mogul Sought Trophy Wife," *Sunday Times* (London), August 16, 2015. British journalist Selina Scott, who knew the princess, recalled Diana saying of Trump, "He gives me the creeps."

167 *"one hundred stitches"*: Trump added that he would stay with her even if she was disfigured.

168 *"speak romantically"*: Interview with Goldberg.

168 *"I'd see him chatting"*: Kate Bohner interview with Mary Jordan, April 20, 2015.

168 *"much less glamorous"*: Trump interview with Mary Jordan, April 2016.

168 *"married to my business"*: Jonathan Van Meter, "Did Their Father Really Know Best?," *New York*, December 13, 2004.

168 *"smart to be shallow"*: Donald J. Trump with Meredith McIver, *Trump: Think Like a Billionaire* (New York: Random House, 2004), xvii–xxiii.

169 *"are all wrecks"*: Marie Brenner, "After the Gold Rush," *Vanity Fair*, September 1990.

169 *"develop as a kid"*: Trump children interviews by Dan Zak, *Washington Post*, April 2016.

170 *"very sensational"*: Susan Crawford interview with Frances Stead Sellers, May 16, 2016.

170 *"confidentiality agreement"*: Joseph P. Fried, "Tell-All Book on Trump Won't Be Telling It All," *New York Times*, February 24, 2002.

170 *threatened to terminate*: Frederick M. Winship, "Trump Ends Ivana's Alimony over TV Interview," UPI, May 14, 1991.

170 *"written consent"*: Ibid.

170 *"we're friendly"*: Dana Schuster, "Ivana Trump on How She Advises Donald—and Those Hands," *New York Post*, April 3, 2016.

CHAPTER 10: A LEAGUE OF HIS OWN

172 *gathered in New Orleans*: USFL owners' meeting notes from January 18, 1984.

172 *Oklahoma oil baron*: Paul Domowitch, "USFL Expects to Cash In on Trump," *Philadelphia Daily News*, November 2, 1983.

172 *a former US ambassador*: "Marvin Warner, 82, Figure in S&L Debacle," *New York Times*, April 13, 2002.

173 *ring a gong*: Charles Leerhsen, "USFL's New Game Plan," *Newsweek*, March 19, 1984.

173 *Oldenburg had arrived*: Jim Byrne, *The $1 League: The Rise and Fall of the USFL* (New York: Prentice Hall Press, 1986), 103–4, 119.

173 *didn't appreciate their complaints*: Ibid., 103.

174 *"given the league credibility"*: USFL owners' meeting notes from January 18, 1984.

174 *average NFL team*: Domowitch, "USFL Expects to Cash In."

174 *the entire USFL*: Paul Attner, "USFL Upbeat, but Sees Tougher Sell," *Washington Post*, February 24, 1984.

174 *"I don't want to be a loser"*: USFL owners' meeting notes from January 18, 1984.

175 *"grand plan for the USFL"*: Letter from Myles Tanenbaum to Tad Taube, January 27, 1984.

175 *baseball games in class*: Peter Brant interview with Michael Miller, April 2016.

175 *an ankle injury sidelined him*: Harry Hurt III, *Lost Tycoon: The Many Lives of Donald J. Trump* (New York: W. W. Norton, 1993), 77–78.

175 *New York Mets*: Robert Masello, "The Trump Card," *Town & Country*, 1983.

175 *keep the team in Cleveland:* Brent Larkin, "Donald Trump's Failed Bid to Buy the Cleveland Indians," *Cleveland Plain Dealer*, October 8, 2015.

175 *preliminary talks with Robert Irsay:* Michael O'Donnell, "USFL Must Win or Fold: Trump," *Chicago Tribune*, June 24, 1986.

175 *$6 million:* Dave Goldberg, "Monday, AM Cycle," Associated Press, June 23, 1986.

175 *"known to the world as a loser":* Ira Berkow, "Trump Building the Generals in His Own Style," *New York Times*, January 1, 1984.

176 *three-year contract:* Joe Nocera, "Donald Trump's Less-Than-Artful Failure in Pro Football," *New York Times*, February 19, 2016.

176 *Shula made about $450,000:* Edwin Pope, "Shula's Future? Nobody Knows," *Miami Herald*, October 23, 1983.

176 *"Money is one thing, gold is another":* Larry Dorman, "Don Shula Won't Join USFL Club," *Miami Herald*, October 25, 1983.

176 *Brian Sipe:* Ben Terris, "And Then There Was the Time Donald Trump Bought a Football Team . . . ," *Washington Post*, October 19, 2015.

176 *"there's a squib in the papers":* Berkow, "Trump Building the Generals."

177 *"Maybe we oughta sign Taylor":* Jim Gould interview with Will Hobson, *Washington Post*, April 2016.

177 *"Mr. Taylor, please hold for Mr. Trump":* "How Donald Trump Destroyed a Football League," *Esquire*, January 13, 2016.

177 *"visionary builder":* Berkow, "Trump Building the Generals."

177 *"his money where his mouth was":* "How Donald Trump Destroyed a Football League."

177 *Technically, Taylor bought himself out of the contract:* Gerald Eskenazi, "Taylor Buys Out Generals' Pact," *New York Times*, January 18, 1984.

178 *"brilliant publicity stunt":* "How Donald Trump Destroyed a Football League."

178 *"weak ownership":* Byrne, *$1 League*, 127.

178 *"prominent USFL executives":* Ibid., 137–41.

178 *who that was:* Ibid., 138.

178 *"You Just Sit There":* Ibid., 141–43.

178 *"Trump nerve":* Ibid., 148, 163.

178 *Bassett owned the Tampa Bay Bandits:* "John F. Bassett, 47, Is Dead; Owner of Sports Franchises," Associated Press, May 15, 1986.

179 *sternly worded letter:* Matt Bonesteel, "Donald Trump Was Such a USFL Bully That a Fellow Owner Threatened to Punch Him," *Washington Post*, March 3, 2016.

179 *Sharon Patrick:* Byrne, *$1 League*, 174, 186–87.

179 *consultant couldn't foresee happening:* Ibid.

179 *a move to the fall:* McKinsey & Company report, USFL internal documents.

179 *"bullshit":* Byrne, *$1 League*, 197–98, 204.

180 *"fall of 1986":* Greg Cote, "USFL Moving to Fall in '86," *Miami Herald*, August 23, 1984.

180 *"Joe Namath of the USFL":* Byrne, *$1 League*, 256–57.

180 *take it easy on Flutie:* "Owner Says Trump Asked to 'Take It Easy' on Flutie," *Miami Herald*, March 17, 1985.

180 *John Barron, the fictitious:* Byrne, *$1 League,* 293.

180 *Simmons got a message:* Ibid., 224.

180 *prenuptial agreement with Ivana:* Hurt III, *Lost Tycoon* (1993), 144.

181 *he didn't remember seeing:* Ben Terris, "Does Donald Trump Cheat at Golf?," *Washington Post,* September 4, 2015.

181 *"You are going to die young":* O'Donnell and Rutherford, *Trumped!,* 171.

182 *phony scores:* Terris, "Does Donald Trump Cheat?"

182 *Tour de Trump:* Kevin Hogan, "The Strange Tale of Donald Trump's 1989 Biking Extravaganza: Inside the Making of the Tour de Trump," *Politico,* April 10, 2016.

182 *beating bids from:* Joe Weinert, "Offshore Race Set for A.C. Trump Wins Rights to Championships," *Press of Atlantic City,* November 19, 1988.

182 *break his back:* Joe Weinert, "Atlantic Batters Powerboats: Deep-V's Outrun Cats in Heavy Seas," *Press of Atlantic City,* October 18, 1989.

182 *flipped over:* Joe Weinert, "Boat Flips off A.C.," *Press of Atlantic City,* October 23, 1989.

182 *"a truly cynical financial standpoint":* Angus Phillips, "Rain Makes Trump's Mouth Water," *Washington Post,* October 21, 1989.

183 *$11 million to host:* Hurt III, *Lost Tycoon* (1993), 201–4.

183 *"Thank you, Mr. Trump":* Ibid.

183 *Desiree Washington:* Russ Choma, "The Time Donald Trump Tried to Get Mike Tyson out of Going to Prison for Rape," *Mother Jones,* December 2015.

183 *championship belt:* D'Antonio, *Never Enough,* 322.

183 *Courtroom 318:* Richard Hoffer, "USFL Awarded Only $3 in Antitrust Decision: Jury Finds NFL Guilty on One of Nine Counts," *Los Angeles Times,* July 30, 1986.

184 *reeked of his omnipresent cigars:* Randy Harvey, "Whom Do You Trust in This Antitrust Case?," *Los Angeles Times,* July 6, 1986.

184 *slide show:* NFL internal documents, *USFL v. NFL* court records.

184 *"the plague":* Donald Trump testimony, *USFL v. NFL* court records.

184 *"not even on my Christmas card list":* Pete Rozelle testimony, *USFL v. NFL* court records.

185 *all Trump's idea:* John Bassett deposition testimony, *USFL v. NFL* court records.

185 *there was an even split:* Patricia Sibilia interview with Will Hobson, April 2016.

185 *"cheap way in":* Ibid.

186 *"We're dead":* Dave Goldberg, "Only Token Damages Against NFL in Antitrust Suit by Rival League," *Associated Press,* July 29, 1986.

186 *"strike out a lot":* Trump and Schwartz, *Art of the Deal* (1987), 48.

186 *"single key miscalculation":* Ibid., 276.

186 *His first national:* Barrett, *Trump,* 342.

187 *"self-aggrandizement, narcissism":* Michael Tollin interview with Will Hobson, April 2016.

187 *"we had a great lawsuit":* Donald Trump in *Small Potatoes: Who Killed the USFL?,* ESPN Productions, 2009.

187 *an estimated $22 million:* Blair, *Trumps,* 333.

187 *an estimated $4 billion:* Mike Ozanian, "The Most Valuable Teams in the NFL," *Forbes,* September 15, 2015.

187 *ultimately bowed out*: Jeff Horwitz, "Donald Trump: No White House Run If He'd Bought the Buffalo Bills," Associated Press, February 7, 2016.

187 *"more exciting"*: Ibid.

CHAPTER 11: THE GREAT UNRAVELING

188 *James Brown's "I Feel Good"*: All material in this paragraph and other parts of this section from Doug Cox, Joe Serpente, and Jeffrey Ludwig interviews with Amy Goldstein, *Washington Post*, April 2016.

189 *Trump Castle Hotel & Casino*: New Jersey Department of Law and Public Safety, Division of Gaming Enforcement, "Preliminary Report on the Financial Condition of the Donald J. Trump Organization Post-restructuring," August 13, 1990, 18.

189 *negative $295 million*: Report on Trump Organization finances, Kenneth Leventhal & Co., June 14, 1990.

189 *"Castle Bond"*: "Trump Skips Payment on Castle Bond," *Press of Atlantic City*, June 16, 1990.

189 *needlepoint of Trump's visage*: "Trump Honored at Birthday Rally," United Press International, June 16, 1990.

189 *"largest surprise is yet to come"*: Henry Stern, "Boardwalk Birthday Party for Trump Day After Missed Bond Payment," Associated Press, June 17, 1990.

190 *"Bought the Plaza"*: "Why I Bought the Plaza," advertisement in *New York* magazine, September 12, 1988.

190 *set in the Plaza*: Theplazany.com/history/.

190 *"in the world"*: "Why I Bought the Plaza."

190 *Trump had intended*: Howard Kurtz, "Loves Won and Lost; The Trump Divorce: Day 2," *Washington Post*, February 14, 1990; and David W. Dunlap, "Trumps Plan to Revamp the Plaza in a Big Way," *New York Times*, December 20, 1988.

190 *so furious*: Barbara Res interview with Drew Harwell, *Washington Post*, March 31, 2016.

190 *next-highest bid*: Interviews with Robert McSween and another banker familiar with the transaction, who requested anonymity, with Jerry Markon, *Washington Post*, April 2016.

190 *a risky move*: Report on Trump Organization finances, Kenneth Leventhal & Co., Schedule II, June 14, 1990.

190 *hotel was charging*: Hurt III, *Lost Tycoon* (1993), 208.

191 *perceived as anti-Japanese*: Yumiko Ono, "Trump's Condos Lose Their Luster for Tokyo Buyers," *Wall Street Journal*, June 22, 1990.

191 *to be repainted*: Bruce R. Nobles and Ray Belz interviews with Jerry Markon, *Washington Post*, April 2016.

191 *make the purchase*: Kenneth Leventhal & Co. report, June 14, 1990.

191 *told them to push harder*: Interview with Nobles.

192 *were redeemed*: Ibid.

192 *and an engineer*: Ibid.

192 *"severe financial distress"*: Division of Gaming Enforcement, "Preliminary Report."

192 *Alexander's department store*: Ibid.

192 *credit at Bankers Trust:* Interviews with Alan Pomerantz, Robert McSween, and a third banker familiar with the negotiations with Jerry Markon, *Washington Post*, April 2016.

192 *"absolutely berserk":* Donald Trump interview with Amy Goldstein and Jerry Markon, *Washington Post*, May 18, 2016.

193 *banks in Britain, Germany, and Japan:* Interviews with bankers, including Alan Pomerantz and Robert McSween, with Jerry Markon, *Washington Post*, April 2016.

193 *had been his idea:* Trump interview with Goldstein and Markon.

193 *sit down with Trump:* Robert McSween and other bankers' interviews with Jerry Markon, *Washington Post*, April 2016.

193 *$3.2 billion debt:* Memo from Casino Control Commission Financial Evaluation Unit on Trump's petition regarding his casinos, August 16, 1990.

193 *who represented Citibank:* Interview with Pomerantz.

194 *"I resign":* O'Donnell and Rutherford, *Trumped!*, 326. As word spread that O'Donnell planned to write a memoir of his experiences, titled *Trumped!*, a Trump lawyer visited O'Donnell to express displeasure. O'Donnell later wrote that the lawyer, Joseph Fusco, warned him that Trump would "look for anything he can to discredit you." Fusco declined comment. O'Donnell and Rutherford, *Trumped!*, 333–34.

194 *saying he fired O'Donnell:* Trump interview with Michael Kranish.

194 *Taj's workforce:* Letter from Donald J. Buzney to Donald Trump, September 7, 1990.

194 *"wasn't satisfied":* Diana B. Henriques and M. A. Farber, "An Empire at Risk— Trump's Atlantic City; Debt Forcing Trump to Play for Higher Stakes," *New York Times*, June 7, 1990.

195 *"I have a lot of money":* Alison Leigh Cowan, "Trump Criticized on Late Payments," *New York Times*, May 4, 1990.

195 *negotiating with his bankers:* Interviews with three bankers familiar with the negotiations with Jerry Markon, *Washington Post*, May 2016.

195 *curb on Trump's habits:* Division of Gaming Enforcement, "Preliminary Report"; and memo from New Jersey Casino Control Commission, Financial Evaluation Unit, on Donald J. Trump petition regarding his casinos, August 13, 1990.

196 *would sign the agreement:* Interview with McSween.

196 *"lien on Mar-a-Lago":* Interview with Pomerantz.

196 Surviving at the Top: Interview with McSween. Trump has said he gave copies of *Art of the Deal*; McSween provided a photograph of the book he was given, *Surviving at the Top*, which was signed by Trump.

196 *create a fiscal plan:* Division of Gaming Enforcement, "Preliminary Report."

196 *on Central Park South:* Steven Bollenbach interview with Amy Goldstein, *Washington Post*, April 2016.

196 *commanding views of the park:* Condominium Unit Deed, October 2, 1990, Release of Part of Mortgaged Premises, October 18, 1990. New York City real estate records obtained through propertyshark.com.

197 *for one day:* Interview with Bollenbach.

197 *the organization's spreadsheets:* Ibid.

197 *"What do we do now?'"*: Interview with Trump confidant by Michael Kranish, Amy Goldstein, and Jerry Markon, *Washington Post*, April 2016.

197 *where they were*: Interview with Bollenbach.

198 *$1.3 billion*: Memo from New Jersey Casino Control Commission on Trump petition.

198 *Atlantic City's gambling earnings*: Richard D. Hylton, "Trump Now Reported Near Bond-Swap Offer," *New York Times*, September 11, 1990.

198 *danger of missing*: Division of Gaming Enforcement, "Preliminary Report."

198 *"And me, I guess"*: Donald Trump interview with Marc Fisher and Michael Kranish, *The Washington Post*, June 9, 2016.

198 *Tempers flared*: Trump initially said he would relinquish 25 percent of his Taj stock; the bondholders insisted on 85 percent. Trump came back with 19.9 percent, which bondholders said was unacceptable. Interviews with bondholders familiar with the negotiation with Amy Goldstein, *Washington Post*, April 2016.

199 *talks broke off*: Interviews with two bondholders familiar with the negotiations with Amy Goldstein, *Washington Post*, April 2016.

199 *billionaire financier Carl Icahn*: Interview with bondholder familiar with the negotiations with Amy Goldstein, *Washington Post*, April 2016.

199 *"greediest men on earth"*: Drew Harwell, "Inside the Rocky Billionaire Bromance of Donald Trump and Carl Icahn," *Washington Post*, April 30, 2016.

199 *casino's prized high rollers*: Interview with Perskie.

199 *when the parties hung up, deadlocked*: Hilary Rosenberg, *The Vulture Investors* (New York: John Wiley & Sons, 2000), 285.

200 *"to save ourselves"*: Ibid., 289.

200 *"maybe the word is depression"*: Robert J. McCartney, "Trump to Put N.J. Casino into Bankruptcy Process; Bondholders to Get Half of Taj Mahal," *Washington Post*, November 17, 1990.

200 *"in July"*: Division of Financial Evaluation, New Jersey Casino Control Commission, "Report on the Financial Condition of Donald J. Trump," April 15, 1991, 3.

200 *and the city would forfeit*: Interview with Perskie.

200 *30 more chips*: Complaint, New Jersey Division of Gaming Enforcement vs. Trump's Castle Associates Limited Partnership, April 3, 1991.

201 *a way to sidestep them*: Supplemental Stipulation of Facts, New Jersey Division of Gaming Enforcement, June 26, 1991.

201 *first batch of chips*: Neil Barsky, "Trump's Dad Chips in $3 Million–Plus to Help Pay Interest on Casino Bonds," *Wall Street Journal*, January 21, 1991; and transcript, New Jersey Casino Control Commission meeting, June 19, 1991, 40.

201 *dropped nearly one-third*: Trump Castle SEC filing, June 1991.

201 *"easy with the chips'"*: Donald J. Trump interview with Robert O'Harrow, *Washington Post*, May 13, 2016.

201 *"this came down"*: Transcript, New Jersey Casino Control Commission meeting, June 26, 1991, 172.

201 *personally punished*: Ibid., 170–73.

202 *"all good deals"*: Trump interview with O'Harrow.

202 *vividly against the night sky*: Mark Cutler interview with Shawn Boburg, *Washington Post*, May 2016.

203 *$54 million in all:* "Trump Files Payment Plan for Taj Mahal Subcontractors with SEC," Associated Press, October 4, 1990.

203 *the company's home:* Docket, Bankruptcy Petition #91-21885, US Bankruptcy Court for the Eastern District of Pennsylvania; and interview with Cutler.

203 *deserved the best:* Linda Stasi, "A Familiar Ring: What Next: Donald," *Newsday*, September 23, 1991.

203 *free publicity:* Interview with Pomerantz.

203 *$10 million:* Ibid.; and interview with Bollenbach.

204 *"were going swimmingly":* Trump interview with Goldstein and Markon.

204 *"the guys love it":* Interview with Nobles.

204 *"no pressure to sell":* Agis Salpukas, Company News, "Shuttle Head Is Appointed by Trump," *New York Times*, September 19, 1991.

204 *Trump was a real estate guy:* Interview with a person familiar with bankers' dealings with Trump over the Trump Shuttle with Jerry Markon, *Washington Post*, April 2016.

204 *It took another year:* Interview with person familiar with Trump's dealings with banks on Trump Shuttle with Jerry Markon, *Washington Post*, May 2016; USAIR Inc. SEC filing, April 1992; and US Department of Transportation Order 92-3-57, March 1992.

205 *"than you needed":* Trump interview with Goldstein and Markon.

205 *string of miscalculations:* Interview with Nobles.

205 *"Happy Celebration to You":* William H. Sokolic, "A Celebratory Trump Bash, His Casinos Make a Rebound from a Financial Licking," *Philadelphia Inquirer*, November 9, 1992; and "Donald Trump Reveling 'Against All Odds,'" *Asbury Park Press*, November 10, 1992.

205 *tidy prepackaged bankruptcies:* "Bankruptcy Court Clears Plan for Trump Plaza," *Wall Street Journal*, May 1, 1992; and Terry Mutchler, "The Castle's Game Plan Wins in Court, Casino Leaving Bankruptcy," *Associated Press*, May 6, 1992.

206 *keep the Plaza:* Interview with person familiar with the Plaza transaction with Jerry Markon, May 2016.

206 *"Let's hear it for":* William Sokolic, "A Celebratory Trump Bash," *Philadelphia Inquirer*, November 9, 1992.

206 *huge debts:* David Cay Johnston, "Trump Walks a Tightrope in Plan to Sell Casino Stock," *New York Times*, April 3, 1995.

206 *casino ventures:* Trump Hotels & Casino Resorts S-1 prospectus filed with the Securities and Exchange Commission, 1996, https://www.sec.gov/Archives/edgar/data/943320/0000950130-96-000349.txt.

206 *DJT:* Ibid.

206 *$14 a share:* "Trump Gets $295 Million in Sale of Stock, Debt," *St. Louis Post-Dispatch*, June 8, 1995. "Trump Pays 15.5% in Junk Bond Sale," *New York Times*, June 8, 1995.

206 *$290 million:* Timothy L. O'Brien, "What's He Really Worth?," *New York Times*, October 23, 2005.

207 *his net worth was:* O'Brien, *TrumpNation*, 151.

207 *Forbes's estimate:* Forbes 400 list, 1996.

207 *$100 million:* James Sterngold, "Long Odds for the Shares of Trump's Casino Company," *New York Times*, March 9, 1997.

207 *$880,000 in cash:* Company SEC filing (10-K, March 29, 1997: https://www.sec .gov/Archives/edgar/data/943320/0000940180-97-000299.txt. "Trump paid $884,550 in cash").

207 *$1.7 billion of his debt:* Daniel Roth, "The Trophy Life: You Think Donald Trump's Hit Reality Show Is a Circus? Spend a Few Weeks Watching Him Work," *Fortune*, April 19, 2004.

207 *paid Trump $7 million:* Trump Hotels & Casino Resorts 10-K filing with SEC, March 31, 1998, https://www.sec.gov/Archives/edgar/data/943320/0001047469 -98-013201.txt.

207 *logged $82 million:* Ibid.

207 *"raises suspicions":* James Sterngold, "Long Odds for the Shares of Trump's Casino Company," *New York Times*, March 9, 1997.

207 *$477,000 for failing:* "FinCEN Announces Penalty against Trump Taj Mahal Associates," January 28, 1998, https://www.fincen.gov/news_room/nr/html/19980128 .html.

207 *$250,000 to settle:* Charles V. Bagli, "Trump and Others Accept Fines for Ads in Opposition to Casinos," *New York Times*, October 6, 2000. Trump Hotels and Casino Resorts paid $50,000; Trump's lobbyist, Roger Stone, and the antigambling group Trump advertised with paid the rest.

207 *negative results:* "SEC Brings First Pro Forma Financial Reporting Case: Trump Hotels Charged with Issuing Misleading Earnings Release," SEC, January 16, 2002, https://www.sec.gov/news/headlines/trumphotels.htm.

207 *lost more than $1 billion:* NYSE data.

208 *stocks and bonds:* Ibid. See also Russ Buettner and Charles V. Bagli, "How Donald Trump Bankrupted His Atlantic City Casinos, But Still Earned Millions," *New York Times*, June 11, 2016.

208 *the company co-owned with NBC:* "Trump Hotels Agrees to Pay $17.5 Million to Stockholders," Associated Press, March 29, 2005.

208 *"basket of goodies":* "Trump Offers $17.5 Million to Shareholders," Associated Press, March 28, 2005.

208 *proceeds from an auction:* Ibid.

208 *piggy bank:* Interview with Sebastian Pignatello by Drew Harwell, *Washington Post*, May 2016.

208 *"He had been pillaging":* Ibid.

208 *paid more than $44 million:* Analysis of SEC 10-K reports.

208 *Trump Ice bottled water:* Trump Entertainment Resorts' proxy statement, April 3, 2007, https://www.sec.gov/Archives/edgar/data/943320/000119312507073468 /ddef14a.htm.

208 *"Entrepreneurially speaking":* Roth, "Trophy Life."

209 *worth at least $2.6 billion:* Jennifer Wang, "The Ups and Downs of Donald Trump: Three Decades On and Off the Forbes 400," *Forbes*, March 14, 2016.

CHAPTER 12: RATINGS MACHINE

210 *"crocodiles and ants":* Mark Burnett interview with Marc Fisher, December 2015.

211 *"bottom-feeders of society":* Trump quoted by Jim Dowd, then NBC's publicity

director and later head of a PR firm, Dowd Ink, interviewed by Marc Fisher, December 2015.

212 *fired the agent:* Donald Trump interview with Marc Fisher, December 2015.

212 *chip away at:* Interview with Burnett.

212 *fine on the show:* Jeff Gaspin interview with Marc Fisher, December 2015. Branson, Cuban, and Martha Stewart: NBC executives interviews with Marc Fisher, December 2015.

213 *not scripted:* Trump, Gaspin, and Burnett interviews with Marc Fisher; two other NBC executives interviews with Marc Fisher, December 2015.

214 *"no teleprompters":* Andy Dean interview with Frances Stead Sellers, December 2015.

214 *"good at it":* Trump interview with Fisher. During the early phase of the 2016 presidential campaign, former Florida governor Jeb Bush described Trump as "an actor playing a role of the candidate for president." He meant it as a criticism.

215 *psychological and medical evaluations: Apprentice* contestants interviews with Frances Stead Sellers, December 2015.

215 *bolster Trump's brand:* Sam Solovey interview with Frances Stead Sellers, December 2015.

215 *"do more publicity":* Elizabeth Jarosz interview with Frances Stead Sellers, December 2015.

216 *"nervous about the ratings":* Jim Dowd interview with Marc Fisher, December 2015.

216 *"rumblings of a soul":* Mark Singer, "Trump Solo," *New Yorker,* May 19, 1997.

216 *"ratings machine":* Trump, on *Saturday Night Live,* NBC, April 3, 2004.

216 *"He's a showman":* Interview with Burnett.

216 *"a lot of fun":* Trump, *Time to Get Tough,* 166.

216 *"it's lucrative":* Trump interview with Fisher.

217 *"was a barbarian":* Trump, on *Larry King Live,* CNN, February 27, 2004.

217 *" 'I'm not acting' ":* Trump interview with Fisher.

217 *"He was mobbed":* Interview with Dowd.

217 *"loved being a TV star":* Interview with Gaspin.

217 *"destroy the meager ratings":* Trump open letter to Martha Stewart, quoted in Keith Naughton, "You Were Terrible," *Newsweek,* February 20, 2006.

218 *"run for president":* Interview with Burnett. Asked if he was supporting Trump for president, Burnett said only, "I have no idea about the politics. I have had great fun—great fun—watching it."

218 *"not tone down":* Ibid.

219 *"the celebrity helped":* Trump interview with Fisher.

219 *role as judge:* Stephen Zeitchik, "Trump's 'Lady' Comes to Fox," *Variety,* June 12, 2007.

219 *create a pilot:* Gay Walch interview with Marc Fisher, January 2016.

220 *wasn't great:* Network executives interviews with Marc Fisher, December 2015.

220 *"he can do this":* Trump interview with Fisher.

CHAPTER 13: THE NAME GAME

221 *the rapper Nelly:* Deposition of Mark Hager, March 3, 2011, *ALM International Corp. v. Donald J. Trump*, 12.

221 *business venture:* Ibid.

221 *Trump no longer:* Ibid.

221 *start with menswear:* Interview of executive familiar with the Phillips–Van Heusen clothing deal, by Rosalind S. Helderman, *Washington Post*, April 3, 2016.

222 *a broker's fee:* Deposition of Hager, 50. During subsequent litigation, Trump testified that he agreed to pay a fee to Hager's company if it brokered a deal with certain conditions, but there were disputes as to whether those conditions were met. See Testimony of Donald J. Trump, April 15, 2013, *ALM International Corp v. Donald J. Trump*, trial transcript, 520–21.

222 *twenty licensing deals:* Deposition of Cathy Glosser, March 8, 2011, *ALM International Corp. v. Donald J. Trump*, 135.

222 *head of licensing laughed:* Testimony of Jeff Danzer, April 15, 2013, *ALM International Corp v. Donald J. Trump*, trial transcript, 593.

222 *what he had been:* Ibid., 595.

222 *Danzer sent:* Ibid.

222 *"a premium veneer":* Paul Tharp, "'Apprentice' Buzz Likely to Mint Trump a New Fortune," *New York Post*, February 11, 2004.

222 *"I do everything":* Testimony of Danzer, 642–43.

222 *Spider-Man on kids' pajamas:* Deposition of Glosser, 9.

223 *wanted a deal:* Testimony of Danzer, 596.

223 *company was wary:* Mark Weber, *Always in Fashion: From Clerk to CEO—Lessons for Success in Business and in Life* (New York: McGraw-Hill, 2015), 71.

223 *Trump announced he wanted:* Mark Weber interview with Rosalind S. Helderman, *Washington Post*, March 8, 2016.

223 *"I was taken aback":* Ibid.

223 *"respect and love Regis":* Ibid.

223 *The more insistent:* Weber, *Always in Fashion*, 72.

223 *"Make it happen":* Testimony of Cathy Glosser, April 10, 2013, *ALM International Corp v. Donald J. Trump*, trial transcript, 111. Trump gave a similar account in his testimony in the case: "I told Cathy Glosser to essentially get the deal done and see if they could get a deal with PVH." Trump testimony, April 15, 2013, 519–20.

223 *"Because I want to win":* Weber, *Always in Fashion*, 73.

223 *contracting with factories:* Rosalind S. Helderman and Tom Hamburger, "Trump Has Profited from Foreign Labor He Says Is Killing U.S. Jobs," *Washington Post*, March 13, 2016.

223 *$1 million a year:* Executive Branch Personal Public Financial Disclosure Report (OGE Form 278e), Donald J. Trump, July 22, 2015, 21.

224 *made an appearance:* Trump menswear: *The Apprentice*, season 10, episode 8, "Dressed to Kill," original airdate November 4, 2010; Trump Ice: *The Apprentice*,

season 1, episode 8, "Ice Escapades," original airdate February 26, 2004; Trump Success: *The Apprentice*, season 12, episode 10, "Winning by a Nose," original airdate April 22, 2012.

224 *all sold well:* In a one-page description of his assets in 2015, Trump claimed the value of his name alone at $3.3 billion. A *Washington Post* analysis of Trump's 2016 disclosure with the Federal Election Commission found that he reported income of between $6.02 million and $34.15 million from licensed real estate and consumer goods between July 2015 and May 2016. See Tom Hamburger, "Trump's Financial Claims Short on Details, Long on Exaggerations," *Washington Post*, June 16, 2015.

224 *twenty-five different licensing deals:* Donald Trump personal financial disclosure form, filed with Federal Election Commission, 2016.

224 *sell Trump Steaks:* Natasha Geiling, "A Definitive History of Trump Steaks," *Think Progress*, March 4, 2016.

225 *Trump, the Fragrance:* Stevenson Swanson, "Trump Becomes Institution, Mogul Launches Online Education Enterprise," *Chicago Tribune*, May 24, 2005.

225 *"to make money":* Ibid.

225 *"we teach success":* Tom Hamburger and Rosalind S. Helderman, "Trump Involved in Crafting Controversial Trump University Ads, Executive Testified," *Washington Post*, May 31, 2016. See also *Washington Post* video by Peter Stevenson: https://www.washingtonpost.com/politics/trump-involved-in-crafting-con troversial-trump-university-ads-executive-testified/2016/05/31/f032a488-2741 -11e6-ae4a-3cdd5fe74204_story.html.

225 *"largest real estate liquidation":* Tom Hamburger, Rosalind S. Helderman, and Dalton Bennett, "Donald Trump Said 'University' Was All about Education. Actually, Its Goal Was 'Sell, Sell, Sell!'" *Washington Post*, June 4, 2016.

226 *"have to control it":* Ian Shapira, "In Downturn, Aspiring Moguls Turn to Trump U. for Wisdom," *Washington Post*, September 26, 2009.

226 *"set the hook":* "Trump University 2009 Playbook," 36; copies of "playbooks" released in *Cohen v. Trump*, 3:13-cv-02519-GPC-WVG, Order on Motion to Intervene, attachments 1–5, May 31, 2016. See also Hamburger, Helderman, and Bennett, "Donald Trump Said 'University' Was All about Education."

226 *"change their lifestyle":* Ibid., 37.

226 *good targets:* "Trump University 2010 Playbook," 36. Copies of "playbooks" released in *Cohen v. Trump*, 3:13-cv-02519-GPC-WVG, Order on Motion to Intervene, attachments 1–5, May 31, 2016. The 2010 playbook was first published by *Politico*. See also Hamburger, Helderman, and Bennett, "Donald Trump Said 'University' Was All about Education."

226 *In the evenings:* Hamburger, Helderman, and Bennett, "Donald Trump Said 'University' Was All about Education."

226 *one of nearly six hundred:* Declaration of Mark Covais in opposition to plaintiffs' motion for class certification and appointment of class counsel, filed in 3:13-cv-02519, *Cohen v. Trump*.

226 *"I really felt stupid":* Emma Brown, "Donald Trump Billed His 'University' as a Road to Riches," *Washington Post*, September 13, 2015. Guillo was one of dozens

of plaintiffs in a class action suit against Trump University. See also Jim Zaroli, "Trump University Customer: 'Gold Elite' Program Nothing but Fool's Gold," National Public Radio, June 6, 2016.

226 *Trump's personal ire:* Adam Edelman, "Donald Trump Hits Back at Dissatisfied Trump University Students, Naming Two Who Appeared in Ads Bashing the 2016 GOP Front-Runner," *New York Daily News*, March 8, 2016.

226 *"really legit":* Emma Brown, "Donald Trump Billed His 'University' as a Road to Riches."

226 *Eric Schneiderman filed:* New York state case 451463-2013.

227 *Trump Entrepreneur Initiative:* Brown, "Donald Trump Billed His 'University' as a Road to Riches."

227 *"handpicked by me":* Hamburger, Helderman, and Bennett, "Donald Trump Said 'University' Was All about Education."

227 *pitch was recorded:* Brill, "What the Legal Battle Over Trump University Reveals About Its Founder," *Time*, November 5, 2015.

227 *none were donated:* Ibid. Brill's piece on Trump University was the first to report Trump's failure to fulfill the charity donation pledge. Alan Garten confirmed to the *Washington Post* that no proceeds went to charity.

227 *intended to pass the proceeds:* Hamburger, Helderman, and Bennett, "Donald Trump Said 'University' Was All about Education."

227 *no special Trump methods:* Michael Sexton deposition taken by office of New York State Attorney General, New York City, July 25, 2012. Sexton also said Trump did not pick instructors.

227 *little real estate knowledge:* Hamburger, Helderman, and Bennett, "Donald Trump Said 'University' Was All about Education."

227 *"valuable education":* Donald J. Trump Statement Regarding Trump University, June 7, 2016, https://www.donaldjtrump.com/press-releases/donald-j.-trump -statement-regarding-trump-university.

227 *"Home Shopping Network":* Tom Hamburger, Rosalind S. Helderman, and Alice Crites, "What Trump Said under Oath about the Trump University Fraud Claims—Just Weeks Ago," *Washington Post*, March 3, 2016.

227 *hotel ballrooms:* Brown, "Donald Trump Billed His 'University' as a Road to Riches."

228 *presented a choice of prizes: The Apprentice*, season 6, episode 14, "Decision Time," original airdate April 22, 2007.

228 *Trump Towers Atlanta:* Douglas Sams, "Proposed Trump Towers Site Listed for Foreclosure," *Atlanta Business Chronicle*, February 15, 2010.

228 *"You are being paid sooner":* Letter from Fernando Hazoury to Eric Trump, December 28, 2009, entered as exhibit G to Document 27-4 in *Trump Marks Real Estate LLC v. Cap Cana S.A., et al.,* 1:12-cv-06440-NRB, filed January 17, 2013.

228 *Trump had been paid millions:* Complaint, Document 1, *Trump Marks Real Estate LLC v. Cap Cana S.A., et al.,* 1:12-cv-06440-NRB, filed August 23, 2012.

228 *suit was settled:* Stipulation of Voluntary Dismissal, Document 32, *Trump Marks Real Estate LLC v. Cap Cana S.A., et al.,* 1:12-cv-06440-NRB, filed June 10, 2013.

229 *several licensing agreements:* E.g., License Agreement between Trump Marks Real Estate LLC and Cap Cana S.A., February 16, 2007, section 16. Filed as exhibit A to

Document 27-1 in *Trump Marks Real Estate LLC v. Cap Cana S.A., et al.*, 1:12-cv-06440-NRB, filed January 17, 2013. Also, License Agreement between Trump Marks LLC and PB Impulsores, S. de R.L. de C.V., October 12, 2006, section 18.

229 *"largely owned"*: Donald J. Trump, letter to the editor, *Wall Street Journal*, November 28, 2007.

229 *did not own:* Disclaimer, "Trump International Hotel & Tower" Waikiki Beach Walk is not owned, developed, or sold by Donald J. Trump. www.trump.com, accessed May 1, 2016.

229 *Asked about the discrepancy:* Deposition of Donald J. Trump, December 19, 2007, *Donald J. Trump vs. Timothy L. O'Brien, et al.*, No. CAM-L-545-06, 89–90/.

229 *"substantial equity contribution":* Tom Hamburger and Rosalind S. Helderman, "How Donald Trump Cashes In Even When His Name-Brand Properties Fail," *Washington Post*, July 23, 2015.

229 *"deals can change":* Ibid.

229 *could walk away:* Ibid. See also licensing agreements such as License Agreement between Trump Marks Real Estate LLC and Cap Cana S.A. and License Agreement between Trump Marks LLC and PB Impulsores S. de R.L. de C.V., October 12, 2006.

229 *first-class accommodations:* E.g., License Agreement between Trump Marks Real Estate LLC and Cap Cana S.A., February 16, 2007, 32. Filed publicly as Exhibit A to Document 27, 1:12-cv-06440, January 17, 2013.

230 *next trip to Florida:* J. Michael Goodson interview with Tom Hamburger, *Washington Post*, April 2016.

230 *rent out their units:* 2nd Amended Complaint, *Abercrombie v. SB Hotel Associates LLC et al.*, 07-60702 CACE, 16.

230 *perfect for Goodson:* Goodson interview with Hamburger.

230 *"luxurious experience":* 2nd Amended Complaint, *Abercrombie v. SB Hotel Associates LLC et al.*, 12.

230 *"with great pleasure":* Ibid.

230 *check for $345,000:* Goodson interview with Hamburger.

231 *honor his dream:* Sheila Rousseaux interview with Tom Hamburger, *Washington Post*, April 2016.

231 *a stretch:* J. Michael Goodson, Sheila Rousseaux, and Naraine Seecharan have all been plaintiffs in litigation against Trump over the project.

231 *"can't lose":* Naraine Seecharan interview with Tom Hamburger, *Washington Post*, April 2016.

231 *crowd celebrating:* Trevor Aaronson, "Chump Tower," *Broward-Palm Beach New Times*, June 22, 2006.

231 *"He's real tough:"* Ibid.

231 *"I gave Donald Trump a call":* Ibid.

231 *"We are celebrating":* Aaronson, Ibid.

232 *diamond cuff links:* Aaronson, Ibid.

232 *Corus Bankshares:* Monica Hatcher, "Florida Moves On after Failure of Bank behind Condo Boom," *Miami Herald*, September 15, 2009.

232 *$166 million:* Doreen Hemlock, "Lauderdale Condo-Hotel That Was to Bear Trump Name Sold at Foreclosure Auction," *Sun-Sentinel*, March 14, 2012.

232 *until early 2017:* Information on progress of the project from Conrad Hotels & Resorts website, http://conradhotels3.hilton.com/en/hotels/florida/conrad-fort -lauderdale-beach-FLLCICI/index.html.

232 *he distanced himself:* "We are not the developers." Deposition of Donald J. Trump, November 5, 2013, *Trilogy Properties LLC vs. SB Hotel Associates LLC et al.,* 39.

232 *"world is ending":* Seecharan interview with Hamburger.

232 *"I panicked":* Rousseaux interview with Hamburger.

232 *advised complainers:* Alan Garten interview with Tom Hamburger and Rosalind S. Helderman, *Washington Post,* April 15, 2016.

232 *a local ordinance:* 2nd Amended Complaint, *Abercrombie v. SB Hotel Associates LLC et al.,* 16.

232 *pleaded guilty:* Transcript of sentencing of Felix Sater, 98-CR-1101, October 23, 2009, 6. Filed as Exhibit M in New York State 152324-2014, February 25, 2015.

232 *margarita glass:* Charles V. Bagli, "Real Estate Executive with Hand in Trump Projects Rose from Tangled Past," *New York Times,* December 17, 2007.

233 *"extraordinary cooperation":* Transcript of sentencing of Felix Sater, 98-CR-1101, October 23, 2009, 4. Filed as Exhibit M in New York State 152324-2014, February 25, 2015.

233 *was not revealed:* Deposition of Donald J. Trump, *Abercrombie v. SB Hotel Associates LLC et al.,* November 5, 2013, 16–17.

233 *kept under seal:* Rosalind S. Helderman and Tom Hamburger, "Former Mafia-Linked Figure Describes Association with Trump," *Washington Post,* May 17, 2016.

233 *"If he were sitting":* Deposition of Donald J. Trump, *Abercrombie v. SB Hotel Associates LLC et al.,* 157.

233 *frequently went:* Helderman and Hamburger, "Former Mafia-Linked Figure Describes Association with Trump."

233 *"build a Trump Tower":* Ibid.

233 *so close:* Ibid.

233 *were both traveling:* Ibid.

233 *"all screwed":* Seecharan interview with Hamburger.

234 *minus legal fees:* Bill Allison, "Legal War over Botched Deal Shows How Trump Wins Even When He Loses," *Foreign Policy,* November 30, 2015.

234 *a circuit court jury found:* Verdict issued in *Deer Valley Realty v. Donald J. Trump,* 12-10560 CACE, 17th Judicial Circuit, Broward County, Florida, March 12, 2014. Information comes also from Jared Beck (plaintiff's attorney) interview with Tom Hamburger, *Washington Post,* April 2016.

234 *"in the world":* Michael Calderone, "A Friggin' Mortgage Company Opening," *New York Observer,* April 6, 2006.

234 *"you're fired":* John Carney, "Trump Mortgage Opens," Dealbreaker.com, April 10, 2006.

234 *"a god":* Jan Scheck interview with Michael Kranish, *Washington Post,* February 2016.

235 *"great time":* Trump interview on CNBC, *Wall Street Journal Report,* April 9, 2006.

235 *gave the business:* Tom Hamburger and Michael Kranish, "Trump Mortgage

Failed. Here's What That Says About the GOP Front-Runner," *Washington Post*, February 29, 2016.

235 *to urge buyers to try:* License Agreement between Trump Marks Real Estate LLC and Cap Cana S.A., February 16, 2007, section 3(i). Filed as exhibit A to Document 27-1 in *Trump Marks Real Estate LLC v. Cap Cana S.A. et al.*, 1:12-cv-06440-NRB, filed January 17, 2013.

235 *$3 billion:* Tom Fredrickson, "Undoing of Trump Mortgage," *Crain's New York Business*, August 5, 2007.

235 *Seven million:* "7.3 million Boomerang Buyers Poised to Recover Homeownership in Next 8 Years," RealtyTrac.com, January 26, 2015.

235 *"a bubble":* Trump interview, *Morning Joe*, MSNBC, July 24, 2015, http://www.msnbc.com/morning-joe/watch/donald-trump-rounds-out-the-week-on-morning-joe-490679363866.

235 *"in a very big way":* Fredrickson, "Undoing of Trump Mortgage." Ridings did not respond to a request for comment.

236 *inflated his résumé:* Ibid.

236 *"a better job":* Frederickson, "Undoing of Trump Mortgage."

236 *Trump licensed his name:* Ana Swanson, "The Trump Network Sought to Make People Rich but Left Behind Disappointment," *Washington Post*, March 23, 2016.

236 *" 'be millionaires' ":* Ibid.

236 *"a long shot":* Julianna Goldman and Laura Strickler, "Behind the Collapse of the 'Recession Proof' Trump Network," *CBS This Morning*, accessed May 5, 2016, http://www.cbsnews.com/news/donald-trump-network-cbs-news-investigation-supplements-multi-level-marketing.

237 *promotional video:* Trump promotional video for Trump Network. Available on youtube.com, https://www.youtube.com/watch?v=KjD8AgBKwO4.

237 *"no one ever apologized":* Swanson, "The Trump Network."

238 *simply licensed:* Swanson, "The Trump Network."

238 *"a little surprised":* Paul Owers, "Lenders Foreclose on 200-Unit Trump Condo," *Sun-Sentinel*, November 19, 2010.

238 *By Thanksgiving 2010:* Ken Grossman interview with Tom Hamburger and Rosalind S. Helderman, *Washington Post*, April 8, 2016.

238 *flashy party:* "Trump Hollywood Treats Guests to a Night to Remember," Social Miami.com.

238 *"A fantastic relaunch":* Ibid.

238 *Within fifteen months:* Daniel Lebensohn interview with Tom Hamburger and Rosalind S. Helderman, *Washington Post*, April 8, 2016.

238 *book of Trump's standards:* Review of book of Trump standards by *Washington Post* reporters Tom Hamburger and Rosalind S. Helderman during tour of Trump Hollywood, April 8, 2016.

239 *$10 and $20 million:* Lebensohn interview with Hamburger and Helderman.

CHAPTER 14: EMPIRE

240 *the structure was only a shell:* Visit by Kevin Sullivan, 2016.

241 *in South Korea:* Trump Organization website: http://www.trump.com/real-estate -portfolio/seoul/trump-world/.

241 *Toronto's City Council:* Jonathan Fowlie, "Trump Tower Planned for Downtown Will Be Tallest in City," *Globe and Mail*, February 7, 2003.

242 *Trump boasted:* "Trump Lauds Saakashvili on Fox & Friends," Democracy & Freedom Watch, May 2, 2012, http://dfwatch.net/trump-lauds-saakashvili-on -fox-friends-59008-8320.

242 *cancellation of many projects:* Interview with Kevin Sullivan, 2016.

242 *comments about Muslims:* Andrew Scott, "Damac Removes Trump Billboards from Akoya Project in Dubai," *National*, December 10, 2015.

242 *"does not understand Islam":* "Turkish Business Partner Condemns Donald Trump's Anti-Muslim Stance," *Guardian*, December 11, 2015.

243 *contestants in filming:* "Emin in Another Life Official Music Video Ft. Donald Trump and Miss Universe 2013 Contestants," YouTube, November 20, 2013, https://www.youtube.com/watch?v=iuZUNjFsgS8.

243 *"'be in my video?'":* Aras and Emin Agalarov interview with Michael Birnbaum, 2016.

243 *Donald Trump of Russia:* "The Donald Trump of Russia," CNBC interview, May 18, 2015, http://video.cnbc.com/gallery/?video=3000380510.

243 *Miss Universe organization:* Aras and Emin Agalarov interview with Michael Birnbaum, 2016.

243 *traveled to Las Vegas:* "Emin USA launch of Single 'Amor,'" Getty Images photo, June 15, 2013, http://www.gettyimages.com/detail/news-photo/aras-agalarov -donald-trump-miss-universe-2012-olivia-culpo-news-photo/170653701.

244 *met Trump:* Aras and Emin Agalarov interview with Birnbaum.

244 *started his business:* Clio Williams, "Relative Values: Russia's Billionaire Property Developer, Aras Agalarov, 59, and His Son, Emin, 35, One of Russia's Biggest Pop Stars," *Sunday Times*, April 8, 2015.

244 *Agalarov's Crocus Group:* "Far Eastern Federal University on Russky Island," Crocus Group press release, May 12, 2011.

244 *Putin presented Agalarov:* "Vladimir Putin Decorated Aras Agalarov with the Order of Order (sic)," Crocus Group press release, October 29, 2013.

245 *about $14 million:* Aras and Emin Agalarov interview with Birnbaum.

245 *preliminary agreement:* Ibid.

245 *As early as 1987:* Steve Goldstein, "Trump May Build Hotels in USSR," Philly. com, July 7, 1987.

245 *Donald Trump Jr. said:* Hazel Heyer, "Executive Talk: Donald Trump Jr. Bullish on Russia and Few Emerging Markets," *Global Travel Industry News*, September 15, 2008.

245 *building a skyscraper:* "US 'Miss Universe' Billionaire Plans Russian Trump Tower," RT.com, November 9, 2013.

245 *scheduled to meet:* Aras and Emin Agalarov interview with Birnbaum.

245 *"very warm feelings":* Ibid.

246 *"never becomes president"*: Ibid.

246 *royal wedding*: "Emin: A Singer with Connections," BBC News, March 1, 2011.

246 *dominant political force*: Heydar Aliyev Foundation biography, http://www.hey dar-aliyev-foundation.org/en/content/index/63/.

246 *"Corleones of the Caspian"*: Michael Weiss, "The Corleones of the Caspian," *Foreign Policy*, June 10, 2014.

246 *comparing Aliyev's administration*: Haley Sweetland Edwards, "Azerbaijan: President Aliyev Compared Unfavorably to Hot-Headed Mobster in WikiLeaks Cable," *Los Angeles Times*, December 3, 2010.

247 *Southern Gas Corridor*: "Southern Gas Corridor," Trans Adriatic Pipeline AG company website, http://www.tap-ag.com/the-pipeline/the-big-picture/south ern-gas-corridor.

247 *In November 2014*: "Trump Hotel Collection Announces Trump International Hotel & Tower Baku," PR Newswire, November 4, 2014.

247 *State Department called*: "2013 Investment Climate Statement-Azerbaijan," U.S. State Department report, March 2013, http://www.state.gov/e/eb/rls/othr /ics/2013/204596.htm. Mammadov did not respond to repeated requests for an interview, relayed to him through officials at his company, friends, via email and Facebook messages.

247 *Mammadov attended*: "Philanthropist Anar Mammadov," Anar Mammadov, WordPress.com, August 14, 2014.

247 *waterfront mansions*: Andrew Higgins, "Pricey Real Estate Deals in Dubai Raise Questions about Azerbaijan's President," *Washington Post*, March 5, 2010.

247 *$1 billion for projects*: Nushabe Fatullayeva, "Mixing Government and Business in Azerbaijan," Radio Free Europe/Radio Liberty, April 4, 2013. The report also disclosed that Mammadov was for a time, when he was barely out of his twenties, an 81 percent shareholder in the Bank of Azerbaijan, which handled much of Mammadov's transportation-related business.

248 *Azerbaijan Golf Federation*: "Inaugural Azerbaijan Golf Challenge Open Praised by Foreign Media," Anar Mammadov Tumblr page, http://anarmammadov .tumblr.com/.

248 *$12 million lobbying*: "Azerbaijan America Alliance," OpenSecrets.org report, 2015, http://www.opensecrets.org/lobby/clientsum.php?id=D000064546.

248 *"caviar diplomacy"*: Robert Coalson, "Baku Smooths Over Its Rights Record with a Thick Layer of Caviar," Radio Free Europe/Radio Liberty, November 8, 2013.

248 *annual gala dinners*: Daniel Swartz, "Speaker Boehner, Congressional Leaders, AMBs reaffirm U.S./Azerbaijani Relationship at Dinner Gala," Revamp.com, November 15, 2012, http://www.revamp.com/story.php?StoryID=2127.

248 *Burton, a Republican from Indiana*: Ilya Lozovsky, "How Azerbaijan and Its Lobbyists Spin Congress," *Foreign Policy*, June 11, 2015.

248 *licensing agreement*: Alan Garten interview with Kevin Sullivan, 2016.

249 *smart business move*: Ibid.

249 *"trying to establish itself"*: Ibid. Garten said he could not remember the name of the intermediary who connected Trump with Mammadov.

249 *Trump had hired*: "Corinthia Hotels Appoint Eric Pere as New General Manager of Corinthia Hotel Prague," Corinthia Hotels press release, November 9, 2015,

http://www.ihiplc.com/news/news-detail/corinthia-hotels-appoint-eric-pere-as
-new-general-manager-of-corinthia-hotel-prague.

249 *"had an interruption":* Khalid Karimli interview with Sullivan.

250 *income from the project:* Rosalind S. Helderman and Tom Hamburger, "Donald Trump's Financial Disclosure Lists Hundreds of Positions and Deals," *Washington Post,* July 22, 2015.

250 *Burton resigned:* Carl Schreck, "Ex–U.S. Congressman Quits Azerbaijani Lobby Group, Citing Nonpayment," Radio Free Europe/Radio Liberty, March 2, 2016.

250 *"never had more":* Trump Hotel Collection literature, https://www.trumphotel collection.com/panama/panama-city-panama-hotels.php.

251 *President Ricardo Martinelli:* "Donald Trump at Press Conference in Trump Panama," YouTube, July 6, 2011, https://www.youtube.com/watch?v=ZfyvAE6 uZLU.

251 *"very important bridge":* Tim Rogers, "Donald Trump to Panama: You're Hired!" *Christian Science Monitor,* February 24, 2011.

251 *invited Donald Trump:* Roger Khafif interview with Sullivan.

252 *Trump name attached:* "Thatcher Proffitt Completed Trump Ocean Club Bond Offering," PR Newswire, November 20, 2007.

252 *the details of the project:* Interviews with Kevin Sullivan, 2016. Khafif would not disclose the percentage of each sale that Trump would receive. Garten declined to discuss any financial details.

252 *about $50 million:* Interviews with Sullivan. The sources asked not to be identified out of fear of retaliation from Trump. "Trump sues everybody," said one, a condominium owner in the Trump building. Garten declined to discuss the financial details of the project.

253 *between January 2014 and July 2015:* Helderman and Hamburger, "Donald Trump's Financial Disclosure Lists Hundreds of Positions and Deals."

253 *management fees:* Donald Trump's personal financial disclosure, *Washington Post,* released on May 18, 2016, https://www.washingtonpost.com/apps/g/page /politics/donald-trumps-personal-financial-disclosure/2033/.

253 *Problems started:* Jeff Barton, "Trump Ocean Club: The Good, Bad and Ugly (Part 1)," *Panama Property News,* September 25, 2014.

253 *filed for Chapter 11:* Maria Chutchian, "Panamanian Trump Hotel's Developer's Ch. 11 Plan Gets Nod," Law360.com, May 30, 2013.

253 *$50 million:* Khafif interview with Sullivan.

253 *the bankruptcy deal:* Jeff Horwitz, "Panama Condo Owners to Trump: You're Fired!" Associated Press, October 11, 2015.

253 *paid $100:* Panama public land records, obtained by the *Washington Post,* April 2016.

253 *Trump's local managers:* Many details of the dispute were first reported by the Associated Press.

253 *had overspent:* Interviews with Sullivan.

253 *managers proposed imposing:* Ibid.

254 *$25 million:* There is some dispute about the amount Trump sought. The Associated Press reported that Trump sued the condo owners for "as much as $75 mil-

lion," and a condo owner interviewed by the *Washington Post* also said Trump had sued for $75 million. But Garten said that was an incorrect reading of the complaint. He said Trump's complaint, which he wrote, sought $25 million on each of several "causes of action." He said it was misleading to add each of those demands together, so the total that Trump sought was $25 million. "I'm not saying that's not a lot of money, but we never sued them for $75 million," he said. The *Washington Post* was unable to obtain a copy of the confidential complaint or settlement.

254 *by the Associated Press:* Jeff Horwitz, "Fired by Panama Condo Owners, Trump Demands $75 Million," Associated Press, November 4, 2015.

254 *board backed down:* Interviews with two people involved in the dispute, Kevin Sullivan, 2016.

254 *"protect our interests":* Interview with Sullivan.

254 *Stevenson, Trump's former:* Interview with Sullivan.

255 *"celebrities will descend":* Karen Grant, "Donald Trumpets New Dawn for Golf," *Aberdeen Evening Express,* April 1, 2006.

256 *"being sawn off":* "Me Take over Millionaire? Don't (Piggy) Bank on It," *Aberdeen Press and Journal,* April 3, 2006.

256 *grand promises:* Martin Ford interview with Jenna Johnson, April 12, 2016.

257 *"he's funny, too":* Severin Carrell, "Heir of Stornoway: Trump's Flying Visit to the Family Home," *Guardian,* June 10, 2008.

257 *"read so much":* Morag Lindsay, "Laid-Back Millionaire Confident of Triumph," *Aberdeen Press and Journal,* June 11, 2008.

257 *"know how to buy":* Craig Walker, "Trump & Ford Clash at Inquiry," *Aberdeen Evening Express,* June 10, 2008.

257 *"like a pig":* Quoted in Anthony Baxter, *You've Been Trumped,* documentary film, Montrose Pictures, 2012.

257 *"obliterated by a slum":* Frank Urquhart, "Donald Trump Jets In and Fires Off 'Slum and Pigsty' Slur," *The Scotsman,* May 27, 2010.

258 *ripped them out:* David Milne interview with Johnson, April 1, 2016.

259 *declined to attend:* Scot Macnab, "Nicola Sturgeon Rules Out Meeting Donald Trump at Turnberry," *Edinburgh Evening News,* June 10, 2016.

259 *"already been won":* Donald Trump, "Why Scotland Will Help Me Become US President," *Aberdeen Press and Journal,* April 11, 2016.

CHAPTER 15: SHOWMAN

260 *throbbing mass:* Aaron Oster, "Donald Trump and WWE: How the Road to the White House Began at 'WrestleMania,'" *Rolling Stone,* February 1, 2016.

260 *"lions in the jungle":* Steve Kraske, "Flamboyant Trump Plays the Presidential Hinting Game," *Contra Costa Times,* February 13, 2000.

260 *"screw them back":* Robert McCoppin, "Amen, Brother! Financial Gods Trump and Robbins Whip Expo Crowd into a Frenzy, but Investors Come for Straight-Shooting Sermons," *Chicago Daily Herald,* November 10, 2005.

261 *"Look up at the sky, Vince":* "Donald Trump Gives Away Mr. McMahon's Money

on Fan," YouTube, posted July 3, 2012, https://www.youtube.com/watch?v =ybtwzNpJ0YA.

261 *"grapefruits are no match"*: "Mr. McMahon and Donald Trump's Battle of the Billionaires Contract Signing," YouTube, posted December 8, 2013, https://www .youtube.com/watch?v=vVeVcVBW_CE.

262 *"gave him a wallop"*: "Donald Trump Hits Wrestling Promoter Vince McMahon," YouTube, posted August 14, 2015, https://www.youtube.com/watch?v=-9CjKf O6ef0.

262 *"He was working crowds"*: Court Bauer interview with Paul Schwartzman, May 2016.

262 *"What Donald stands for"*: Ibid.

262 *"hostile takeover"*: "The Battle of the Billionaires Takes Place at WrestleMania," YouTube, posted July 19, 2011, https://www.youtube.com/watch?v=5NsrwH9 I9vE.

262 *"He exceeded all expectations"*: Bauer interview with Schwartzman.

262 *an electric shaver*: "The Battle of the Billionaires Takes Place at WrestleMania," You Tube, posted July 19, 2011, https://www.youtube.com/watch?v=5NsrwH9I9vE.

262 *"a great entertainer"*: NBC News transcripts, April 2, 2007, https://www.nexis.com /results/enhdocview.do?docLinkInd=true&ersKey=23_T24134647381&format =GNBFI&startDocNo=76&resultsUrlKey=0_T24134669170&backKey=20 _T24134669171&csi=157446&docNo=99.

263 *"my esteemed pleasure"*: *The Fresh Prince of Bel-Air*, season 4, episode 25, "For Sale by Owner," https://www.youtube.com/watch?v=Tu1gj010oa8.

263 *in cameos*: Donald Trump's IMDb page, http://www.imdb.com/name/nm0874339 /?ref_=rvi_nm.

263 *"there are knives"*: *Ghosts Can't Do It*, dir. John Derek (1989: Triumph Releasing), https://www.youtube.com/watch?v=co0aDXPTK5o.

263 *"particular about his hair"*: Shelley Jensen interview with Paul Schwartzman, May 2016.

264 *"real estate mogul"*: Ibid.

264 *"Mr. Trump here wrote* Art of the Deal*"*: *Spin City*, season 2, episode 14, "The Paul Lassiter Story," January 21, 1998.

264 *"this crazy, paranoid guy"*: Walter Barnett interview with Paul Schwartzman, May 2016.

264 *"he could be difficult"*: Andy Cadiff interview with Paul Schwartzman, May 2016.

264 *"A cosmopolitan and Donald Trump"*: *Sex and the City*, season 2, episode 8, "The Man, the Myth, the Viagra."

264 *"want to study them?"*: Victoria Hochberg interview with Paul Schwartzman, May 2016.

265 *"you're really beautiful"*: New York City Inner Circle Show 2000, dir. Elliot Cuker, https://www.youtube.com/watch?v=4IrE6FMpai8.

265 *"a traveling judge"*: Elliot Cuker interview with Paul Schwartzman, May 2016.

265 *"I'm not doing that"*: T. Sean Shannon interview with Paul Schwartzman, May 2016.

265 *"making fun of him"*: Ibid.

266 *"great to be here"*: Saturday Night Live, season 29, episode 16, https://www.nbc
.com/saturday-night-live/season-29/episode/16-donald-trump-with-toots-and
-the-maytals-63841.

266 *straw hat and overalls*: 57th Annual Emmy Awards, CBS, September 18, 2005, https://www.youtube.com/watch?v=AiZqFGLAeAc.

266 *"pop-culture oddity"*: Diane Werts, "The Emmys; The Donald 'Idolized,'" Newsday, September 19, 2005.

266 *"really needed to win"*: Megan Mullally interview on *Conan*, January 18, 2016, https://www.youtube.com/watch?v=47meFVgINLU.

266 *nuptials live*: Neil Wilkes, "Trump Regrets Not Televising Wedding," *DigitalSpy*, February 5, 2005, http://www.digitalspy.com/tv/news/a19014/trump-regrets-not
-televising-wedding/.

266 *fifteen hundred crystals*: Julia Ioffe, "Melania Trump on Her Rise, Her Family Secrets, and Her True Political Views," *GQ*, April 27, 2016.

266 *serenading the couple*: Michael Callahan, "Flashback: When Hillary and Bill Hit the Wedding of Donald and Melania," *Hollywood Reporter*, April 7, 2016.

267 *"no-maintenance woman"*: Trump, *Trump: The Art of the Comeback*, 141.

267 *"She was a homebody"*: Edit Molnar interview with Mary Jordan, September 2015.

267 *"a celebrity myself"*: Melania Trump interview with Mary Jordan, April 2016.

268 *"We like the same things"*: Ibid.

268 *"Donald the best"*: Louise Sunshine interview with Frances Stead Sellers and Paul Schwartzman, May 2016.

268 *"Sometimes he listens"*: Melania Trump interview with Jordan.

269 *"the great beauties"*: Trump interview with Bob Woodward and Robert Costa, April 2016.

269 *"more models' lives"*: Comedy Central Roast of Donald Trump, March 15, 2011, http://www.cc.com/shows/roast-of-donald-trump.

269 *"'I have less money'"*: "In Bed with Joan: Episode 7," published April 17, 2013, https://www.youtube.com/watch?v=ZJdVL2O7Nok.

270 *"You suck!"*: Video of ceremony posted April 9, 2013, https://www.youtube.com
/watch?v=ZBl6cL9GYs0.

270 *selling off his shares*: Drew Harwell, Rosalind S. Helderman, and Tom Hamburger, "Trump's Business Booms as He Runs for President, Financial Disclosures Show," *Washington Post*, May 19, 2016.

270 *"I sold it"*: Trump interview with Frances Stead Sellers, November 2015.

CHAPTER 16: POLITICAL CHAMELEON

271 *This had been the setting*: Schwartzman, "How Trump Got Religion."

271 *The first signs*: Weiss, "The Lives They Lived: Fred C. Trump." Trump sold his interest in the Empire State Building in 2002.

271 *Hundreds of mourners*: Angela Mosconi, "Trump Patriarch Eulogized as Great Builder," *New York Post*, June 30, 1999.

271 *ten stained glass*: http://www.marblechurch.org/welcome/history/.

271 *shared stories*: Blair, *Trumps*, 203.

271 *Mayor Rudolph Giuliani:* Mosconi, "Trump Patriarch Eulogized as Great
     Builder."

272 *When it was Donald's turn:* Blair, *The Trumps*, 203.

272 *"The name just sells":* Robin Pogrebin, "Protests Supplanted by Praise; Trump
     Place Becomes Real, and Even Popular," *New York Times*, June 25, 1999.

272 *"toughest day":* Mosconi, "Trump Patriarch Eulogized as Great Builder."

272 *his best friend:* Trump interview with Shawn Boburg, Robert O'Harrow,
     Drew Harwell, Amy Goldstein, and Jerry Markon, *Washington Post*, May 18,
     2016.

272 *"loneliness and responsibility":* Trump interview with Fisher and Kranish, June 8,
     2016.

272 *to see himself differently:* Donald Trump, *The America We Deserve* (Los Angeles:
     Renaissance Books, 2000), 23.

272 *a condolence letter:* Ibid., 24.

272 *died when an airplane:* Mike Allen, "Bodies from Kennedy Crash Are Found,"
     New York Times, July 22, 1999.

272 *the glowing obituaries:* Trump, *The America We Deserve*, 23.

272 *death was perhaps:* Trump interview with Boburg, O'Harrow, Harwell, Gold-
     stein, and Markon. In the interview, Trump, when asked whether his father's
     death prompted him to run for president, said: "I would imagine perhaps it did,
     but maybe inwardly."

273 *"Today's Super Rich":* Rona Barrett interview with Robert Samuels, *Washington
     Post*, May 18, 2016.

273 *"we just sit back":* Trump interview with Rona Barrett, October 6, 1980, Reelin' in
     the Years Productions.

273 *wanted a winner:* George Arzt and Cindy Darrison interviews with Shawn
     Boburg, *Washington Post*, May 18, 2016.

273 *opposing candidates:* Analysis of New York City, New York State, and federal cam-
     paign finance data by Alice Crites, *Washington Post*.

273 *"someone who was going to continue":* George Arzt interview with Shawn Boburg,
     Washington Post, May 19, 2016.

274 *Armed with subpoena power:* Transcript of "Hearing on Campaign Finance Prac-
     tices of Citywide and Statewide Officials," State of New York Commission on
     Government Integrity, March 14, 1988.

274 *But Trump "circumvented":* "Corruption and Racketeering in the New York City
     Construction Industry," *Final Report of the New York State Organized Crime Task
     Force* (New York: New York University Press, 1990), 120.

274 *a different name:* Transcript of "Hearing on Campaign Finance Practices of City-
     wide and Statewide Officials," State of New York Commission on Government
     Integrity, March 14, 1988.

274 *In June 1985:* Ibid.

274 *More than thirty years:* O'Harrow, "Trump Swam in Mob-Infested Waters."

274 *He gave more than:* Martin Tolchin, "10 Pay Fines for Excessive Campaign Dona-
     tions," *New York Times*, March 18, 1993.

275 *Trump Tower that summer:* Michael Dunbar interview with Robert Samuels,
     Washington Post, April 29, 2016.

275 *They had a deal:* Dunbar interview with Samuels.

275 *A few weeks later:* Michael Oreskes, "Trump Gives a Vague Hint of Candidacy," *New York Times*, September 2, 1987.

275 *"There's nothing wrong":* "There's nothing wrong with America's foreign defense policy that a little backbone can't cure," newspaper advertisement, The Trump Organization, *Washington Post,* September 2, 1987.

276 *Trump told a* Washington Post *reporter in 1984*: Lois Romano, "Donald Trump, Holding All the Cards, The Tower! The Team! The Money! The Future!," *Washington Post*, November 15, 1984.

276 *"Hint of Candidacy":* Oreskes, "Trump Gives a Vague Hint of Candidacy."

276 *"have had enough":* Amy Hart, "Trump Tells Rotarians He's Not Running for President," *Foster's Democrat Daily*, October 24, 1987, provided by Michael Dunbar.

276 *"running for president":* Hart, "Trump Tells Rotarians He's Not Running for President."

277 *planted a seed:* Michael Dunbar interview with Robert Samuels, *Washington Post*, April 29, 2016.

277 *"a large ego":* Letter from Frank Donatelli to Tom Criscom, November 19, 1987, ID#547309, White House Office of Records Management Subject Files, Reagan Presidential Library.

277 *"Dear Donald":* David K. Li, " 'Donald Trump Will Be a Winner' Predicted Richard Nixon," *New York Post*, September 9, 2015.

277 *"helluva chance of winning":* Trump interview with Oprah Winfrey, *The Oprah Winfrey Show*, April 25, 1988.

278 *why he was there:* Trump interview with Larry King, CNN, August 17, 1988.

278 *"principles of the Republican Party":* Ibid.

279 *"roving bands of wild criminals":* Michael Wilson, "Trump Draws Criticism for Ad He Ran after Jogger Attack," *New York Times*, October 23, 2002.

279 *Trump was "greedy":* Alan Finder, "The Koch-Trump Feud," *New York Times*, June 1, 1987.

279 *"executed for their crimes":* Wilson, "Trump Draws Criticism for Ad He Ran after Jogger Attack."

279 *"hatemongering ad":* Al Sharpton letter, "Sharpton Urges Don King, Tyson to Boycott Trump," *New York Amsterdam News*, May 13, 1989.

279 *New York's problems:* Fox 5 News, WNYW, transcript and tape, May 1, 1989.

279 *"You better believe that":* Oliver Laughland, "Donald Trump and the Central Park Five: The Racially Charged Rise of a Demagogue," *Guardian*, February 17, 2016. Video: http://www.theguardian.com/us-news/2016/feb/17/central-park-five -donald-trump-jogger-rape-case-new-york.

279 *Trump's assertion "garbage":* The NBC-TV special *R.A.C.E.* aired during the first week of September 1989. Video of the show was obtained from the Vanderbilt University television news archives. See also Walter Goodman, "A Poll of Viewers' Feelings about Racial Issues," *New York Times*, September 8, 1989.

280 *"candy from a baby":* Stephen Rex Brown, "Exclusive: Members of the Central Park Five Shocked Donald Trump Is Leading GOP Candidate, Despite Having 'No Compassion,' " *New York Daily News*, August 18, 2015.

280 *Decades later:* Video: "Central Park Five Member Recalls Trump," *Guardian*, February 17, 2016.

280 *"Wouldn't you say I'm a little controversial":* Trump interview with King, July 27, 1990.

280 *"biggest scandal ever":* Transcript, "Oversight Hearing before the Subcommittee on Native American Affairs," Washington, DC, October 5, 1993, 242–47.

280 *The comments echoed:* Ibid. The hearing record includes a transcript from Trump's appearance on *Imus in the Morning*.

281 *cocaine lines and syringes:* Neil Swidey, "Trump Plays Both Sides in Casino Bids," *Boston Globe*, December 13, 2000.

281 *ostensible telephone survey:* James M. Odato, "Trump, Associates Detail Campaign," *Times Union*, November 29, 2000.

281 *Institute for Law and Safety:* Bagli, "Trump and Others Accept Fines for Ads in Opposition to Casinos."

281 *a Republican operative and fixer:* Roger Stone interview with Tom Hamburger and Mary Jordan, *Washington Post*, May 11, 2016.

282 *Trump had paid:* Bagli, "Trump and Others Accept Fines for Ads in Opposition to Casinos."

282 *The state lobbying:* Settlement Agreement between Trump Casino and Hotels and New York Temporary State Commission on Lobbying, November 13, 2000.

282 *"It's been settled":* Bagli, "Trump and Others Accept Fines for Ads in Opposition to Casinos."

282 *misdemeanor charge:* Kenneth Lovett, "Republican Game to Pounce on Donald Trump over $250,000 Fine He Paid for Illegal Lobbying to Stop Indian-Run Casino," *New York Daily News*, March 8, 2016.

282 *"destroy the progress":* Bagli, "Trump and Others Accept Fines for Ads in Opposition to Casinos."

282 *Under a 1997 pact:* Ruling and Order, March 31, 2004, Trump Hotels & Casino Resorts vs. David A. Roscow, et al., U.S. District Court, Connecticut, Case No. 3:03CV1133.

282 *Miami-based firm:* Lobbying Disclosure Act database, U.S. Senate, http://sopr web.senate.gov.

282 *tribe won federal:* Complaint: Trump Hotels & Casino Resorts vs. David A. Roscow. In 2005, three years after winning federal recognition, the Department of the Interior reversed its decision following an appeal by Connecticut's attorney general.

283 *more than $600,000:* Ronald Platt interview with Shawn Boburg, *Washington Post*, May 19, 2016.

283 *"held back payment":* Matt Flegenheimer and Steve Eder, "Donald Trump's Trips to Capitol Hill Years Ago Foretold of Campaign," *New York Times*, May 11, 2016.

283 *"not a matchmaker":* Letter from Tony August to President Clinton, April 2, 1993, Clinton Presidential Library, Donald J. Trump collection.

283 *prominent officials:* Jonathan P. Hicks, "After Skipping President's Talk, Giuliani Meets Clinton in Private," *New York Times*, March 11, 1994.

283 *Clinton's personal secretary:* Clinton Presidential Library, Donald J. Trump collection.

284 *"How about me with the women?"*: Glenn Kessler, "Trump's Flip-Flop on Whether the Bill Clinton Sex Scandals Are Important," *Washington Post*, May 24, 2016.

284 *this could be Trump's moment*: Roger Stone interview with Robert Samuels, *Washington Post*, May 2, 2016.

284 *was still popular*: http://uselectionatlas.org/RESULTS/national.php?year=1992.

284 *particularly familiar with the rise of Jesse Ventura*: *CNN Tonight*, CNN, August 18, 2005.

285 *previous two presidential elections*: http://www.fec.gov/press/bkgnd/fund.shtml.

285 *"spirit has to be brought back"*: *Larry King Live*, CNN, October 8, 1999.

285 *Oprah Winfrey*: *Larry King Live*, CNN, October 8, 1999.

285 *publicity stunt*: Al D'Amato interview with Robert Samuels, *Washington Post*, May 20, 2016.

285 *"divide our country"*: Paul Alexander, "Trump Towers," *Advocate*, February 15, 2000.

286 *renegotiation of trade agreements*: *Larry King Live*, CNN, October 8, 1999.

286 *Trump interrupted*: *Meet the Press*, NBC, October 24, 1999.

286 *partial-birth abortion was*: Roger Stone interview with Tom Hamburger and Mary Jordan, *Washington Post*, May 11, 2016.

286 *"Let's cut to the chase"*: Trump, *The America We Deserve*, 15.

286 *"a woman's right to choose"*: Ibid., 30.

287 *election campaign awaited them*: Phil Madsen interview with Robert Samuels, *Washington Post*, April 30, 2016.

287 *"Just be honest"*: Dean Barkley interview with Robert Samuels, *Washington Post*, April 28, 2016.

287 *Trump expressed concern*: Ibid.

287 *"Are these people stiffs"*: Cragg Hines, "Trump, Ventura Stir Political Pot," *Houston Chronicle*, January 8, 2000.

287 *an op-ed in the* New York Times: Donald J. Trump, "What I Saw at the Revolution," *New York Times*, February 19, 2000.

287 *He won both*: http://www.fec.gov/pubrec/fe2000/2000presprim.htm.

288 *graciously let it pass*: Judith Hope interview with Shawn Boburg, *Washington Post*, May 19, 2016.

288 *"in my business"*: Trump interview with Fisher and Kranish, June 9, 2016.

288 *He also invited*: Joshua Gillin, "The Clintons Really Did Attend Donald Trump's 2005 Wedding," *PolitiFact*, July 21, 2015.

288 *joined the Democratic Party*: New York City Board of Elections voting history.

288 *"said to myself"*: Trump interview with Boburg, O'Harrow, Goldstein, Markon, and Harwell.

288 *policing and the commercialization*: Fernando Ferrer interview with Shawn Boburg, *Washington Post*, May 17, 2016.

288 *eve of the runoff*: Michael Cooper and Randal C. Archibald, "Runoff Campaign Turns Confrontational and Strange as Candidates Trade Charges," *New York Times*, October 10, 2001.

289 *wondering to himself*: Fernando Ferrer interview with Shawn Boburg, *Washington Post*, May 17, 2016.

289 *handwritten letter*: Interview with Eliot Spitzer, *Washington Post*, May 19, 2016.

289 *slammed Spitzer:* Donald Trump, Twitter account, July 10, 2013.

289 *"I give to everybody":* YouTube, presidential debate, August 6, 2015, https://www.youtube.com/watch?v=jiwMCAkK9uE.

290 *"give not to show up?":* Frank Sanzillo interview with Marc Fisher, *Washington Post*, April 2016.

290 *Trump and his major companies:* Analysis of New York City, New York State, and federal campaign finance data, Alice Crites, *Washington Post.*

290 *"The only thing":* Charlie Rangel interview with Robert Samuels, *Washington Post*, May 9, 2016.

290 *a "disaster":* Trump interview with Robert Samuels, *Washington Post*, May 25, 2016.

290 *Five days after the invasion:* Michelle Ye Hee Lee, "A Timeline of Trump's Comments on Iraq Invasion: Not Loud, Not Strong, No Headlines," *Washington Post*, February 25, 2016.

290 *Recalling the 2004 vote:* Trump interview with Samuels.

290 *"wonderful qualities":* Maureen Dowd, "Trump Fired Up," *New York Times*, December 23, 2006.

290 *voted for him:* Trump interview with Samuels.

290 *changed parties:* Voter registration records, New York City Board of Elections. Information on Trump's historical party registration is based on a document provided by the Board of Elections in the City of New York. The document, a description of "Activities to the Voter Record," contains internal coding corresponding to changes in Trump's voter registration since 1992. A spokeswoman at the Board of Elections declined to explain the coding, but Jerry Skurnik, a New York City–based political consultant who cofounded a company, Prime NY, that collects and distributes information on agency records, examined the document at the request of the *Washington Post.*

291 *"make friends":* Trump interview with Fisher and Kranish, June 9, 2016.

291 *Trump's celebrity:* Jonathan Weisman and Scott Greenberg, "NBC/WSJ Poll: A Donald Trump Surprise," *Wall Street Journal*, April 6, 2011.

291 *Among Tea Party:* "NBC/WSJ Poll: Trump Tied for 2nd in 2012 GOP Field," www.nbcnews.com, April 6, 2011.

291 *a "jobkiller!":* https://twitter.com/realDonaldTrump/status/131778860189626369?lang=en.

291 *"one of the greatest threats":* https://twitter.com/realDonaldTrump/status/137640805908234240?lang=en.

291 *"show his birth certificate":* Seamus McGraw, "Trump: I Have 'Real Doubts' Obama Was Born in U.S.," *Today News*, April 7, 2011.

291 *Obama announced that:* Karen Tumulty and Anne E. Kornblut, "Obama, Frustrated by 'This Silliness,' Produces Detailed Hawaii Birth Certificate," *Washington Post*, April 27, 2011.

291 *"phenomenal":* Roxanne Roberts, "I Sat Next to Donald Trump at the Infamous 2011 White House Correspondents' Dinner," *Washington Post*, April 28, 2016.

292 *"greatest passion":* Lisa de Moraes, "Donald Trump: I Will Not Be Running for President," *Washington Post*, May 16, 2011.

292 *"contract with* The Apprentice*":* Trump interview with Marc Fisher, *Washington Post*, December 2015.

292 *"something great":* Rachel Weiner and Phil Rucker, "Donald Trump Endorses Mitt Romney," *Washington Post*, February 2, 2012.

292 *$5 million to a charity:* "From the Desk of Donald Trump: Major Announcement," posted October 24, 2012, https://www.youtube.com/watch?v=MgOq9pBkY0I.

292 *Obama ignored the request:* CBS News, "Donald Trump 5m Offer to President Falls Flat, Joke to Many," October 25, 2012.

292 *"felt good":* Gayle Fee, Laura Raposa, and Megan Johnson, *Boston Herald*, November 7, 2012. Trump also described his attendance in Boston, and his frustration at the loss in an interview with Jenna Johnson, *Washington Post*, May 13, 2016.

292 *"total sham and a travesty":* Donald Trump, @realdonaldtrump, November 6, 2012, https://twitter.com/realDonaldTrump/status/266035509162303492?lang=en.

292 *"Let's fight like hell":* Trump, November 6, 2012, https://twitter.com/realDonald Trump/status/266034957875544064?lang=en.

292 *"Our nation is totally divided!":* Trump, November 6, 2012, https://twitter.com /realDonaldTrump/status/266034630820507648?lang=en.

CHAPTER 17: THE WORTH OF A MAN

293 *$8.7 billion:* Donald J. Trump Summary of Net Worth as of June 30, 2014.

293 *"amazing job":* Transcript of Donald Trump presidential announcement speech, June 16, 2015, https://www.washingtonpost.com/news/post-politics/wp/2015 /06/16/full-text-donald-trump-announces-a-presidential-bid/.

294 *"TEN BILLION DOLLARS":* "Donald J. Trump Files Personal Financial Disclosure Statement with Federal Election Commission," Trump press statement, July 15, 2015, https://www.donaldjtrump.com/press-releases/donald-j.-trump -files-personal-financial-disclosure-statement-with-federal.

294 *every December:* State of New Jersey Department of Law and Public Safety Division of Gaming Enforcement Report to the Casino Control Commission, October 16, 1981, 35.

294 *paid no income tax:* Ibid., 37. Drew Harwell, "Trump Once Revealed His Income Tax Returns. They Showed He Didn't Pay a Cent," *Washington Post*, May 21, 2016.

294 *from his father:* State of New Jersey Department of Law and Public Safety Division of Gaming Enforcement Report to the Casino Control Commission, PDF32.

294 *Atlantic City debt:* Ibid., 25.

294 *"keep score" in life:* Donald Trump tweet, September 13, 2014, https://twitter.com /realdonaldtrump/status/510935518360895488.

295 *about $500 million:* Randall Lane, "Inside the Epic Fantasy That's Driven Donald Trump for 33 Years," *Forbes*, October 19, 2015.

295 *"divide whatever [Trump] said":* Harold Seneker interview with Allan Sloan, *Washington Post*, 2016.

295 *"breaking every record":* Jennifer Wang, "The Ups and Downs of Donald Trump: Three Decades On and Off the Forbes 400," *Forbes*, March 14, 2016.

295 *"won't lose a dollar"*: Robert Lenzner, "He's His Own Trump Card: New York's Biggest Wheeler-Dealer Looking for Bigger, Better Deals," *Boston Globe*, October 23, 1988.

295 *"I hope so"*: David Letterman interview with Donald Trump, November 10, 1988, at the eighteen-minute mark, https://www.youtube.com/watch?v=GmNN2MCJ -7U&feature=youtu.be&t=16m12s.

296 *"your own lap"*: *MacNeil/Lehrer NewsHour* interview with Abe Wallach, 1989. https://www.youtube.com/watch?v=KlwCXgZwSCc (10:05).

296 *defamation of character:* Interview with Abe Wallach, 2016.

296 *did not recall:* Trump interview with Fisher and Kranish, June 9, 2016.

296 *Trump himself called:* Abe Wallach, "How to Get Hired by Donald Trump," unpublished manuscript.

297 *offered him a job:* Ibid.

297 *calculated his net worth:* State of New Jersey Casino Control Commission Report on the Financial Position of Donald J. Trump, April 15, 1991; Wallach unpublished manuscript provided to *Washington Post.*

297 *"additional source of coin"*: Richard L. Stern and John Connolly, "Manhattan's Favorite Guessing Game: How Rich Is Donald," *Forbes*, May 14, 1990.

297 *$500 million:* "Trump Loses Billionaire Status, *Forbes* Says," United Press International, April 27, 1990.

297 *six consecutive years:* Wang, "The Ups and Downs of Donald Trump: Three Decades on and off the Forbes 400."

297 *"very inaccurate survey"*: Glenn Plaskin, "Playboy Interview: Donald Trump," *Playboy*, March 1990.

297 *"net worth"*: Trump and Leerhsen, *Surviving at the Top*, 30.

297 *$832 million in debt:* State of New Jersey Casino Control Commission, Trump Petition to Transfer Casino Security and Equity to banks, August 16, 1990, 37.

297 *due diligence:* Interview with Abe Wallach, 2016.

298 *informal financial statement:* Ibid.

298 *the building for renovations: Bloomberg Business News*, "40 Wall Street Is Sold to Trump," December 7, 1995, as published in the *New York Times.*

298 *"turned down the heat"*: Trump interview with Fisher and Kranish, June 9, 2016. Wallach gave a similar account in the "40 Wall Street" chapter of his unpublished manuscript.

299 *at least $500 million:* Steve Cuozzo, "Donald Trump Could Sell 40 Wall St. to Fund His Campaign," *New York Post*, May 23, 2016.

299 *"many years"*: Trump interview with Fisher and Kranish.

299 *$214 million:* Trump financial disclosure form.

299 *"control his image"*: Robert Slater, *No Such Thing as Over-Exposure: Inside the Life and Celebrity of Donald Trump* (New Jersey: Prentice Hall, 2005), xiii–xxiv.

299 *"last minute"*: Robert Slater speech at the Library of Congress, "The Hazards and Joys of Writing Books on Donald Trump and Martha Stewart: One Author's Perspective," October 25, 2005, http://www.loc.gov/today/cyberlc/transcripts /2005/051025slater.txt.

299 *punish those who questioned:* Abraham Wallach with Robert O'Harrow Jr. and Drew Harwell, *Washington Post*, May 2016; Wallach unpublished manuscript.

300 *1,900 lawsuits:* Nick Penzenstadler and Susan Page, "Exclusive: Trump's 3,500 Lawsuits Unprecedented for a Presidential Nominee," *USA Today*, June 2, 2016.

300 *complex business deals:* Roger Parloff, "Highlights in Trump Litigations," *Fortune*, http://archive.fortune.com/2016/highlights-in-trump-litigations/.

300 *"sue the ass off"*: Jerry Useem, "What Does Donald Trump Really Want?," *Fortune*, May 3, 2000.

300 *What was he really worth?:* Timothy L. O'Brien and Eric Dash, "Is Trump Headed for a Fall?," *New York Times*, March 28, 2004.

300 *Trump Taj Mahal:* Ibid.

300 *success or not?:* O'Brien interview with Drew Harwell and Robert O'Harrow, *Washington Post*, May 2016.

300 *fall of 2005:* O'Brien, *TrumpNation: The Art of Being The Donald* (New York: Warner Business Books, 2005).

301 *weekend meeting:* O'Brien, *TrumpNation*, 153.

301 *net worth came up:* Ibid., 154.

301 *"gross misrepresentations"*: Jason D. Greenblatt, *Trump v. O'Brien*, on appeal, Appendix to brief of plaintiff/Appellant Donald J. Trump, Volume VII, pdf 315.

301 *"riches are hard to find"*: O'Brien, "What's He Really Worth," *New York Times*, October 23, 2005.

301 *$5 billion: Donald J. Trump v. Timothy L. O'Brien*, Brief of Defendants/Respondents in Opposition of Appeal, 9 (001 O'Brien Appeals Brief).

301 *litany of questions:* Trump deposition, 19.

302 *"my own feelings"*: Ibid., 10.

302 *"I don't say anything"*: Ibid., 27.

302 *"People can form"*: Ibid., 26.

302 *line of credit:* Ibid., 35.

303 *"aware of that"*: Ibid., 36.

303 *$788 million:* Ibid., 37.

303 *"assets are worth"*: Ibid.

303 *as high as $2.5 billion:* Ibid., 66.

303 *March 20, 2009:* Brief of Defendants/Respondent Timothy L. O'Brien et al., 1–2, doc 001.

303 *"ability to close deals"*: On December 16: Brief in Support of Plaintiff/Appellant Donald J. Trump in Support of Appeal, 7, doc 000.

303 *"Given the vast"*: Brief of Defendants/Respondent Timothy L. O'Brien et al., 1–2, doc 001.

304 *"billionaire's club"*: *Trump v. O'Brien et al.*, Appellate Division decision, September 7, 2011, http://law.justia.com/cases/new-jersey/appellate-division-published/2011/a6141-08-opn.html.

304 *"low-life sleazebag"*: Trump interview with Harwell, O'Harrow, Boburg, Goldstein, and Markon.

304 *"unbelievably dishonest"*: Ibid.

304 *filed for bankruptcy:* Jeffrey McCracken, "Trump Feud Faces a Court Threat," *Wall Street Journal*, February 14, 2009.

305 *"worthless to me now"*: Drew Harwell, "As Its Stock Collapsed, Trump's Firm Gave Him Huge Bonuses and Paid for His Jet," *Washington Post*, June 12, 2016.

305 *Atlantic City:* Drew Harwell, "Inside the Rocky Billionaire Bromance of Donald Trump and Carl Icahn," *Washington Post*, April 30, 2016.

305 *quality and success:* Ibid.

305 *"how come they went bankrupt":* Alexandra Berzon and Christina S. N. Lewis, "Debating the Value of Trump Name," *Wall Street Journal*, February 26, 2010.

305 *sold Trump Castle:* Drew Fitzgerald, "Landry's Buys Trump Marina Hotel in Atlantic City for $38 Million," *Wall Street Journal*, February 14, 2011. "Trump's Castle Is Shifting to Publicly Held Company," *Bloomberg Business News*, June 26, 1996. (Sold in 1996 for $525 million.)

305 *four of the city's twelve casinos:* Brent Johnson, "Which Atlantic City Casinos Have Closed and Which Are Still Open?," *Star-Ledger*, June 3, 2015.

305 *Icahn reemerged:* Carl Icahn interview with Drew Harwell, *Washington Post*, 2016.

306 *questions about his net worth:* Donald J. Trump Summary of Net Worth as of June 30, 2014, https://www.scribd.com/doc/296070432/Donald-J-Trump-Summary-of-Net-Worth-as-of-June-30-2014.

306 *two properties:* Interview with Actovia Commercial Mortgage Intelligence founder Jonathan Ingber, May 3, 2016.

306 *Vornado:* "Vornado to Acquire 70% Controlling Interest in 1290 Avenue of the Americas and 555 California Street," press statement, March 16, 2007, http://www.vno.com/press-release/clndi9rcjl/vornado-to-acquire-70-controlling-interest-in-1290-avenue-of-the-americas-and-555-california-street.

306 *Trump Palace:* Interview with Ingber, 2016.

306 *more than $50 million:* Donald Trump personal financial disclosure filed with the FEC in 2015, 22.

306 *$1.4 million:* Drew Harwell, "Trump Once Revealed His Income Tax Returns. They Showed He Didn't Pay a Cent."

306 *Every major party nominee:* Glenn Kessler, "Trump's False Claim That 'There's Nothing to Learn' from His Tax Returns," *Washington Post*, May 12, 2016.

307 *"nothing to learn":* Julie Pace and Jill Colvin, "AP Interview: Trump Says Big Rallies His Key Campaign Weapon," Associated Press, May 10, 2016.

307 *little as possible:* Trump interview with Chuck Todd, *Meet the Press*, January 24, 2016, http://www.nbcnews.com/meet-the-press/meet-press-january-24-2016-n503241.

307 *"It's ridiculous":* Trump interview with *Face the Nation*, CBS, August 23, 2015.

307 *"ardent philanthropist":* 2014 archive of Trump website biography, http://web.archive.org/web/20140721012816/http://www.trumpcom/Donald_J_Trump/Biography.asp.

307 *charity auctions:* David A. Fahrenthold and Rosalind S. Helderman, "Missing from Trump's List of Charitable Giving: His Own Personal Cash," *Washington Post*, April 10, 2016.

307 *Serena Williams:* Ibid.

307 *charity that bore:* Ibid.

307 *"No, I don't want to":* Trump interview, May 13, 2016.

307 *until four months later:* David A. Fahrenthold, "Four Months after Fundraiser, Trump Says He Gave $1 million to Veterans Group," *Washington Post*, May 24, 2016.

307 *"nasty guy"*: Ibid.

308 *$6 million:* David A. Fahrenthold and Jose A. DelReal, "Trump Rails against Scrutiny over Delayed Donations to Veterans Groups," *Washington Post*, May 31, 2016.

308 *"continue to attack"*: Ibid.

308 *"representing Donald Trump"*: Trump interview with Robert O'Harrow and Drew Harwell, *Washington Post*, May 2016.

CHAPTER 18: "TRUMP! TRUMP! TRUMP!"

310 *season of missteps:* Ed O'Keefe, "Jeb Bush Announces Presidential Bid: 'We Will Take Command of Our Future Once Again,'" *Washington Post*, June 15, 2015.

310 *had been lured:* Ben Terris, "Donald Trump Begins 2016 Bid, Citing Outsider Status," *Washington Post*, June 16, 2015.

310 *a little different:* Corey Lewandowski interview with Dan Balz and Jenna Johnson, May 19, 2016.

310 *"crazy policy"*: Ronald Kessler, "Donald Trump: Mean-Spirited GOP Won't Win Elections," Newsmax, November 26, 2012.

311 *regarded prepared texts:* Trump interview with Balz and Johnson, May 23, 2016.

311 *"bringing crime"*: Transcript of Trump announcement, http://time.com/3923128 /donald-trump-announcement-speech/.

311 *"not a politician"*: Don and Kathy Watson interview with Balz, June 16, 2015.

311 *"wouldn't underestimate"*: Steve Scheffler interview with Balz, June 16, 2015.

312 *"very inflammatory"*: Clinton interview with Jon Ralston, *Ralston Live*, Ralston reports.com, June 18, 2015.

312 *"whatever you want"*: Trump interview with Balz and Johnson. A Macy's spokesman said that Lundgren would have no comment on the exchange with Trump.

312 *"That was blowback"*: Trump interview with Balz and Johnson.

313 *"take our country back"*: "Donald Trump, Phoenix, Arizona, July 11, 2015, Full Speech—Donald J. Trump for President," published on July 17, 2015, https:// www.youtube.com/watch?v=sPED92gRpsY.

313 *"the crazies"*: McCain, quoted in Ryan Lizza, "John McCain Has a Few Things to Say about Donald Trump," *New Yorker*, July 16, 2015.

313 *"weren't captured"*: "Presidential Candidate Donald Trump at the Family Leadership Summit," C-SPAN.org, http://www.c-span.org/video/?327045-5/presidential -candidate-donald-trump-family-leadership-summit.

313 *strengthen the Veterans Administration*: Lewandowski interview with Balz and Johnson.

314 *"actually may go up"*: Chip Saltsman interview with Balz, May 17, 2016.

314 *"didn't apply to this one"*: Michael Glassner interview with Balz and Johnson, May 23, 2016.

314 *risky move:* Trump interview with Balz and Johnson.

314 *"politically correct"*: Republican Presidential Candidates Debate, Fox News, August 6, 2015.

315 *nose or ears:* Philip Rucker, "Trump Says Fox's Megyn Kelly Had 'Blood Coming Out of Her Wherever,'" *Washington Post*, August 8, 2015. Also, Trump on *Today*, NBC, August 10, 2015, http://www.today.com/news/donald-trump-megyn-kelly -blood-comment-wasnt-meant-be-insult-t37681.

315 *"virtually every question":* Danny Diaz interview with Balz, May 25, 2016.

315 *"all the arrows":* Lewandowski interview with Balz and Johnson.

316 *so much airtime:* Nicholas Confessore and Karen Yourish, "$2 Billion Worth of Free Media for Donald Trump," *New York Times*, March 15, 2016.

316 *"completely eye-opening":* Mike DuHaime interview with Balz, May 17, 2016.

316 *August night:* Heather Haddon and Beth Reinhard, "Donald Trump and Jeb Bush Duel at Competing Events in New Hampshire," *Wall Street Journal*, August 19, 2015.

316 *campaign structure:* Lewandowski interview with Balz and Johnson.

317 *"can't be replicated":* Ibid.

317 *"place went crazy":* Trump interview with Balz, June 10, 2016.

317 *"pigpen with a pig":* Ed O'Keefe, Dan Balz, and Matea Gold, "Fall of the House of Bush: How Last Name and Donald Trump Doomed Jeb," *Washington Post*, February 21, 2016.

317 *"adapt to reality":* Glassner interview with Balz and Johnson.

317 *"cancer on conservatism":* Rick Perry, "Defending Conservatism against the Cancer of Trump-ism," RickPerry.org, July 22, 2015.

318 *"get more attention":* Scott Walker interview with Balz, December 29, 2015.

318 *"exactly wrong":* Whit Ayres interview with Balz, May 18, 2016.

318 *more a "mood":* James Ceaser interview with Balz, March 4, 2016.

318 *"churn the waters":* Todd Harris interview with Balz, May 17, 2016.

319 *Syrian refugees:* Jenna Johnson, "Donald Trump Says Tough Gun Control Laws in Paris Contributed to Tragedy," *Washington Post*, November 14, 2015.

319 *"loss of control":* Focus group report provided by confidential source.

319 *"total and complete" ban:* "Donald J. Trump Statement on Preventing Muslim Immigration," December 7, 2015, https://www.donaldjtrump.com/press-releases /donald-j.-trump-statement-on-preventing-muslim-immigration.

320 *"Trump is unhinged":* Bush tweet, December 7, 2015, https://twitter.com/jebbush /status/673990065517891584.

320 *"how people feel":* Adviser to Trump interview with Balz and Johnson, May 23, 2016.

320 *"destroy ISIS":* Republican Presidential Candidates Debate, CNN, December 16, 2015.

320 *"no new piece":* Todd Harris interview with Balz, May 17, 2016.

320 *"wasted time":* Trump interview with Balz, Robert Costa, and Philip Rucker, October 5, 2015.

320 *" 'in the top ten' ":* Donald Trump concession speech, Des Moines, Iowa, February 1, 2016.

321 *"Where's Chuck?":* "Donald Trump Endorsed by Actor John Wayne's Daughter at Museum," YouTube, January 19, 2016, https://www.youtube.com/watch?v =CDRjSXlUIXw.

321 *took the lead:* Des Moines Register–Bloomberg Politics Iowa Poll, January 30,

2016, http://www.desmoinesregister.com/story/news/elections/presidential/caucus/2016/01/30/donald-trump-reclaims-lead-latest-iowa-poll/79562322/.

321 *"never done this"*: Trump interview with Balz and Johnson.

321 *underestimated the turnout*: Lewandowski interview with Balz and Johnson.

322 *"false stories"*: Trump interviews with Balz and Johnson, May 23, June 9, and June 10, 2016.

322 *"would lose respect"*: Trump interview with Balz, June 10, 2016.

323 *"first time I thought"*: Trump interview with Balz, June 9, 2016.

323 *"'blew the state'"*: Trump interview with Balz and Johnson, May 23, 2016.

323 *"he's got walls"*: Ibid.

323 *"only wished and prayed"*: "Donald J. Trump Response to the Pope," February 18, 2016, https://www.donaldjtrump.com/press-releases/donald-j.-trump-response-to-the-pope.

324 *"This is toughness"*: Lewandowski interview with Balz and Johnson.

324 *debunked the story:* David Mikkelson, "Pershing the Thought," Snopes.com, October 31, 2001.

324 *Pants on Fire:* Louis Jacobson, "Donald Trump Cites Dubious Legend about Gen. Pershing, Pig's Blood and Muslims," *PolitiFact*, February 23, 2016.

324 *"it's an analogy"*: Lewandowski interview with Balz and Johnson.

324 *"eke out a win"*: Whit Ayres interview with Balz, May 18, 2016.

324 *"multi-candidate race"*: Jeff Roe interview with Balz, May 26, 2016.

325 *"'establishment' candidate"*: Danny Diaz interview with Balz, May 25, 2016.

325 *"sat it out"*: Mike DuHaime interview with Balz, May 17, 2016.

326 *"bad dudes"*: Debate transcript, CNN, March 10, 2016.

327 *"got no bounce"*: Jeff Roe interview with Balz, May 26, 2016.

327 *"glimmer of hope"*: Trump interview with Balz and Johnson, May 23, 2016.

328 *"presumptive nominee"*: Paul Manafort interview with Balz, April 8, 2016.

328 *"going to be over"*: Trump interview with Balz, June 9, 2016.

329 *starting to pivot:* Philip Rucker, Dan Balz, and Robert Costa, "Trump Is Playing 'a Part' and Can Transform for Victory, Campaign Chief Tells GOP Leaders," *Washington Post*, April 21, 2016.

329 *cigar bar:* Manafort interview with Balz and Johnson, May 23, 2016.

330 *"temperament unfit"*: Romney quoted in Monica Langley, "Behind Mitt Romney's Increasingly Lonely Challenge to Donald Trump," *Wall Street Journal*, May 28, 2016.

330 *"learn about issues"*: Armitage quoted in Michael Crowley, "Armitage to Back Clinton over Trump," *Politico*, June 16, 2016.

330 *fired Lewandowski:* Philip Rucker, Jose A. DelReal, and Sean Sullivan, "Donald Trump Fires Embattled Campaign Manager Corey Lewandowski," *Washington Post*, June 20, 2016.

330 *the country's enemies:* Karen DeYoung and Jose A. DelReal, "Trump Says He Was Right about Obama and Terrorists, Citing Questionable 2012 Intelligence Cable," *Washington Post*, June 15, 2016.

330 *responded by revoking:* Paul Farhi, "Trump Revokes *Post* Press Credentials, Calling the Paper 'Dishonest' and 'Phony,'" *Washington Post*, June 13, 2016.

330 *"most un-American thing"*: Graham quoted in Patrick Healy, Maggie Haberman,

and Jonathan Martin, "Democrats Jump on Allies of Trump in Judge Dispute," *New York Times*, June 6, 2016.

331 *"textbook definition"*: Ryan quoted in Mike DeBonis, "Ryan Says Trump's Attacks on Judge Fit 'the Textbook Definition of a Racist Comment,'" *Washington Post*, June 7, 2016.

331 *"'rest of your life'"*: Trump interview with Fisher and Kranish, June 9, 2016.

EPILOGUE: LAW AND ORDER

336 *lifted verbatim*: Karen Tumulty, Robert Costa, and Jose A. DelReal, "Scrutiny of Melania Trump's Speech Follows Plagiarism Allegations," *Washington Post*, July 19, 2016.

339 *"the strategy is"*: *The O'Reilly Factor*, Fox News, July 18, 2016.

340 *"life was business"*: Trump interview with Fisher and Kranish, June 9, 2016.

340 *"sense of pageantry"*: Ibid.

340 *"they are narcissists"*: Trump with McIver, *Think Like a Billionaire*, xvii–xviii.

342 *favored the attack*: Eugene Kiely, "Donald Trump and the Iraq War," FactCheck .org, February 19, 2016.

342 *"But she's not"*: Trump on *60 Minutes*, CBS, July 17, 2016.

342 *"No self-discipline"*: Interview with Charlie Rose, *CBS This Morning*, CBS, July 19, 2016.

343 *18 black people:* Jonathan Capehart, "Guess How Many African American Delegates Are Going to Be at the Republican Convention," *Washington Post*, June 6, 2016.

343 *4 percent:* Washington Post–ABC News national poll, July 11–14, 2016.

343 *"more racist"*: James Evans interview with Kranish, July 18, 2016.

343 *"absolutely" a Muslim:* Michael Edison Hayden, "Antonio Sabàto Jr. Says He's 'Absolutely' Sure Obama's a Muslim After RNC Speech," ABCNews.com, July 18, 2016.

345 *"out of control"*: *60 Minutes*, July 17, 2016.

346 *35 million Americans:* Stephen Battaglio, "35 Million TV Viewers Watch Donald Trump's Acceptance Speech at GOP Convention," *Los Angeles Times*, July 22, 2016.

347 *"I want it short"*: Trump interview with Fisher and Kranish, June 9, 2016.

347 *no time to read:* Trump interview with Fisher and Kranish, April 21, 2016.

INDEX